Appointment at Armageddon

CONTRIBUTIONS IN AMERICAN STUDIES

Series Editor: Robert H. Walker

The Columbian Exchange: Biological and Cultural Consequences of 1492
Alfred W. Crosby, Jr.

The Politics of a Literary Man: William Gilmore Simms
Jon L. Wakelyn

Visions of America: Eleven Literary Historical Essays
Kenneth S. Lynn

The Collected Works of Abraham Lincoln, Supplement 1832-1865
Roy P. Basler, Editor

Art and Politics: Cartoonists of the *Masses* and *Liberator*
Richard Fitzgerald

Progress and Pragmatism: James, Dewey, Beard, and the American Idea of Progress
David W. Marcell

The Muse and the Librarian
Roy P. Basler

Henry B. Fuller of Chicago: The Ordeal of a Genteel Realist in Ungenteel America
Bernard R. Bowron, Jr.

Mother Was a Lady: Self and Society in Selected American Children's Periodicals, 1865-1890
R. Gordon Kelly

The *Eagle* and Brooklyn: A Community Newspaper, 1841-1955
Raymond A. Schroth, S. J.

Black Protest: Issues and Tactics
Robert C. Dick

American Studies Abroad
Robert H. Walker, Editor

APPOINTMENT AT ARMAGEDDON

Muckraking and progressivism in the American tradition

LOUIS FILLER

CONTRIBUTIONS IN AMERICAN STUDIES NO. 20

GREENWOOD PRESS
WESTPORT, CONNECTICUT • LONDON, ENGLAND

Library of Congress Cataloging in Publication Data

Filler, Louis, 1911-
Appointment at Armageddon.

(Contributions in American studies; no. 20)
Includes bibliographical references and index.
1. United States—Politics and government—1865-1900. 2. United States—Politics and government—20th century. 3. Progressivism (United States politics) I. Title.
E661.F52 322.4'4'0973 75-23865
ISBN 0-8371-8261-1

Library of Congress Catalog Card Number: 75-23865
ISBN: 0-8371-8261-1

First published in 1976

Greenwood Press, a division of Williamhouse-Regency Inc.
51 Riverside Avenue, Westport, Connecticut 06880

Printed in the United States of America

Contents

Illustrations

Introduction

Even though progressivism is apparently established in history as a potent force in American life, it has fallen on strange days so far as its status in living affairs is concerned. Among the acknowledged classics in the field—in a sadly relativistic world—are Lincoln Steffens's *Autobiography* and Finley Peter Dunne's *Mr. Dooley* essays. But Theodore Roosevelt has been degraded from one of America's greatest figures to the prototype of a racist and imperialist. Tom Watson has been firmly established at the highest academic levels as the typical white southerner and Progressive. And the entire movement of progressivism and its attendant muckraking have been described as calculated to strengthen the powers of government in order to strengthen the powers of business over government and in opposition to the will or weal of the American majority.

Such interpretations do not appear by accident or flourish adventitiously. We need to understand what proponents of the anti-Progressive view seem to see and why. In general, until recently modern history studies in the field had enjoyed an era of hypothesis. It appeared useful to work large views of American development as struggles for status, consensus-seeking, or a search for law and order. More recently the large hypotheses have given way to relatively small monographs exploiting groups of assembled papers and correspondence in one or another repository and dealing with housing, poverty, charity, farm problems, particular Progressives such as Elmer Benson and Robert M. La Follette, child labor, "moral purity," prohibition, and others.

These have in many cases been useful investigations. But in some instances they have included doubtful aspects. Thus the study of a group of papers may well make a doctoral candidate an "authority" in a field. If, however, he extrapolates to the entire field in an effort to extend his authority he may well make critical errors. We all have our views on many social problems, but these are stronger and better documented in some areas than in others. If we are called as witnesses to some of our weaker fields, our general credibility may suffer as a result. A responsible examination sees its problem as a whole rather than as a shadowy footnote in a docket of accusations. Josephine Shaw Lowell, for example, believed in the sanctity of sex. So did Frances Willard. And Anna Garlin Spencer. But to treat these great women in so narrow a framework of research would be inhuman—and close to infamous.

Involved, then, in due analysis of the Progressive phenomena is a sense of perspective on its content and real experience. Obviously progressivism did not come out of nowhere. It represented a restructuring of old impulses and American associations to serve a new time. Whether our latest needs and dilemmas require something drastically newer, something repudiating old progressivism—perhaps repudiating progressivism entirely—is one of the interesting questions that a study of progressivism must answer. The old secured achievements of progressivism are probably acknowledged largely from mere duty. Ida M. Tarbell's famous examination of the Standard Oil Company, which is little read, can help us little in determining our relationship to oil, expecially since oil's very significance as a fuel has obvious time limitations. Soon, relatively soon, there may be no oil. If any living core of Tarbell's study survives, it will have to be of a principled rather than a substantive nature.

Ray Stannard Baker's studies of the "color line" are patently obsolete; for better or worse we have been in process of "modernizing" racial relations. Labor has come up from being an oppressed minority seeking compassion and aid in survival struggles to a powerful force in defining government policy. Almost nothing relates "Big Bill" Haywood and Jimmy Hoffa. And although there could be interesting comparisons projected between Samuel Gompers and George Meany, at this time they are not made. Students correctly identifying Tarbell, Baker, and Gompers in Graduate Record Examinations have not had to strike imaginative equations between old issues bemusing the American public and new ones.

All issues inevitably become obsolete. The problem is to abstract from them some essence that makes them illuminating to present debate. It is important to determine, then, whether it is a living truth to see in old progressivism the narrow program of prejudice and authoritarianism that some modern scholars have fancied. All examinations of evidence are not necessarily limited and partial. A democratic debate will balance the biased preferences of any particular investigator with the criticism and supplementary information of others in the field.

Imbedded in such a benign process is what can only be called a cultural approach. This can help if the reader's sensibilities make decent connections between people and their life work. It can harm if dogma is permitted to run roughly over human nature and needs, reading into them whatever dogma's social attitudes deem good. Thus, Ben B. Lindsey of Colorado worked as hard as any person of his time to ensure the civil rights of children in the face of bureaucratic processes that made it possible to treat them as felons or as mere pawns of judicial machinery. At the same time Lindsey felt it necessary to set up solid social conditions that gave the more insecure, embittered, strong-headed, and dangerous children before the courts a time to pause in their delinquent exploits and to reconsider what they wished of society or were able to demand of it. In due course, Lindsey, for having put such children in reform schools, for having separated them from more patently promising yet undefined youth, was to be accused . . . of having interfered with their civil liberties.[1] It is a serious accusation that should not be permitted to rest in academic archives, to create slovenly images in academic minds eager to stay abreast of modern libertarian hopes.

The cultural component merits another word because it involves not only an appropriate regard for human nature and personality as they unfold in our time but an awareness of inevitabilities in human experience as seen over decades and centuries of history. Modern men and women have too often geared themselves to "existential" thinking at the expense of clear realities. They have traded dreaming and analysis for immediate tangibles—food, gossip, diversions—

without closely counting the cost. Poetry is rarely chosen over "kicks." Yet D. H. Lawrence once observed that poets were scientists of a kind, able to assess vital activities of personalities for accurate results. To separate the cultural principle from the social-scientific principle is to wound both areas while we seek to make more firm our grasp on the life about us.

To write of progressivism as though it were mere politics, merely bread-and-butter issues, of muckraking as though it were mere journalism—the oldest charge against it—is to forget that people simply do not live by bread alone. They are enticed by hope, obscured motivated attractions, fads, even logic. Eric Hoffer in our time has noted that boredom is a factor in group decisions. To grasp the ordinary course of social cause and effect and relate it to the second level of human need requires a grasp of the more subtle purposes of human nature that the poetry, the narrative, the essay of a given era help clarify. Separating "history" from culture, puzzling over whether the historian belongs among humanists or social scientists, causes us to act schizophrenically and to get schizophrenic results. Progressivism was fiction as well as "fact." It was "The Man with the Hoe" as well as David Graham Phillips's "The Treason of the Senate." But it was also other creative work by Edwin Markham and many others: work that could take such a title as "The Man with the Hoe" out of the category of cliché and give it a meaning for its time and ours.[2]

Our problem with progressivism is in its very implications; ours is not an era that has reason to anticipate progress. The word, accordingly, tends to exude a breath of dishonesty: of false promises, tricky substance, sterile heartiness. Yet it engrossed the energies of some of the most useful and dedicated citizens of their time. How wrong-headed they may have been on one or another issue it is good to consider. But even when they made blatant errors, it behooves us to be modest in our estimates of their failures and to recall our own vulnerability to criticism.

Guglielmo Ferrero, in his study of the rise and fall of Rome, felt it necessary not so much to rehabilitate Nero as to suggest that, considering our limited and biased sources of information, some of his nefarious reputation could not be credited.[3] We, with our vastly greater resources ought to be chary of thesis writing not so much intended to expose new truths as to make new opportunities for ambitious writers, not so much to bring the past to bear on the present as to exploit the past for partisan aims. We may not believe in progress but we cannot do without improvements in our lot.

NOTES

1. *Reviews in American History* 1 (June 1973): 271ff.
2. See Louis Filler, "Edwin Markham, Poetry, and What Have You," *Antioch Review* (Winter 1963-1964); 447ff.
3. For example, he rejects as wholly incredible the rumor that Nero had any responsibility for the burning of Rome, July, 64 A.D Guglielmo Ferrero and Corrado Barbagallo, *A Short History of Rome* (New York, 1919), 2:208-211.

part I
PAST AND PRESENT

Great Expectations

American traditions preceded American nationality and were subject to its hopes and dangers. As with all societies, colonists produced elite classes and debased ones. But unlike most societies, theirs was a congeries of peoples in competition with others and with their very own, all stirred by change and anticipation. To tour the British colonies in America was to move among Anglicans, Quakers, Presbyterians. Congregationalists, and a score of other denominational groups. It was to know Frenchmen, Britons, Scots, Scotch-Irish, and Irish who sometimes "passed" as Scotch-Irish (a step up on the social scale).

Among the humbler folk, it was to see freedmen and freeholders, and indentured servants who planned to become freemen, as well as farmers resentful of feudal obligations. All of these classes, in large or small measure, contributed to social alliances that were often stronger in rhetoric than in reality. What they had in common were great expectations. Such alliances produced serious and sometimes bloody quarrels, between Tidewater aristocrats and frontiersmen, between yeomen and administrators, between colony and colony—the Mason-Dixon line (1767) was a major settlement of claims argued between Pennsylvanians and Marylanders.[1]

But none of these clashes resulted in the devastating proscriptions that drove whole classes of citizens from European countries in times of civil war and that often helped augment the population of the British American colonies. Colonial quarrels created what was almost a tradition of dissatisfaction leading to confrontations and revolts.

There were numerous insurrections, rebellions, uprisings, and even seditions, before and after the American Revolution.[2] "Bacon's Rebellion"—often noted as having significantly preceded the events of 1776 by a round century—was a model of such occurrences. Nathaniel Bacon, a kinsman of Francis, traveled from England to Virginia and settled on its near frontier. As a wealthy freeholder he was entitled to a seat in its House of Burgesses, the first representative body in the New World, though it left underrepresented the farmers who lived insecurely outside the capital of Jamestown. In the house, Bacon (a complex and forward young man; it was said those qualities had forced his emigration) not only demanded greater democracy than the governor, William Berkeley, cared to permit, he also asked for protection from the Indians, who came civilly to Jamestown to trade but who harassed the English pioneers on the frontier. Berkeley was a firm conservative who had pointedly hoped there would be no printing press in the colonies for a hundred years.

Bacon took it upon himself to organize his outpost neighbors and lead them to counterattack their Indian foes. Following hectic meetings and intrigues, Berkeley proclaimed Bacon and his followers traitors. This left Bacon no alternative but to set up a camp outside Jamestown and prepare to win over public opinion at home and that of King Charles in England. Unexpectedly, Bacon was laid low with fever and died. He was the spirit of his uprising, and with him gone it collapsed and was cruelly revenged. Bacon's democratic vision, helped perhaps by his florid style and coupled with his early death at age twenty-nine, created a legend of independency, as well as of youthful social action.[3]

Half-forgotten in this growth of American tradition of dissent are the Indian tribes, inevitable victims of the determined drives westward of Spanish, French, British, and lesser migrations. Belief in the superiority of the Christian faith over the pagan accounted in part for such forgetfulness. The bitter effort of Indian sachems from time to time to wipe out the white invaders contributed even more to national amnesia on the subject. Half-lost in all such differences, from Florida to Maine, were attempts made from earliest times in both British and Indian camps to understand each other and to create kindly feelings between nations. Such benign gestures had to rise above the most disillusioning experiences, such as the following, as seen by a distinguished historian:

> The advance of the whites along the coast alarmed the Pequot Indians, who lived in the central part of Connecticut. The origin of the trouble does not clearly appear, but the settlers were convinced that the times demanded a most signal chastisement. Massachusetts lent a hand, and in 1637 a combined force of whites from Massachusetts and Connecticut, with 280 Indian allies, ancient foes of the Pequots, surprised the enemy in a fort near the Rhode Island boundary line and of the 400 men, women and children within it not more than five escaped alive. The Pequots were then pursued vigorously. Overtaken in a swamp near New Haven, another great slaughter occurred, and the result of the two engagements was the complete extinction of the Pequot tribe as such. It was grim dealing, but it gave the whites peace from the Indians for many years.[4]

For not too many years. Yet the interim between the Pequot War and King Philip's War, which began in 1675, saw the saintly mission of John Eliot, "Apostle to the Indians," in addition to the usual frontier outrages. Eliot was indeed partisan to his religious faith, but in the process of Christianizing pagans, he did study their language and arts, and he did labor to reach them in humanistic and individual terms. There will doubtless always be those, however, who for sentimental or other reasons, will prefer the spirit of Philip, chief sachem of the Wampoags of Massachusetts. He answered Eliot's pleas that he adopt Christianity by grasping Eliot's coat and saying harshly, "I care no more for your Gospel than I care for that button."[5]

Philip, leading his braves into a war that horribly devastated the frontier, caused the destruction of numerous English settlements and left families throughout Massachusetts to mourn their dead. He not only ended thirty-eight years of relative peace but lost his Indian followers an opportunity to participate in the colony's growth. Ultimately they became themselves a species of immigrant, with the problem of uniting with other Americans for strength in order to appeal to American traditions for gain or status.

Indians enslaved each other and were themselves enslaved, though temperament and other factors made them less manageable and less profitable workers than Africans and the much more numerous whites who suffered kidnapping or other cruel misadventures to become part of the colonial labor force. Even larger was the body of workers who signed articles of indentureship, making them for a time the property of masters throughout the provinces. Open fields and frontier were both a trap and an opportunity. They required ardent and continuous labor, but they also opened vistas of freedom that finally produced the generous libertarian slogans of a Thomas Jefferson. He was far from alone. Few, North or South, admired slavery or openly defended it. And though many took pride in their own heritage or religious faith, they also perceived the human offense inherent in enslavement, particularly in lush contrasts afforded by vistas of tilled acres and endless frontier.

Hard work and responsibility they always expected from both lower and elite orders, but slavery, they thought, would die of its own infirmities. Patrick Henry, himself a product of democratic opportunity, which made him able to defy his aristocratic betters in speeches that stirred colonists everywhere, railed against slavery as incompatible with religion. He would not attempt to justify his own ownership of slaves. The later tremendous achievement of Thomas Jefferson and his fellow slaveholders in passing the Northwest Ordinance of 1787 (which debarred slavery from that western empire) testified to their sincerity and effectiveness. One patriot charge against the British crown was that it would not end the "iniquitous and disgraceful" traffic of slaves from Africa. Economic interests, it must be noted, were never far from moral. Richard Henry Lee, protesting slave importations in the Virginia legislature in 1759, asked why neighboring colonies, though settled later than Virginia, were "far before us in improvement." The reason, he thought, was "that with their whites they import arts and agriculture, whilst we, with our blacks, exclude both."[6]

Economics alone, however, could not activate a vital portion of the Americans to shake off British authority as foreign. A Lee might gamble his life, property, and distinctions against the chance of shaking off frustrating taxes and laws drawn up in London governing domestic military posts, land speculation, legal documents, and other weighty matters. But what stake had a redemptioner—for example, a white man or woman who had bartered freedom for ship passage to America—in such affairs? John Bach McMaster later spelled out in great detail the lot of such unfortunates. When their ship arrived, for example in Philadelphia, they were offered for sale. If no buyer appeared, they were often sold to speculators who drove them about the country in chains and haggled with this farmer and that for the price of a redemptioner:

> The contract signed, the newcomer became in the eyes of the law a slave, and in both the civil and criminal code was classed with negro slaves and Indians. None could marry without consent of the master or mistress under penalty of an addition of one year's service to the time set forth in the indenture. They were worked hard, were dressed in the cast-off clothes of their owners, and might be flogged as often as the master or mistress thought necessary. . . . Father, mother and children could be sold to different buyers. . . .
>
> In the Middle and Southern States almost all labor, skilled and unskilled, was done by slaves, redemptioners or indentured servants. The advertisements of redemptioners mention weavers, gardeners, spinners, carpenters, smiths, wheelwrights, shoemakers, and school teachers, stonecutters, bricklayers, tailors, hatters, harness makers—men and women skilled in every sort of labor then needed in the country.[7]

For such human conditions, the Declaration of Independence could not suffice; it offered too little. Indeed, it is problematic whether it thrilled revolutionary patriots more than it constituted a justification for malcontents of later eras—malcontents who exploited the fact that somewhere in the declaration it was stated that "all men are created equal." They did not trouble to study the document enough to note any of its specific charges against the British king. These included the accusation that "he has excited domestic insurrections among us [that is, of Negro and other slaves], and has endeavored to bring on the inhabitants of our frontiers the merciless Indian savages, whose known rule of warfare is an undistinguished destruction of all ages, sexes and conditions."

If this was a partisan statement of American social circumstances in a revolutionary era, it nevertheless also appealed to universal ideals of brotherhood for vindication. More calculated than the Declaration of Independence to win the endorsement of common men and women were the appeals of Thomas Paine, appeals masking as "common sense" but reeking with emotional hatred of class distinctions and of the monarchy that Paine thought symbolized them. "O! ye that love mankind!" Paine's pamphlet *Common Sense* (1776) exhorted. "Ye that dare to oppose not only the tyranny but the tyrant, stand forth!" Paine's eloquence galvanized not only the humble but also the cautious, those with substance and position to lose.

He mocked British democracy as a farce, its boasted constitution as no more than an instrument for "innumerable robberies and executions." All this was meaningful to indentured servants who had, after all, felt driven to leave Great Britain in search of a better living and had even sold themselves in order to do so. Innumerable editions of Paine's pamphlet and his other inflammatory writings were a promise that American life, separated from the British empire, would be more open, different, free of stultifying doctrines and betrayals. Paine's words gathered regiments for Washington and his generals. They were vital to commitments that ended in the drawing up of the Declaration of Independence. They should have made Paine unforgettable to later generations.

Vernon Louis Parrington saw Paine as a latter-day John Lilburne, English Puritan and ultrarepublican Leveler. Lilburne had seen even Oliver Cromwell as an agent of aristocracy. Parrington understood that Paine had been of inestimable value to the Revolution. He could not understand why Paine's continued advocacy of what would later be termed "permanent revolution"—as in *The Rights of Man* (1791-1792), honoring the French Revolution—and especially Paine's denunciation of the Bible in his *The Age of Reason*, why such writings should have caused his drop in reputation among Americans. "His thousands of followers among the disenfranchised poor could not protect his reputation against the attacks of the rich and powerful," thought Parrington.[8]

They could not protect him from themselves. Paine's mind, emotional rather than clear and logical, enchanted them with its eloquence but troubled them in their ambitions. His *Agrarian Justice* (1797), generously advocating wholesale expropriation and distribution of land, would have distributed the land they longed to seize and individually hold. New York State gave Paine the four-hundred-acre farm, confiscated from Tories, on which he settled in New Rochelle, and in 1805 it was an empty-handed and disgruntled odds-job worker, not an aristocrat, who sought to kill him by firing a bullet through his window. The Jefferson administration sent no representative to attend Paine's funeral in 1809. The lowly and poor were also conspicuous by their absence.

> Poor Tom Paine! here he lies,
> Nobody laughs and nobody cries;
> Where he's gone and how he fares,
> Nobody knows and nobody cares.[9]

Other idealists, prototypes of progressivism, had reason to taste the bitterness of popular forgetfulness. Philip Freneau, "poet of the revolution," yearned to be an American bard, and he did succeed in writing the first native verses that leave a taste of American woodlands, the feel of American thought. He also wrote unrestrained doggerel that sought to bury King George and the British in eternal infamy. Later, as a stipendiary of Thomas Jefferson, Freneau sought equally to spew venom and contempt on Federalists, whom he saw as undermining the gains of the revolutionary era. Freneau's journalism was all too partisan and unsubtle to be memorable. It denounced the purse-proud and the aristocratic as though there were no Jeffersonians with full purses and family pride. It "exposed" the plots of Federalists who, Freneau alleged, longed to return the Republic to royalists. Such rantings could persuade only those who were already persuaded.

But there was a humanistic side to Freneau, which deserved more regard than it received from an easily diverted public, always looking beyond to new interests and sensations, and no doubt cynically aware that much professed idealism was no more than the growl of stomachs hungry for affluent fare. Yet Freneau's "Robert Slender" papers—early familiar essays—offered ideas intended to serve a gracious society rather than a competitive one. "Robert Slender" contributed his mite to a better world and even in small degree to a definition of what would in time be called "muckraking":

> Having heard that there was a tavern at about the distance of a

mile or so from my favorite country spot, where now and then a few neighbors meet to spit, smoke segars, drink apple whisky, cider or cider-royal, and read the news—a few evenings ago, I put on my best coat, combed out my wig, put my spectacles in my pocket, and a quarter dollar. . . . But I had not gone half the way, when, by making a false step, I splashed my stocking from the knee to the ankle. . . . Odds my heart, said I. . . . Had I . . . but half the income of the United States, I could at least so order matters, that a man might walk to his next neighbor's without splashing his stockings or being in danger of breaking his legs in ruts, holes, gutts, and gullies. I do not know, says I to myself . . . but money might with more profit be laid out in repairing the roads, than in marine establishments, supporting a standing army, useless embassies, exorbitant salaries, given to many flashy fellows that are no honor to us, or to themselves, and chartering whole ships to carry a single man to another nation. . . . I could then, says I, still talking to myself, see the reason why the old patriots, whose blood flowed so freely in purchasing our independence, are cast aside, like a broken pitcher, (as the Scripture says) and why the old tories and active refugees are advanced to places of power, honor and trust. . . .[10]

NOTES

1. Compare with Woodrow Wilson, *A History of the American People* (New York, 1901), 1: 63-64, which interprets such events in Virginia as early as 1622, during the time when Englishmen first "swarmed" into the colonies.

2. Charles M. Andrews, ed., *Narratives of the Insurrections, 1675-1690* (New York, 1915).

3. Forgotten was the fact that the Bacon rebels infringed illegally on Indian lands. For a classic statement of the Bacon incident, see T. J. Wertenbaker, *Torchbearer of the Revolution* (Princeton, 1940). Wilcomb E. Washburn, *The Governor and the Rebel* (Chapel Hill, 1957), takes Berkeley's part as a proper defense of law and order but seems unlikely ever to overcome the sympathy Bacon's personality and attitude inspires. The view, variously expressed, that Bacon led elements of the "western" ruling class in competition with Jamestown rulers, rather than a democrat or proto-Progressive movement, assumes a species of the latter which may not exist, as subsequent chapters may indicate.

4. John S. Bassett, *A Short History of the United States* (New York, 1913), 70.

5. Ezra Hoyt Byington, *The Puritan as a Colonist and Reformer* (Boston, 1899), 256. It merits notice that "class" differences do little to explain Indian-white antagonisms. The "common people" opposed not only Christianizing Indians "but also all such English as were judged to be charitable to them." Peter N. Carroll, *Puritanism and the Wilderness* (New York, 1969), 213.

6. Burton J. Hendrick, *The Lees of Virginia* (New York, 1935), 103.

7. John Bach McMaster, *The Acquisition of Political, Social, and Industrial Rights of Man in America* (New York, 1961), 34-35. It merits notice that McMaster through his researches unfolded a point of view offensive to some species of radical, because he seemed to honor American progress; Staughton Lynd believed that his work ought not to be reprinted; see Lynd, "The Bourgeois Philosopher," *Book Week*, January 10, 1965.

8. Vernon Parrington, *Main Currents in American Thought* (New York, 1927), 1:341.

9. W. E. Woodward, *Tom Paine: America's Godfather, 1737-1809* (New York, 1945), 268. This was a canard of 1794, circulated in England when it was imagined he had been executed in France. In fact, the pro-Paine bibliography is enormous and accretes additional books and pamphlets down to the present. Much of it is, to be sure, polemical rather than broadly humanistic.

10. Robert Slender, *Letters on Various Interesting and Important Subjects, etc.* (Philadelphia, 1799), 128-129.

Vehicles for Change

A section of the country that could claim such figures as Patrick Henry, Thomas Jefferson, and Andrew Jackson, moving freely about in their environs and attaining national fame or office, could hardly be described as a concentration camp. Yet civil dissent created images of the South as dominated by "lords of the lash," and similar concepts were nourished in the North following the Civil War. Although slavery did indeed become characteristic of life in the southern states, its defense came relatively late and was relatively brief. White labor akin to slavery was universal in the seventeenth and eighteenth centuries and seemed destined to drive black servitude out of circulation, whites being more numerous and their exertions more profitable.

The American Revolution appeared likely to be the final blow undermining black slavery. The success of the cotton gin gave a new vitality to the southern slave system, withered out of use in the North, but it was not until 1831 that the vitalized abolitionist movement unwittingly inspired the explicit argument that slavery was not a painful heritage of the past, which needed to be diminished or exiled, but a "positive good."[1]

The Indian issue also seemed centered in the South. Georgia responded to the will of its land-hungry white settlers who were excited by the discovery of gold in western Georgia lands held by the Cherokee and who demanded that the Indians be removed and their lands freed for new settlement. The harsh measures of the Georgia legislators early in the 1830s, supported by the Andrew Jackson administration, stirred sympathy among northerners for the driven

Indians. Senator Theodore Frelinghuysen, justly honored as the pious stateman from New Jersey who practiced as well as preached philanthropy, cried out against violence and urged "fair contract" for the Cherokee. Ralph Waldo Emerson deplored forcible removal. But such worthies gave less attention to the fact that northern Indians had already been removed as far as Illinois. In 1832 the war against the Sauk and Fox Indians, led by the chieftain Black Hawk, caused the government to order still further removal to trans-Mississippi areas.[2]

Late-twentieth-century dissidents who practiced criticism of American policy found no problem in these paradoxes. Northerners and southerners were "racists" all; their sectional quarrels could not obscure their common will to dominate and oppress their more feeble antagonists. Such judgments not only failed to describe the philosophies of the peoples involved, their life-styles and expectations, such as would normally be expected in analyses of Elizabethans or Nigerians. The generalizations gave no guiding principle for distinguishing between leaders among the beleaguered Negroes and Indians who sought accommodation with the whites and those who did not. They did not distinguish between whites who were determined to wipe out their black or red foes on whatever grounds and whites who out of love or a sense of justice labored to build bridges of humanity to and about them. The fact was that there was "racism" and competition everywhere and among all peoples. It was blatant among patriots but implicit in intensive ethnocentric arguments and ways of life. It took rude forms in the movement of settlers and military expeditions but was often modified by individual affections and kindly ministrations. In the South it resulted in several levels of social interaction.

John Roy Lynch was born in Louisiana of an Irish father and a slave of mixed blood whom his father loved tenderly. His father's will was betrayed by his brother, who sold his wife and children into slavery. Young Lynch received his opportunity during the Reconstruction era when, supported by federal troops, he became speaker of the House of Representatives in Mississippi at the age of twenty-two. He was later the state's first Negro to be elected to the United States Congress. His view of southern life was realistic and included awareness of the fact that politics and tradition were potent, but that human nature found its own avenues for expression. As he wrote:

> It is a fact well known, by Southern people at least, that in nearly all cases in which white men were and are heads of colored families, they are not only faithful, loyal, and devoted to their families . . . but they usually take the necessary steps to see that the family cannot, after his death, be deprived of whatever wealth he may have accumulated. . . . To those who are familiar with the fact, it is not at all strange to find a number of colored families in every southern state who are not only in comfortable circumstances, but some of them are what may be called wealthy.[5]

In their defense of slavery, southern ideologues argued that their social and industrial system was vastly more humane than that in the North, where employers coined to exhaustion the strength of their helpless employees, male and female, and flung them into the streets to die. Aggravating reports of the exploitation of children in mines and mills also helped modify northern discontent with the slavery system. Southern defenders often gained by the bitterness of such labor leaders as George Henry Evans, who saw his workingmen associates as the truly oppressed class in America.

During the reform era of the pre-Civil War decades, there was scarcely a Negro who could adhere to the Democratic party and scarcely an Irishman who could find political work to do among the Whigs. Jacksonians and their later apologists deemed the abolitionist movement "a conservative plot,"[4] calculated to turn attention away from the national issues of the Bank and the currency. But though these could little affect hand-to-mouth poor, to say nothing of slaves, they did affect national conditions of prosperity and depression, during which reform movements pulsed or contracted.

In a nation of minorities—in which the Indians were themselves divided into numerous, wholly distinguishable tribes—national issues were necessary to give some cohesion to popular developments. National issues provided a vocabulary for popular unrest, popular ambitions. They gave common cause to otherwise alien and distrustful people, separated by sects and sections and by a sense of greater deservedness because parents or grandparents had come earlier than other immigrants, or could speak a more highly esteemed language, or had been city folk rather than peasants in their old country. It was all but fatal that the issue of issues should have become not abolition, not free trade, certainly not currency, but the political destiny of the western American terrain. At first glance this should have saved the nation from mortal dissension. With so endless a frontier, it would have seemed there would be enough land for all: slaveholders, Free Soilers, Indians, free Negroes. As Senator Thomas Corwin of Ohio put the matter in his speech (one of the greatest of the century) protesting the war with Mexico: "Sir, look at this pretense of want of room. With twenty millions of people, you have about one thousand millions of acres of land, inviting settlement by every conceivable argument—bringing them down to a quarter of a dollar an acre, and allowing every man to squat where he pleases."

Nevertheless southern and northern partisans chose to make of the public terrain a moral issue, a vehicle of change. In Kansas they created martyrs and heroes, some of whom rounded out their lives at Harpers Ferry and Civil War battlefields.

Minorities were not only black, or red, or various shades of white separated by religion, social status, language, and habits. They were also men and women whose condition received attention in the reform periods and beyond. Although women were present in all events and developments in America, their emergence as a progressive or revolutionary force was a matter of time and circumstances. Certainly, males appeared to be more conspicuous in any casual glance backward into the past. Leaders in politics, business, and the social arts were overwhelmingly male. Laws were so totally biased toward men that one student of the subject charged the famous *Commentaries* of Sir William Blackstone (1765) with having "extinguished the married woman's personality."[5]

Yet any unimpassioned reconsideration of American experience indicated that the subject was more complex than any female militant could credit who was bent on expanding women's prerogatives and impatient with arguments or facts not contributing to her cause.

American frontier conditions, for example—conditions that dominated much of American experience—were not of a sort to indulge male or female vanity. Both men and women were necessary to survival, and roles were parceled out in terms of need almost as much as for decorative purposes or esteem.[6]

Social evolution produced conspicuous women as well as conspicuous men. No one who knew anything of Roger Williams could fail to have heard also of Anne Hutchinson—who was also a powerful religious dissenter and wilderness pioneer—and probably harbored a blind spot on the question of who her husband was and what he had done in life as her consort. A flood of women played essential roles in the American Revolution. And if they failed to play roles comparable to those of men in legislative assemblies, it did not follow that this left them more unfulfilled than had their meager services in the armed forces.

Moreover, a vast percentage of women were obviously in superior situations as compared with a comparable percentage of males of lesser social position than their own. Male slaves, children indentured servants, apprentices, and even craftsmen were constrained to give due reverence to mistresses as well as masters. Hindsight estimates of women's condition as generally pitiful or outrageous as compared with that of men seem impertinent at the least. For greater perspective, one needs to consider the human condition that often defeated males, perhaps as often defeated females, depending on how one assesses human wants and fulfillments.

The same arguments retarded modernization of man-woman relations in pre-Civil War decades and after as retarded expansion of the suffrage, the ending of legal slavery, the liberalization of master-workman relations, public education, compassion toward debtors, the sick, and the insane. At two extremes were hardfisted and malevolent reactionaries, and greedy or irresponsible radicals. Both extremes nurtured memorable leaders. On one side stood John C. Calhoun of South Carolina, who would have frozen all human contracts and understandings if he could in the interest of social stability. On the other side stood such an idealist as Thomas Skidmore, an early New York mechanic. In company with Frances Wright and Robert Dale Owen, son of the great "utopian" Robert Owen, Skidmore sought to create the Working Men's party. His *The Rights of Man to*

Property (1829) would have redistributed wealth, doling it out in equal amounts to all.

The heroes and heroines who made one or another cause their own, and made it vibrant with talents and resolution, had to move against the human nature of the middle groups of society, which were tempted to concentrate on their own problems, to avoid becoming too much involved in other people's problems, and to relax in the relative comfort of inherited habits of thought.

The eruption of the great reform movement of 1830-1860 produced an unprecedented torrent of conspicuous female talent, infusing every radical cause directly and, in addition, creating the cause of woman's suffrage and women's rights. The list of famous and effective female writers, speakers, petitioners, and organizers in behalf of reforms is endless. It is strangely obscured in the landmark *History of Woman Suffrage* (1881-1887), edited by Elizabeth C. Stanton and others, which focused on the massive and continuous agitation in favor of the vote. It diverted public attention from the equally massive female energies put into journalism, investigation, committees, and other social conduits for changing opinion on social deportment.

The social order urgently needed those fresh female talents for new and unforeseen conditions. It is futile to imagine a Deborah Franklin, a Mercy Warren, an Abigail Adams, or any other distinguished women of Revolutionary times as asserting personalities in the fashion of the women reformers of later times.[7] And yet even the latter generation of activist females operated within impulses and relationships that did not differ radically from those of other women of early and even contemporary times.

Abby Kelley was a schoolteacher who followed the urgings of Garrisonians and became an eloquent public speaker in opposing slavery. Her accession to the chairmanship of a committee of the American Anti-Slavery Society at its 1840 annual meeting split the society in two. "Conservative" abolitionists—actually as firm in their antislavery principles as Garrison himself—refused to accept a chairwoman. Yet as the wife of the radical abolitionist and farmer Stephen S. Foster, she did not differ in her routines from numerous other women of the time. Lucy Stone also began as an abolitionist lecturer. She was as individualistic as any great women of her era, not only in pioneering public lectures on women's rights but maintaining her own name in marriage, her husband heartily concurring. But though she undoubtedly advanced the suffrage cause, it is not clear that she broke any ground at all for sexual innovations or wished to do so. If anything, her career underscored the validity of traditional sociobiological expectations, leaving nothing for later experimenters to exploit.

Lydia Maria Child did as much as any female of her time for womanly distinction as writer, abolitionist, and public figure. She courageously gave up her popularity as an author on such subjects as cooking and the raising of girls to affront her conventional readers with her testimony against slavery, a testimony that strongly influenced such figures as Reverend William Ellery Channing and Charles Sumner. Yet she had little interest in the suffrage for women. She held no duty higher than that to her distinguished but utterly impractical husband David Lee Child, a reform lawyer without a legal practice, a pioneer farm innovator without an income. Such combinations of traditional and unconventional attitudes made the Childs formidable to neighbors who lacked their sense of social commitment but whom they could reach to a degree through reason and example. Ultimately, the Childs's attitude toward slavery and social change became that of a majority of the North. To that extent, they were precursors of progressivism and memorable to later Progressives.

There were highly practical reasons for changes in attitude toward women and women's work, which were obscured by traditional and family expectations but which forced themselves on various classes of females as industry multiplied and cities grew where there had been none before. Although neither cities nor industry reached in pre-Civil War years the impersonality that later became a supreme problem in human relations, they were sufficiently novel in structure to require new arms and mentalities for efficient administration. Lady editors, female poets, woman attendants in hospitals and asylums, and teachers who became sufficiently numerous almost to rank with men as not requiring designation by sex—such workers were not necessarily progressive or concerned with advancing the cause of education or of women.

Clara Barton (1821-1912) was outstanding in advancing her own status and prestige though she became a symbol of social philanthropy. She began her career as a frustrated teacher in a New Jersey school, which she had made the first public school in the state but which was then calmly preempted by her male superior. She became a copyist in the Patent Office in Washington. When the Civil War began, she personally solicited comforts and supplies for soldiers and delivered them by horse and wagon at the war fronts. She also aided medical men and exposed herself to dangers in the field. Vague reports identified her with the great United States Sanitary Commission but hers was a lone and protracted effort.

After peace was declared, she independently persuaded President Lincoln to permit her to make a project of locating prisoners of war and had Andersonville, Georgia, a prisoner-of-war compound, dedicated as a national cemetery. Barton helped spread her own fame by making personal appearances on lecture platforms until her voice failed in 1868. She suffered one of her recurring breakdowns when work was completed, leaving her emptyhanded, and went abroad for her health. In Europe she made contact with the Red Cross and under its flag served on both sides of the lines during the Franco-Prussian War. Back home she made herself an agent pressing for an American Red Cross and congressional approval of the Geneva treaty, which called for neutral aid to the wounded and needy in wartime. She obtained Senate ratification in 1882.

Thereafter, though she was in her sixties, and amazingly into her eighties when she continued to hold to the form and features of youth, she personally dispensed aid in domestic flood, fire, and tornado situations, and in Russia and elsewhere during famine. Using funds publicly acquired as suited her improvised program, Barton took deep and naive satisfaction in attaining international celebrity as an angel of mercy.

She was an inspiration to several generations of girls and young females and merited all the acclaim her matchless energies attracted. But she was no progressive in the sense of her contemporary Dorothea Dix, whose eloquence won over legislatures to the idea of caring for the helpless and insane. Dix's monuments were hospitals and institutions committed to such missions. They extended public responsibility in fields that had once been private but that could no longer be so if human feelings and civic controls were to be maintained. Barton spoke for the individual, the private sector; and it was quite proper that "her" Red Cross should finally have been taken from her, to be administered by others. Dix's vision went beyond to a more complex, a more responsible civilization.

Both Barton and Dix were vehicles for change, but it was the latter who promised more for the future. Dix was both agitator and achiever. Somewhere between the propaganda function she served and the building of asylums that she inspired lay a formula for progressivism. It involved change and modernization, using the common materials of lawmakers and their public. Several generations of writers, politicians, and civic workers, women as well as men, refined the formula before it attained its classic period.

NOTES

1. Louis Filler, ed., *Slavery in the United States of America* (New York, 1971).
2. The logistics of government policy and public opinion merit further study. Georgiana C. Nammack, *Fraud, Politics, and the Dispossession of the Indians: The Iroquois Land Frontier in the Colonial Period* (Norman, Okla., 1969), offers itself as a model for issues and treatment that can be applied to other areas of the country. See also Bernard W. Sheehan, *Seeds of Extinction: Jeffersonian Philanthropy and the American Indian* (Chapel Hill, 1973).
3. John Hope Franklin, ed., *Reminiscences of an Active Life: The Autobiography of John Roy Lynch* (Chicago, 1970), 22. This work was written in the author's old age, following a long and successful career as congressman, civil servant, real estate dealer, and lawyer.
4. Arthur M. Schlesinger, Jr., *The Age of Jackson* (Boston, 1945), 424-425.
5. Mary R. Beard, *Woman as a Force in History* (New York, 1946), 78ff.
6. William A. Fowler, *Woman on the American Frontier* (Hartford, 1878).
7. Phebe A. Hanaford, *Daughters of America* (Augusta, Maine, 1883), helps perspective by passing in review hundreds and even thousands of female careers in ways that stimulate thought about their individual achievements; this process of assessment is helped further by such a compilation as *Our Famous Women* (Hartford, 1886), chapters of which were prepared by "Twenty Eminent Authors," all female. It quickly becomes apparent that "eminence" is controversial to nonpartisans.

Liberal Syndrome: The Politics of Hope

Poor there always were, though their troubles and predicaments were often impugned by the feeble use they made of their opportunities in "flush times" and by their often precipitous escapes into drink and drugs, morphine being available for euphoria as well as pain. Nor was their cause helped by their lack of sympathy for alien poor of various types: alien in religion, in heritage, in race. Nevertheless, there were those who sought to aid the poor—through charity, so linked with patronage and contempt as to lose all moral credit, or through display of their sorrows, so patently legitimate in the case of exploited children and needy mothers. Help was rarely commensurate with the poverty produced by a careless, competitive society bemused by frontier and other opportunities.

There was a marked contrast in social policy between the Americans and the English. The latter, hemmed in by a more rigid class structure and by ocean, produced so imperial a reformer as Lord Shaftesbury. His half-century crusade against poverty and the degradation it induced gave form to the movements that created curbs in factory management, and schools and other agencies for the young and helpless. His wiping out of the institution of "climbing boys"—chimney sweeps—was but one of his many achievements.[2]

Charles Dickens's revelations of poverty and its effects, wept over on both sides of the water, drowned the subject in sentimental distinctions between good people and bad. Thomas Carlyle wrote inspiringly on the virtues of hard work but made a moral issue of what was often a patent matter of human anguish capable of modification. And his scorn of "inferior" people, as he saw them, ultimately contributed to destroying much of his prestige among those concerned for the traditions of freedom. Even in his own time he was reproached by the Italian republican Mazzini: "Mr. Carlyle comprehends only the *individual*; the true sense of the unity of the human race escapes him. He sympathizes with all men, but it is with the separate life of each, and not with their collective life."[3]

Most deadly to the cause of the poor whites was the sympathy they evoked in order to justify slavery. Harrowing tales of children in the mills and the mines, of girls driven to prostitution and boys to burglary by their life pressures, of women mangled at looms and wasted by hunger at piecework wages—all such accounts, though appalling, were diluted by appeals to race prejudice and prideful nationalism. Parliamentary investigations of conditions in the homes and workplaces of British labor spoke more eloquently than any journalistic or literary account of social misery, but they were undermined when contrasted with benign, self-serving portraits of slavery as slaveholders chose to see it. John C. Calhoun, who sought a capitalist-plantation owner alliance by equating the need for slaves in the South with the need for "white slaves" in the North, could not understand why so convenient a program did not flourish, if only to save the Union.[4]

Such dilemmas were reflected in the always expanding democratic politics of the nation. The "Jackson Revolution" of 1828 differed signally from the "Revolution" of 1800, which saw Thomas Jefferson's ascension to the presidency. Jefferson and his men were concerned with principles and programs to guide a relatively established society, though their democratic rhetoric sometimes fired hopes of advancement in their supporters which they could not control. And their formal separation of church and state retarded such stabilization of society as was obtained in Great Britain where Anglican church and crown combined to make "the Establishment" a meaningful phrase.[5]

Highly informed Jeffersonians had debated with their federalist opponents such questions as the rights and privileges of government and due policies toward manufacturies at home and Napoleon abroad. They presumed themselves to be the best as social leaders and administrators, and to prove their quality through learning and eloquence. In contrast, the politicians who combined to make Andrew Jackson President were at least as concerned for public opinion as for public issues, for, by the time voters went to the polls in 1828, continuing pressures and debates and petty insurrections had all but made white male suffrage universal.

As the Virginia aristocrat John Randolph of Roanoke venomously observed, the notorious tariff of 1828 sponsored by the Democrats—the "tariff of abominations"—was intended neither to help nor diminish industries; it "referred to manufactures of no sort or kind, but the manufacture of a President of the United States."

There were, nonetheless, principles discernible in the Jackson alliance intended to augment democratic opportunity and to create a language of public debate suitable to it. Unquestionably, it did not include Negroes; the North-South Jackson political alliance directly excluded them. Nor did it create a coherent policy toward Indians. Jackson himself had made much of his reputation as an Indian-killer; he had won not only the admiration of the common people but of many Indians who appreciated his courage and warlike skills and who joined him in battles with other Indians and in his immortal stand at New Orleans.

The egalitarian ideal, then, if it was to extend to such deprived elements in society, would require non-Jacksonians as advocates. And it did find them among many of the nation's major bards and conscience keepers, many of them educated and adhering to stable features of religion and family. Concerned for universal principles rather than for politics or expediency, they sought to recognize the humanity of patently oppressed classes rather than compete with them. Samuel Ringgold Ward, a Negro abolitionist, recognized this fact from personal experience:

> The early settlers in many parts of America were the lowest of the English population: the same class will abuse a Negro in England or Ireland now. The New England States were settled by a better class. In those states the Negro is best treated, excepting always the State of Connecticut. . . . The middling

> and better classes of all Europe treat a black gentleman as a gentleman. Then step into the British American colonies, and you will find the lowest classes and those who have but recently arisen therefrom, just what the mass of Yankees are on this matter. Also, the best friends the Negro has in America are persons generally of the superior classes, and of the best origin. These are facts. . . .[6]

Jacksonians, though they not infrequently included notables from "better classes," generally looked elsewhere for inspiration. They were more materialistic in outlook and, in emphasizing the separation of church and state, served both those who made little of religion and the Irish whom their politicians patronized in opposition to Whig Protestants. Jackson Democrats fought harder than did their Whig enemies for the abolition of imprisonment for debt; Whigs were troubled by the need for substitutes for prisons—substitutes that would keep the light-fingered and the light-headed from squandering other people's money. Jacksonians approved of the expansion of educational opportunities, which inevitably meant that those with funds would have to pay for the instruction of other people's children. Democrats were also more practical and vocational minded in educational goals than were such famous Whigs as Horace Mann, to whom education meant first of all religious and patriotic devoutness and a respect for law, whether terrestrial or higher.

Above all, Jacksonians hungered for a fluid democracy and tangible opportunities. Their leader's sensational war on the Second Bank of the United States was probably more symbolic than real; it is doubtful that the Bank was about to dry up the sources of free enterprise and private initiative either on the frontier or in the secured eastern cities. But the political battle that closed down the Bank and made "monopoly" a hated word among the democratic masses created an attitude that would motivate later duels between independent businesses and railroads. And though Jackson made a fetish of "hard money"—silver and gold—as the only true and honest currency, his *intention* of better satisfying the needs of the poor and uneasy would in time reappear in endless programs and debates over "soft" paper currency.

Common to earlier and later eras, then, were liberal assumptions that government interventions of particular kinds were necessary to prevent private power from overwhelming the needy and the uninformed. How much in itself hard money or soft aided a generation of spenders and gainers has never been determined. Antagonists for or against one or the other did, however, create stereotypes of monopolists, greedy bankers, beset farmers, and harassed workingmen,[7] which they fancied or despised. In this way they helped to display choices for empathy to voters and activists.

The syndrome of progressivism, then, meant first of all a feeling for expanding opportunities that might help an individual's private ambitions and that would feed his dreams and generally serve the politics of hope. It meant a recognition of material realities—what Grover Cleveland would a half-century later refer to as a condition confronting the country rather than a theory. Cleveland emphasized, as John C. Calhoun had earlier, the economics of "free" trade: a program as controversial as "soft" money. "Free" trade did not mean the same thing to all people, and, as the world grew smaller, international trade became a function of international politics and was reduced to a secondary issue. But in its time, implemented with pompous rhetoric about the economics of wool for warmth and food for babies, it did agitate all *voters* indiscriminately. The politics of hope had no place for those who placed ideals above community, or the individual above society, and readily sacrificed even some of its own partisans when necessary.

Frances Wright was as materialistic as any other Democrat. She was an egalitarian with the best of them. But her disregard for their conventional clichés and her flouting of religion limited her usefulness to them. She pressed courageously for freedom in sex; later crusaders in the field would give her the same lip service they gave "Tom" Paine. But such stances left her largely peripheral to more important Progressive decisions and oddly closer to the moral crusaders who reprobated her as a disgrace to womanhood, though she was anything but a slut.

Raw progressivism was possible only in good times. When they failed, Progressive types needed to edge nearer to the moral crusaders they normally scorned or patronized. Moral reformers tended toward absolutes. Slavery was evil. Drunkenness was a sin. There could not be too much dedication to principle. Such tenets produced upright and even awesome figures in education, temperance, peace, literature, woman suffrage, religious liberalism, and a score of other areas including, most spectacularly, abolition. It was thus fantastic, at the least, to accuse any of them, especially so indispensable an abolitionist-businessman as Lewis Tappan, who happened to believe in God and to honor the Sabbath as being "part of an authoritarian philosophy that fostered the proslavery spirit in the nation at large and the proscriptive spirit in the antislavery movement."[8] The eloquence and deeds of reformers ranging from Ralph Waldo Emerson to Wendell Phillips inspired and motivated multitudes.

"Go love thy infant, love thy woodchopper, be good-natured and modest; have that grace; and never varnish your hard, uncharitable ambition with this incredible tenderness for black folk a thousand miles off. Thy love afar is spite at home." Thus Emerson's *Self-Reliance*, in words reminiscent of his friend Thomas Carlyle's views. And as between Jacksonism and moral reform, it was the first that contained the most potent seeds of progressivism, for implicit in Jacksonism was a sense of human nature that moral reformers rejected. Henry Thoreau in his obscure Walden sanctuary, of no public consequence until after his death, became a legend that could refresh and console persons wearied by life's problems and temptations. True, they needed a species of idealism to accompany them in their quest for status and security. How else could they hope to interest others in their cause? But they needed as much issues that could be a hearth of hope for a variety of social types, including their own. They needed leaders who through personal charisma and familiar experiences could bind them as a party. A William Lloyd Garrison who rejected parties, a Lucy Stone who rejected traditional views of women's role, and all the reformers who upbraided tipplers for wasting their substance and ruining their families could hardly help pass laws friendly to debtors, to land-hungry bankrupts, to troubled mechanics who escaped from their troubles in gin mills: all of these with votes and fearful of the practical competition unleashed slaves and women might offer.

Moral reformers often found means for reaching popular mentalities. They appealed to good and better natures. But, generally, moral reformers' influence was on the outlook of crowds and legislatures. They revealed disparities between professed American ideals and the tragedies of the maimed and oppressed and demanded that auditors and readers live emotionally with such realities. They refined useful arguments for practical men.

Progressives had their own utopian anticipations, but they functioned in the realm of the material. It is a curious fact that posterity has preferred to recall Robert Owen, whose New Harmony, Indiana, cooperative colony failed catastrophically, and to forget George Rapp, Owen's predecessor in New Harmony, whose "Harmonist" colonies there and in Pennsylvania totally succeeded, materially and in a spirit of well-being. The evident reason is that Rapp's followers were religious in motivation, whereas Owen's were dedicated to materialism, and their leader at the time was an atheist.[9]

Owen had been a successful businessman in Scotland before he concluded that all material existence could be organized to satisfy human needs through rational living arrangements, he himself to decide what constituted rational living. The collapse of his New Harmony colony, based on such premises, did not discourage him. Further organizational efforts and programs in England entitled him to a pioneer status in the annals of socialism and the welfare state. Truer Progressives were satisfied to press for laws and causes that continuously raised leaders and slogans to voice their hopes and keep their dissatisfactions fresh.

There were nevertheless still the poor, and, in the case of the Irish, they were still aliens in an ungenerous world. Thoreau sought to talk to one of them near Walden but gave up in disgust; the man had no sense, he said. No wonder many like the Irishman turned for recognition and support to Democrats who flattered them and occasionally gave them jobs or, when jobs failed, loaves of bread; a constantly changing and responsive people derived the word "loafers" from the act.

The Irish immigrants also precipitated leaders and would-be leaders who, in New York City, were constrained to challenge and meet with the Democratic leaders of Tammany Hall. It had heretofore been entirely in the hands of upper-class, native-born Protestants like Aaron Burr and the less remembered Matthew L. Davis, the latter several times Grand Sachem of Tammany before being disgraced and jailed for fraud against banks and insurance companies on a grand scale. Whatever the deficiencies of Tammany leaders, they did not fail to give verbal regard to their potential voters, and to do so better than could their opponents among the moral reformers.

Thus Wendell Phillips, major orator of abolition, vigorously denied that white workers could be equated with black. Slaves were helpless; white workers could defend themselves through their acknowledged rights. "To economy, self-denial, temperance, education, and moral and religious character, the laboring class, and every other class in this country must owe its elevation and improvement."[10] Phillips later modified his view to acknowledge the difficulties under which labor worked to establish its rights. But in 1847 it took another high-minded reformer, Reverend George Ripley, founder of the cooperative Brook Farm, to remind Phillips that it was "idle to talk of the laborer, on the lowest round of the social ladder, about getting to the top of it by the observance of morality."[11]

It was nevertheless a shorter distance from Ripley to Phillips than from Ripley to the labor champions of this earlier time. They generated earnest leaders of workers' opinions like George Henry Evans, an English immigrant and pioneer labor publicist whose thought ran to unions, the legitimacy of strikes, and land reform. They also nurtured such a demagogue as Mike Walsh, whose services are harder to discern. He had been brought from Ireland when a child, had been a wanderer, and had interested himself in New York politics, where he unfolded an earthy, cynical, demogogic personality. This little-schooled malcontent preferred agitation to work, clowning at rallies, and acting out the restless dreams of some deprived Irish by indulging personal greed and exotic fantasies and by pouring out indiscriminate hatred of all who enjoyed well-being.

He had been a reporter for several years in Aurora, New York, and in Washington, D. C. In 1843 he founded *The Subterranean*, named to give a philanthropic cast to his tirades. The next year he briefly merged his paper with George Henry Evans's more dedicated *Working Man's Advocate.* He was soon in prison serving a term for libel and seems to have voluntarily separated himself from the alliance with Evans on grounds that Evans suppressed some of his fulminations, as Evans had to if he was to further his labor reform causes. Yet Evans was not disillusioned by his irresponsible associate's antics and continued to praise Walsh as an advocate of "the great truths that are to redeem the downtrodden masses." Evans added: "True, he [Walsh] has been vilified; and it would not be one of the wonders of the world if he *had* some faults or *had* committed some youthful indiscretions. Without taking the trouble to investigate this point, I can afford to admit such charges, and then, after balancing accounts, claim for him a remainder of many more good qualities than those who make the charges even make pretension to."[12]

Evans would not turn his back on a tainted associate or even consider how deeply tainted he might be. What was interesting about Walsh's otherwise banal career was that he turned his fury on the politicos of Tammany Hall, accusing them of subverting the democratic process by their machinations. That they did so regularly was well known. Critics of democratic politics not infrequently expressed admiration for the corruptionists as representing the true democracy, especially since they repaid their supporters with human attention and gifts. Walsh's denunciations of Tammany had little purpose but to call attention to himself. His organization in 1840 of a "Spartan Band" to exert pressure on Tammany patronage and nominations was little more than a form of blackmail. Tammany chieftains from time to time made deals with Walsh, but they never permitted him to root among them. Walsh's monument was the gang, which roughed up dissidents at meetings and at the polls, but he was quickly superseded in usefulness by such other gangs as Captain Isaiah Rynder's "Empire Club," which Walsh despairingly denounced as "hireling ruffians organized by the depraved and mercenary office-holding Hunkers of Tammany Hall . . . kept . . . in victuals, clothes, money and rum, to commit outrage upon such defenceless grey-headed citizens, cripples and apple women, as may be found bold and unguarded enough to openly express an opinion conflicting with the wishes or mandates of their Hunker employers, and also to multiply their votes as often as possible on the day of election."[13]

Walsh himself used the system adequately enough during his brief heyday; he was elected to the New York State Assembly for several years, then to the House of Representatives in Washington during the 1853-1855 term where he dreamed fair dreams of being none other than President. As he wrote, in his letters home:

> I concluded to dismiss—when President—every chap attached to the [H]ouse who should not pay a proper respect to me in my present position, and also to remind him what it was for on discharging him. . . .
>
> In a moment I was sitting down. The grave members of my cabinet had gone home, after receiving my instructions. I forgot politics—let the cares of the State go to the devil until next day—and was enjoying myself in the most glorious and phylosophical style with two bright luscious looking young ladies, each of whom were putting naughty, though very pleasing thoughts into my head, by leaning on my neck and twisting my hair into ringlets with their fingers, under the innocent supposition, no doubt, that Presidents have no feelings like other men. . . .
>
> "Hallo! By Jove, I'm the first President that ever understood how to enjoy himself."[14]

Walsh's readers in New York very likely appreciated his reverie as tallying in part with reveries of their own. But life was real, and they had wives and children to look after. They responded as well, therefore, to such rant as the following:

> I come here determined to reduce the county meeting to its legitimate purposes—to appeal from the decision of a corrupt committee, who dispose of nominations to the highest bidder, as the hireling soldiery of Rome used to sell the imperial diadem. This is a thing which should have been done at every county meeting which has been held here for several years past; but because I am the first man to repel an insult offered to the working classes, and resist a wanton high-handed, and palpable act of injustice, you are terrified at what you consider the daring recklessness of the innovation. [Tremendous cheering accompanied with hisses and threats.] And why do you consider a manly proper and patriotic act a dangerous innovation? Because

> you are slaves. [Terrific uproar] Yes, abject willing slaves—slaves by choice, while you foolishly flatter yourselves that you are democrats. [Cries of pull him down, pull him down, this is no place for such remarks.] Keep still, gentlemen—don't worry yourselves—*this is just the place for such remarks*; but you have acted so long like automatons, that to act like men seems to you to be a new state of being. [Then turning around to Slamm, Ming, Riel and others, who were hissing.] When the Locofocos first started, they had not the courage nor the ability with all their organizations to come into Tammany Hall and purify it, but they sneaked like thieves into an obscure corner hole in the Bowery, where, like their predecessors, the leaders of the movement to tickle their followers, put forth doctrines which they detested in their hearts, and never followed for a moment. Then the chief cry against them was "why did they leave Tammany Hall," and now when I come here—I who have always religiously practiced what I preach, you exclaim "This is no place for such remarks." Truly, gentlemen, the man who would consult you, and try to mould himself to your views, would not be lost for employment. But I wish you to distinctly understand me when I tell you that Tammany Hall belongs to us—we being the only honest, virtuous portion of the democratic party, and I wish you also to distinctly understand that we are determined to keep possession of it until you are able to dispossess us—and that I believe is as good as a lease for life, is'nt it boys? [Terrific cheering, hisses and cries of "yes," mingled with "go it Mike," "turn him out etc.," which finally ended in two or three beautiful fights. The uproar here was so great, that the reporters were unable to note a word for several minutes.][15]

No one seems to have spelled out whatever came of Walsh's verbalisms. All noted his heavy drinking and vain actions. Following his term in Congress, when he was unseated by "Honest John" Kelly, he went on a spree throughout Europe and as far as Constantinople, nominally in behalf of a man who dreamed of building ships for the Russian navy. Walsh returned a physical wreck and made a dissipated coda of the last passages of his life. In 1859 he was found dead in an areaway, following a night of roistering, his gold watch and diamond ring missing. There were fine Irish who honored their people with their lives and who were honored in turn by other Americans. It seems unkind to the efforts of labor in America to dub Walsh "one of America's first proletarian leaders."[16]

NOTES

1. Blanche D, Coll, "The Baltimore Society for the Prevention of Pauperism, 1820-1822," *American Historical Review* 61 (October 1955): 77-87.

2. Edwin Hodder, *The Life and World of the Seventh Earl of Shaftesbury, K.G.* (London, 1887), 583-588. Abolitionist philanthropists like Harriet Martineau argued that his attacks on manufacturers were those of the landowner who kept his own peasants in serflike circumstances, but these accusations are not borne out by the facts. Shaftesbury as courageously attacked hardfisted squires—including his own father—as he did intransigent mill-masters.

3. Mazzini was given this insight by his own dream of a unified Italy; see his "On the Genius and Tendency of the Writings of Thomas Carlyle" in *Essays Selected from the Writings of Joseph Mazzini* (London, 1887). Even more harmful to Carlyle's good repute was his scorn of abolitionists as frauds concerned for misery abroad rather than the misery of the poor at home, and his firm view that Negroes were congenitally inadequate; see his "Occasional Discourse on the Nigger Question," published originally in *Fraser's Magazine* in 1849; see *Critical and Miscellaneous Essays* in his *Works* (New York, n.d.), 16: 461ff.

4. Calhoun's "reverse Marxism" is evident in all his appeals to Congress for an understanding between North and South; see Richard K. Crallé, ed., *Speeches of John C. Calhoun Delivered in the House of Representatives and in the Senate of the United States* (New York, 1857), volume four of *The Works of John C. Calhoun*, 6 vols. (New York, 1854-1857), 532-533. A remarkable work, the author unidentified, is John C. Cobden, *The White Slaves of England,* first issued in Auburn, New York, in 1853, which appeared in at least six editions, largely composed of searing abstracts from parliamentary hearings of conditions in English mines and factories, and obviously intended to combat abolitionist sentiments, a species of muckraking in reverse.

5. For its revitalization in the United States late in the twentieth century, see Richard H. Rovere, *The American Establishment and Other Reports* (New York, 1962), 3-21.

6. Samuel Ringgold Ward, *Autobiography of a Fugitive Slave* (1855; reprint ed., Chicago, 1970), 31.

7. It helps perspective to realize that many "workingmen" were, in

reality, master-workmen who employed others to carry bricks and dig holes. In effect, they were employers, capitalists, entrepreneurs and would be so revealed in post-Civil War decades. Many of them were, of course, quite capable of working and managing at the same time, and they were the best of the crew; see Joseph Dorfman, "The Jackson Wage-Earner Thesis," *American Historical Review*, 54 (January 1947): 296-306.

8. Aileen S. Kraditor, *Means and Ends in American Abolitionism* (New York, 1967), 75.

9. William E. Wilson, *The Angel and the Serpent: The Story of New Harmony* (Bloomington, Ind., 1964), John S. Duss, *The Harmonists: A Personal History* (Harrisburg, Pa., 1943). Especially interesting is the treatment by John Humphrey Noyes in *History of American Socialisms* (Philadelphia, 1870), Noyes himself being notorious for his "free love" theories and practice, and famous for the success of his Oneida (New York) Community plate silver, once advertised as "forever" in wedding advertisements.

10. John R. Commons, ed., *Labor Movement, 1840-1860* in Commons et al., eds., *The Documentary History of American Industrial Society* (Cleveland, 1910), 8: 220-221.

11. *Ibid.*, 221-222. See also the account of an Irish workers' strike in 1846, they having received sixty-five cents per day wages and then been challenged with the strikebreaking of new German immigrants. "Of course the Military were called out, the Irish overawed, the Germans protected in their work, and thus the matter stands." *Ibid.*, 8: 225-226.

12. Commons et al., *History of Labour in the United States* (New York, 1918), 1: 529-530.

13. *Ibid.*, 529.

14. Michael Walsh, *Sketches of the Speeches and Writings of Michael Walsh: Including His Poems and Correspondence, Compiled by a Committee of the Spartan Association* (New York, 1843), 92.

15. *Ibid.*, 26-27.

16. Arthur M. Schlesinger, Jr., *The Age of Jackson* (Boston, 1945), 491; cf. Robert Ernst, "The One and Only Mike Walsh," *New-York Historical Society Quarterly*, 36 (January 1951): 43ff. See also pages 148-149.

The People's Press

Along with the new politics of the common people came a new press; it is a matter of judgment as to which came first. The instrument of agitation during the era of the Revolution had been the pamphlet, read aloud in taverns and uniting those who could read with those who could not. The pamphlet maintained its popularity throughout the reform era. Great stores of pamphlets accumulated in such private collections as that of William Henry Seward covering all subjects from canals and other matters of town and country development to the great moral and political questions. Pamphlets controverted pamphlets, often in a continuing series of ripostes. Outstanding speakers and debaters brought their opponents up to the mark, reminding them of assertions they had made years and even decades before.

In the 1830s the penny press emerged to seek a wider audience, which would read for information but also for amusement, for ideas, for a sense of the way the world was going, which might affect its destiny. The new popular press brought forth an amazing variety of newspaper talent—from William Leggett, an ardent reformer who helped give dimensions to Jacksonian democracy, to Edgar Allen Poe, whose "Balloon Hoax" briefly diverted New York readers in 1844, one year after the more celebrated "Moon Hoax" of Richard Adams Locke. His circumstantial, imaginative account of vegetation and finally "man-bats" purportedly seen through a telescope caused a sensation, with scientists preparing to learn more of the phenomena observed on the moon, according to Locke, by astronomers stationed at the Cape of Good Hope. The articles were so well written that "even the six-cent sheets which pretended to despise it, took for granted the truth of the reports."[1] As significant for the future of journalism was the fact that the *New York Sun*, which printed the articles, momentarily obtained the largest newspaper circulation in the world, which was then nineteen thousand.

The future had even more to cope with James Gordon Bennett, father of "yellow journalism" though not, be it noted, of muckraking. He was a Scotch immigrant who did much to stimulate the increasing hunger for novelty and diversion. Bennett began life as an idealist; he had originally come to America because it was the homeland of Benjamin Franklin. He quickly grasped what people really wanted—sensation, excitement, lurid charges and imputations.

Henry J. Raymond of the *New York Times* envied Bennett the success of his *New York Herald*, initiated in 1835. Raymond expressed the wish that the devil would come to him every evening as he did to Bennett to let him know what the public would like to read the next morning. There was, however, more than evil counsel in Bennett's triumphs. He did indeed feature murders. But he also sent journalists out in boats in New York harbor to board newly arrived ships and pick up succulent news items about Europe before the ship's newspaper cargo had been unloaded and distributed. Bennett was the first to employ telegraph services. And if, in addition, he practiced unscrupulous journalism and was mean minded toward blacks and abolitionists, it could not have been because he differed widely in opinion from that of most of his readers. Bennett had a rascally touch to his character, but he was also in his own fashion a romantic. Only this explains his hasty return to his office to be the first to report that he had just been caned by a competitor whom he had maligned.[2]

Alexis de Tocqueville in his *Democracy in America* (1838) looked down on the popular journalists as half-educated, vulgar, and unprincipled adventurers, and Charles Dickens in *Martin Chuzzlewit* (1844) was no more complimentary of the popular press. But it had distinguished adjuncts, the most distinguished being William Cullen Bryant, whom a complex nation would choose to remember only as a poet, to be sure the first poet to win universal acceptance in that role in view of Freneau's failure to attract seconds or support.

In his time, Bryant was not only famous as a poet. A man of high dignity, he was New York's first citizen and, as editor of the *New York Post*, its philosopher and conscience for almost a half-century. He had been born in a Federalist household in western Massachusetts and raised among rivers and fields. He joined the Jacksonians because he could not resist their egalitarian goals. His standards of speech and writing helped raise the credibility of the entire journalistic establishment. Yet another scion of Federalism, William Jay, had occasion to express indignation that Bryant had allowed slave-catching advertisements to be printed in the *Post*.[3] Bryant was as true a progressive as the times brought forth, though of the moderate stripe that necessarily, in a nation of numerous and subtly distinctive tendencies, formed the bulk of the power-carrying alignment.

Bryant's associate William Leggett belonged to its more radical, more aggressive faction: limited in numbers and direct influence but well regarded even by his foes. He received little patronage and meager opportunities, yet when he died he was accorded almost universal respect. Leggett was a sensitive young man who yearned to serve the poor and fought illness and material difficulties in order to do so. He helped organize the Locofoco radical wing of the Democratic party in New York, joined the fight against the Second Bank of the United States, and opposed municipal corruption as degrading to government and an added burden on the needy. Leggett also protested riots against abolitionists, though in so doing and in order not to lose all his influence among Democrats he found it necessary to emphasize publicly that he was himself in no way associated with them or their program. Privately he sought means for creating a position that would be politically effective and morally just. He struggled manfully with his dilemma:

> What I am most afraid of is, that some of my friends, in their too earnest zeal, will place me in a false position before the public on the slavery subject. I am an abolitionist. I hate slavery in all its forms, degrees, and influences; and I deem myself bound by the highest moral and political obligations, not to let that sentiment of hate be dormant and smoldering in my own breast, but to give it free vent, and let it blaze forth that it may kindle equal ardour through the whole sphere of my influence. I would not have this fact disguised or mystified, for any office the

> people have it in their power to give. Rather, a thousand times rather, would I again meet the denunciations of Tammany Hall, and be stigmatized with all the foul epithets with which the anti-abolition vocabulary abounds. . . . That I should discharge this duty temperately, and should not let it come in collision with other duties; that I should not let hatred of slavery transcend the express obligations of the Constitution, or violate its clear spirit, I hope and trust you think sufficiently well of me to believe. . . .[4]

All he would write, Leggett promised, would bear out his principles. He died soon after, however, in 1839, too soon to enhance his progressive principles with political abolitionism. Its tenets of Free Soil and free enterprise could have given him a platform on which numerous writers were able to stand, and write and speak with a fervor not much different from that of the moralists.

Numerous editors contributed technical and literary aspects to the rising popular journalism. Samuel Bowles of the *Springfield* (Massachusetts) *Republican* made his paper outstanding for its clear writing and liberal, independent views; he later made himself all but a symbol of protest against corruption in business and government. Joseph Medill and others built the *Chicago Tribune* into a force in what was then the American West; a later photograph would show Abraham Lincoln studying the paper with attention. Indeed the paper rose with his star and joined him in attaining national prominence.

The editor of editors, however, was the unlikely Horace Greeley, an absentminded, impetuous journalist who came from a Vermont farm to become the unofficial voice of the North through his Whig *New York Tribune.* Greeley's almost incredible naiveté caused him to embrace every fad of his era, including spiritualism, mesmerism, and phrenology. A legend was later established that as a result of the violent attacks on him conducted by Republican party publicists in 1872 when he ran for President on the Liberal Republican party ticket, he suffered a nervous breakdown and died in despair in a sanatorium. A study of his passionate outpourings of that sad time, on the contrary, suggests that he had never been clearer in his self-recriminations. He had given too little thought to his future and that of his family by aimlessly lending his money in all directions, including alleged reformist experiments: money that never came back. He had neglected his wife in pursuit of numerous projects of doubtful relevance and driven her toward insanity and death.

His lecture tours had been lucrative and high-minded—from them derived a volume, *Hints toward Reform* (1850). But they added up to little more than entertainment for his comfortable audience and vanity and ambition for himself; Greeley was notorious for his greedy and futile hunger for political office. He had meant well, he had meant well, Greeley wildly repeated during his final agonies. "My life has been a fevered march," he had said. And again, he "had been tempted by the glittering bait of the Presidency" when he should have put his own house in order: "And now, having done wrong to millions while intending only good to hundreds, I pray God that he may quickly take me from a world where all I have done seems to have turned to evil, and wherein each hour has long been and henceforth must be one of agony, remorse, and shame."[5]

Essentially, Greeley had been the country boy who had been shown respectable big city delights from a high place and had been unable to resist their self-righteous enticements. But before his tragic collapse, he showed matchless ability to sense public preferences and discontents and minister intellectually to them. He virtuously scorned tobacco, liquor, and dancing. But he permitted his readers to dream about utopian communities through the essays of Charles A. Dana and Albert Brisbane. The latter was a follower and translator of Charles Fourier's ideas about people living in harmony in "phylansteries." Greeley himself helped turn the experimental community of Brook Farm into a Fourier community, which swiftly disintegrated and died.

He gave newspaper space to the humanistic essays of George Ripley and to Margaret Fuller, who wrote pioneer essays on women and woman's potential. Karl Marx from abroad informed Greeley's essentially conservative readers on foreign affairs. Those readers, in New York, but also throughout the North as well as in the South among leaders and publicists requiring information on northern thinking, received an unequaled selection of writings expressive of the region's temperament and concerns. Thoreau, who came down from Concord, Massachusetts, to sample New York's interests and ways, was one of the few to resist its temptations. He quietly refused to compete with its buccaneers and reformers, preferring to return to Concord (which was not impressed by his choice) and his own largely interior dialogue.

How complex was the interrelationship of parties and journalism and reform can be seen in the quarrels that separated Horace Greeley and James Fenimore Cooper. The humbly born Greeley was associated with the party that Jacksonians rhetorically identified with the rich and well born, whereas Cooper, proud resident and landholder of Cooperstown, New York, counted himself a follower of Jackson. To be sure, Cooper was surrounded by Whig farmers in upper New York State, farmers who resented their feudal obligations to old Dutch landlords who held colonial grants in perpetuity. Cooper saw the farmers as destructive revolutionaries, though their goal was no more than the private possession of the lands they worked and which they were eager to purchase.

Cooper grimly defended the rights and privileges of aristocrats as landlords, and himself conducted lawsuits intended to prove that efforts to break contracts in perpetuity and ordinances in support of them were legally and morally wrong. But Cooper was not so much a Jacksonian as he was a Jeffersonian out of time. In turgid fiction and in lucid prose essays he brilliantly identified democracy with the rule of the best, among whom he quite accurately included himself. Yet his farmer antagonists were people of courage and independence. In their hunger for freeholds they would not stop for law or tradition. In time, they would become famous for their conservatism and contempt for New York City liberality. But in the 1830s they themselves defied laws and authority in order to force the lordly Van Rensselaers and Van Scheiffelins to release them and their children from old colonial dues. In their efforts they earned the endorsement, if not the cooperation, of Horace Greeley and the hatred of the great novelist.[6]

NOTES

1. George Henry Payne, *History of Journalism in the United States* (New York, 1920), 248.

2. Bennett's story is instructively told in Oliver Carlson, *The Man Who Made News* (New York, 1942).

3. Jay to Lewis Tappan, August 22, 1836, Tappan Papers, Library of Congress. Allan Nevins, *The Evening Post* (New York, 1922) is more sympathetic to Bryant's evasion of abolitionist tenets. Bryant became a Free Soiler in 1848 and one of Lincoln's most ardent supporters. That Bryant's views need to be seen in perspective is shown when they are compared with those of Philip E. Bell, founder of *The Colored American,* second Negro newspaper in America. Bell not only refused to publish criticisms of moderate abolitionists for repudiating William Lloyd Garrison; he would not publish Negro abolitionists' endorsement of Garrison. For this Bell was denounced by Boston Negroes. New York Negroes were divided on a proper attitude toward Louis Kossuth, the Hungarian republican revolutionary who was visiting in the United States and refusing to comment on the slavery issue, arguing that it was a domestic question. (Carter G. Woodson, ed., *The Mind of the Negro as Reflected in Letters Written during the Crisis, 1800-1860* [Washington, 1926], 190-193, 287-290.)

4. Leggett to ——, October 24, 1838, in Theodore Sedgwick, Jr., ed., *A Collection of the Political Writings of William Leggett* (New York, 1840), 2: 335-336. Frank Luther Mott's reference to Leggett as a "proletarian" writer indicates the need for more careful discriminatory observations in the field; see Mott, *American Journalism* (New York, 1941), 258.

5. William Harlan Hale, *Horace Greeley, Voice of the People* (New York, 1950), 351-352.

6. For a defense of the antirent rebellion, which reached its height in the 1840s, see Henry M. Christman's dramatic and well-researched *Tin Horns and Calico* (New York, 1945). The rights of the patroons are explained with less eloquence, but with detailed scholarly analysis, in David M. Ellis, *Landlords and Farmers in the Hudson-Mohawk Region, 1790-1850* (Ithaca, 1946). Cooper's "Littlepage" novels are interesting as providing a fictional view of the antirent events and as helping reveal relations between "literary" criticism and social attitudes. Antirent sympathizers sneered at Cooper's social novels while continuing to patronize his Leatherstocking tales. Best known of Cooper's prorent fiction is *Satanstoe* (1845), but *The Chainbearer* (1845) and *The Redskins* (1846) also repay reading.

"'Common Scold'"

James Gordon Bennett's formula for a newsworthy tale was a beautiful woman murdered under mysterious circumstances. "Beautiful" women, in fact, became a staple of popular journalism whether they were indeed beautiful or not. Frances Wright (1795-1852) almost certainly gained some of her notoriety because she was comely and carried an aura of scandal, thanks to her libertarian views.

"Fanny Wright" became a byword with conservatives and those they influenced, but not before she and her enthusiastic writings on liberty had won the attention of such older liberals as the Marquis de Lafayette and Thomas Jefferson. The Scot-born young woman was impressed by Robert Owen's plans for reorganizing human society, and in 1827 she began a colony in Nashoba, Tennessee, near what became Memphis. Her plan was for equal conditions for rich and poor, Negro and white. The colony quickly degenerated into licentiousness and incompetent management. Wright went on to New York with Robert Dale Owen, himself empty-handed from New Harmony, Indiana, and its failures. The two proposed a program of free thought, workingmen's organization, and equal rights for women.

Owen's career as a radical wound down as he returned to Indiana and became an influential politician and emancipationist: a clearly progressive figure in the turbulence of events that produced the Republican party. Wright's radical adventure was surprisingly brief. She drew audiences in 1829 and 1830 in New York who came to see her and hear her shocking ideas. She returned to Europe, where she became herself an aristocrat, briefly and unhappily married to the

Frenchman D'Arusmont. Her subsequent visits to the United States were inconsequential. It is doubtful that she made an impact of any sort on the fight for women's rights, or, indeed, rights of any kind. Although her program was intended to rid the world of superstition and put it on a sound, materialistic base, she rates as a utopian rather than as contributory to a practical understanding of human needs.

Her contrast with Anne Royall is impressive. One was young and pretty, the other was old and unattractive. One enjoyed famous associates, the other fought cruelty and contempt. One became a legend of liberalism and vaguely imagined achievement. The other was lost in oblivion. Yet probably it was the latter whose cause was more deeply rooted in American realities and who better merits recollection.

It is perhaps appropriate that the prototype of the muckraker should have been a woman who had experienced pioneer dangers, who had enjoyed for years the prestige and privileges of ladyhood, and who had then suffered in the extreme the penalties of unfair and outdated connubial laws. Progressives always faced the problem of assessing social needs along a line of constantly changing conditions. And with elite families always under pressure from ambitious underlings who yearned to dance on their graves, the needs of both rich and poor required understanding for an equation that would be of general interest.

Anne Royall was a reformer not out of philosophical conviction but out of necessity. The cause she espoused was her own, but it directly touched that of numerous others without her resources of courage and endurance. Although her cause was social, she was unable to institutionalize it, and she died with it: one of the race of American "eccentrics." Nevertheless, she did enough to win the title "Grandma of the Muckrakers."[1]

She was born in 1769 Anne Newport, daughter of a Marylander who was possibly an illegitimate son of one of the noble Calverts of that state. A Tory, he moved his family during the American Revolution to the western Pennsylvania frontier, and there he died possibly during an Indian massacre. Such were the scenes of Anne's childhood. Her mother, a Virginian, remarried, but following her second husband's death she moved down the Shenandoah Valley to western Virginia seeking relatives or friends. In 1785 she settled as a servant in the household of Captain William Royall, a wealthy and educated farmer who had served in the Revolution and was said to have been well acquainted with George Washington.

Royall made a protégé of young Anne, then sixteen years old and twenty or more years his junior. He introduced her to his library and instructed her in his views while almost certainly living with her. Royall was a Deist, an admirer of Thomas Paine, contemptuous of established churches, and a dedicated Freemason. He was also among those southerners who, believing in the principles of the Revolution, had voluntarily freed his slaves. In 1797 he caused a sensation by marrying the twenty-eight year old Anne. Thereafter she lived happily as his consort, enjoying books and the amenities of country life.

In 1813 he died and her idyll came to an end. He had left her everything in his will, and she was able to undertake travels in a coach attended by three servants. But bitter relatives of her dead husband instituted court actions to strip her of her property. For the next decade she apparently enjoyed the warmth and leisure of Alabama. Catastrophe overtook her in 1823 when, at the age of fifty-four, she learned that the courts had decided against her as an adultress, depriving her of all her inheritance.

In this dark time she clung to her status as the wife of a Revolutionary soldier and began an action to receive a widow's pension from the government. She won some support in Washington, notably from former President John Quincy Adams, now a congressman from Massachusetts. When she was finally awarded $2,400 in 1848 by act of Congress, half of it was turned over to Royall's triumphant legal heirs. The remainder, except for ten dollars, was taken up by her lawyers.

Meanwhile she had reorganized her life's challenges with amazing fortitude. She was a lone person with no experience but travel. Through the 1820s, without funds or patronage, using every means of conveyance from steamers to simple walking shoes, she traveled throughout the country taking notes of people and places of every description. Within five years she had set down her meetings and impressions in no fewer than ten volumes. ***Sketches of History, Life and Manners in the United States*** (1826) and ***The Black Book, or, A Continuation of Travels in the United States*** in three volumes (1828-

1829) were filled with memorable scenes reflecting her vibrant interest in life and capturing the country's variety even while it yielded to new means of transportation and populations, exchanged men's small clothes for long trousers and discarded wigs, and made other changes for women and children in deference to the will of an ever-burgeoning democracy.

Mrs. Royall was, at this stage of her work, a mirror of events rather than a social critic. But included in her plan were purposes that can only be called social and that verged on reform. She tirelessly set down tales of personal vicissitudes and adventure, local history, Indian raids, literary personalities, and events. The larger cities she broke down into institutions, notable landmarks, and other features. She praised where she could, but life and eager observation had given her standards for assessment. Moreover, her now permanently insecure status helped sensitize her to the human needs of others. Thus her account of the poorhouse in Washington was a model of early muckraking; it was not only technical in detail but provided a personal sense of repugnance that could be imparted to others:

> This wretched establishment only exists to disgrace Washington. I found several wretched children in this dreary and comfortless asylum, without one cheering voice, or hand of kindness to comfort or cherish them. Some were stretched on straw, unable to rise, others were bedecked with crocus, (I think they call it) the coarsest stuff I ever saw. The whole group had a squalid appearance, which filled me with disgust, and the smell of the place was insupportable. I asked one of the unfortunate women whose business it was to attend to these sufferers, what made the rooms smell so ill; but she was too simple to understand me. The intendant and his wife are Irish; he appeared to me to be wholly unfit for the place, and his wife a perfect she dragon. It is much to be lamented, that in such cases care is not taken to select persons of humanity, who are capable of administering comfort and consolation to affliction. The house is large and beautiful, and in the finest situation in the city, but death would be mercy compared to the situation of the unfortunate inmates. I was told that part of the house was appropriated to a

> work-house, for the punishment of disorderly persons, but I had neither the courage nor the inclination to see more of a place so replete with human woe and with an aching heart I turned my back upon those cheerless, friendless sufferers. . . . Three thousand dollars are appropriated annually for the support of this establishment![2]

Mrs. Royall did not seek out the sordid. Her accounts of hospitals, deaf and dumb institutions, schools, and other places varied with their quality as she perceived it. But her effort to function as a public informant had elements of novelty, which she had perforce developed because of her situation. Washington Irving also traveled, also observed employing a literary style she could not approach. But her substance was sometimes far more urgent. It gave her a species of fame that soon curdled into notoriety as she pursued her work.

She sought people and eventually commented upon most of the conspicuous persons of her time, expecially in politics, whom she met in her travels or in Washington.[3] She repeatedly returned to the capital in order to prosecute her case or to publish her books. Her vignettes of public men were often defined by her hopes of patronage or resentment for having been rebuffed. Many of those she met were repelled by her forwardness and unsympathetic to her needs and in their rudeness to her shared responsibility for having made her the sharp-tongued and bitter person she became. By 1829 she was sufficiently well known to publish her latest travels as *Mrs. Royall's Pennsylvania Tour* in two volumes. The following year saw publication of her *Letters from Alabama, Mrs. Royall's Southern Tour* in three volumes (1830-1831). These completed her work in the genre.

In 1829 occurred the incident with which she was thereafter maliciously identified. She had publicly denounced a group of Presbyterians who maintained a church near her own home in Washington and who hated her for the antichurch views she treasured from her late husband—views that also comported with her generally pro-Andrew Jackson, civil-rights sympathies. They had her brought to court on an old law that prescribed ducking in water for any person convicted of being a "common scold." It did not help her case that she was eloquent and defiant; she had not hesitated to term her chief antagonist a "d——d bald-headed son of a b———h." Ducking was actually provided for with the building of a ducking stool at Navy Yard Hill. The judge, however, with some shadow of modernity, ordered payment of ten dollars in lieu of the older tradition of humiliation. The fine was paid by Andrew Jackson's Secretary of War, John Eaton, in an act underscoring elements of the Democratic administration that contributed to the politics of compassion. Eaton himself that year married the daughter of a Washington tavern keeper and created a greater controversy in democratic annals than poor Anne could ever hope for when wives of the Washington political elite concluded to ignore the engaging but unelevating Peggy Eaton.

They won their case, but Anne Royall's religious opponents could not know and were not made uneasy by the knowledge that they were pillorying themselves for a posterity that would not—regrettably late—sympathize with the harassment of a person on the grounds of sex.

In 1830 Mrs. Royall, now age sixty-one, settled in Washington, acquired an old printing press and worn type, and with a faithful companion she had found, Mrs. Sarah Stack, began to issue pamphlets and other printed matter for sale to townspeople. She was already an ungainly, familiar figure who boldly accosted politicians and others, seeking to sell them her books. Her disreputable status was, in many ways, her best legacy to society. Those who were annoyed by the aged peddler too well perceived that she was in her own person a program representing better than Frances Wright the cause of the lonely and bereft, widows constrained to earn a living, women who lacked human opportunities. Theirs, also, was the contempt too often felt for the unprotected female and the fear of people who refused to die or otherwise disappear and so relieve them of their uneasy sense of injustice done.

On December 5, 1831, Mrs. Royall set down a landmark in American journalism with a new publication. Her weekly, *Paul Pry,* ungainly named like herself, contained some characteristics of her earlier work, including personalizing admirations and antipathies, contempt for church institutions, a demand for Sunday mails, and reverence for Freemasonry; Masons had helped sustain her through her trials. In addition, she urged tolerance for Catholics and such

Jacksonian causes as "hard" money and antagonism toward the Second Bank of the United States. Not surprisingly, she also passionately asked justice for widows.

But Mrs. Royall was more than a special pleader. With a concern for order and equity in the home, she had roamed the corridors of Congress remarking skulduggery and the deals of practical men. Her opening salute promised that "we shall expose all and every species of political evil and religious fraud without fear or affection." In succeeding years she refined this enterprise, nosing out or suspecting evidence of corruption and what would later be called graft, and printing her charges for all to read.

There were, of course, numerous persons of probity and virtue in public life, but it was not always easy to determine what separated legitimate self-interest from venality. Daniel Webster was one of the half-dozen outstanding statesmen in the nation and its greatest spokesman. But he thought it not amiss to accept stipends from the Second Bank. He believed in it and worked freely in its behalf.[4]

Party loyalties generally dictated that party leaders be seen in their best light, the opposition at their worse. Mrs. Royall's unceasing search for materials with which to fill her columns served her and the general public of which both were part. Although *Paul Pry*'s revelations were often doubtful and sometimes patently wrong, the method she employed as public watchdog concerned for the facts was one vital to the democratic process, which, by its nature, tended to run down toward clique conspiracies, demagoguery, and simple malfeasance in office.

John Quincy Adams saw Mrs. Royall, somewhat sympathetically, as a "virago errant . . . , redeeming herself from the cramps of indigence by the notoriety of her eccentricities and the forced currency they gave her publications." Rather, she was as much a public servant as any in Washington—as Adams himself—and helped to define the terms of public service. That she did so in pursuit of a living wage was all to her honor, yet, strangely, contributed to the lack of esteem she was accorded. Men and women who gave respect to the fiery orators of abolition withheld it from the limping old lady in a shabby green plaid; she had once suffered a broken leg after being flung down stairs by an anti-Mason with whom she had argued. Seeing her as she carried her green umbrella and a number of books

PAUL PRY.

VOL. I.] WASHINGTON, DECEMBER 3, 1831. [No 1

PAUL PRY.

PUBLISHED EVERY SATURDAY, BY

MRS. ANNE ROYAL.

FULTON'S FIRST STEAM BOAT.

Judge Story's Discourse.

The first muckraking publication. (Courtesy of the Library of Congress) and papers for ready sale, they concluded that she lacked dignity. Yet, had anyone been interested, Mrs. Royall could in her own right have offered some such thought as Abby Kelley Foster did at the Woman's Rights Convention of 1850: "Sisters, bloody feet have worn smooth the path by which you come here."

Paul Pry ran until November 19, 1836. It was succeeded on December 2 of that year by *The Huntress*, which then continued to July 2, 1854, when Mrs. Royall was eighty-five years of age. These publications are yet to be adequately assimilated into the American tradition of democratic journalism. They served their own time better than that time thought it necessary to appreciate. Their author was meagerly compensated; and when she at last ceased battling the world and died on October 1, 1854, she had nothing. She was buried as a pauper in the congressional cemetery. With Hamlet, or his female equivalent, she could have said: The rest is silence.

NOTES

1. Heber Blankenhorn, "Grandma of the Muckrakers," *American Mercury* (September 1927), 87-93.

2. Anne Royall, *Sketches of History, Life, and Manners in the United States* (Washington, D.C., 1826), 143.

3. See appendixes A, B, and C for indexes to pen portraits, places described, and descriptions of members of Congress and others in Sarah Harvey Porter, *The Life and Times of Anne Royall* (Cedar Rapids, Iowa, 1909).

4. It is interesting that though this mixing of private motive and public by Webster should have caught the partisan attention of a Jackson historian, he noted a bastion of Jackson democracy, Samuel Swartwout, only as "the corrupt Collector of the Port [of New York]." He thus avoided the question of whether corruption might not have been as serious a pursuit for Bank antagonists as for Bank proponents. Swartwout was, in fact, a Jackson favorite, and his defalcations of over a million dollars in official capacities—a sum worth vastly more in 1945 terms—merited philosophical remarks on the operations of democracy, and certainly of the Democratic party of the time; compare Arthur M. Schlesinger, Jr., *The Age of Jackson* (Boston, 1945), 84, and pp. 88-89 above.

William Lyon Mackenzie

The very prototype of the muckraker-Progressive, however, was not the woman who conquered her place in life and doubtless—long after it could serve her—in history, but a small, passionate agitator and publicist whose idealism and impetuosity in 1837 raised a rebellion in Canada. Like much of William Lyon Mackenzie's life and works the rebellion was abortive and inadequately planned, but it had enduring effects. The events of 1837 began Canada's march to independence and assured Mackenzie his place among the country's immortals. As bizarre as were the chances that enabled him to make his imprint on United States history, though, even more than Anne Royall was he to be deprived in its annals of the honor due a pioneer and benefactor.

Mackenzie (1795-1861) was a Scotsman of humble birth and of quick mind, whose experiences as a merchant, bookseller, canal manager, and engineer took him to London and then to Canada, to which he emigrated in 1820. There he engaged in business and interested himself in politics. In 1824 he issued the *Colonial Advocate*, through which his retentive memory and striking eloquence—a combination of Scotch Presbyterianism and egalitarian principles—gained him attention. As a member from York (Toronto) of the provincial parliament he poured out a constant flow of criticism of the official classes, being expelled from the legislature no fewer than five times, though he continued to hold the sympathy of his constituents. A proponent of reform and instigator of popular unrest, Mackenzie visited London in 1832 to present a petition of grievances,

W. L. Mackenzie

and he secured the dismissal of the province's attorney general and solicitor general.

In 1834 he was chosen first mayor of the newly designated city of Toronto, and two years later began in his newspaper *The Constitution* a campaign against election and other policies that limited Canadian political opportunities. In August 1837 Mackenzie published a manifesto in *The Constitution*, which was essentially a declaration of independence from Great Britain. With other insurgents Mackenzie publicly demanded a convention that would settle all matters at issue. The lieutenant governor refusing his demand, he determined to march on the city, seize its arsenal, and arrest the crown's officers.

On December 7, 1837, a skirmish took place between Mackenzie's cohorts and government troops about four miles from Toronto, during which several lives were lost. The rebels retreated to Navy Island in the Niagara River. There they were joined by some five hundred Americans, before whom Mackenzie proclaimed a provisional government. Cannonading from loyalist troops and the actions of the American commander, General Winfield Scott, broke up the rebel camp. On the American side, Mackenzie made tireless and unrestrained efforts to continue the rebellion. Though he had brought with him his large family, and was close to penury, he kept up an endless flow of correspondence and publication. In 1839 he was tried in Rochester, New York, for having incited American citizens to an attack on a foreign power. He was sentenced to eighteen months of prison.

Dank and constrictive conditions prevailed there, but Mackenzie maintained his courage and unexampled energy. Petitions poured out upon President Martin Van Buren for a pardon, which Van Buren refused, probably because it might have offended the British government. (This fact would later be exploited in partial explanation of Mackenzie's "attitude" toward Van Buren.) After a year of incarceration, Mackenzie was released—an outcast from Canada with a price on his head and in need of a living in a country he did not much respect. "The more I see of the South," he wrote privately, "the more I see it is our great enemy. It is southern slaveholding influence that keeps Cuba dependent, distracts Mexico, and enslaves

Texas. That influence has crushed thus far the American feeling for Canada."[1]

Nevertheless, he made the decisions of a concerned person, leaned toward the Democratic party, and, through incessant journalism and contacts managed to interest Robert Tyler, son of the new President John Tyler, in his financial plight. Hopes and enterprises took him to New York, where he obtained work with the New-York Mechanics' Institute and issued several numbers of *The Sons of the Emerald Isle, or Lives of One Thousand Remarkable Irishmen*, brimming with outpourings from his large store of anecdote and commentary. Mackenzie had hopes of an inspectorship of customs in New York at $1,100 a year. This was deflated into an archival task at $700 and moved him and his dependents rapidly from elegance in William Street in Manhattan to more modest furnishings in Williamsburg across the East River. At the Customs House Mackenzie was shown vast piles of correspondence left behind by the previous collector of customs, which he quickly identified as extraordinary. It involved some of the most distinguished names in the Democratic party and revealed them in confidential postures writing of intimate financial and political matters.

It took a person like Mackenzie to perceive its importance. Jesse Hoyt, formerly a storekeeper in Albany and a protégé of Martin Van Buren and the highly successful Benjamin F. Butler, formerly United States District Attorney for the Southern District of New York, had no outstanding qualities other than doglike devotion to his sponsors. It was an indication of how casually the system of patronage and political advancement had grown since George Washington's day that, on taking leave of customs, Hoyt did not trouble to remove or destroy his accumulation of incriminating letters. Obviously he expected his successors to be too busy with their own affairs to give time to old transactions. Thirty years before there had been quick profits in land deals and trading privileges, inside information about banks and government projects. There were still fortunes in these, but, in addition, government appointments had multiplied, the nation was more affluent, opportunities to gain from political preferment mixed with patriotic and egalitarian rhetoric. A General Andrew Jackson stood forth in relief as a man of action and strength.

A Jesse Hoyt worked busily in the shadows, serving his betters and profiting from their favors.

Mackenzie's was the insight of an outsider whose vision was sharpened by his reform ideals. He was akin to Thomas Paine and to the then current moral reformers, except that the latter in their pursuit of such causes as temperance and abolition tended to disdain politics as sullied by compromise. Sullied it was, but Mackenzie had been made a firebrand by his insistence on purity in politics. He had now in his hands the means for exposing the system of political chicanery as it had quickly unfolded in the United States under pressure of the popular suffrage.

Mackenzie was later to be accused of having filched private papers, of having irresponsibly put them before the public, or of having done so for reasons of spite and malice. The comparison with the later Daniel Ellsberg phenomenon is startling, though the one was concerned for domestic chicanery, the other with what he fancied to be inadequate foreign policy. Both exploiters of official and quasi-official materials seem to have been at one in their desire to improve public understanding and reform according to their lights. Mackenzie, for one, protested that none but civic motives impelled him and proved it by rejecting opportunities for gain from his revelations. As he said:

> I hear much said in Congress, the Newspapers, private circles, &c., about going to war for Oregon, for Texas, for Canada, for Mexico, for our rights, and so forth—and there was a time when I did not dread war. But when I look at the successful efforts of such men as I am describing in this volume, to corrupt the whole mass of society, to substitute the machinery propelled by a band of covetous, unprincipled, factious politicians, for the healthful influences of our free, elective institutions; I tremble lest their power over the public press and other appliances should hasten the Union into a war. It is reform at home, equal laws, and faithful public stewards that America requires. It is enemies within that our country should set about subduing, far more than enemies without.[2]

Mackenzie provided evidence that he had shown the letters to the present collector of customs and to others and had sent copies to the President of the United States himself, James K. Polk. All had approved of his project of copying the letters and striving to make them better known. It does not seem to have occurred to Mackenzie that their amiability was directed at least as much by political and sectional considerations—Polk was an unqualified proponent of slavery; Van Buren, though he had freely cooperated with his slaveholding Democratic colleagues, was more and more affected, as a northern political leader, by Free Soil sentiment—as by indignation about underhanded and thieving politics.

Mackenzie's documents were fascinating in themselves, but to them he added his remarkable sense of individuality, which helped give form to what might otherwise have appeared as an amorphous mass of private negotiations with no clearly defined theme or direction. He thus dramatized the issues of citizenship and public responsibility. Benjamin F. Butler was a dignified, unimaginative machine politician and not memorable except as raising questions about why he should have advanced publicly at all.[3] Jesse Hoyt was a more disturbing type: worse than insignificant, useless in public service, and increasingly numerous—a lengthening shadow on the Republic. Mackenzie limned him well:

> [He] made himself . . . necessary to Mr. Van Buren and his son [John], the present Attorney General. . . . Mr. M. Van Buren is very penurious and covetous—Jesse would run all over New York to recover a $5 or $10, which his late employer had reluctantly lent to some poor fellow when in trouble—would hire lodgings for him on terms of economy—would see to the washing of his clothes—the buying of his wines and groceries, or the stopping or getting subscriptions for his newspapers. John Van Buren bets, gambles, speculates in the stocks—in all this Jesse has been his humble slave. He electioneered, voted, betted, schemed, ran, stood, fetched, or carried, to order—was "more banks" or sub-treasury, Crawford or Jackson, Rufus King and negro freedom or "to jail with the missionaries," just as his patrons gave the signal. His object was pelf and power—theirs power and pelf—patriotism, the welfare of the millions . . . probably never entered into their thoughts.[4]

Hoyt was a notorious defaulter whom Van Buren had sustained in credit and office for years. The prize Jacksonian of New York, however, was Samuel Swartwout, who had begun his career as a seller of paints and dyes in New York, served well in the army during the War of 1812, then entered heavily into politics. As collector of customs of the port of New York he made off with more than a million dollars—a distinct record for that era. Among Hoyt's papers Mackenzie found raw evidence of the patronage services that had kept Swartwout in good standing while he had pursued his real career—evidence that named names and detailed relationships in wholly unprecedented amount. But, in addition, he found evidence that a higher standard of political morality could have curtailed Swartwout's work:

> I think there can be no doubt but that Mr. [Secretary of the Treasury Levi] Woodbury's office knew that Swartwout was a heavy defaulter long before he left for Paris—for it seems to be an object with him to remain quiet till after the elections of Nov. 1838. Mr. Hoyt and his friends could not have remained ignorant of the real state of Swartwout's affairs after June, 1838, the end of his (Hoyt's) first quarter. They must have seen that Swartwout was $646,754 behind for cash paid him in bonds. Mr. Ogden, Swartwout's cashier, was Hoyt's cashier till March, 1839—he knew the whole; and yet Gilpin the Solicitor was not sent to New-York till Nov. 1838. If the department received the accounts required by law, Mr. Woodbury must have known of a defalcation, even in 1837—but as he was lenient to other men who had embezzled large sums, but professed to be active [Democratic] partizans, perhaps it was his wish to be so with Swartwout and his friends. When Mr. Swartwout declined to send his last quarter's account to Washington in April, 1838, why did Woodbury not send an officer to get it till November? . . .[5]

It is difficult to give a full sense of the wealth of Mackenzie's book and its successor, *The Life and Times of Martin Van Buren: Correspondence of His Friends, Family and Pupils* (1846). A later pro-Van Buren historian, Edward M. Shepard in his *Martin Van Buren* (1888), dismissed Mackenzie as the publisher of "purloined letters, writing his pamphlet with the most obvious and reckless venom," and he quoted a Canadian foe of Mackenzie's, writing earlier, as having him lie "out of every pore of his skin." But even had Mackenzie done so, such venom gave no account of the cascade of private correspondence with which Mackenzie inundated the country. The correspondence ramified through politics, through personal ambitions, through foreign affairs, notably those of Texas. It was coherent in showing the growth of American politics from the time of the "caucus" political system of the 1820s—when small groups of elected officials in Congress and elsewhere chose their candidates for President and lesser posts—to the era of conventions, which gave a semblance of democracy to the elective process.

Thus, readers of Mackenzie's book could learn that Van Buren had, in 1824, favored for President the Georgian politician William H. Crawford over Andrew Jackson. Van Buren had been eager to acquire a branch of the Second Bank of the United States for New York. He had harbored equivocal feelings about the discontented farmers of upstate New York, though he was nominally sympathetic to them in their battle with the landlords. Mackenzie's materials relative to these causes contrasted dramatically with the routine political connections and what would later be termed payoffs for services rendered or declared. His cast of characters ranged from famous to infamous, from such buccaneer journalists as James Gordon Bennett and Mordecai M. Noah of New York to Francis P. Blair of Jackson's own Kitchen Cabinet, from strong-arm New York Democrat C. C. Cambreling to United States Post Master Amos Kendall in Washington. And over all such worthies hung the temperate and binding figure of Martin Van Buren, a man of modest deportment and philosophy, master of the New York Democratic machine, who had for a while monitored the relations of slave and antislavery states.

Typical of the tone that working politicians had assumed was that of Swartwout, who used some of his stolen funds to invest in Texas. A sample of his correspondence indicates the offhand manner in which Texas enterprise was furthered, to be implemented by arms and adventurers, including the ineffable Davy Crockett of Tennessee; Swartwout indited his epistle, February 11, 1836, to a Colonel Frost Thorn, of Nacogdoches, Texas:

My Dear Sir: I received a draft from you yesterday for 1000

> dollars at 60 days, which was promptly accepted, but there was no letter of advice accompanying it. This I regret, as I do not know what it is for, although I presume it is intended for the Texan cause. If so, please to inform me by return post—General Mason leaves this for Nacogdoches tomorrow morning. He goes on for the purpose of locating his grants, I have requested him to speak to you about Carahalls business, about which I will thank you to write me; I have paid your third draft, or rather my third note due 28th January. My interests are now very large in Texas, and I pray you do all you can to sustain Mason. You must not forget that *we* who have hitherto purchased and paid for our lands were in a great degree, the cause of your getting so many gallant men into your country. . . .
>
> Do my dear friend let me hear from you what is my atogue *now* worth, that is when you shall have made and maintained your independence? . . .[6]

Mackenzie's 152-page pamphlet in small type caused intense interest, rapidly selling fifty thousand copies. Hoyt sought and was granted an injunction halting further distribution of the work. The copies in circulation therefore immediately doubled in price. Meanwhile Mackenzie had busied himself in producing his *Life and Times of Martin Van Buren* (1846), composed of 308 pages of additional materials from his archives and elsewhere. It was more smoothly prepared and showed the competence gained from preparation of the preceding volume. Like it, it was heavily interlarded with moral judgments, many of them with debatable tone and detail.

Friends had rushed to Van Buren to inform him of the publication of Mackenzie's first volume. In his memoirs, Van Buren maintained a calm attitude toward the sensation, holding that it was caused by Mackenzie's bitterness for having been refused pardon while he was jailed. Van Buren was brief and positive in response: "The general sentiment elicited by their publication, on the part of both my political opponents and friends, was that I could well have afforded to defray the expenses of bringing out in such form, my portion of the correspondence."[7]

Van Buren put the matter too positively; the correspondence did not help him with his political enemies. Yet he was probably more accurate in his general assessment of his position as compared to Mackenzie's. The latter had intended a moral revolution. What he had succeeded in accomplishing was to introduce in full, circumstantial form the reality of American politics to the American public. His revelations did not purify the political process; if anything, they aided would-be job- and contract-seekers to make more expeditious tracks than before to those in position to help them.

Americans of the 1840s took the abolitionists to heart, but less so the politicos. Mackenzie was much upset by John Van Buren: "Prince John," attorney general of New York, who took life lightly, used his father's government franks for private mail and bet on elections that presumably involved the public's sacred will. All of this roused Mackenzie to moral sentiments and condemnation, but it is doubtful that they did much harm to Van Buren. He was charming, did not take his market losses to heart, and probably did little more swearing than others of his time and place. Passages in his correspondence showed him to say:

> My Dear Jesse.— . . . I know nothing of the d——d stock, except that Bremner was dealing in it, and it had been rising for a month, and I hardly tho't my buying would knock it down forthwith. . . .
>
> They say "the blood of the Martyrs is the seed of the Church," and heaven knows I have been freely tapped in the good cause. THE REM. [removal] OF THE DEP. [deposits] cost me a fortune, and now I don't see but I must lose another hunk of my little earnings.[8]

Mackenzie was shocked that the younger Van Buren was as ready to bet for or against members of his own party, and even his father offered the observation during the great election triumph of 1828 that the Jackson majority of New York State was such that "the residue of the votes [the indignant emphasis is Mackenzie's] were *only useful on the score of bets.*"[9] Mackenzie was upset, as were the Whigs and reformers. It is fair to judge that a majority of the public was not.

Mackenzie served Greeley and the *Tribune* as a correspondent, then, having been granted amnesty, returned to Canada. He continued his career there as a conscience in politics, a disturber of the peace, affectionately regarded by his countrymen. His brief career as an American was lost between American forgetfulness and Canadian indifference. As later on, when Thomas W. Lawson stirred them with incredible revelations, the public listened, they learned, they went on. New crises bemused them. New opportunities beckoned.

NOTES

1. Charles Lindsey, *The Life and Times of Wm. Lyon Mackenzie* (Toronto, 1862), 2: 270.
2. William L. Mackeinzie [sic], *The Lives and Opinions of Benj'n Franklin Butler . . . and Jesse Hoyt . . . with Anecdotes or Biographical Speeches of F. P. Blair . . . C. C. Cambreling . . . W. H. Crawford . . . William L. Marcy . . . Martin Van Buren . . . and Their Friends and Political Associates* (Boston, 1845), 34.
3. Though a Democratic wheelhorse, a cabinet member, and founder of the law school of New York University, Butler is best remembered as father of William Allen Butler, himself best recalled for his versified reprimand of frivolous society belles, *Nothing to Wear* (1857). See also his amiable *A Retrospect of Forty Years, 1825-1865* (New York, 1911).
4. Mackeinzie [sic], 35.
5. *Ibid.*, 135. The bonds, patently withheld and the major part of Swartwout's gigantic theft, were a notable item in customs finances and could not have passed notice.
6. *Ibid.*, 84. All Democrats were not of Swartwout's temper. Theodore Sedgwick openly scorned the Texas speculators as "abominable frauds." *Ibid.*, 63.
7. John C. Fitzpatrick, ed., *The Autobiography of Martin Van Buren,* (New York, 1969), 539. Van Buren sought gently to separate himself from Hoyt, but his letter to Hoyt of February 3, 1827, puts a different color on their connection: in it he declared that as a Senator he had ceased giving financial endorsements. "Your case, however, does not admit of hesitation. Wishing you all sorts of happiness, I remain your sincere friend," Mackeinzie, *Lives and Opinions,* 35.
8. *Ibid.*, 61.
9. *Ibid.*, 65.

Moments of Truth: Progressivism and War

The Civil War dragged on almost three times as long as the later World War I so far as American participation was concerned. Yet the earlier confrontation, though it lacerated the nation, probably did far less harm to the American psyche than did the latter. Nor could the 53,000 American dead and the 204,000 wounded (often hidden and lost in Veterans Administration hospitals) be compared in the national despair engendered—a despair so killing to Progressive hopes—with that resulting from the sacrifice of a half-million Union and Confederate troops and the wounding of at least a half-million more.

The earlier war produced a rash of war profiteers and shoddy military and political intrigues. It produced worthless purveyors of rhetoric, many of whom had served nowhere during the actual war but whose pompous denunciations of southern traitors and praise of northern heroes should have bored or shamed those who had truly sacrificed. Joseph B. Foraker, governor of Ohio, made himself conspicuous as the "Fire Alarm" who was unwilling to forget less crucial aspects of the war and in 1887 dramatically refused to return captured Confederate flags at President Grover Cleveland's suggestion.[1]

The Civil War was a personal war to most participants. It engaged their feelings and ideals and left a residue of respect and achievement. It became a prideful legend to the freedmen that, for reasons of expediency or otherwise, the freedmen employed in their continuing struggle for increased status.[2]

By contrast, American participation in World War I became a legend of futility and deception. The sinking of the *Lusitania*, once an excuse for intervention, became a symbol of devious government behavior intended to rouse public prejudice against Germany and edge the nation blindly toward the Allied cause.[3] Statues raised at home to the khakied veterans of Chateau Thierry, St. Mihiel, and Sedan memorialized abstractions, as compared with statues raised everywhere, including the sites of battles, to the soldiers who had worn the blue or grey. Machine guns, long-range cannon, poison gas seemed to spell the end of the nineteenth-century humanism, though World War II was to produce impersonal horrors that made almost romantic the earlier war's cliché of there being a bullet "with my name on it" that the overseas Yank could welcome almost as an individual.

The liberal goal of World War I—to "save the world for democracy"—became a mockery of progressivism such as the "freeing of the slaves" never—even under the greatest provocation of disillusionment and radical malice—quite became. The segregation of Negroes in the armed units of the American Expeditionary Forces produced bitterness among black veterans and little glory for them at home. E. Franklin Frazier, eminent Negro sociologist, recalled with bitterness the habit of neighbors in his southern city of addressing him as "general," "colonel," "major," and anything else that came to their minds except his actual rank of captain.

By contrast, the strength of the Republican party in post-Civil War decades and, however calculated or contrived, its policy toward blacks, enabled the latter to wear emblems of service in the war for the Union proudly and with profit. As late as 1884, the Republican presidential convention thought it proper or expedient to make a late slave and Reconstruction functionary of Mississippi keynote speaker of the convention.[4]

The journalism of the Civil War was one of its accomplishments. It pushed into the background the "personal journalism" that had so often earlier made editorials more important than sluggishly acquired "news." During the war readers had learned to look eagerly for word of battles, fought or imminent, and through lists of casualties for the names of friends or relatives. The views of editors had taken second place to those of America's war correspondents—men like Whitelaw Reid, who had begun as country newspapermen. Reid had for the *Cincinnati Gazette* reported the battles of Shiloh and Gettysburg so effectively that Horace Greeley had invited him to join the *Tribune.* Journalists like Reid had ferreted out military plans and army movements. They had done some harm with their articles. General Robert E. Lee had startled federal commanders by his eerie anticipations of their assaults. It turned out that he had merely read of them in northern papers. Yet journalistic enterprise had also prevented generals from becoming too far removed from public opinion. And their aggressive reportage had kept General U. S. Grant from being buried in bureaucratic reports intended to rob him of military credit due him.

The journalism of World War I was a letdown from an era of communication that only a few years earlier produced such entrepreneurs of news as Joseph Pulitzer and E. W. Scripps and such famous newspapermen as William Allen White in Kansas, Fremont Older in San Francisco, and Abraham Cahan in New York, the latter the editor of the famous *Jewish Daily Forward.* Now Upton Sinclair flatly indicted the newspaper profession in his *The Brass Check* (1919), holding that it was enslaved to commercial interests. He accused the great Associated Press of having lied consistently before and during the war respecting issues and culpability, and especially of having vilely slandered the Russian revolutionary leaders.[5] Although such social critics as H. L. Mencken mocked Sinclair as foolish and without social sophistication, less doctrinaire students of the press of the time were not more sympathetic to the problem of patriotic editors who reported the war and its progress.

The military gained honor and prestige from Civil War service and in return infused strength in the progressive tenets that the war touted: tenets of egalitarianism, comradeship, dedication. It helped the postwar progressive cause to be able to point to General James Baird Weaver as leader of the Grangers and Populists. General Grant was excused his administrative failures as President because his name spelled national survival above all else. But General Rutherford B. Hayes was chosen Republican standard-bearer for his mildly reform term as governor of Ohio; after Grant, Republicans needed a reform candidate. And General James A. Garfield, from the same state and a former principal of what became Hiram College, four years later suggested to voters education and the better traditions of Republicanism. Republican attacks on his successor, Grover Cleveland, centered partly on the fact that he had not served in the war. As late as 1896, William McKinley's supporters could praise his services as the "young Major" of Civil War fame as well as his kindly efforts in behalf of the poor during the then recent severe economic depression.

Following World War I, as soon as the trumpets and parades ended, as soon as roles ended and offices closed, its heroes lost their aureole. There was some perfunctory talk of making presidential timber of General John J. Pershing, but it died quickly. Both parties sought Herbert Hoover in 1920 as the "great humanitarian" who had fed starving Belgians, Russians, and others, and as an executive whose abilities better fit the age than military heroics. Cynicism respecting war aims, not to mention results, was appraised as intelligence among the cognoscenti. And though American Legionnaires were still warmly welcomed by businessmen who appreciated their flow of money during conventions, as well as their muscle during labor disputes, they did not gain the type of regard deemed necessary to administrators and public relations personnel. Their best-remembered figures were Eddie Rickenbacker, who proved competent in the business end of civil aviation, and Sergeant Alvin York, who lacked civil competence of any sort. Sadly, the Unknown Soldier, symbolizing the losses in humanity incurred by the war and the uselessness of memorials and eternal lights, probably was better known than either of the former.

Progressives had aided the prosecution of World War I; indeed, it could not have been fought without them. Intervention could not even have taken place without their formulation of purposes and their spelling out of virtuous means to prosecute war.[6] Postwar reaction to their cause impugned much, if not most, of their fame and sent most of them into retirement. It left no such monument as the ending of slavery for anyone to point to. The few Progressives who survived as public personages did so for other reasons.

The causes that had made their reputations still needed to be furthered and gave employment and letterheads to a variety of publicists and politicians. But even Robert La Follette, who had fought against intervention in the European war and who was the very symbol of the Progressive tradition, could not generate a national following.

Progressive causes were still, in measure, pursued after World War I: social and political equity, race issues, moral standards, sectional problems, and others. But they were increasingly pursued by agencies activating individuals rather than the other way around: agencies such as the American Civil Liberties Union and the Urban League. They were less and less intended to engage the single, separate person, except as a voter and contributor. And for him or her, the choice was less between being a Progressive or a conservative as between being identified as aiding reaction (however defined) or radical change.

Overall, the Progressive component in American life and politics did not lose by the Civil War. It created a literature that was essentially positive, as in the fiction of John W. De Forest and Ambrose Bierce and the poetry of Walt Whitman. Even Stephen Crane's subtle *Red Badge of Courage* (1895) was misread as a study in the making of a hero, rather than as the sardonic comment on life as meaningless that it actually was.[7]

In contrast, the literature of World War I was wholly disillusioned, featuring such distinguished authors as John Dos Passos, E. E. Cummings, and Ernest Hemingway, among many others. The memoirs of General Pershing and others were respectfully reviewed in the established press, but ritualistically and without seminal results of any kind.

Post-Civil War progressivism sustained energies intended to keep life meaningful and fruitful. It directly inspired some of the reformist thinking of Edward Bellamy and his "Nationalism" followers, who approved a substantial amount of social regimentation when it seemed to advance public policy.[8] Not a few reformers took pride in their racial heritage and vowed that it would not be sullied by base wars or indefensible industrial and other relations. The war experience led directly into the distinguished career of Josephine Shaw Lowell. It enabled friends of reform to face up bravely to the dark and negative implications of Darwinism.

Egotistical thinking and mean-minded sectionalism continued in post-Civil War decades to muddle social criticism. Southerners "muckraked" the North for hypocrisy in racial relations and sordid materialism as a way of life. Sidney Lanier, Confederate soldier and poet, deplored commercialism and gave heart to his compatriots in odes praising emotional truths and in words that directly inspired Woodrow Wilson. Northerners continued unctuous in their formal disdain for the southern caste system but were less faithful than the latter in watering the graves of their wartime dead. And so others, in the Middle west and beyond. But all these sections produced artists and social figures who saw beyond nostalgia and clichés. They created new ideas and slogans befitting a new time.

Proud figures could be identified with World War I events: Douglas MacArthur, George C. Marshall, and George S. Patton, Jr., among others, gave distinguished service. In time they became unforgettable figures, commanding memorials that were visited respectfully by millions of Americans. They seemed likely to provide a focus for a renewed patriotism and gratitude in time. For the more immediate decades they were lost in international patterns and rendered trifling when not contemptible by the shining marble encasing the million dead at Verdun. They complicated the meaning of progressivism for the late twentieth-century generation.[9]

NOTES

1. "No Rebel flags will be surrendered while I am Governor." Philip D. Jordan, *Ohio Comes of Age, 1873-1900*, 5:297, in *The History of the State of Ohio*, ed. Carl Wittke (Columbus, 1943). For statistics, see Thomas L. Livermore, *Numbers and Losses in the Civil War in America, 1861-65* (1900; reprint ed., Bloomington, 1957), and *Statistical Abstracts of the United States* (Washington, D. C., 1967), 262.

2. Harry A. Ploski and Roscoe C. Brown, Jr., comps. and eds., *The Negro Almanac* (New York, 1967), 539ff.

3. Even more serious charges seemed implied in Colin Simpson, *The Lusitania* (New York, 1973)—charges involving the deliberate sacrifices of passengers in order to inflame public sentiment toward war. Richard Hofstadter, *The American Political Tradition* (New York, 1948), 120-122, sug-

gests that Lincoln maneuvered the Confederates into a first action of rebellion at Fort Sumter, but the charge does not seem to have aided the cause of those who later worked to create a sense of disrespect toward Lincoln.

4. John Hope Franklin, ed., *Reminiscences of an Active Life: The Autobiography of John Roy Lynch* (Chicago, 1970), 279ff.

5. Frank Luther Mott, *American Journalism* (New York, 1941), 616, held that with respect to English guidance of American opinion on the war "no one can tell" its extent. However, Philip Gibbs's *Now It Can Be Told* (New York, 1920) had begun revelations of censorship from the establishment side, which swelled into a chorus of exposures as others more singlemindedly took up the theme. Norman Hapgood, *The Advancing Hour* (New York, 1920), on the American side, spelled out a congealed program of censorship and fraud, which Progressives vainly fought. A notorious example contributed by Walter Lippmann showed the *New York Times* as unwilling to report English-Bolshevik peace negotiations as not new and constituting "an effort to further the Soviet propaganda throughout the world" (p. xviii). The same *Times* page somehow managed to quote verbatim alleged plans for world revolution by a Soviet emissary traveling incognito in Germany at secret meeting of German "chieftains of Communism."

6. See, for example, Arthur Bullard's *Mobilizing America* (New York, 1917) for a brief, important statement in this connection. Bullard was a highly respected socialist who joined the crusade and helped clarify objectives for it; see especially "The Mobilization of Public Opinion," 26ff.

7. An effort to impugn the literature of the Civil War is Daniel Aaron, *The Unwritten War* (New York, 1973). However, since it basically disavows the aims and achievements of the war because of its alleged failures to secure a full egalitarianism for Negroes, its thesis in terms of art is rendered complex and subject to debate. For example, it honors Nathaniel Hawthorne for his lack of enthusiasm for the war and assesses him as therefore more realistic and profound than such partisans as Ralph Waldo Emerson and James Russell Lowell. The simple truth is that Hawthorne was a "doughface," and as a regular Democrat and close friend of former President Franklin Pierce uninterested in Negroes and willing to live with slavery so long as it stayed below the Mason-Dixon line. See Louis Filler, "The Civil War as Myth and Reality," *Reviews in American History* 2 (September 1974): 401-408.

8. This fact was discovered by Arthur E. Morgan during studies that resulted in his remarkable *Edward Bellamy* (New York, 1944). Retired Civil War officers who had turned to mysticism in their later years were among the early discoverers of Bellamy's *Looking Backward* (1888).

9. The problem of the relationship of wars to Progressive tendencies involves historians as well as history and also popular opinion, which is subject to change. For example, Robert F. Kennedy, as a young United States Attorney General visiting Indonesia, outraged Texans at home by referring to the Mexican War (1846-1848) as "unjustified. . . . I do not think

we can be proud of that episode." Allan Nevins, the historian, disagreed. He held that Kennedy's views were "old fashioned" and "traditional in Massachusetts"; and that though such views had once been widely assumed as true in the United States, new evidence had revealed Mexico in a less innocent light (*New York Times*, February 17, 1962). Subsequent argument and discussion introduced the fact of Mexico's subjugation of its province of Yucatan. As an added ingredient of controversy, readers of the press were enlightened respecting Yucatan's contemporary, twentieth-century partiality to a form of human slavery.

part II
INDUSTRY

The Machine in the Garden

City and countryside were never so separated or divided as legend made them. Benjamin Franklin was wholly a city person. He contributed to city density in the late eighteenth century by building a row of three houses off High Street, later Market Street, in Philadelphia, sacrificing greenery and open space in the process.[1]

In his bucolic, well-thumbed *Poor Richard*, Franklin doffed his hat to the larger rural population and its attitudes but without letting their expectations interfere with his own. Thomas Jefferson, though more wholly committed to the farming interest, inhabited a world of Deism and mechanics, which most of his farmer associates in Virginia found of little use in their practical concerns. Beacon Street in Boston, Wall Street in New York, and High Street in Philadelphia were executive suites of rural America but quite able to foist their views upon their farmer clients as occasion required, during the Revolution and after.

Nevertheless, city and countryside shared enough in common to create related ideals of competition and cooperation. Ideals were not total realities. Slavery subsisted beside freedom. Free enterprise flourished next to monopolies. Both elements could be discerned in the career of such a businessman as John Jacob Astor who in 1848 died the richest man in America, worth some $20 million.

A poor German boy, Astor went to New York in 1783. In the next forty years he gained fur-trading rights from upper New York State to Oregon, which his friend Washington Irving celebrated in *Astoria* (1836). He also shrewdly invested in Manhattan property, which brought him fortunes and his descendants vast annuities while they busied themselves with social life.[2]

Ideals, however, were not impotent, or brought low by Astor's triumphs. They affected legislation framed to serve democratic principles and social movements designed to fill those principles with content.

The career of the Fourteenth Amendment to the Constitution exemplified this process. Made law in 1868, it was apparently designed to ensure the civil rights of the new freedmen. As applied in the crucial Slaughterhouse cases of the 1870s, however, the United States Supreme Court seemed to water down the amendment's potential for positive action in the freedmen's behalf. The Court endorsed "carpetbag" legislation in Louisiana, which monopolized slaughterhouse privileges for its friends, despite the protests of native, white southern slaughterers who declared that their rights to a livelihood (presumably guaranteed by the Fourteenth Amendment) had been infringed. The carpetbaggers were technically friends of the state's blacks, who stood to gain by this invocation of states' rights doctrine. But they stood ultimately to lose when and if political power reverted to the native whites.

Not only Negroes, but labor generally, stood to lose by accepting monopolistic privileges; full-grown monopolies would in time become their most formidable opponents. Thus laborers, and blacks as laborers, had a way to go before they fully realized their identity of interests, their stake in the minority opinion of the Court, which held that the slaughterhouse monopoly transgressed the "sacred right of labor."[3]

Ideals and realities clashed and intermingled. To the extent that sectional interests could be clearly separated from national—or, in the case of blacks, minority interests—they resulted in power struggles and diverse interpretations. This could be seen in the landmark Granger cases, which reached their historic height in *Munn* v. *Illinois* (1877) and seemed clearly to pit farmers against city manipulators.

The Court was asked, in effect, to judge how free grain-storage owners were to charge farmers exorbitant prices for handling their grain: how liable were entrepreneurs to state legislation. The Court therefore had to determine what powers farmers had to curb railroad tycoons and others through state laws and commissions empowered to judge the fairness of rates for services drawn up by private persons or corporations. The Court concluded that where the "public interest" was involved, free enterprise must be less free:

> It matters not in this case that these plaintiffs in error had built their warehouses and established their business before the regulations complained of were adopted. What they did was from the beginning subject to the power of the body politic to require them to conform to such regulations as might be established by the proper authorities for the common good. They entered upon their business and provided themselves with the means to carry it on subject to this condition. If they did not wish themselves to submit themselves to such interference, they should not have clothed the public with an interest in their concerns. . . .[4]

In this way, a "conservative" Court found for farmers harassed by great impersonal combinations of capital and management. To be sure, the Court also found for the latter in other cases, as due process and other legal considerations subsequently entered into its councils. It interpreted the Fourteenth Amendment to serve railroads much more than it served freedmen. Yet this was also true of the great agitations for change that characterized the era. Parties and social schemes designed to aid troubled or oppressed classes in their struggles with establishments provided slogans and techniques that embellished and invigorated the latter. Whether they originated in the city or the country, they were preempted by national spokesmen and contributed to the tentative programs for change that they proposed.

Massive changes in population would, for a time, enable city spokesmen to set the tone for public debate on national issues.[5] But even while the growing metropolises counted their people and square miles, their landmarks and financial houses, their sweatshops and model department stores, their leaders and publications, their political managers had to take into account the smallest of the states and the fewest of inhabitants. No state had more than two senators in Washington—a fact that would later give ringing significance to the fight for the popular election of senators. Quite often, also, the sparsely settled areas contained waterpower, stands of trees, crucial metals, strategic locations, or simply votes that forced urban lords and their political henchmen to adopt modest miens in negotiating contracts or favors with front men for such interests.

Not infrequently, vital congressional committees were headed by politicians whose constituencies could have been housed in a few city blocks or who grew in unspectacular settings. Shelby M. Cullom was a Wayne County, Kentucky, boy who became an Illinois politician and a United States Senator and who headed the committee that created the Interstate Commerce Commission (1887). George Hunt Pendleton, a congressman from Cincinnati and an antiwar Democrat, was author of the "Ohio Idea" of paying in paper "greenbacks" all government bonds that did not specify payment in gold or silver (1869): an inflationary proposal that soon became a reform issue. Henry Laurens Dawes of Pittsfield, in western Massachusetts, chaired the Senate Committee on Indian Affairs and pressed for what became the Dawes Act of 1887, allotting lands to Indians willing to take up civil responsibilities and renounce their tribal system of holdings. Nelson Dingley from Maine, Chairman of the Committee on Ways and Means and from a state with far less than three-quarters of a million population, in 1896 prepared the high tariff schedule that controlled that aspect of government until 1909. And so many others, from states including Wyoming, which had about a hundred thousand population. The leader of Congress, Nelson W. Aldrich of Rhode Island with its half-million population, survived Democratic election victories in 1890 and 1892 to rise with the Republican tide in 1896 and become the key figure in formulating all federal legislation.

The social and political agitations of the post-Civil War period were not too different in kind from those that had, as far back as the time of Aaron Burr as leader of Tammany Hall, created Democratic alliances between New York bosses and Virginia aristocrats, and later between Republican lawyers from upstate New York and from downstate Illinois. The great difference was that provided by a heightened technology, swifter territorial and material growth, and new immigrant populations drawn especially from southern Europe.[6]

A new industry, a new labor. Railroads across the plains and mountain ranges that could literally determine the destinies of new towns and even states. The farmer, for the most part Anglo-Saxon in heritage, Protestant, and white, waiting for the sounds of the train that might bring him news, clothing, companionship, or, contrariwise, a higher rate of charges for carrying his produce to market . . . such a farmer was no longer the indispensable man of Benjamin Franklin's old, flattering image: the man all must honor, if only on election day.

But neither was he alone in his anguish during depression times or in his inordinate optimism and self-esteem when hard times lifted. The "farmer's cause" seemed to grow in post-Civil War decades and to reach a desperate climax during the Populist revolt of the 1890s. But this was less because of the unique quality of farmers' problems than of the multiplication of cities, which made them more conspicuous than when there had been none but farmers anywhere. As one farmer's son recalled, in enduring prose:

> Good times came again. In eighteen eighty-two there was a good crop of wheat, and some corn, in spite of a blazing hot September. Wheat prices rose above a dollar, and land buyers of early spring paid for their farms with the first crop. Prairie schooners moved west again, and several neighbors who had left the year before came back, bought livestock for twice what they had received for their own, and settled down to farming, resolved never to leave again. . . . Henry and Rosie prospered moderately. From the sale of wheat and hogs, Henry got enough to pay the seven-hundred-dollar note that he owed to Rosie's father, and to buy a horse-drawn corn planter.[7]

Bad times came again and prostrated many farmers. But more survived to fill state legislatures with their own kind, blending ideals with personal ambitions. In the Midwest, which even so hardheaded a historian as Charles A. Beard was to view as the perfect flowering of

Jeffersonian democracy, successful businessmen in both the Democratic and Republican parties joined to control the farmers' discontent and keep it from spilling over into excessive radical action.[8] They were aided by the ambivalence of the farmers themselves, who first cried for railroads and then complained self-righteously about their deceptive policies; and who went on to invest recklessly in stocks and bonds, which rose intemperately in value before crashing in fraudulent schemes or successive depressions.

Hamlin Garland drew a picture of infinite bleakness in the farm stories of his *Main-Travelled Roads* (1891). In his pioneer statement of literary goals, *Crumbling Idols* (1894), he called his method "veritism." Nevertheless, the farmer was no more truly without hope than anyone else. Farms multiplied in post-Civil war decades, as did all other types of property in an era highlighted by unprecedented expansion of territories and states, thanks to the thundering movement of railroads.[9] Nor were the farmers bleakly alone. Through the 1870s, they had met and worked together as Patrons of Husbandry, and, as Grangers, they fought for the right to regulate the policies of common carriers. Numerous local farmer organizations enabled them to meet and enjoy companionship while discussing their mutual troubles, while the women cooked and discussed their own affairs and the children disported themselves. They were not parochial in any stereotyped sense. Their Northern Alliance of Farmers, begun by New Yorkers, derived from their Granger experiences.[10] The Southern National Farmers' Alliance and Industrial Union and the Colored Farmers' Alliance, though not wholly linked in goals, contributed to a formidable farmers' interest.

It seems wise, therefore, to read Hamlin Garland's subsequent *A Son of the Middle Border* (1917) not as part of his once-touted "sell out" of Populist ideals[11] but as a warmer, truer picture of what the western farmer once was and had become. He had been dissatisfied, often in trouble, prone to tragedy as his children became aware of his diminishing power or drifted off to the city to leave him with fewer companions than before. Yet the farmer reorganized to employ new machinery, to augment his sources of communication and entertainment. He joined with sons and daughters to set stakes in land ownership and politics.

As early as 1848, Karl Marx and Frederick Engels in their *Com-*

munist Manifesto had declared it the historic task of the "proletariat" to emancipate the farmer from his "rural idiocy." In time it became evident that there was also a species of "urban idiocy" that required national attention.

It would be as inaccurate to see the farmer as backward in any stage of his westward movement as to deride New Dealers of the later 1930s for having failed to take into account 1970s problems with welfare and job insurance. Yet a serious chasm of self-concern separated farmer and worker. Thus, the sheer quantity of farmers' publications was impressive; by 1890, there were perhaps a thousand farmer-partisan papers, organized in a National Reform Press Association.[12] Yet their impact on national opinion was slight and furnished no prelude to muckraking. Their "news" about railroad and political skulduggery was no news at all but predictable flattery and exhortation. There was nothing in them for the nonfarmer but a private vocabulary about "short hauls" and "long hauls," foreign to his thought and concerns.

The workers' own publications were, similarly, alien not only to the farmer and his associates but to others of his own class or trade. Tailoring, for example, had numerous divisions, in 1890 involving 121,586 tailors proper, 63,611 female adjuncts of tailoring, 289,083 dressmakers, 149,704 seamstresses, "in all 623,984 persons, a larger number than in any other manufacturing industry."[13] Most of these, however, were workers and their history one of struggle for trades unions; the master workers and merchants of pre-Civil War years were lost in a sea of manufacturers and contractors whose exploitation of workers caused them, like the farmers, to work as whole families, in order to survive.

The distance between town and country increased not only materially but psychologically, despite Swedes, Dutch, Poles, and others on farms and moving west who should have added an international quality and sophisticated touch to life in rural territories. "That *damned* East," David Graham Phillips would have a farmer protagonist say as late as the Progressive era, even though farm lands were being employed from Maine to Florida.[14] For the first time in American history, popular city jokes would patronize the farmer and treat him as a fool, someone who came to the city to gawk at its wonders and who could in his naiveté be sold the Brooklyn Bridge.

The farmer, in his turn, took pride in his racial heritage, his history, his religion, and looked down on many of the new immigrants as worthless interlopers: the "hick" antagonistic to the "Mick."

If the farmer no longer inhabited a garden of Eden or a land of milk and honey (such images haunted artists like John Steinbeck far into the twentieth century) the farmer was far from being reduced to the "valley of ashes" of F. Scott Fitzgerald's later imaginings.[15] The city, too, was a scene of struggle for life and development.

NOTES

1. Sam Bass Warner, Jr., *The Private City* (Philadelphia, 1968); for an interesting reconstruction of the area, see 2, 15.

2. Kenneth W. Porter, *John Jacob Astor: Business Man* (Cambridge, Mass., 1931).

3. Jacobus TenBroek, *The Antislavery Origins of the Fourteenth Amendment* (Berkeley, 1951). See also Louis Filler, "William Burnham Woods," in L. Friedman and F. L. Israel, eds., *Justices of the United States Supreme Court* (New York, 1969), 2:1327ff. Woods, a strategic figure in the Slaughterhouse cases, was stereotyped as a "southern judge" and thus part of the postwar conservative reaction. Lost was the fact that Woods, as an Ohioan, helped keep Ohio in the war—the state's noncooperation would have been catastrophic to the federal cause. He also served as a federal general whose military work helped keep Kentucky and Tennessee from seceding, which would have been equally catastrophic. Woods accompanied Sherman's army through Georgia and on to Washington. He then served as a Reconstruction judge in the South before joining the Supreme Court.

4. Filler, "Morrison R. Waite," in Friedman and Israel, eds., *Justices*, 2:1243ff.

5. Urban population in 1820 was 693,000 against a rural population of 8,945,000. By 1880 the cities counted 14,130,000 of concentrated population against the farmers' more dispersed 36,026,000. The decade from 1910 to 1920—crucial in the saga of progressivism—saw the cities overreach the farms by a 54,158,000 to 51,533,000 margin. *Statistical Abstract of the United States* (Washington, D.C., 1967), 24. The meaning of such statistics, however, must be sought in terms of culture and social power.

6. The power of nonurban areas was well understood in post-Civil War eras and informed some of the thinking of later muckrakers. As David Graham Phillips, one of them, put the matter: "Today Nevada has fewer people than it had in 1870. No rain, no vegetation, no available wealth, and Nevada is going down, down. It casts about 10,000 votes altogether, but—it sends two Senators to the United States Senate, just as New York or Ohio

does. And it casts three electoral votes—*enough to have changed the result in the Presidential Election of 1876!*" David Graham Phillips, "Grover Cleveland," *Saturday Evening Post* 175 [August 16, 1902]: 5.

7. John Ise, *Sod and Stubble: The Story of a Kansas Homestead* (Lincoln, Neb., 1936), 139.

8. Horace Samuel Merrill, *Bourbon Democracy of the Middle West, 1865-1896* (Baton Rouge, 1953).

9. For a popular statement of this fact, see Freeman Otis Willey, *The Laborer and the Capitalist* (New York, 1896), 290 ff.

10. John D. Hicks, *The Populist Revolt* (Minneapolis, 1931), 97. Hicks is definitive for what it accomplishes but requires the added dimension of such works as Ima H. Herron, *The Small Town in American Literature* (Durham, 1939), 218-226, and Lucy L. Hazard, *The Frontier in American Literature* (New York, 1927), 261ff.

11. John Chamberlain, *Farewell to Reform* (New York, 1931), 95ff., though considered "left wing" at the time, makes efforts to treat this question fairly.

12. Hicks, *Populist Revolt*, 131.

13. William D. P. Bliss, *The Encyclopedia of Social Reform* (New York, 1897), 1301.

14. David Graham Phillips, *The Second Generation* (New York, 1907), 155.

15. F. Scott Fitzgerald, *The Great Gatsby*,, in *The Bodley Head Scott Fitzgerald* (London, 1958), 1:36.

Public Service and the Scapegoat

> Believe this, young man . . . try to believe this—to begin with—*that railroads build themselves*. . . . What do I count for? Do I build the railroad? You are dealing with forces, young man, when you speak of Wheat and the Railroads, not with men. . . . Men have only little to do with the whole business.[1]

American affluence took new forms in postwar decades, particularly as the proliferation of railroads west exposed the entire continent to exploitation. The fact that this did not result in universal well-being haunted many observers and drew out many explanations, some defensive, others antagonistic. One of the results of the disparity between wealth and degradation was to begin the career of scapegoats selected to explain public troubles, a career that had no end in sight.

Scapegoats of this species were not conspicuous before the war. Malefactors and traitors there were in plenty, but they were not seen as unique impediments to universal well-being. Egalitarians did not believe that life would improve dramatically when the revered but feared General Washington stepped down from the presidency. Nor were traitors well remembered. Though Jefferson did what he could to besmirch Aaron Burr's good name, Americans in time found him easy to confuse with Benedict Arnold.

Abolitionists made a symbol of slavery rather than of John C.

Calhoun. Temperance advocates belabored demon rum. Jacksonians made a symbol of the Second Bank of the United States more than they did of its president Nicholas Biddle. Moreover, the Bank was a semipublic institution and more or less subject to law and lawmakers. Later corporations were private institutions, more independent, more difficult to reach, more alarming in their ability to conjure up nameless terrors in the public mind.

Although workers slaved inordinately in the mills and mines of the prewar decades, none of their masters took on the fatal character with which John D. Rockefeller was later endowed. Earlier public symbols tended to be of a positive nature. Dorothea Dix represented institutional reform, Horace Mann education, and others evangelical religion, statesmanship, oratory, democratic opportunity. The new need for scapegoats was partially a function of a more impersonal character in later American society. With new and alien immigrants struggling for footholds and elements of older stocks fearing for theirs and alienated one from the other, binding forces for hatred as well as regard seemed necessary.

The silent but relentless growth of business, particularly as a result of the impetus provided by the Civil War, did not go unnoticed, and it roused concern among conservatives as well as earlier-style reformers. Said the *New York Times* in a May 3, 1864, editorial:

> The growing wealth and influence of our great corporations . . . is one of the most alarming social phenomena of our time. . . . Men acting for a company work with an independence of conscience which they would shrink from displaying as individuals. . . . Our public companies already wield gigantic power, and they use it like unscrupulous giants. . . . They are generally, from the nature of the case, close monopolies, and all attempts to escape from their tyranny by starting rival or supplementary enterprises, are every day becoming more hopeless. They control the Legislatures, and crush all schemes that seem in the least likely to interfere with their gains. . . .[2]

First to achieve national suspicion as formidable beyond public control were the railroads, earlier chastened by eastern state laws and local ordinances as well as by the competition of roads and waterways. Now, in the 1870s, they emerged as the greatest of all American businesses, and they sprawled over the Great Plains and beyond, difficult to grasp and regulate.

The American dilemma, as public wealth grew and became more available, was that all Americans except a relatively few idealists and malcontents hungered for private gain and advancement. Most had to look on helplessly as some among them went far ahead in wealth and emoluments, thanks to background and personal qualities: program, patience, imaginative hold on economic essentials, courage, or a superior brand of unscrupulousness. And even when an average American could find someone to look down upon, by fooling a farmer or city dullard, outwitting a horse trader, avoiding legal writs and licenses, or using bankruptcy as a means for evading debts, his ego was still in jeopardy. One man was fooled by a patent rat trap; he himself may have fooled a detective while "hustling" illegally by leaving a fraudulent itinerary for the detective to find and eagerly follow. Still another could laugh at an entire audience of "hicks" who believed him when he explained that his "phonograph" would not play because it had caught a cold.[3]

But such triumphs and defeats were trifling beside the mighty gains won and lost in the gyrations of the stock market and the raw power exercised in the building and operations of business, particularly the railroad business.

It is difficult to comment upon so vast and unending a history of railroads except in terms of its Progressive components, which lie buried in a mountain of raw economic and social forces. The problem of assessing either economics or the forces activated lay in the relation of law to performance, especially when appropriate law and standards for applying it were unclear or even unformed. Credit Mobilier became the most memorable of symbols for designating corruption in government-railroad relationships, though by their nature all railroads concerned government, and numerous bankruptcies throughout the era of railroad building made their finances lurid. Such weighty problems as solvency were enmeshed in the very bill that created the Union Pacific Railroad, signed in 1864 by President Lincoln.

Credit Mobilier, a construction company, was organized to carry out the purposes of the bill, and in doing so faced the problem of risks involving labor costs, Indians, sickness, weather, all of which had to be overcome to make a profit. In an era of exposure that blew storms about the Grant administration and its associates, Oakes Ames, a congressman of a distinguished Massachusetts family and business background, became the scapegoat. His foes held that the owners of stock had made inordinate profits from the government-supported action and that the highest of administration men—including Vice-President Schuyler Colfax, his successor to the office Henry Wilson, and James A. Garfield who was to become President—had all profited from the plot. Legend presumed some $40 million dollars or more in costs unaccounted for. A congressional investigation censured Ames and another as ringleaders in the lengthy transaction.

All such sensational charges and details, involving contradictory tales by participants, were savored rather than examined. Seized upon and repeated innumerable times was the passage from an Ames letter that said of his sale of stocks: "I have used this where it will produce most good to us, I think." The actual details of investment, the denials of participants, faded from recollection.[4]

One of Ames's major defenders in vain denied the surplus figure of $40 million, which, in his accounting, became something less than $10 million on an expenditure of some $70 million during four years of anxious labors. Said he stoutly:

> The object of the Ames party was to build as good a road as possible, and have it fully completed and equipped. . . . A decade has shown the wisdom of their faith. The Union Pacific Railroad is now paying all its running expenses, all its interest, is making ample provision, in sinking funds, for the extinguishment of the government loan at its maturity, and is paying about eight per cent. dividends upon its stock, which has ready sale at open market at nearly par.[5]

The Democratic historian Claude G. Bowers explained the Ames censure as having been a warning to other corrupt (Republican) congressmen against turning state's evidence, for Ames had been candid in making public his many transactions, which had been harshly used against him. His candor, on the other hand, became one of the many arguments made in his behalf by his apologists. There was public fury against him, but it moved and developed curiously. It first immolated him; Ames died of aggravation soon after his disgrace. But then his townspeople named a memorial hall for him. The Massachusetts legislature exonerated him. The Union Pacific Railroad raised a monument to Ames at Sherman Summit, Wyoming. This would have particularly pleased Ames, for he seems to have wished "to connect my name conspicuously with the greatest public work of the present century."[6]

Wilson, a famous antislavery figure and Radical Republican, was not attacked in his vice-presidential office, and Garfield, despite Democratic hounding, went on to become President and a martyr figure. The public was no more willing to give up its railroad legends than it was to return Texas to Mexico, but it was equally unwilling to foreclose the future in the legends's behalf.

Progressivism, if it could be described in such enterprises, resided somewhere between the businessman's vision of progress, meaning improvements, expansion, production—a vision that created such titans of industry and invention as Andrew Carnegie and Thomas A. Edison[7]—and the moralist interpretation of events featuring Henry Adams and his brother Charles Francis Adams, Jr., the latter at least in his first phase as social critic. Their *Chapters of Erie* (1871) is the first modern book of "muckraking," describing in the impeccable English of the day and their class the sordid activities of the "lords" of the Erie Railroad and (in "The New York Gold Conspiracy," a tale that directly involved the White House) the fashion in which their relationship to Tammany Hall "was the equivalent to investing Mr. [Jay] Gould and Mr. [James] Fisk with the highest attributes of sovereignty."

Yet as a forerunner of "muckraking" their distinguished book showed other qualities, for, in attacking the gross subversion of the judiciary to brutal business adventures, the Adamses failed to say how business could be better conducted. Cornelius Vanderbilt, in his impatience with legal opinion, was in effect asking that his ambitions for expansion be unbridled—something that the Adams tradition was unwilling to grant. It asked for an ordered society: a society of the well bred and those born to command. The Adamses despised the uncouth Goulds; Charles Francis Adams, Jr., was to feel the effects of Gould's power when it unseated him as head of the Union Pacific Railroad in 1890. No more did the Adamses approve of socialist pretensions; they were of the type of those whom Friedrich Engels derided in his *Socialism, Utopian and Scientific* (1891): aristocrats who wished to turn back the clock to simpler and more class-ridden days.

The Adamses wished to stop not only socialism; had they been able to have their way, they would have stopped capitalism. One of Henry Adams's contributory papers (written with Francis A. Walker, son of a noted reformer and economist and himself chief of the United States Bureau of Statistics, with other distinctions in the offing) denounced the issuance of paper money by the government for purposes of fighting the Civil War. Taxation and loans would have sufficed for government needs, these then-young social critics thought. Indeed, the government had chosen to dishonor its credit voluntarily with the use of its "tortuous and disreputable expedient" of greenbacks. Walker and Adams admitted that such infusions of unsupported (by gold or silver) currencies into society could "produce a temporary and feverish excitement, which, during a certain length of time, may facilitate borrowing, though at a frightful ultimate cost."[8] That cost was inflation, but its alternative was restrictive economic circumstances, which neither the nation's entrepreneurs nor its farmers and tradesmen were willing to tolerate.

Chapers of Erie was addressed to leaders of society rather than to the general public, and it contained democratic content only to the extent that it foresaw a financial oligarchy that had to be broken up if democratic processes were to survive. What the Adamses and their friends did not grant was that the intemperate expansion of industry by rude, frontierlike types could not be stopped and could be modified only by popular will and directed legislation.

The second Grant administration was identified with corruption, a result of its highlighted scandals. It is evident, however, that favors and self-service were not so much peculiar to the time as made vulnerable to criticism by augmented Republican opportunities and the lack of such a crisis as the Civil War to divert attention to more momentous questions of life and death. Victims of such circumstances were many, as political neophytes sought to advance themselves while also working in established routines, which now failed them. Brevet General John McDonald was one such victim, falling from the position of a supervisor of internal revenue to a jail sentence for participating in an operation that defrauded the government of revenue due from the production and sale of whisky in St. Louis and other leading cities. It was of interest that there had been a whisky ring in Andrew Johnson's administration, which had raised money for campaign purposes. A new group of Republicans had entered into arrangements that built on earlier ones but branched beyond to form a newwork of revenue agents who divided unreported whisky production and taxes due with distillers and others. The channels of bribery wound throughout the Internal Revenue Service and reached up to President Grant's private secretary, General Orville E. Babcock, who had served under Grant during the war.

An exposé in the *St. Louis Democrat* (a Republican paper) roused Secretary of the Treasury Benjamin H. Bristow to an investigation. A rudely conceived plot, the whisky ring was readily exposed and its protagonists prepared for prosecution. The problem was what to do with the President. It was the bitter contention of General McDonald that Grant had been privy to all the transactions and had himself profited from them, though his gains from them, if any, had apparently involved gifts rather than a systematized series of bribes. McDonald had letters and recollections of conversations, but none of them proved much beyond Grant's well-recognized loyalty to his associates.

Congressmen, even Democrats, were reluctant to become implicated in a drive to get Grant out of the White House; he was too sweepingly admired as a saviour of the Union. It would have impugned the war itself to have brought Grant low, for the horde of war profiteers was only too well known, and tolerable only as unmemorable adjuncts of a basically glorious effort.

McDonald's exciting accounts of funds passed, of handsome women enjoyed were well read. But politicians willing to sacrifice some of their own to foes and public opinion dragged their feet at the prospect of issuing warrants against Grant. This was so, even though McDonald reported (after the event; he claimed loyalty for having withheld testimony during his trial) that he had personally told Grant that there was "a barrel" of information available sufficient to convict many distillers and liquor rectifiers. And what, the President had asked, ought to be done with this evidence? McDonald, thinking of the bribe receivers as well as the bribe givers, had suggested that it ought to be "shoved into a red-hot stove." The President had answered, according to McDonald, that that would not be good policy but that it ought to be "sealed up securely and placed in a vault where no one could be at it."[9]

Whether the President did in fact say this and other things imputed to him could not be known, and it was not earnestly pursued. Congressmen concluded to be satisfied with a deposition by him detailing his relations with Babcock. McDonald observed of this deposition, which covered no more than nineteen pages of his own book, that the President professed no recollection of key points or simply decided not to answer key questions. The documentary evidence was clear enough, as witness a letter from Babcock signed with a pseudonym but backed by a reproduction:

> Dear Friend:
>
> Keep steady on. Do not lose your grit. Some of the gaugers and distillers want to squeal, and have, by such action, defeated the *plans* in a measure. *They will not be allowed to turn informers and then go free themselves.* Who ever goes to your city will be instructed to make no such promises. When the attention of the public is called to Milwaukee, Chicago, Evansville, Cincinnati, as it will in a very short time, no special attention will be called to your city.
>
> You want to help any one that goes to your city, and trust to the reliability of the friend whom you telegraphed. Sorry your officials have to leave the service. Steer your ship in the tempest, any one can do it in the calm.[10]

Nonetheless, Babcock was saved from conviction by Grant's personal intervention.

The case of Grant's Secretary of War, William W. Belknap, was more harrowing. Belknap was forced to endure the rigorous test of congressional impeachment and a spectacular trial before the Senate on charges of having accepted bribes constituting high crimes and misdemeanors while in office. Among the particulars was the sale of commissary rights in army camps, a charge that once again brought back dreary echoes of the late war.

Belknap's counsel was among the most distinguished in the land. Jeremiah S. Black had been the United States Attorney General under President Buchanan. Montgomery Blair was the son of Francis Preston Blair, a strong arm of Jackson's Kitchen Cabinet, and the younger Blair had himself been a Postmaster General. Earlier he had been counsel for Dred Scott. There was no point of law or procedure that these lawyers conceded, including the right of Congress to impeach a Secretary who had resigned; hundreds of pages of exchange were required to establish that one point, while Babcock's counsel scoured history to find precedents exculpating him from any responsibility, let alone suspicion.

Instructive was the change in political climate respecting impeachment since the days when the Radical Republican press had clamored for President Andrew Johnson's Presidential head. An example of that press's rhetoric could be judged from the comment of *The Independent*, influential organ of Henry Ward Beecher and Theodore Tilton, both soon to be principals in "the trial of the century," with Tilton charging that Beecher had committed adultery with his wife: "The People are waiting anxiously for the impeachment of the President. . . . Meanwhile, if Andrew Johnson makes an attempt at war against the Republic, let him be tried by a court martial, and shot by twelve soldiers in a hollow square."[11]

No such peremptory approach was possible toward Grant, whom the Radical Republicans had politically created, or toward his subordinates. The key to the Belknap defense was the sacredness of due process. Nothing had been proved. Documents, relationships, testimony proved nothing. With extraordinary confidence in the forgetfulness of the general public, to say nothing of Mackenzie and the thousands of copies of his books still floating about in public places, Black, a Democrat, even brought up the Swartwout infamy as a miscarriage of justice in order to depict the shoals in which his own client's reputation sought passage:

> You know, as everybody knows, that the truest and best men that ever lived have fallen under such proceedings as these. . . .
>
> Here in 1839, or thereabouts, a Mr. Swartwout was charged with being a defaulter to the amount of $1,300,000. He was not; he had never spent or appropriated to his own use any dollar of the public money; but his papers were in a state of utter confusion; he was not able to prove his innocence, and so he ran away incontinently. . . .[12]

There were good and honorable men in the Senate and among managers of the impeachment proceedings, and they listened and probed patiently as the former Secretary's counsel argued that there had been no plot, that Belknap had investigated complaints, that there had been no complaints from some posts (the investigation concentrated on one post, Fort Sill, in order to establish the dereliction from duty), that stationed commandants and men had been satisfied with the commissary services, that the managers were proceeding against their client as Edmund Burke had once proceeded in the celebrated trial of Warren Hastings and been rebuked by the House of Commons . . .

The managers answered with spirit and point. One retorted that he would be happy to have parallels drawn between Burke and himself, but that failing, he would "simply remain the humble individual that I am." One of the most distinguished of the managers, Senator George F. Hoar of Massachusetts, held determinedly to the line of inquiry, underscoring that it involved the most serious charges that could be directed against an officer of the government. Yet the issue was not Belknap's rather obvious malfeasance but the right of impeachment. Hoar spoke out eloquently in its behalf:

> The convention that framed the Constitution depended upon the process of impeachment to secure the people against two great dangers: usurpation of executive power and official corruption. Their debates, the debates in the State conventions, the countless arguments addressed to the people through the press, all show that the men of that generation expected the Constitution to stand or fall as it had solved the problem of

> protection against these two dangers, executive usurpation and use of office for corrupt personal ends. . . . Treason and bribery are expressly named and coupled together in the Constitution as the two great heinous crimes against the existence of the nation itself.[13]

Still, Belknap was voted not guilty, and twenty-three of the twenty-five senators who so voted asserted they had felt it necessary to do so because Belknap had resigned and hence was not a government official when impeached. The public—their constituency—could not endorse corruption, but it had no stomach for crucifying it, and certainly not when it involved a soldier who had served with merit at Shiloh, Corinth, and Vicksburg and, under Sherman, in Georgia and the Carolinas.

The public had enjoyed an excessive prosperity following the war and, after the great stock-market crash of 1873, struggled with an economic depression that bitterly tormented the poor. Business generally suffered shocks and bankruptcies. But railroads had become the carriers of all major business, its symbol and support. And railroad proprietors knew no way to meet their own crisis but to cut off portions of their elite employees and reduce salaries. Liberalism all but disappeared in the ensuing confrontation.

The liberal, progressive impulse had manifested itself in 1872 when discontented Republicans had gathered in Cincinnati to express their criticism of the directionless party leaders. Present had been Carl Schurz, carrying an aura of the German revolution of 1848 and Civil War service, E. L. Godkin, an Englishman turned American, brilliant editor of the young *Nation*, and a dedicated Free Trader, and others representing talent and prestige. (The aged Bryant was there to lend his dignity and distinction to the assembly.)

Their third party of Liberal Republicans could have chosen the best of candidates, Charles Francis Adams, Sr., whose services during the war as ambassador to Great Britain could have made him formidable; he had all but singlehandedly kept Great Britain from recognizing the Confederate government as legitimate. Instead, the Liberal Republicans chose the worst of candidates, Horace Greeley, whom Republicans mercilessly ridiculed for his personal eccentricities and such actions as having put up the bail for Jefferson Davis when an effort went underway to make the southern wartime Confederate president liable to capital charges.

It seems fair to conclude that postwar prosperity was too much for the progressivism of its time. Progressivism manifested itself elsewhere—in city reform measures, in labor-capitalist projects for bettering relations, in farmer organization, and in the search for panaceas. But the nation as a whole was still too committed to the past, to Civil War memories, to its frontierlike enterprises to give up its traditional bonfires and parades, its prejudices, its ebullience. Armageddon was still far ahead.

NOTES

1. Frank Norris, *The Octopus* (New York, 1928), 2:285.
2. Quoted by Robert V. Bruce, in Ernest Kohlmetz, ed., *The Study of American History* (Guilford, Conn., 1974), 533.
3. J. P. Johnston, *Twenty Years of Hus'ling* (Chicago, 1888), 514 and passim.
4. They are carefully reviewed in Robert William Fogel, *The Union Pacific Railroad, a Case of Premature Enterprise* (Baltimore, 1960), with results that discern neither angels nor devils but do perceive a desire for profit.
5. J. B. Crawford, *The Credit Mobilier of America* (Boston, 1880), 72, 87. Neither this work nor others in the same vein are noted in Matthew Josephson, *The Robber Barons*(New York, 1934). For an important reexamination of the "robber baron" analogy with American businessmen predicting that it must diminish in importance with time, see Hal Bridges, "The Robber Baron Concept in American History," *Business History Review* 32 (1958): 1-13.
6. Allan Nevins, in *Dictionary of American Biography* (New York, 1928), 1:251. A formidable reassessment of Ames and his work is Charles Edgar Ames, *Pioneering the Union Pacific* (New York, 1969).
7. That there was such a sense, relating capitalist enterprise with progressivism, may be seen in the criticisms of entrepreneurs, as in James H. Bridge's *The Inside History of the Carnegie Steel Company* (1902), which "muckraked" Carnegie, denying that he had aided invention in the field or encouraged its uses. The fall of status by businessmen in progressivism can be traced in the decline of Edison in the public consciousness from his previous position as awesome inventor and inspiration.
8. Charles F. Adams, Jr., and Henry Adams, *Chapters of Erie, and Other Essays* (Boston, 1871), 332.

9. Gen. John McDonald, *Secrets of the Great Whisky Ring . . . with . . . Fac-similes of Confidential Letters and Telegrams Directing the Management of the Ring* . . . (St. Louis, Mo., 1880), 143.
10. *Ibid.*, 159.
11. "The Public Situation," *Independent,* September 19, 1867.
12. *Proceedings of the Senate Sitting for the Trial of William W. Belknap, Late Secretary of War . . . Forty-fourth Congress, First Session* (Washington, D.C., 1876), 43.
13. *Ibid.*, 176-177.

Panaceas

The American West continued to feed emigrants' expectations, providing opportunities for experiments in life and what would in time be termed lifestyles. The expanding West attracted malcontents, theorists, enthusiasts, and others in groups and as individuals, able to test out their dreams. And this was in ways impossible among better-ordered and -policed communities in the seaboard states, not to say in Great Britain or Europe. Hence the cascade of "utopian" communities that gave a picturesque aspect to pre-Civil War reform and that nourished progressive thinking as it suggested the untapped potential of expanding democracy.[1]

The new post-Civil War era of explosive technology and mass labor produced serious traumas in living conditions and expectations everywhere in the country. It excited dreamers and activists to new efforts to counter the harsh realities of mill-town living and city slums. Anxieties were stirred in farmers and retail merchants by the power and scope of trusts. Their fears touched writers whose thoughts rooted instinctively in the rhetoric and examples of earlier thinkers, men and women like Josiah Warren and Fanny Wright. The former tried in Cincinnati, Ohio, to create a "time store" where goods could be exchanged for the time estimated which individuals and communities had given to make them. Thomas Skidmore, a mechanic in New York, had dreamed of a political party that would force an equal division of the land. Sex and family reformers in Oneida, New York, had been critical not only of capitalistic property relations but of the accompanying human arrangements that derived from them. New utopias—for they continued to multiply despite theories[2]—were usually responsible enterprises that attracted earnest talents and commitments stemming from deep hopes for happiness or distinction.

But probably to a degree unparalleled elsewhere, Americans sought panaceas: solutions to their social problems that would cut through to their dissatisfactions, give them what they thought they needed, and ask of them a minimum of duty and responsibility in exchange. They wished not to be poor but also not to be prevented from achieving the great bonanza, the lucky strike, the unsought, unexpected, unmerited good fortune that would raise them above their less requited comrades.

Panaceas became identified with patent medicines: concoctions sold by hearty, entertaining traveling salesmen; John D. Rockefeller, Sr.'s father was one of them. Men like Rockefeller retailed "medicines" that would allegedly clear the blood, remove pimples and moles, grow hair—anything the purchaser wanted done. And without asking anything of him or her other than the modest price of the bottle: not restraint, not physical exercise, not intelligent use of time and opportunity.

In their restless search for panaceas, Americans explored all possibilities. The progressive claimed that education was the panacea for the nation's ills. The ignorant (and not a few of the educated) bought charms, magic potions, phrenological charts, and sought the advice of fortune-tellers. For the nation's troubles there were numerous prescriptions. One of the most remarkable of them was the outlawing of spirits, originally called "temperance," but enthusiastically widened to mean prohibition and calculated to produce a clean, upright, successful America. Whatever the limitations of temperance, it was a major cause for earlier abolitionists, suffragists, and institutional reformers. It accrued an enormous prestige, which was maintained in post-Civil War decades and divided the countryside from the more permissive town.

Silver became a major panacea for America's financial troubles of the late nineteenth century. Congress's abandonment of its legal ratio of sixteen to one with gold was interpreted by "silverites" as the cunning plot of financiers to control the currency by maintaining the dominance of gold as a legal standard and preventing the flow of money to the general public. The "people" necessarily included the millionaire owners of silver mines, who stood to gain by hitching their holdings to the more stable gold bullion. Whether the holders of gold could have known that great silver mines would be discovered, which would further depreciate the value of silver, is not known. But there can be no doubt that creditor farmers, especially in the South and West, were eager to undermine the value of gold by whatever means.

Silver was not at first a radical measure. When William McKinley was a young Congressman from Ohio, he approved the Bland-Allison Act of 1878, which committed the government to purchasing quantities of silver and coining it into silver dollars, though not forcing them into a legal relationship to gold. McKinley later became an ardent defender of the gold standard. The silver issue highlighted the great William Jennings Bryan campaign of 1896, though whether his triumph, if it had occurred, could have affected basic currency reform can never be known. At bottom creditors were seeking inflation: "cheap" money that would enable them to pay off what they deemed to be unfair and undemocratic debts and to acquire ready money for their private wants and preferences.

Free Trade was another of the great postwar panaceas, producing Free Trade Leagues, Free Trade political planks, and other signs of social vitality. As late as 1909, the Payne-Aldrich tariff, interpreted as favoring industry at the expense of the lower prices the poor were supposed to anticipate from a lower tariff schedule, impugned William Howard Taft's presidential campaign promises and hurt his credibility with voters. As late as 1912 a call for Free Trade was a major slogan of Woodrow Wilson's presidential campaign.

The tariff question had distinguished key southern politicians from their northern counterparts in the prewar era. In the Republican postwar decades, "Protection of Home Industries" was identified with prosperity, jobs to employed workers, and patriotism. Free Trade was equated with reform by its partisans, though it continued to attract southern spokesmen who declared themselves "oppressed" by northern manufacturers. They demanded the competition of products from abroad that they believed Free Trade would engender and from which they could profit.

As an issue, Free Trade never attained the magnitude in America that it achieved in Great Britain, where the repeal of the protectionist Corn [wheat] Laws in 1846 was literally taken by its advocates to mean more bread in the mouths of the poor. It made "Manchester Liberals" and statesmen of the manufacturers John Bright and Richard Cobden, who believed that international trade competition would not only lower prices on necessities but lead to international peace, thanks to the free flow of goods and understanding between countries. The emphasis of these great advocates was on freedom; both achieved high flights of eloquence in opposition to laws regulating factories. Such laws, they thought, interfered with individual rights, among other evils.[3]

In the United States neither wheat, nor wool, nor any other necessity could be dramatized in the same fashion as abroad. Free Trade did not become the slogan of beset farmers who were eager for protection of their farm products from those brought in foreign ships or across the Canadian border. It was not the slogan of workers who in "good times" accepted the doubtful protection of their jobs from foreign merchandise often manufactured by "cheap labor" and who in "bad times" fought for labor organization and collective bargaining. Free Trade made a major convert of a President, Grover Cleveland, who distinguished himself more for his independence than for his social politics. Like his British predecessors, Cleveland meant freedom more than he meant social benefits, but unlike them he primarily meant neither peace nor bread, and he produced muddled results in both connections. With Cleveland and with some others of the postwar generation committed to traditional law and uninvestigated order, Free Trade was a dogma rather than a boon to humanity, and as such added little to the annals of progressivism.[4]

The search for magic wands, for short-cuts to fame and security, may be termed a national mania; no other nation produced such a torrent of publicity seekers, opportunists, self-deceived minor prophets whose careers were calculated to make cynics of all but the most steadfast of optimists. Benjamin F. Butler of Massachusetts (unrelated to the Butler of Mackenzie's shoddy saga) was a prototype of such false leaders, one of the "political generals" of the Civil War: civilians who received army commands solely because of their political strength. Butler had no military record and no place in antislavery chronicles. Yet he seized its temporary popularity during the war to make pronouncements and give orders dangerous to the war's conduct. This gave him an astounding popularity.[5] After peace, he proposed himself as a demagogic partisan of labor, though without status in its ranks, and actually achieved the governorship of his state in 1882. Two years later he was the nominee for President of the Anti-Monopoly and Greenback parties, both representing highly regarded and substantial panaceas of the time.

That these well-meaning groups, speaking for genuinely troubled citizens, would have hit upon so unprincipled a politician as Butler as a spokesman, with his cheap shots at bankers and capitalists—of which he was himself a most affluent and unscrupulous one—indicated limitations in their social thought. Butler had learned a simple rule while manipulating government funds for his personal profit, practicing blackmail, and underpaying workers in the factories that received his investments, and that was that people could be wooed with verbiage and with social gestures that cost him nothing. "Glorious old Ben!" wrote Susan B. Anthony because he had endorsed woman suffrage. Samuel Gompers, acknowledging Butler's exhortations in labor's behalf, endorsed his candidacy for President. As James Russell Lowell appositely observed of his Massachusetts's most popular representatives in Congress: "The two best known are Butler and a vender of patent medicines."[6]

Nevertheless, panaceas produced two immortals not unconnected with the career of progressivism, though distinct from it. Henry George and Edward Bellamy had in common their need to perceive a moral purpose in life. Both were oppressed by the implications of the Darwinian hypothesis, which suggested that man was no more consequential than the creatures among which he had evolved. George, however, thought he had discovered universal laws that ensured man's ultimate triumph over nature and his own frailties: his *Progress and Poverty* (1879) is the one major work in economics that ends with a chapter affirming religious faith. Although this fact would seem to impugn George's investigations at the outset, it differed only in the article of faith from Karl Marx's belief that the triumph of the proletariat was "inevitable." Both writers believed that their logic and data supported their conclusions.

George's personal odyssey made a moving tale, which his followers and admirers could recount for decades: his youthful travels as a common seaman seeking understanding; his discovery of abstract thinking, which persuaded him that man differed from animals; his distress as a young, unemployed married man with a child to feed; his beginnings as a printer and journalist, and growth in intellectual power and reputation as a San Francisco thinker and spokesman; his staggering revelation that land would increase in value as more and more immigrants came west to work it, but that the implied progress would only result in an increase in poverty.

George sketched his ideas in a pamphlet published in 1871, *Our Land and Land Policy*; following the financial crash of 1873, with its protracted depression, he set to writing his master work. *Progress and Poverty* was prayerfully finished in 1879, and found no publisher. George published the book himself in an edition of five hundred copies. It was then taken over by a commercial house and soon made its author a prophet to numerous people at home and abroad.

George's key idea—that land belonged to everyone and gained its value from community efforts, and thus could not decently be appropriated for the unqualified use of any one person or group of persons—suggested the "single tax" solution with which he was simplistically identified. Government would justly assess land holdings in terms of the value with which society had endowed it. Improvements would not be taxed. George's idea, then, was not to preempt property but to return to the community what was legitimately its own: to save free enterprise from its exploiters rather than to harm the free enterprise system. Not a few conservatives recognized and respected George's purpose. As one of them stated in the respectable *Cyclopaedia of Political Science*, not long after George had succeeded in disseminating his views:

> We need not . . . shut our eyes to the fact that in the remote future the time may come when individual ownership in land may become a burdensome monopoly. It is to be hoped, however, that when that time does come, those who then are uppermost in the field of politics and of government will be so vastly superior in character and mind to the present prevailing politicians and so-called statesmen that the ownership in land may then safely be transformed from a personal into a government monopoly.[7]

George did not think it necessary to wait for millennial conditions. In effect he anticipated just assessments of property, which would be matters of public record, and his great work did in fact influence the modernization of revenues from land. In time, it influenced in Great Britain the famous Lloyd George budget of 1909, noted for its social legislation, and it turned special attention on Ireland, notorious for being burdened with "absentee landlords." In addition it influenced affairs as far away as Australia, which George visited in the course of his tireless evangelical pursuits.

But the George program—like other notable panaceas—was more than the single tax. It was a point of view that would often be lost on succeeding assessors of land who had never heard of him. His program showed an awareness of human trouble and of the need for keeping avenues to it open. George moved to New York City, where he established the weekly *Standard* as a vehicle for his ideas. He wrote memorable books on the land question, on protection and free trade, linking "true protection" and "true free trade" with his own crusade, and all with a forceful and even stirring prose unknown among run of the mill economists. His work contributed light and excitement not only to the struggles of laborers and farmers, but to classes of industrialists to whom industry meant reform as well as profit. (See p. 154.)

George also seriously influenced the programs of urban reformers. In 1886 he ran for mayor of New York and, without a party organization, polled 68,110 votes against the Democratic party's Abram S. Hewitt's 90,552. (Theodore Roosevelt, then age twenty-eight and running for the Republicans, polled 60,435 votes.) George also inspired other municipal struggles, which during the Progressive era resulted in the emergency of no fewer than fifteen "single tax" cities. None of them attained their goal of what would have amounted to a confiscatory assessment of property. All of them, however, carried on campaigns that resulted in more modern systems of tax valuation, with other reform gains counted in franchise awards, election procedures, and aid to citizens.

At the same time, it could be profitably argued that George's major achievement—that which most repaid a modern reading of his books—was emotional and intellectual rather than directly and tangibly effective. And it was the fact of inspiration that mainly connects him with the gathering Progressive tradition, as it pooled contributions in social thought from various sources. The single tax itself seems unlikely of any fruition in such terms as George envisioned.[8] But George's keen observations of real conditions and relationships, and the compassion with which he communicated his insights have an eternal resonance.

Much the same could be said of that other creator of a major panacea, Edward Bellamy, whose fantastic literary success and its aftermath said much about the American people of the time who precipitated both. Bellamy was a thoughtful Massachusetts boy, the son of an impecunious minister, who worried much about the meaning of life. In early private notes, Bellamy set down the thought that one ought not to give up the possibility that life ended in the grave. He also, though still a very young man, formulated for himself a "religion of solidarity" (1874), which guided him through most of his relatively short life. Bellamy confided his hope that when he was dying someone would read his paper to him.

Most people made too much of individual differences, he believed. They emphasized their uniqueness, whereas they would be wiser to emphasize those elements they and the universe had in common. Cooperation, not combat, was the key to human life. Altruism was a necessary feature in human fulfillment; nature itself had instilled that element in humanity's psyche. Such were avowals that Bellamy took obliquely into his career as a fiction writer.[9]

His era was perceptive in suggesting that he might prove to be the successor to Nathaniel Hawthorne. It sensed that, like Hawthorne, Bellamy was haunted by the question of whether life had meaning; a growing feeling of futility had contributed to debilitating Hawthorne so that he died without natural cause.[10] Bellamy's brooding mind conceived tales that not only struggled with life's meaning but sought answers to its dilemmas. He had questioned infant damnation, sin, resurrection. A visit to Europe at age eighteen had shocked him with revelations of poverty and realizations that his own country suffered the same agonies of want. In 1879 he wrote *Dr. Heidenhoff's Process,* which foretold modern "shock" treatments for neurosis, in the tale obliterating morbid fancies by means of electricity. It had seemed pitiful to Bellamy that one had to suffer all one's life for a single mishap, an error, a mistake. That same year he printed in the papers his story "The Duke of Stockbridge,"[11] which recounted with tone and a sense of dialect the uprising of Captain Daniel Shays in 1786 against poverty, cruel taxes, and foreclosures that in western Massachusetts followed the Revolutionary War. Bellamy abjured patriotic rhetoric to depict the disappointment and feeling of betrayal that some of the troubled classes had felt. So Bellamy worked between the psychological and the overt to build his personal vision of life.

The astounding success of his fictional *Looking Backward 2000-1888* (1888) was a tribute not only to himself but to the public that made it the greatest such literary triumph between Harriet Beecher Stowe's *Uncle Tom's Cabin* (1852) and Upton Sinclair's *The Jungle* (1906). Americans wanted economic and social goals, but they also needed images that fed their emotional wants: images of people and places, and their interrelationships. So fiction ceased being fiction, and became reality. The story line of *Looking Backward* became a commonplace; indeed, it was not original with Bellamy.[12] Its inner texture repaid understanding.

Julius West awakes to find himself alive a hundred years hence. But the world has been transformed. The city is one of peace and organization. People get what they wish from the cooperative stores. As children, they serve the state; later they follow rational and satisfying vocations. As elder citizens they develop policy for the community. The other life, the time of desperation and clash, disappeared during a period called the Great Revolution, when its total inadequacy became too patent to endure.

West asks questions, and Dr. Leete, his guide through the new time, gently enlightens him, and corrects his false attitudes and misconceptions. A remarkable achievement was the fact that Bellamy somehow transmuted the tone of Boston as it was and made persuasive the thought that on it could have been erected this tranquil superstructure. Bellamy's imagination conjured up improvements, including music that could be piped into individual homes. In the atmosphere of peace and individual self-expression Bellamy created, the conception of what would become the radio did not seem far-fetched. As important in the story as it had been in Henry George's exposition was religion; in *Looking Backward* it became a personal attainment of oneness with the universe. People turned to whatever minister or leader they preferred, and became tuned to the freshest and most persuasive spiritual formulations.

Although the delineation of a utopia was an old human impulse, Bellamy contributed a novelty by having his protagonist return, briefly, to the old world of 1888, where he was horrified anew by its anguish and bestial competitiveness. Bellamy here delivered himself of a phrase that was to reappear in another stirring context—the Democratic convention of 1896 that nominated William Jennings Bryan—when he had West declare that he had seen humanity hanging from a cross of gold. It was with relief that his readers learned that this return to the past was a dream, a nightmare, and that he, the reader, for the duration of his imaginative adventure into the future was secure in a world worthy of humankind.

Succeeding events revealed a nation—and especially a literate, fiction-reading nation led by middle-class ideals—determined to adjust its relations to government and to each other. The social unrest was real enough, as were economic fears and a sense of ominous crises. But as real were the fears and insecurity caused by the questions raised by the Darwinian hypothesis, by unprogressive churches, and by feelings of alienation created in impersonal cities and by ever-widening distances. *Looking Backward* was vague on key points. It offered little information on crucial questions of social incentives, problems of law and order, of individual neurosis and conflicting attitudes toward life. Yet it was precisely because *Looking Backward* could accommodate itself to various and even conflicting programs that it succeeded. It concentrated on the fact that there *was* a common need and that disparate groups had to join if they were to meet it.[13]

It was significant that the novel first impressed religious seekers in Boston who included retired Civil War officers. Bellamy himself had once applied to West Point and had been refused for reasons of health. His utopia required an element of organization and authority that might repel extreme libertarians but encouraged those who saw the increased complexity of urban and industrial life as requiring some giving up of individualistic ways.

Clubs sprang up in support of Bellamy's program, by January 1891 numbering 162 and showing particular strength in California.[14]

Bellamy was conscious that Americans were by nature suspicious of socialism and that it could not be sold to them under that name. He avoided, therefore, the concept of nationalization though it was at the heart of his panacea; thus he termed his growing movement "nationalism," with its appeal to the patriotic motive in readers and followers. In 1892, at the convention of the People's (Populist) party in Omaha, Nebraska, the Bellamyites were in attendance and wrote into the party's platform its nationalizing features calling for public ownership of railroads, the telegraph, and the telephone.

This was the high point of the Bellamy crusade. Thereafter, the silver panacea took over in Populist terrain and frenzied the nation in the election year of 1896. Bellamy's contribution was mainly inspirational. This was shown by the more moderate reception accorded his *Equality* (1897), which tried to answer at length and in practical terms such questions and doubts as the earlier book had raised. Although *Equality* contained eloquent passages and appeals to humane thinking, it caused no movement of people. Americans were not Bellamyites. They were seekers for reassurances that could accompany them on their individualistic treks—treks that, they hoped, would leave them with as many options as possible. Bellamy had little direct effect on Progressive activities, less than did George, who roused municipal reformers to demanding curbs on monopoly and contriving tax reforms.[15] But Bellamy, as much as George, contributed ideas and sensibilities that appealed to generous public sentiments among people and encouraged the reformers among them.

NOTES

1. Arthur E. Bestor, Jr., "Patent-Office Models of the Good Society," *American Historical Review* 58 (April 1953): 500-526, theorizes that "utopias" were a product of frontier conditions, and with their "passing," disappeared and could not be revived. For a criticism of this theory, see Louis Filler, "Pilot Plants, Utopias, and Social Reform," *Community Service News*, 12 (1954): 45-49. See also Walter P. Webb, *The Great Plains* (Boston, 1931), which extended such thinking to the entire society of cowboys and ranchers, holding that for a time they had created a democratic society different in kind from that establlished in the East. The vision of a benign

West is set down fictionally in Eugene M. Rhodes, *The Proud Sheriff* (Boston, 1935).

2. Robert Fogarty, ed., *American Utopianism* (Itasca, Ill., 1972).

3. Their solution to the evident miseries of workers in factories run by cruel and inflexible owners was, in addition to free trade, education, the virtues of benign internationalism, and immigration. The latter would decrease the number of workers available for employment and force up wages and humane treatment of factory operatives. See John Morley, *The Life of Richard Cobden* (New York, 1881), 1: 464-468; J. A. Hobson, *Richard Cobden, the International Man* (London, 1919), 162-163, 339-340.

4. Allan Nevins, *Grover Cleveland, a Study in Courage* (New York, 1932), did all that could be done for its subject's policies and his famous phrases: "It is a condition which confronts us, not a theory," "What is the use of being elected to anything, unless you stand for something." However, also to be taken into account are such thoughts of Cleveland's as his adherence to "Democratic principle and Democratic good faith," which enabled him to say that "in accordance with our declared party purposes, sugar is a legitimate and logical article of revenue taxation," enabled him to oppose an income tax, and to order federal troops as a strikebreaking agency into the Pullman strike of 1894 over the objections of Illinois Governor John P. Altgeld. (Allan Nevins, *Letters of Grover Cleveland, 1850-1908* Boston, 1933), 336-360.

5. Butler may have turned down an offer from President Lincoln for the vice-presidential nomination in 1864 in the belief that he would be nominated for the presidency proper in place of Lincoln; see Louis Taylor Merrill, "General Benjamin F. Butler in the Presidential Campaign of 1864," *Mississippi Valley Historical Review*. 33 (March 1947): 537-570.

6. Robert S. Holzman, *Stormy Ben Butler* (New York, 1954), 202.

7. Simon Sterne, "Monopolies," in John J. Lalor, ed., *Cyclopaedia of Political Science* (New York, 1890), 2:898.

8. Arthur Birnie, *Single Tax George* (London, 1939), succinctly sums up major criticisms of the panacea's limitations.

9. Arthur E. Morgan, *Edward Bellamy* (New York, 1944), not only traces its subject's evolution but also the relationship of his ideas to the needs of his time. See also Joseph Schiffman, "Edward Bellamy's Altruistic Man," *American Quarterly* (Fall 1954): 195ff.

10. Henry G. Fairbanks, *The Lasting Loneliness of Nathaniel Hawthorne: A Study of the Sources of Alienation in Modern Man* (Albany, N.Y., 1965).

11. Published as a book in 1900, following Bellamy's death.

12. Morgan, *Plagiarism in Utopia* (Yellow Springs, Ohio, 1944).

13. Louis Filler, "Edward Bellamy and the Spiritual Unrest," *American Journal of Economics and Sociology* 8 (April 1949): 239-249.

14. William D. P. Bliss, *The Encyclopedia of Social Reform,* (New York, 1897), 918. For an example of the rise and decline tendency within the

Bellamy movement, William F. Zornow, "Bellamy Nationalism in Ohio 1891 to 1896," *Ohio Archaeological and Historical Quarterly* 58 (April 1949): 152-170.

15. Ransom E. Noble, Jr., "Henry George and the Progressive Movement," *American Journal of Economics and Sociology* 8 (April 1949): 259-263.

The Goo Goos

There was reform that did not portend revolution and was not intended to. It was unsensational when contrasted with the travail and challenge of the "new immigrants" from Middle Europe and Italy, the harsh rise of the city tenements, the dramatic confrontations of labor and capital, industrial innovation, and the farmers' crusades. But "genteel" reform was a flywheel of society, which kept it from grinding upon itself destructively. Its proponents were ladies and gentlemen. Although they would later appear to have been pulverized by democratic forces, in the post-Civil War period at least (and much beyond, if properly perceived), they made their impress on their times. The very malice and contempt that they attracted from later academics helped to indicate that feelings had been ruffled, and for cause.

Abram S. Hewitt, for example, was no small man. The son-in-law of Peter Cooper, inventor and railroad builder, Hewitt helped him build the Cooper Union, which was one of the stars and emblems of New York's democratic education. Cooper was one of the more honorable class of businessmen and employers. He helped advance steel-making processes and served the North well during the Civil War as a manufacturer of cannon. A Democrat, he served as mayor of New York, resisted the skulduggery and pressures of Tammany Hall, and was dropped by that organization following his term of office.[1]

He was a "goo goo," to employ the phrase Charles A. Dana, former Brook Farm idealist, contemptuously used to describe such civil personages who refused to recognize the inevitability of special favors in public business. As applied to founders of Good Government Clubs, "goo goo" suggested childishness, goody-goody ethics, and an inability to cope with the real world. It also suggested the hypocrisy implied by affluent living and pious principles in a world of sorrow and need. Charles Edward Russell, prime leader of the later muckrakers, scorned these reformers as self-esteeming moralists who hated corruption so long as it could be traced to Irish politicians and the poor but who cared nothing about fundamental social inequities and a government eager to defend the privileges of the rich.[2]

Such opinions did not exhaust the subject. For one thing, they were premised on the expectation that goo goo critics of the left would accomplish more than did the goo goos. Whether those critics did may be judged in ensuing pages. Russell's accomplishments are yet to be considered. Those still further "left" of Russell appeared to believe that they merited special regard *because* they held drastic egalitarian views. Yet one reviewing the career of a Daniel De Leon (1852-1914) might well wonder what precisely he achieved at all. De Leon's central thought was that reform retarded the great day of capitalistic collapse and ought not to be respected. Workers ought to be educated to anticipate a general strike, which would lay the archaic society completely in the dust. Upon it would be raised an industrial commonwealth of socialism and plenty. But De Leon's Socialist Trade and Labor Alliance accomplished close to nothing, as did his later Worker's International Industrial Union and Socialist Labor party. De Leon often wrote eloquently and merits some place as a labor educator.[3] Otherwise, it is difficult to see how people like him rated higher on a social scale of achievement than any liberal of lesser pretensions.

One of the greatest figures of the pre-Progressive era, Josephine Shaw Lowell, was closer to the despised goo goos than to any socialist or radical liberal complex. Yet even less-remembered persons than she among the genteel reformers could claim significant accomplishments, and a body of leaders who could hardly be termed "submarginal" in any sense. Any movement that took in Charles Francis Adams, Jr., and perhaps his brother Henry, Dorman B. Eaton, George William Curtis, Richard Rogers Bowker, founder of the great Bowker publishing company and an outstanding liberal, Helen Hunt Jackson, William Dudley Foulke, *Nation* editor E. L.

Godkin, Theodore Roosevelt, and Woodrow Wilson, at least in their early pre-Progressive phases, could be written off only by the truest utopians—utopians who could not believe that democracy required a number of social forces, not necessarily sympathetic to one another, but adding necessary ingredients to reform.

The difficulties attending genteel reform can be readily summarized. Its partisans made much of an educated elite, equipped and able to rule. They were philanthropic toward blacks rather than fundamental, willing to help with education and aid but not to join a to-the-death struggle to reinvigorate achieved constitutional rights. They often scorned aggressive labor and the "dangerous classes" of the political discontented. John Hay's *The Bread-Winners* (1884) was later made notorious by militant liberals who saw Hay as seeking a docile labor. In addition, the genteel reformers supported the harsh use of police and military force in social confrontations.

The genteel reformers made much of manners, of deportment, of superficial etiquette, which in itself set up a screen between civil rights and the true democracy, as in their lack of concern for the free speech and obscenity issue: one that later Progressives honored along with socialists interested in greater public tolerance of their own opinions.[4]

Finally, they lacked a broad social program, and they made little effort to reach the masses with their views. Henry Adams, in his novel *Democracy* (1880), rejected them entirely as part of the reason for the low estate to which government had fallen.

Nevertheless, the genteel reformers spoke for a sense of standards and tradition in a time that desperately needed both. And their emphasis on individual worth and responsibility resisted whirlwinds of conflict that threatened to deprive contestants of that support. Ex-President Rutherford B. Hayes, for example, did, indeed, make much of "character," arguing that neither law nor education could amply substitute for it. It is doubtful that this emphasis on individual worth "paralyzed" gentility so far as "action" was concerned.[5] An emphasis on "character" could be rhetorical. Demands for education could mean a turning away from salary and labor conditions. An overconcern for manners could mark the shallow spirit. But the obverse was also true. A viable society would not be patient with the self-pitying and the wilfully illiterate. Boors did not merit encouragement. Action was not always preferable to thought and deliberation. Hayes was not a key figure in genteel reform, but he was a most useful citizen who contributed to the well-being and progress of the black community, worked for justice to the Indian, and lent his prestige to prison reform.[6] In a time that was creating a new tradition of industrial violence, fostering ugly dreams on both sides of the battle lines, it is difficult to see how the meliorative efforts of a Hayes and of others of the gentility can be faulted. They pointed to a moderating program, which became the ultimate hope of a society that could less and less afford disruption and clashes and that needed above all to honor character.

The two greatest accomplishments of the goo goos were undoubtedly social civility and civil-service reform. Their image of dignity and proper deportment seems stuffy today and an impediment to the true needs of overworked and underpaid laborers who needed not manners but means, not Sunday church but rest, not docile sons and daughters but resources for rising out of poverty and low social esteem. But those who "rebelled" against their lot did not always do so with foresight, and they strewed the city streets and institutions with their broken bodies and minds. Those laborers and their wives who fought to hold on to their traditions and sense of decorum, who submitted themselves to humdrum lives and respect for others' property, and who set examples of stability and peace to their children often revealed qualities of heroism more than of supine resignation, and made transitions to a place in the social order lighter and more tangible for their children and neighbors than did flashy and reckless careers of the Mike Walsh type.

The destructive antagonism between social interests urgently needed civility as an antidote to crude scorn and hatred between sections, between farmers and city folk, and between viciously competing ethnic and other groups. The Saturday bath, the tight new shoes and collar, the starched dress, the living room used only for special occasions—such rituals and events helped maintain family morale and ambition. And nothing symbolized them better than the settled gentility. They, too, had their problems and anxieties; and their lack of full answers to the troubled postwar decades may well have afflicted them with a species of neurosis.[7] In the case of their Francis Parkman, however, they had a man of towering courage who fought his way past blindness—possibly neurotic blindness—to write what were among the greatest writings of American history: a cultural heritage. Parkman, like others of his caste, spoke for a sense of standards in a time that needed to be reminded of their worth.

Genteel publications, too, played a role in offering a balance of culture and public concern as a mediating force between troubled intellectual opposites. The veteran *North American Review, Harper's Monthly, Century,* the *Atlantic,* and the *Forum* often published work by distinguished personages who were more fixtures of society than dynamic components. But these publications also made bold to treat momentous issues of their time. Twenty percent of the *North American Review*'s articles dealt with such matters as trusts, labor, the inequality of wealth, political reform, and the challenge of the city. The *Forum* gave 13 percent of its space to such questions, the *Atlantic* and *Century* 5, and even the insistently literary *Harper's* 2 percent.[8]

To be sure these publications had no agitational features to identify them with the coming Progressive articles, and they were not popular in format. But they did use writings by such proponents of change as Henry George, Hamlin Garland, and the economist and professor Richard T. Ely, who reprobated monopolies and asked for mediation of labor disputes. Ely was one of the most influential social commentators on campuses of the late nineteenth century. His trial for economic heresies at the University of Wisconsin in 1894 was a landmark in academic freedom. Even his socialist opponents confessed that "his treatment of Socialism has done much to obtain a hearing for it among the unreasonable."[9] Most such critics were in time themselves tossed dustlike into the social wind, and their strictures survived only to muddle the problem of a valid, long-staying critique of American thought and movements.

There were others in the genteel spectrum who contributed to the clarification of American problems, not definitively but, at the least, not irresponsibly, as in the case of Isaac L. Rice, industrialist and founder of the *Forum,* who advocated nationalization of railroads. Contributors to his pages stood for government ownership of telegraphs and independent regulatory commissions, without fearing to be tarred as socialists or anarchists. Whatever the limitations of many of their writings, they provided a leaven of ideas and information from which more pointed writings came. And their sharp literacy and precision became a base from which the popular magazines could and successfully did take off.

Civil service was uniquely an achievement of the genteel reformers. Their Thomas A. Jenckes, a patent lawyer and congressman, drew up the bill in 1867 that began slow but steady progress toward creation of a civil service—or "snivel service," as witty enemies called it. George William Curtis of *Harper's Monthly* and *Harper's Weekly* headed the Civil Service Commission that drew up specifications for competitive examinations, and Carl Schurz, as Secretary of the Interior under Hayes, pressed for civil service in his department. Theodore Roosevelt as civil service commissioner dramatized the issue, fighting the traditions of patronage that, whatever the virtues alleged by defenders of corruption who discriminated between theirs and others', drained strength from the government's operations and required the treatment of a Mackenzie or a Roosevelt from time to time.[10]

The most distinguished of civil-service reformers was Dorman B. Eaton (1823-1899), a Vermonter and graduate of Harvard Law School. He became a noted New York lawyer who in 1864 and after worked for the association of New York Citizens and became strategic in the battle against Tweed. Eaton's civil labors led to the creation of the New York Department of Health, its fire department, its department of docks, and its police judiciary, all of which became models for the country. In addition he fought with others to establish a merit system.[11]

This was "structural reform"—an emphasis on forms and organization, which some later academics would strive to make appear peripheral, if not irrelevant, either to social reform, concerned for the well-being of needy social elements, or even to "fundamental" reform, which would, presumably, put the nation into a state of egalitarian, if not welfare, stability and content. The means by which so joyous a condition would be obtained was not always spelled out, especially in accurate assessment of American goals and traditions. More serious was a myopia that failed to recognize that structural reform was a prior condition to social reform of a more humanitarian type. Stephen Smith, a genteel reformer, in his *The City That Was*

(1911) portrayed a New York of the prewar decades that had blundered into an expansion involving immigrants and industry so that it sat in a cesspool of filth and iniquity. Although compassionate or fearful city fathers had sought to control these evils, their incidence had risen above the efforts made, all but futile in the face of the fraud practiced by political rings and their patronage. The social reform that went underway, tentatively in the 1890s and in full flood after, is seen ungratefully if not viewed in connection with the work of earlier reformers.[12]

In 1873 Eaton was appointed chairman of the first Civil Service Commission, which was, however, dependent on congressional allotments of funds and was discontinued the next year. Three years later, Hayes commissioned Eaton to visit England and study its civil service. He returned to write his classic *The Civil Service in Great Britain: A History of Abuses and Reforms and Their Bearing upon American Politics* (1880). Still later he drew up the Pendleton Act (1883), which established the civil service, and he was appointed first charman of its commission, serving until 1886. Thereafter he joined such others as Albert Shaw of the *American Review of Reviews* as a student of municipalities and their proper functions, and he wrote *The Government of Municipalities* (1899).

Although such works might seem academic to millennium-minded academics who viewed them through a haze of benign boss politics (see page 146), they were vital to maintaining concepts of social decorum as a brake on a swiftly moving democracy, which was producing at random such enigmatic American successes as "Diamond Jim" Brady, the speculator, Frank Leslie of tawdry newspaper fame, and Allan Pinkerton, who began his career as an abolitionist and escort to President Abraham Lincoln and later provided strikebreakers for beleaguered industrialists. Democracy spawned Victoria Woodhull, who moved out of a career as a common spiritualist trickster and sexual exploiter to pose as an advocate of woman's rights and who muddied worthy causes in the process. It produced whole categories of financial schemers, labor opportunists, Indian exploiters, and others.

Indian reform made less of an impact on that postwar era than did many other issues, mainly because the nation was still required to deal with the western tribes as active foes. All the more valuable, therefore, in that difficult time were the services of the civilian reformers who sought to improve the quality of Indian agents and to rid the Bureau of Indian Affairs of appointees who despoiled their charges by fraudulent contracts and corrupted them with liquor and debauchery. These new "friends of the Indian" were not Quakers. They comprised various public and private citizens, including Carl Schurz and Henry L. Dawes, who made themselves spokesmen for the harassed Indian.

The reformers worked ardently for their goals in the face of public indifference—too often underrated by later assessors of reformers' achievements—fear of Indians, and the mercenary goals of adventurers. The reformers' hope lay in breaking up tribal relations and their reservation base and settling Indians on 160-acre homesteads by allotment of land "in severalty," that is, on an individual basis; in making Indians citizens and thus protected by law; and in providing an education system that would bring Indians into the general American community. The Dawes Act (1887), which made Indians wards of the state and protected by it, was a major achievement in this direction, but the dreams that inspired it inevitably became part of the general competitive drives among American ethnic elements and moved slowly toward fulfillment.[13]

What gave body to the work of the genteel reformers in this field were two works, one expository, the other fiction, which dramatized the question of American responsibility toward the tribes. Helen Hunt Jackson was considered a poet, and she was a friend of Emily Dickinson. But though both were in the genteel tradition, the differences in their verse were the differences between art and artifacts: a distinction that haunted much, though far from all, of genteel poetry. What was important was that Mrs. Jackson's concern for emotional themes, and her penchant for poetics gave her prose a power not available to the mere journalist, however accurate or forceful his point.[14]

Mrs. Jackson's discovery of Indian problems, her involvement in them, her organization of the Boston Indian Citizenship Association, and circulation of tracts in behalf of Indians, all contributed to maturing her writing. Her publication of *A Century of Dishonor* (1881) bore the marks of her emotional commitment to the Indian cause. Yet she had also studied the official records carrying the details of clashes between settlers and natives and between government officials and their chiefs. *A Century of Dishonor* mixed indignation with documentary proof.

Later critics could argue that she had ignored whole volumes spelling out Indian treachery, Indian massacres of whites, and the sheer facts of white-Indian confrontation,[15] yet her tale made sufficient impression to increase the level of philanthropic commitment to Indians, to make Mrs. Jackson a commissioner of Indian affairs, and to contribute strongly to passage of the Dawes Act. Americans wanted more than a recital of data, and it was this fact that made *A Century of Dishonor* a direct precursor of muckraking. That hers was not the full story did not detract from the fact that it was a story that needed telling.

Even more impressive was the phenomenon of *Ramona* (1884), her novel of Indian misadventures in California, especially since it *was* fiction as compared with alleged fact:

> When one compares the success of *Ramona* with that of *A Century of Dishonor*, the superiority of imaginative literature over nonfiction in arousing the public is obvious. *Ramona* has gone through three hundred printings; countless stage and screen versions testify to its power. *A Century of Dishonor* [has been] out of print since the year of Mrs. Jackson's death.[16]

The muckrakers, too, later thought it urgent to generalize their feelings and outlook in fiction and, as will be seen, joined several of their tales and novels in a line of descent that by common agreement went back to Stowe's *Uncle Tom's Cabin.* However this fact is interpreted, there could be no question but that *Ramona*, by humanizing Indians and by juxtaposing them with whites in vital, personal ways, helped Americans to refresh their attitudes toward Indians.

Although Mrs. Jackson's temperament was sharply different from that of E. L. Godkin, the contrast helped suggest that there was diversity in genteel, elitist circles and that they could only falsely be stereotyped into some single, senseless caricature. Godkin was a strangely cold, analytical student of events who had left England for the United States following a short, brilliant career as a journalist who had reported the Crimean War at age twenty-one.[17] He became the first editor of the *Nation*, originally founded to help adjust Negro freedmen to ordinary life in America. The *Nation* quickly lost that character, becoming instead an outstanding repository of critical articles that attracted hundreds of first-class talents of the caliber of Henry James, Francis Parkman, Charles Francis Adams, Jr., the mathematician Charles Peirce, Thomas Wentworth Higginson, William James, and numerous others in all intellectual fields.[18]

Godkin had but one cause: Free Trade and the peace it would presumably bring to the world. He had but one fear: the excesses of democracy. This narrow but precise and highly informed program enabled Godkin to cover American events without partisanship other than that following from his distaste for democratic corruption, the protection of home industries, and the international troubles they must cause. His position gave him a curious tolerance; he would, for example, not join the rabble in its contempt for the Chinese. Godkin's evident breadth was, however, deceptive. Godkin knew no Chinese; his position was purely theoretical. His hatred for political corruption was more genuine, and it made him a pioneer in municipal reform, and of methods to prevent cheating at the polls. As editor of the *New York Evening Post*, a position he assumed in addition to his work on the *Nation*, he attacked Tammany Hall with fury, in 1890 actually being arrested for criminal libel as a result of a series of biographic sketches he caused to be published revealing the sordid backgrounds of some of its chieftains.[19]

All such matters contributed to the coming era of muckraking and progressivism. Yet they could be distinguished from the latter in that the goo goos sought to influence an elite on public matters and to find ways to stabilize American life as it was. They were less capable of learning how to utilize the new energies of ordinary Americans and immigrants that had to be molded for American service. It would take Progressives to do that.

Godkin cared nothing for the new immigrants who had been brought to serve the factories. He cared little for their health. He was obsessed by the need to maintain the law. So was his social equal Theodore Roosevelt, but the latter was also determined to deal with life as it was. Hence, when he was apprised by Samuel Gompers in 1882 of the horrid conditions in cigar making by immigrants in their homes—conditions that made filthy and oppressive with tobacco dust the habitats of whole families enslaved in the trade—Roosevelt was persuaded that a law was necessary to prevent such desecration of family life.[20] Godkin's fear that such laws would whittle away individual freedoms made him a figure of the past—a past that contained admirable pages of civil-service reform, anticorruption, and admirable prose, as well as some poetry. But Roosevelt's more perceptive understanding enabled him to stay abreast of changing events and to affect them.

Most fatal to the genteel name was its reputation for moral hypocrisy and repression of natural knowledge and activity. This emphasis upon pruriency was not unique to postwar gentility but rather helped show the increasing alienation of the elite from the poor and especially the immigrants. Richard Welling was one of the imposing genteel reformers of that era and after; his monument was the teaching of civics in schools. But it was not he, it was his great-grandfather, John Welling, who caused Lawrenceville, New Jersey, to acquire its name to replace what Welling thought was the embarrassing original name of "Maidenhead."[21] His great-grandson was of a somewhat more hearty disposition. Gentility did come to be identified with sexual repression. And yet the symbol of aggressive inhibition was not any of the famous ladies or gentlemen of the pre-Progressive decades but a rugged son of Connecticut farmers, fundamentalist in religion and firm in his conviction that especially the young could become depraved by tempting illustrations, tales, and unprofitable activities being joined with lust.

To be sure, such citizens as Abram Hewitt and Anson Phelps Stokes helped subsidize Anthony Comstock's war against what he defined as vice, and others of well-to-do classes joined or supported his Society for the Suppression of Vice. Nevertheless, distinguished members of the gentility were ordinarily too busy with larger issues of labor, government policies, elections, and cultural pursuits to work closely in the field. Henry Adams had a cold and distrustful view of sex, but the Philadelphia poet and diplomat George Henry Boker, though rating as a gentleman, was more exploratory in the field. Between these two, the genteel classes furnished an exciting range of personalities and moral experiences.

Comstock represented a range of middle-class elements, mainly of Anglo-Saxon derivation, fearful for traditional standards of family and social life. Some of them had been earnest in pre-Civil War crusades and could recall the futile and ridiculed efforts of the Mary Magdalen Society to end prostitution in New York. Some abolitionists were involved in such moral reform and could actually quote William Lloyd Garrison (though not wisely, for Garrison's reach was further than the quote indicated) as opposed to regulating prostitution, for "if one sin can be licensed, why not another?"[22]

Comstock, however, went much further than the old-time reformers; he would not only have regulated prostitutes but all society. Farm boys and girls unleashed in the new, scarcely structured cities and immigrant families caught between Old World expectations and the new, competitive American society had mutual problems on moral issues. Comstock had many faults and limitations, but one of them was not indifference to the miseries of the immigrant young who were trapped in gambling, sexual, and saloon-centered frauds. There was indeed a "purity" crusade, which attracted a few former abolitionists, though far from all. Parker Pillsbury had been one of the most uncompromising of abolitionists. Yet he fought for Ezra Heywood, arrested by Comstock in 1877 for publishing *Cupid's Yokes,* an argument favoring "free love." It would thus be grossly inaccurate, utterly myopic to refer to the "purity" movement as a "new abolitionism." Eye-catching though the phrase may be, the movement, such as it was, lacked the central function of the antislavery drive. "Purity" was, rather, a by-product of broader-gauged movements, including the woman's rights movement and the temperance crusade, carried over from prewar decades.

Comstock's difficulty was that he joined too many issues in order to attack what he clearly saw as the liberal position. He not only attacked licentious writings; he attacked all writings he deemed licentious and would have put recognized classics in private collections, to be used only through vested authority. He would have closed theaters that trafficked in "low" plays and stopped the sale of boxes of candies that included prizes (the "primary department of gambling"). He would have closed poolrooms and impeded "infidels" from corrupting the young.

Among the 3,600 men, women, and children Comstock arrested

over the years for circulating "lewd and lascivious" publications, for publishing abortion information or misinformation, for selling contraceptive devices, or otherwise contributing to vice, there were doubtless many unsavory characters. But their misdemeanors were arbitrarily determined and their legal rights regularly infringed. Comstock's definition of virtue was so patently narrow as to limit possibilities for a working social ethic.

His vendetta against "the great infidel," Robert J. Ingersoll, reflected badly upon Comstock's understanding of freedom. Ingersoll's rationalistic criticisms of the Bible challenged a generation of auditors who also knew of Ingersoll's reverence for the Republican party and for family life. Indeed, Ingersoll approved the notorious law Comstock pushed through Congress in 1873 for stopping the interstate traffic in "lewd" publications. In 1880 Ingersoll resigned as vice-president of the National Liberal League because it sought the repeal of Comstock's law.

Gentility suffered by false identification with Comstock's crusades. He himself became an object of ridicule when, in 1905, he caused the New York Public Library to place George Bernard Shaw's *Man and Superman* on restricted circulation, and, the next year, raided the Art Students' League to seize its latest issue of *The American Student of Art*, containing reproductions of nudes done by students.[23] It was unfortunate that such antics created libels against the most distinguished of genteel reformers, which society ultimately, for its own well-being, would wish to disown.

NOTES

1. Allan Nevins, *Abram S. Hewitt: With Some Account of Peter Cooper* (New York, 1935).

2. In addition to agreeing with this indictment, John G. Sproat, *"The Best Men": Liberal Reformers in the Gilded Age* (New York, 1965), emphasizes the incompetence of reform political victories as compared with the firm growth and social validity of well-organized, corrupt political machines.

3. Daniel De Leon, *Speeches and Editorials* (New York, 1903-1934).

4. The Free Speech League, attracting the support of such muckrakers as Brand Whitlock and Lincoln Steffens, was organized in 1911 by the

maverick crusader Theodore Schroeder; see introduction by Jerold S. Auerbach to Schroeder, *"Obscene" Literature and Constitutional Law: A Forensic Defense of Freedom of the Press* (New York, 1972).

5. David F. Thelen, "Rutherford B. Hayes and the Reform Tradition in the Gilded Age," *American Quarterly* 22 (Summer 1970): 150ff.

6. Harry Barnard, *Rutherford B. Hayes and His America* (Indianapolis, 1954), 503ff.

7. Stow Persons, *The Decline of American Gentility* (New York, 1973), 285ff. See also John Tomsich, *A Genteel Endeavor: American Culture and Politics in the Gilded Age* (Stanford, 1971).

8. John G. Clark, "Reform Currents in Polite Monthly Magazines, 1880-1900," *Mid-America* 47 (January 1965): 4-5. This article treats the *Arena* as one of the "polite" publications, a judgment in which it does not seem possible to concur.

9. Arthur M. Lewis, *Ten Blind Leaders of the Blind* (Chicago, 1908), 65ff. See also Benjamin G. Rader, *The Academic Mind and Reform: The Influence of Richard T. Ely in American Life* (Lexington, Ky., 1966).

10. William Dudley Foulke, *Fighting the Spoilsmen* (New York, 1919), is a vivid personal record of the movement. For a scholarly treatment, see Ari Hoogenboom, *Outlawing the Spoils: A History of the Civil Service Reform Movement, 1865-1883* (Urbana, Ill., 1961). See also Gordon Milne, *George William Curtis and the Genteel Tradition* (Bloomington, Ind., 1956), 139ff.

11. *Dorman B. Eaton, 1823-1899* (New York, 1900); Stephen Smith, *The City That Was* (New York, 1911); F. M. Stewart, *The National Civil Service Reform League* (Austin, Tex., 1929).

12. Melvin G. Holli, *Reform in Detroit* (New York, 1969), 157ff. This work derogates structural reform while honoring worker-directed and other humanitarian efforts, which it identifies with "urban politics." It fails to recognize that social reform has been itself subjected to contempt by those who honored the city bosses and that progressivism, in flower, based itself on national rather than merely municipal perspectives.

13. Francis P. Prucha, ed., *Americanizing the American Indians: 1880-1900* (Cambridge, Mass., 1973), is an excellent collection of pro-Indian writings. See also Robert W. Murdock, *The Reformers and the American Indian* (Columbia, Mo., 1971).

14. Helen Jackson, *Mercy Philbrick's Choice* (Boston, 1876), was certainly inspired, in part, by her view of Emily Dickinson, and her poems in the novel, imputed to Dickinson, contrast startlingly with Dickinson's own.

15. Allan Nevins, "Helen Hunt Jackson, Sentimentalist vs. Realist," *American Scholar*, 10 (Summer 1941): 269ff.

16. Andrew F. Rolle, ed., *Jackson, A Century of Dishonor* (New York, 1965), xx.

17. Louis Filler, "The Early Godkin: Toward an Evaluation of a Significant Victorian," *Historian* 17 (Autumn 1954): 43-66.

18. Gustav Pollak, ed., *Fifty Years of American Idealism: The New York Nation, 1865-1915, Selections and Comments* (Boston, 1915).

19. Rollo Ogden, ed., *Life and Letters of Edwin Lawrence Godkin* (New York, 1907), 2:169ff.

20. Bernard Mandel, *Samuel Gompers* (Yellow Springs, Ohio, 1963), 31.

21. Robert Muccigrosso, "Richard W. G. Welling: A Reformer's Life" (Ph.D. diss., Columbia University, 1967), 6.

22. David J. Pivar, *Purity Crusade: Sexual Morality and Social Control, 1868-1900* (Westport, Conn., 1973), 71.

23. Robert Bremner, ed., *Traps for the Young,* by Anthony Comstock (1883; reprinted, Cambridge, 1967), xxvii-xxviii.

Josephine Shaw Lowell

The crisis of the cities called forth numerous workers in charity and philanthropy to study the problems of poverty and to consider solutions. Dorothea Dix had, in prewar years, done much to create new standards of institutional care. But the growth of the country and its public institutions threatened to inundate the gains that had been accomplished. County poorhouses were hideous enough, but when seen in terms of the children who were assigned to them, they were crushing in the hopeless prospects they unfolded. As the report of the Ohio Board of Charities observed in its 1869 summary:

> What is to be done with [the children]? Think of their surroundings. The raving of the maniac, the frightful contortions of the epileptic, the driveling and senseless sputtering of the idiot, the garrulous temper of the decrepit, neglected old age . . . and you have a faint outline of the surroundings of these little boys and girls. This is home to them. Here their first and most enduring impressions of life are formed.[1]

Frederick Howard Wines, who brought administrative ability and a concern for facts to prison reform, Mary Richmond, who formulated the first comprehensive principles of casework, and Owen R. Lovejoy, who dedicated himself to the eradication of child labor—such activists were central figures in a growing and necessary social work. But none did so much for the broader field of social responsibility than a well-brought-up Boston girl from families in business that were also intellectual and ardent in social contribution.

IN MEMORY OF JOSEPHINE SHAW LOWELL
MDCCCXLIII – MCMV
FOUNDER OF THE CHARITY ORGANIZATION SOCIETY
MDCCCLXXXII
SHE GAVE TO IT SO LONG AS HER LIFE LASTED
HER QUICKENING SPIRIT – HER CALM WISDOM
AND HER ALL EMBRACING SYMPATHY

She was a girl who had little reason to anticipate a lengthy and strenuous career as an innovator in the larger American community.

Josephine Shaw's family lived in West Roxbury, near Brook Farm, and counted its tenants their friends. "Effie" was a good student and gained from travel abroad. After they moved to Staten Island, New York, she continued her education there as well as in Boston. "She is the genius of the family," her mother wrote fondly. "She can cook, cut out things [she was then ten], trim hats and new caps, speak French, German, and Italian, and write poetry." When the Civil War broke out, the Shaws were heavily involved. Her father organized relief for Negroes and contributed to organizing the Freedmen's Bureau. Her brother, Robert Gould Shaw, commanded the first Negro regiment, the Fifty-fourth Massachusetts, sent into action. He died with it July 18, 1863, during the desperate storming of Fort Wagner. Friends angrily reported that the Confederates had "scornfully" buried him among his black troops.[2]

Josephine joined the Woman's Central Association of Relief, an auxiliary of the United States Sanitary Commission, in her first contact with philanthropic work.

In November 1863 she married Colonel Charles Russell Lowell, a nephew of the poet Lowell, who had had a brilliant career at Harvard and, afterward, as a superintendent of iron works. In spring 1861 he was commissioned a captain of cavalry and later became a colonel, having compiled an excellent record against Mosby's Confederate guerrillas and under Sheridan in the Shenandoah Valley. Unscathed despite the loss of a dozen horses shot from under him in three years of battle, he decided to propose. As he wrote a friend, "I am going to marry upon nothing . . . and I know now that it would be unwise to allow a possible want of 'daily bread' in the future to prevent the certainty of even a month's happiness in the present."[3]

He brought his twenty-year-old wife with him to camp in Virginia, where she did all the housewifely chores and served others as well. The chaplain wrote of her hospitality to other officers, the pleasure she gave wounded foreign troops by speaking with them in their native tongues, and the comfort she provided disabled and dying soldiers whose wounds she attended and whose letters she wrote. She and her husband wrote continuously to each other while he was away on military missions.

During the battle of Cedar Creek, Virginia, October 19, 1864, while in advance of his general's division, Lowell suffered wounds but refused to leave his command. A final charge brought more wounds, from which he died the following day. Six weeks later, his wife gave birth to a daughter.

She returned to New York City, bent on continuing the cause she felt her brother and husband had advanced, and involved herself in work aimed at adjusting the former slaves to emancipation. She raised funds for the New York branch of the National Freedman's Relief Association and joined others who set up and encouraged Negro education in Virginia. She picked up old companions from her days of relief work before marriage and joined them in the activities of the New York Charities Aid Association. She quickly revealed a gift for seizing salient details of conditions in poorhouses and prisons, taking up for a new time the work that prison reformers had so vastly accomplished in a previous and more individually oriented generation.[4] Josephine Lowell did not direct her operations nationally, as Dorothea Dix had done, but her analyses and creative solutions were so strong and of such a nature as to have a marked influence on all legislation in the fields she made her own.

Her first thrust related to the loose system of charity that had sprung up to service the burgeoning populations in New York City and outlying districts: a system of casual grants, dispensed by volunteer workers with no training and often with no motives beyond curiosity or patronage. Mrs. Lowell's first response to such conditions was fury at what she saw as something worse than "openly advocated communism," in that "the idle, the improvident, and even vicious man has the right to live in idleness and vice upon the proceeds of the labor of his industrious and virtuous fellow citizen."[5]

She later perceived that worthy people could be as readily stricken and deprived of usefulness as though by natural calamities. Mrs. Lowell's greatest characteristic was her capacity for growth. A woman of moderate height, with notably clear complexion and an aura of spirituality that evidently derived from the swift conclusion of her marriage, she lived quietly in New York, habitually wore black, which did not detract from her appearance, raised her daughter, and was wholly absorbed by her broadening social concerns. Most distinctive for the outside world was her prose, which became increasingly firm, clear, and insistent upon principles. She repudiated charity, especially charity that made no demands upon the recipient. Society had a right to know what social benefit resulted from its largesse. The goal of social expenditures had to be not well-being but rehabilitation, "even if the process be as painful as plucking out an eye or cutting off a limb."[6]

By 1876 her reports had made a sufficient impression to encourage Governor Samuel J. Tilden to appoint her as the first woman member of the New York State Board of Charities. She worked not only for more institutions for the insane, for women, and for feebleminded women; she insisted also on programs designed to increase the social responsibility of those deemed physically competent. Her program called for institutional surveillance during which principles of cleanliness, discipline, and productivity would be taught and practiced: everything that could promise to return the prostitute or thief to the world as a worker and participant. Involved in her viewpoint was the controversial "moral purity" concept, which some of a later generation would argue as an infringement on civil rights. Mrs. Lowell shared controversial views of sexuality, probably derived from the idealized life she shared with her dead. She agreed with those who held that women did not have a sex drive comparable to that of men.[7] The principle on which she operated, however, which did not discriminate between males and females, that people must pull their own weight, deprived the conviction of any sting it might carry. She held firmly to the program of usefulness. And, studying the terrible round of strikes that kept police and militia busy and the toll of deaths by cold and starvation that characterized winter hardship, she turned slowly to the cause of labor. "I must try to help [the working people], if I can," she wrote, "and leave the broken down paupers to others."

She retired from the Board of Charities, and in 1890 led the founding of the Consumer's League of New York, especially organizing women for women's rights in industry and building the consumers' boycott as a weapon for persuading hardbacked industrialists to take their needs into consideration.[8] She took the part of the embattled strikers during the Homestead, Pennsylvania, steelworkers' strike of 1892—a strike that seemed ominously like civil war to Americans who had thought of their land as one of opportunity.

But, with other liberals, she labored for mediation as a means for blunting the sharp edge of industrial warfare. Indeed, her study of the subject, *Industrial Arbitration and Conciliation: Some Chapters from the Industrial History of the Past Thirty Years* (1893), was a basic work that merited recollection not only for its history and conscientious consideration of experiences abroad and at home but for the thorough, dispassionate attention and analysis she accorded this crucial topic.

In 1894 she led in organizing the Women's Municipal League, thus entering directly into urban politics, which was obviously part of the future. She was now a clear precursor of progressivism, with other major figures among women seeking to stir the middle classes into a sense of their responsibility for the new world being fashioned by laborers, machines, and their administrators. Anna Howard Shaw as leader of the suffragists and Frances Willard as educator for women were but two among gathering thousands who were creating rallying points for campaigns that were apparently less momentous than those of the Populists but that keenly touched the self-image of women and the nature of their roles in society. Willard's "Do Everything" slogan, her propaganda for the ballot as the "Home Protection" policy dramatized the women's cause. Mrs. Lowell's less glamorous campaigns cast wider nets, involving men and women without discrimination. They met constantly at her home, planning civil service, woman's rights, and labor drives. So natural were her relations and projects that it was hardly noticed at all that her life honored gentility as well as womanhood.

She stayed abreast of her causes and lived to see them accepted as staples of the national scene. By 1905 the Progressive stage swarmed with women engaged in every kind of activity: political, literary, institutional, theoretic. Mrs. Lowell was no longer conspicuous; like Edward Bellamy she belonged to the future more than to the vibrant time of muckrakers and liberal enterprises. She died that year, and was buried beside her husband at Mount Auburn Cemetery in Cambridge, Massachusetts. Her generation, at least, had no difficulty in finding their two causes, abolition and social philanthropy, related.

NOTES

1. Quoted in Robert H. Bremner, *From the Depths: The Discovery of Poverty in the United States* (New York, 1956), 49. A discussion of the rise of charity organizations by one of its pioneers, Charles D. Kellogg, is in Bliss, ed., *Encyclopedia of Social Reform*, (New York, 1897), 220ff.

2. It was after seeing the Saint Gaudens' bronze memorializing Shaw in Boston that William Vaughn Moody wrote "An Ode in Time of Hesitation," denouncing American imperialism in the Philippines; see *The Poems and Plays of . . . Moody* (Boston, 1912), 1: 15-25.

3. Edward W. Emerson, *Life and Letters of Charles Russell Lowell* (Boston, 1907), 309.

4. For an overview of the movement she inherited, see Frank Dekker Watson, *The Charity Organization Movement in the United States: A Study in American Philanthropy* (New York, 1922).

5. Bremner, *From the Depths*, 47.

6. Josephine Shaw Lowell, *Public Relief and Preventive Charity* (New York, 1884), 94.

7. David J. Pivar, *Purity Crusade: Sexual Morality and Social Control, 1868-1900* (Westport, Conn., 1973), 156.

8. Maud Nathan, *The Story of an Epoch-making Movement* (New York, 1926), which tells the tale of the Consumer's League, was dedicated to Mrs. Lowell.

Tom Watson and the Negroes

There was no class or group anywhere in the nation that did not suffer and gain by the hectic expansions and economic collapses of the time. But the South became a peculiar focus of attention by virtue of its late insurrectionary effort and by Republican-fostered fears that it might gain by political strategem what it had lost in the war. The fear created in the North a species of kindliness toward Negroes, more political than real, which expressed itself in editorial and convention rhetoric and which Negro representatives naturally did their best to give substance.

The career of Tom Watson of Georgia became almost symbolic of the tortuous path that the South took in order to reestablish white supremacy despite federal troops and Republican legislatures. The South was no monolithic white horde. It was composed of struggling families and individuals, many dedicated to war on one another, and with destinies not infrequently interrelated with those of blacks.

Watson came of a once-proud family of slaveholders, in postwar times reduced to poverty and insignificance. Young Watson was an emotional boy and dreamer who read gluttonously, wrote verse, and burned to do great deeds. He attended a small Baptist college and taught school for several years. He then began a long march as a criminal lawyer, which, by 1889 when he was thirty-three years old, saw him a man of relatively large fortune and public esteem: a man of action who had carried a gun against a rival lawyer. Watson was known for his dramatic speeches and exciting personality. He became the redeemer of his family. The thin, nervous, flame-headed Georgian brought them back in triumph to their prewar home. He also publicly thrashed a white landlord who had humiliated his brother Top, once a sharecropper for the bully.

There were many other whites of his state and section whom Watson hated and whom he held to be betrayers of the South and of all humanity. Like many others of his frame of mind, he despised northern capitalists whom he saw as draining the lifeblood of the honest southern yeoman, and he loathed southerners who co-operated with the vultures of the North. There had been a national chorus of mutual congratulations when the disputed election of 1876 had been settled without bullets. The Democrats, and especially the southern Democrats, had exchanged the presidency, which went to Rutherford B. Hayes rather than Samuel J. Tilden, for the postmaster generalship, railroad subsidies, levee bills, and internal improvements. But even so there were "plenty of impoverished cotton farmers who were slow to see how any railroad subsidy would help them clothe their ragged children."[1] Watson undertook to be their mouthpiece and to urge them to believe that they had more in common with the beset farmers of the West than with their own conservative politicians.

E. L. Godkin, among those northerners who traveled South to observe its temper and development, flatly reported that most southerners were no longer entranced by a past slavery or with bedewed memories of the lost Confederacy: "Their minds are really occupied with making money, and the farmers show it, and their designs on the Negro are confined to getting him to work for low wages."[2] Nevertheless there were such others as Watson, who needed to live by imspiration as well as avarice and who thrilled to his denunciations of a heartless creditor class.

Not only were western farmers continuing the movement toward third-party politics, which had been inaugurated by their granges and which had already given them the Greenback-Labor tickets of 1880 and 1884. The Negro farmers had bestirred themselves as well and, as of 1886, organized in Texas a Colored Farmers' Alliance. By 1889 it was able to claim more than a million members and to hold a national convention that applied for and received a charter from its white counterpart to become a national organization. A white Baptist minister who had worked ardently for that goal was appointed national superintendent but all the other officers were Negroes.[3]

In 1890 Watson was elected to Congress as a Populist, but, though he bid fair to become a national leader of the South, he would not stint a campaign that had roused the Georgia conservatives against him, and he made common cause with the Negroes whom he held as oppressed as the poor whites by home and national capitalists. Watson's Georgia opponents were reluctant to join their state causes with national—that is, northern—leadership. Watson boldly led his own followers into the third-party Populist alliance, thereby declaring war on the Democrats in Congress and at home.

So ardent was Watson's call for white-black unity against oppressors that, in his reelection campaign of 1892, he would have "pledge[d] the white listeners to defend the Negro's constitutional rights, making them hold up their hands and promise."[4] An hysterical Democratic campaign against him included violence at the polls, lynching, and fraud, all of which lost Watson his congressional seat. So dedicated was Watson to his campaign that he denounced his South Carolina equivalent, "Pitchfork Ben" Tillman, who had also fought his way back from a debased social status and who also had rallied the poor whites against their economic masters, but who earlier made a scapegoat of Negroes for having as governor disenfranchised the Negroes of his state.

Watson was again defeated by fraud in 1894, though he continued to win popular admiration for his castigations of trusts and recreant Democrats. In 1896 he was given the vice-presidential nomination by Populists who also concluded to support William Jennings Bryan's Democratic candidacy. Watson campaigned for Bryan, but he himself gained nothing from the great campaign.

Embittered, he turned to writing history in which he viewed the French Revolution as a mighty parallel to his own crusade. At the same time, he abandoned his idealistic views of Negro-white cooperation. Watson turned into the most vitriolic of anti-Semites and Negrophobes. The imaginative bent that had made in his mind a gargoyle of free enterprise and stereotyped those who were engineering the creation of a new capitalism now easily conjured up repulsive images of new enemies of the Republic satisfying to his tired and soured rural constituency. Although Watson was made wealthy by his publications and lived in a mansion, he never stinted his denunciations of capitalism, and he was to end his life among opponents of what he thought of as capitalist war. Eugene V. Debs memorialized him as a friend of the poor and foe of the rich.[5]

His major biographer characterized him as a Progressive and a white racist, both of which he was. The unfortunate implication—reaffirmed elsewhere—was that progressivism *was* racism, which satisfied an obscure academic hunger for such an interpretation.[6] The fact was that not only was Watson no leading figure in the national Progressive movement—his status among southern Progressives also needed spelling out.

That there were savage and barbaric southerners, there could be no doubt. How many such there were was a momentous question in any assessment of social elements making up the general southern population. We have seen Tweed of New York defended as a voice of realistic politics, in opposition to the genteel reformers who scorned new immigrants—and Tweed's Irish myrmidons were not famous for their love of Negroes. Tweed-like figures arose in the South and, like their northern counterparts, put out money for hospitals and other benefits while generously helping themselves to public moneys. Indeed, it was not until the 1890s that the great "freeze" set on Negro rights in the South. Before then, black legislators and civil personages in a number of southern states were able to exercise various voting and other prerogatives in behalf of their constituencies and themselves.[7]

The South as well as the North required reform, if only because the painful experiences of Reconstruction and its aftermath had created long traditions of electoral fraud necessitating changes in ballot procedures. South Carolina took pride in having first introduced the direct primary, twelve years before it was adopted in Wisconsin, first of the northern states to put the system into practice. It was not too often remarked in the North that the famous Galveston plan for civic reorganization that followed as a result of the destruction wrought by a tidal wave in 1900 was a southern innovation, as was the subsequent Miami plan.

A remarkable feature of Negro disenfranchisement was that machine politicians and conservatives in the South had learned to handle the Negro vote as part of their general program of languid social improvements. And thus Progressives, in seeking votes for their new policies making for tax improvements, railroad control, education, and other areas, felt it necessary to oppose machine control of the Negro suffrage. Only one southern governor in the Progressive tradition, Hogg of Texas, firmly made continued Negro voting rights part of his campaigns, and he freely expressed his hatred of mob violence.[8]

Behind such figures were numerous others who found violence and repression repugnant and who prided themselves on what they saw as the true southern heritage. There were many imbued with the Progressive impulse who in the next decades would give character to the South as journalists, educators, statesmen, and artists. One would, fatefully, become President of the United States. Woodrow Wilson, as a Princeton professor would, in 1897, while addressing the American Historical Association, ringingly declare that "[t]here is nothing to apologize for in the past of the South—absolutely nothing to apologize for"—a view that did him no harm with members of the association.[9]

Somewhere between Wilson, who preached work and duty to the Hampton Institute assembly he addressed in 1897, and Willis D. Weatherford, who gave fifty years of service to poor whites and poor blacks in behalf of education and cooperative labors, lay the uncommitted South that would define Negro-white relations. Weatherford's Southern Sociological Conference, meeting in Memphis in 1914, raised questions in the minds of local businessmen who sought to segregate the Negro delegates from the white. One officer of the congress offered to "follow the lead of you southern gentlemen." Weatherford, his face flushed, turned to his colleague and demanded, "*I'm* a Southern gentleman, sir. Why don't you follow *my* lead?"[10]

Some followed Weatherford's lead, making his one of the happier tales of southern social history. But no story of the southern Progressive impulse could be complete without a record of the numerous Negro educators and others who gave strength and morale to their own and earned the regard of substantial portions of the white community. That this was achieved by accommodation, there can be no doubt. But it was an accommodation that took courage and intelligence and that gave sinews and direction to southern Negroes. It built a Negro community that grew and gathered resources for endurance and advance in property, educational facilities, and churches.[11]

Perhaps the greatest of post-Civil War Negro leaders was forced to build his career in the North. Daniel A. Payne, born of free parents in Charleston, South Carolina, learned his lessons so well and so widely that the inspiration he afforded free Negroes and slaves as a teacher in his native city alarmed the state's leaders, who in 1834 passed an ordinance making his work illegal. In the North he became a minister and teacher who, in Baltimore, was rejected by its African Methodist Episcopal church as pastor for being too genteel and as one who would not let his congregation sing "the cornfield ditties." Payne next turned to one of his distinguished projects, collecting all available records of the birth and growth of his denomination; it was later published as the invaluable *History of the African Methodist Episcopal Church* (1891). In 1863 he became the founder of Wilberforce University in southwest Ohio, a bastion of Negro education.[12]

Following the war, Payne returned in triumph to Charleston, and there he began a movement of organization and missionary efforts that established the AME church throughout the South. It was, to be sure, a separatist drive, though aided by southern Methodists and involving a solid amount of goodwill.[13] Ultimately, the two churches gave to the South so great a symbol of race reconciliation as Weatherford, among men and women who were not of his stature but memorable.

Booker T. Washington was, of course, the great name in Negro affairs of the time, nationally as well as in the South. However, it was the interrelated careers of numerous others that enabled the black communities to weather the aftermath of Reconstruction with fortitude. Christopher H. Payne was one of many leaders whose varied lives reflected southern as well as Negro conditions. His mother had been the daughter as well as the slave of a James Ellison of Monroe County, Virginia (now West Virginia), where Christopher was born in 1848. Ellison instructed his daughter and set her free. Christopher's father, a cattle drover, died when he was two years old.

His mother taught him to read so early that he could not recall when he could not read.

He was forced to serve Confederate officers, it was said, during the war, but in 1864 he returned home to work on a farm. He then began a schedule of work and study, which in 1868 gained him his teacher's certificate. Payne alternated teaching and farm work until 1875 when he was converted, and soon after he was licensed to preach and take full responsibilities as a pastor and Sunday school missionary. His studies continued at Richmond Institute, later Virginia Union University. He supported a growing family, a mother, and a grandmother while reaching out also to the rural Negroes as a teacher, minister, and community organizer. He later estimated that he had preached some fifteen hundred sermons, converted five hundred people, and organized nine churches while in his peregrinations helping to build up numerous others.

Dignified, earnest, and almost white of countenance, Payne was known to many throughout his state. In addition, he published several weekly newspapers and wrote for others in clear and forceful prose. His main crusade was for education and for preparations that would increase industry and competence among his people. He took this program with him into politics, where he was received with courtesy by the white leadership of the new state, which, because of its Free Soil attitudes, had been carved away from Virginia and should have been named Lincoln but was instead designated West Virginia.

Its Republicans appreciated Payne's ability to deliver the state's Negro votes to them. Payne was an alternate to the national Republican convention of 1884 and was endorsed by the state's machine for minister to Liberia in 1889. That year, however, he was offered, and he accepted the deputy collectorship of internal revenue at Charleston, West Virginia. The next year the state university conferred the Doctor of Divinity degree upon him. In 1891 Payne saw one of his dreams completed with the opening of a mechanical and agricultural college for Negro youth.

Payne next turned to law and in 1896 was admitted to the bar. He also served in the state legislature, the first of his race to do so. He was later appointed consul at St. Thomas in the Danish West Indies. When the United States purchased the island he lost his position but stayed on as a practicing lawyer and police judge.[14] His key services to his people had ended years before, but as an aging man with a family, it behooved him to care for himself and his own where society generally, and his own people in particular, were unwilling or unable to do so.

No tale of Negro progressivism could be complete if it did not notice the numerous women of character and talent who helped sustain the fabric of its goals and personalities.[15] Anna Julia Cooper (1858-1964), a native of North Carolina, attended St. Augustine Normal School, married a minister, and in 1881 entered Oberlin College, where she studied and taught. She became a professor at Wilberforce University and taught first at her own St. Augustine Normal, then for many years at the famous Dunbar High School in Washington, D. C. In 1925, at age sixty-six, she received her Ph. D. at the Sorbonne in Paris.

Her *A Voice from the South, by a Black Woman of the South* (1892) expressed views that some later radicals would find too patient and conciliatory, but it contained its own spirit and sustaining doctrines. She was impatient with her own Protestant Episcopal church for its lack of missionary zeal in competing with the vigorous and far-flung AME church, with its "peculiar faults of worship—the rank exuberance and often ludicrous demonstrations" it permitted. She pleaded for the girls of the Negro communities to be honored, taught, and granted opportunities beyond those of marriage.

With classic references and apt metaphors, she applauded the Reverend Anna Shaw of the National Woman's Council and later Susan B. Anthony's successor, for having resisted segregationist tendencies in women's organizations. Mrs. Cooper took pride in the growing number of Negro professionals, Negro colleges, Negro property holders. She struggled bravely to distinguish oppression from questions of civility, agreeing that no one need be forced to endure unwanted company and even projecting to the viewpoint of the train conductor, forced by his own need to subsist, to direct her to a segregated car.

All of this was to rouse impatience among militant elements in later decades. Yet her plea for civility and education for discerning differences between brutal treatment and misguided treatment was

Yours sincerely
A. J. Cooper.

as necessary for them as for her. Their militancy could not have advanced without the enlightened cooperation of others. Numerous passages out of her observations and experiences were of a nature that had to precede the more consummate demands for civil rights. They carried their own eloquence:

> Stung by such imputations as that of [John C.] Calhoun that if a Negro could prove his ability to master the Greek subjunctive he might vindicate his title to manhood, the newly liberated race first shot forward along this line with an energy and success which astonished its most sanguine friends. . . .
>
> That one black man has written a Greek grammar is enough to answer Calhoun's sneer, but it is leisure, the natural outgrowth of work and wealth, which must furnish room, opportunity, possibility for the highest endeavor and most brilliant achievement. Labor must be the solid foundation stone—the sine qua non of our material value; and the only effective preparation for success in this . . . lies in the establishment of industrial and technical schools for teaching our colored youth trades. This necessity is obvious for several reasons. First, a colored child, in most cases, can secure a trade in no other way. We had master mechanics while the Negro was a chattel, and the ingenuity of brain and hand served to enrich the coffers of his owner. But today skilled labor is steadily drifting into the hands of white workmen—mostly foreigners. Here it is cornered. The white engineer holds a tight monopoly both of the labor market and the science of his craft. . . .[16]

All in all, it is difficult to judge how much of the writer's outlook was obsolete, how much individual and her privilege as an educated and self-supporting person. She, and others like her, were to be later impugned by figures in their own community who held them to have been too modest in their demands, too straitlaced in their ethics, their dedication to work, their ways of life. It seemed likely that they would outlive the calumnies of which they were indirectly targets, to take their place with white counterparts as signal-lights of progress and humanity. They could be termed Progressives.

Such were several of thousands of Negroes with whom the Watsons needed to live. That they dealt infamously with them there could be no doubt. What was unwise was to accept the Watsons as symbols of their section. A certain visibility and power they of course had—and even certain uses as acting out aspects of the troubles and frustrations of their section.

But was the career of a George Washington Cable (1844-1925) not to be honored as significant for southerners? It had involved the writing of such emancipating fiction as *Old Creole Days* (1879) and *The Grandissimes* (1880). It had risen to heights, as Cable protested against the disgrace of Negro discrimination and the ugly convict-lease system in his *The Silent South* (1885). Not to consider Cable part of the southern heritage is as senseless as to throw aside Henry D. Thoreau because his "career" had been almost entirely posthumous. As has been earlier noted, Thoreau had had no effect whatever on his own generation; Emerson had sadly regretted that he had lived as in a millpond.

As the North was more than the sum of its political bosses, so the South was more than its demagogues. In the rise of industry, education, and the arts, the South attained a more promising future for its blacks and whites, and in that achievement a more humane progressivism than Watson could represent.

NOTES

1. C. Vann Woodward, *Reunion and Reaction* (Boston, 1951), 188.
2. Quoted in Louis Filler, "The Early Godkin: Toward an Evaluation of a Significant Victorian," *Historian* 17 (Autumn 1954): 61.
3. Hanes Walton, Jr., *The Negro in Third Party Politics* (Philadelphia, 1969), 39.
4. *Ibid.*, 43.
5. John P. Roche, *The Quest for the Dream* (New York, 1963), 91.
6. C. Vann Woodward, introduction to *Life and Labor in the Old South*, by Ulrich B. Phillips (Boston, 1963). Interestingly, Woodward also denounced abolitionists as frauds in his "The Antislavery Myth," *American Scholar* (Spring 1962): 312ff., thus putting into one package of failure two of the major reform movements in American history, for which he was honored by various liberal movements, including the NAACP.
7. C. Vann Woodward, *American Counterpoint, Slavery and Racism in*

the North-South Dialogue (Boston, 1971), 185. Cf. Arthur S. Link, "The Progressive Movement in the South, 1870-1914," *North Carolina Historical Review* 23 (1946): 172ff. For an analysis of the Negro vote in southern politics, see "The Alabama Election," *Literary Digest* 5 (August 13, 1892): 414.

8. Robert C. Cotner, *James Stephen Hogg, A Biography* (Austin, Texas, 1959), 225-226, 313, 353ff. See also William Larsen, *Montague of Virginia: The Making of a Progressive* (Baton Rouge, 1965), 70ff.

9. Arthur Link et al., *The Papers of Woodrow Wilson* (Princeton, N.J., 1971), 10:93.

10. Wilma Dykeman, *Prophet of Plenty: The First Ninety Years of W. D. Weatherford* (Knoxville, Tenn., 1966), 76.

11. For a valuable review of the post-Civil War Negro leadership, see William J. Simmons, *Men of Mark* (Cleveland, 1887). The forthcoming *Dictionary of American Negro Biography*, ed. Rayford W. Logan and Michael R. Winston, will apply modern scholarship to supplement pioneer collections. See also Richard Bardolph, *The Negro Vanguard* (New York, 1959), 61ff., for assessments of some of the era's notables.

12. Payne details these and other matters in his *Recollections of Seventy Years* (Nashville, 1888).

13. Joel Williamson, *After Slavery: The Negro in South Carolina during Reconstruction, 1861-1877* (Chapel Hill, 1965), 188-189.

14. Simmons, *Men of Mark*, 241-243; Payne's obituary appeared in the *Journal of Negro History* 11 (January 1926): 225.

15. For a useful survey, see Hallie Q. Brown, *Homespun Heroines and Other Women of Distinction* (Xenia, Ohio, 1926).

16. Anna Julia Cooper, *A Voice from the South* (Xenia, Ohio, 1892), 260-262.

Labor, Immigrants, and Reform

> Confrontation between labor and the [Radical Republicans] produced a maddening imbroglio from which emerged a new style of politics, typified by the famous Republican Stalwarts, a peculiar ideology inherited from radicalism by the labor movement itself, and a genteel critique of Radicals, Stalwarts, and labor, which styled itself liberalism.[1]

Liberalism did somewhat better than seems indicated in the above quotation. Analysts were "maddened" because they had dreams—usually utopian—of some kind of social rationale that would bring eternal bliss to all components of society and perhaps purgatory for those who merited one.

Nevertheless it was true that the tensions and hatreds created between capital and labor did, in the 1870s and even after the creation of the American Federation of Labor in the next decade, step up confrontations that could only be called radical and that impugned the value of mediating figures. Some such there were, who worked along with modish attitudes as best they could. William Sylvis of the National Labor Union expressed disgust at carpetbaggers who permitted their daughters to "entertain young negro gentlemen in their parlors," but he also urged the need for limiting antagonism between blacks and whites, and he denounced military strikebreaking and legal efforts to prohibit strikes as inevitably bringing on violence between labor and employers.[2]

That violence exploded in 1877 when railroad workers broke past their more conservative leaders to confront federal troops and state militia in such actions as the nation had not seen before. Railroads were peculiar in that their labor perforce operated "along the line," spread out in waystations as well as in terminals. Most other labor was to be found concentrated either in mills and mines or in the cities. There their struggle for advancement in American terms—labor abroad had to express its fantasies by way of different vocabularies—moved through union aspirations or in hopes of rapport with the employers.

Bricks were exchanged for pistols in Baltimore, where the Baltimore & Ohio Railroad originated, and the strike spread rapidly west and north. Pitched battles were fought between strikers and militia sent from Philadelphia to Pittsburgh, where bullets killed twenty-six of the militants and law-and-order personnel.

> Fire followed looting. Now and then flames burst from an emptied car. Whenever there was a gap, the crowd carried brands to the next string of cars. Toward the Union Depot thousands watched approvingly as a score or so of half-drunken men spread fire among the rolling stock. Billowing oil smoke shadowed the flushed and yelling mob. Up at Twenty-sixth Street firemen had begun playing their hoses on the roundhouse ten minutes after Brinton's command left it, but it was already doomed. . . . No one seemed to mourn the railroad's losses except old Bobby Atchison, who lamented helplessly as the flames swept over his beloved engine Number 281. . . .[3]

Similar scenes took place in Chicago, Buffalo, Scranton, San Francisco, and elsewhere, with similar devastation. President Hayes, elected a liberal as an Ohio reformer to dull the edge of the Grant fiasco, had sent federal troops to Martinsburg, West Virginia, a great railroad terminal, to restore law and order.

"The railroad strike of 1877 was the tocsin that sounded a ringing message of hope to us all," said Samuel Gompers many years after. He himself, however, for much of his life and after was to be scorned

Samuel Gompers as a young labor leader.

as a labor politician, a "labor faker," one who was willing to negotiate rather than fight and who was cold to the unemployed and the unskilled, to say nothing of the yellow and black.[4] Yet as between the Emma Goldmans and the Allan Pinkertons of the time—the anarchists and the strikebreakers—it is likely that Gompers best represented the hope of labor's growth and stability, its possibility of rapprochement with the other great sectors of American society—a rapprochement that had been and would continue to be the goal of progressivism.

Oh, the merchant, he's a dodger,
Yes, a well-known dodger,
Oh, the merchant, he's a dodger,
Yes, and I'm a dodger, too.
He'll sell you goods at double the price,
And when you go to pay him
You'll have to pay him twice.[5]

The abrupt expansion of cities in post-Civil War America, thanks to new immigrants, street railroads, and augmented industry, changed the cities' social and political complexion. Expansion produced "bosses" who became center spokes of such political machines as had not been seen before. There had been ruffians at the polls in earlier decades; Edgar Allen Poe had died at their hands, a trifling incident in their brutal activities during an election in Baltimore in 1849. But the new cities required a more complex organization because of the greater value of city franchises, jobs, and contracts that could be manipulated.

The first organization of rings to attend to the business of secret information and bribes was quite crude, but it dealt with the eternal question: how to strengthen the ring and make its leaders and supporters affluent. As Viscount Bryce later explained in describing the origin and operation of the Philadelphia "Gas Ring," which he treated as a classic example, local government there had fallen into the hands of obscure men, while the "best" citizens were bemused by wartime duties. The new men had taken the highest city posts, putting their own "creatures" into water, highway, tax, and other departments. Their mayor filled the police department with partisans. The key to their operations was the gas trust, administered by James M'Manes, who made of it an enormous source of revenue for himself and his appointees, as well as the base of their power:

> Nearly all the municipal offices were held by their nominees. They commanded a majority in the Select council and Common council. They managed the nomination of members of the State legislature. Even the Federal officials in the custom-house and post-office were forced into a dependent alliance with them,

> because their support was so valuable to the leaders in Federal politics that it had to be purchased by giving them their way in city affairs. . . . Mr. M'Manes held the pay rolls under lock and key, so that no one could know how many employés there were, and it was open to him to increase their number to any extent. The city councils might indeed ask for information, but he was careful to fill the city councils with his nominees, and to keep them in good humour by a share of whatever spoil there might be, and still more by a share of the patronage.[6]

This story was to be repeated an interminable number of times in other cities and also in terms of "statehouse" rings. "Boss" Thomas C. Platt's machine in New York and "Boss" Matthew Quay's in Pennsylvania, both Republican, became conspicuous as prototypes. The activities of such politicians would have seemed calculated to stir citizen uprisings. As was recounted by Andrew D. White, distinguished educator and president of Cornell University who had been a member of the New York Senate and minister to Germany, with more honors ahead:

> Few [of the bosses] have gained their positions by fitness or by public service; many have gained them by scoundrelism; some by crime. . . . It has been my lot also to have much to do with two interior American cities of less size—one of about 100,000 inhabitants, the other of about 12,000. In the former of these I saw a franchise for which a $1,000,000 could easily have been obtained, given away by the common council. I saw a body of the most honored men in the state go before that council to plead for ordinary justice and decency. I saw the chief justice of the highest court of the State, one of his associate judges, a circuit judge of the United States, an honored member of Congress, two bishops, the president and professors of a university, and a great body of respected citizens urge this common council not to allow a railroad corporation to block up the entrance to the ward in which the practitioners lived, and to occupy the main streets of the city. . . to the danger of life. . . . All was utterly in vain.[7]

Such activities were far from unopposed. What was momentous,

Roosevelt and Wilson met, most significantly, March 3, 1896, in Baltimore, during a protest meeting against the attempt of City Council spoilsmen to appoint all persons holding municipal offices. Roosevelt was then Police Commissioner of New York, Wilson a highly esteemed Princeton professor with roots in Johns Hopkins University. Both urged persistent pressure against the council. The accompanying Baltimore cartoons put the future presidents in similar garb and postures.

however, was the source of the opposition—and of the bosses' defense. No one denied that the bosses, to be sure with the aid of brutes and cheats at the polling places, were representative of their poor and immigrant constituencies; and that reformers tended to come from the elite classes and to harbor impatience, and even contempt, for the milling crowds of new Americans. Such attitudes were soon to produce a new journalism to strengthen communication between older American strains and new.

But though reformers won significant victories over organizations top heavy with corruption, the bosses found means for reconstructing their power and moving on to further profits in the course of urban development. In time, they received remarkable endorsements. Thus one political scientist hailed Boss William Marcy Tweed of New York—the very prototype of greed and civic abandon—as a "master communicator" and organizer of the masses, as contrasted with the lily-handed reformers who disdained their social inferiors. Another of the academic community rang the same changes, adding that the ward heelers "could point to substantial visible benefits which people in need actually received from the party organization."[8]

Whatever the truth about the "services" rendered by people by their politicians, there could be no doubt about the partisan nature of alliances and repudiations that retarded civic organization of a fundamental sort. Thus, despite the immigrant vote, terror at the polls, bought judges and tainted police, an attack on the Tweed machine led by the *New York Times* editor George Jones and his inspired cartoonist, the German-born Thomas Nast, brought about the overthrow of the Tweed machine and the jailing of Tweed. The Democratic party split into warring factions highlighting such figures as James O'Brien and "Honest John" Kelly who added not a cubit of character to New York political life.

But voters could not have failed to notice during the election year of 1872 that brought Tweed low Jones's ardent campaign for the reelection of President Grant or the terms the righteous editor used to describe his Republican party chief:

> As the President has faithfully striven for peace, so he has with equal fidelity striven in all other things to discover and carry out the wishes of the people. As he promised, he has

> performed. He has had no policy to oppose to the country, and he has enforced all laws with conscientious firmness. He has done more. He has introduced the beginnings of a civil service reform more thorough in its method, more comprehensive in its scope, more elevated in its purpose than four years ago Mr. [Thomas A.] JENCKES, the most sanguine and enthusiastic of civil service reformers, dared to propose, much less to hope for. Small men may sneer at this, and greater ones may think more could have been done. But the persistent, laborious, honest hearted President has gone far ahead of the party leaders, and a good way ahead of the people. Almost alone, in the face of distrust and cold support, and active hostility, quietly cautiously, but with unflagging determination, he has done more for reform than all other men in the country have done, or could do.[9]

A later *Times* historian, Elmer Davis, would in 1921 delicately note that "to the scandals which flourished in Washington, . . . the editors of the *Times* could not be blind; . . . though their Republican principles made them sometimes delay . . . condemnation rather too long in the hope that the party would do its own housecleaning." The same could doubtless have been said of the Democrats who, from 1872 to 1876, fattened their constituency in part on the anti-Republican slogan of good government.

What was evident was that partisanship had not touched basic social conditions and that the "muckraking" of Thomas Nast in *Harper's Weekly*, though it created the political symbols of the donkey and the elephant and a few immortal cartoons, was no more than a tool of editorial and political policy. Nast's cartoons of Greeley during the tragic campaign of 1872 were cruel, and they helped drive the *Tribune* editor into his grave. And Nast himself, following a successful decade of cartooning, was forgotten in amazingly short order and had to bestir himself in order to live.[10]

So flourished national politics while the cities changed and grew. The new immigrants were stereotyped not only by their foes but by their flattering friends. Yet any honest portrait would have honored their humanity by recognizing that they brought along scoundrels as well as persons of distinction and that overall they represented, as had past generations of immigrants, decent aspirations of the sort that a Mike Walsh or a William Marcy Tweed could not comprehend. Of the newer sort there were such personalities as Terence V. Powderly (1849-1924) who had a proud moment in the early 1880s as head of what then seemed the solidly based Knights of Labor. Its organizers romantically imagined that the labor question could be settled by generously opening their ranks to employers and the unemployed as well as craftsmen; in effect, they offered a crude first draft of later industrial unionism. The more realistic American Federation of Labor, reorganized in 1886 from an earlier "Federation of Organized Trade and Labor Unions of America and Canada," more bluntly asked workmen to prove themselves solvent and able to maintain their membership in good times as well as bad, before being welcomed into the federation. It concentrated on exclusive crafts unions and rebuffed workers who lacked skills or funds. Powderly's lack of sophistication was shown in so plaintive a reminiscence as the following, which contrasted with AFL endurance measures:

> Many persons . . . believed . . . it was the aim of the Knights of Labor to strike for eight hours on May first [1886; Powderly denied the rumor which federationists and others eagerly supported and profited by]. . . . There was never a time when the Knights of Labor were so flagrantly misrepresented, or the aims and purposes of the order so misunderstood. Designing and unscrupulous persons flocked into the order in all parts of the country. The time-serving politician, the trader in votes, the seeker for office, the spoils-hunter . . . all thronged into the assemblies.[11]

Powderly and his Knights went down, as Gompers and the AFL grew in organization and influence. Fortunately for Powderly, he made up in warmth and a talent for comradeship what he lacked in worldly capacity. He served as mayor of Scranton, studied law and practiced it in the 1890s before being appointed by President McKinley United States Commissioner General of Immigration, and otherwise repaid his people with fair services.

Typical also of the better elements of the new immigration, and in the urgent field of culture, was John Boyle O'Reilly, of ancient Irish family, who in 1866, aged twenty-two, sought as a revolutionary to act as a subversive in the British army. He was discovered and sentenced to death but was then transported to Australia. O'Reilly's escape aboard an American whaler in 1869 was reported to Irish everywhere including America. Despite misadventures he landed safely in Philadelphia, went on to Boston where he worked on the Irish *Pilot*, and himself became its owner in 1876. He loyally defended home rule for his native land but became thoroughly committed to America and one of its most highly esteemed Irish-Americans.

In his own time, O'Reilly was most conspicuous as a poet, a fact that reflected on the literary standards of the Gilded Age but not on the amiable attitudes of genteel editors toward the Irish. O'Reilly was firm in his tolerance toward and appreciation of other minority peoples and immigrants, in Boston and elsewhere, and he was wholly unpretentious in his friendliness toward persons of every class. His accidental death left a sense of loss. Popular subscription raised a memorial to him in the Boston Fenway, and affectionate busts of O'Reilly appeared in several institutions.[12]

There was a labor problem. There was also a problem of labor's relationship to the city. There could be no whole solution, only valid alternatives, in a society that included gentle people but also vengeful psychopaths of the kind who assassinated President James A. Garfield and self-appointed saviours, actually harmful to labor's future, of the type that sought to murder Andrew Carnegie's working associate Henry C. Frick during the great Homestead strike of 1892.

Several of society's sectors could help little to advance its better relations and future. The radicals, dreaming of utopia or even of labor solely in terms of its economics, could do little for the status of immigrants, struggling with novel conditions as well as with each other. Their impulse was toward violence, which threatened lives and property. It often found some justification in the cruelty of company police and the use of strikebreakers but constituted in itself a less than complete program. Nor were dedicated conservatives of any more use: those who held that immigrants had the sole responsibility for maintaining an environment and morality without aid, without helpful circumstances, and without fundamental regard for other immigrants who had preceded them.[13]

Such basic conditions required a force that could better mediate differences between Americans. David Graham Phillips later, and before he had begun the "muckraking" phase of his career, remarked on the character of the common brand of conservative reformer:

> The great misfortune of good causes is that they attract so many fatal friends—the superciliously conscientious; the well-meaning but feeble-minded and blundering; the most offensive because least deceptive kinds of hypocrites. . . .
>
> New York was seized with one of its "periodic spasms of virtue." The city government was, as usual, in the hands of the two bosses who owned the two political machines. One was taking the responsibility and the larger share of the spoils; the other was maintaining him in power and getting the smaller but a satisfactory share. The alliance between the police and criminal vice had become so open and aggressive under this bi-boss patronage that the people were aroused and indignant. But as they had no capable leaders and no way of selecting leaders, there arose a self-constituted leadership of uptown Phariseeism and sentimentality, planning the "purification" of the city.[14]

There were better people than such in all the major cities seeking more substantive approaches to their social problems. Jacob Riis won deserved national fame for his journalistic battle against slums in New York. An immigrant who had suffered bitter poverty in the city, he had fought his way to status among newspapermen. He investigated conditions on New York's East Side of such tragic depth as to make pessimists and cynics of some of his more hardened colleagues. Riis, instead, always hopeful, always carrying a certain innocence in his bearing, reported in the *New York Tribune*, then in the *Sun*, with shock and horror and a keen eye for human interest sanitary conditions, family tragedies, the fate of working women and children, and even treatment of the dead victims of hunger and cold. *How the Other Half Lives* (1890) made his reputation and made him a lifelong friend of Theodore Roosevelt, himself just moving out of the goo-goo cause of civil service to the municipal problem of social control. *Out of Mulberry Street* (1898), *The Battle with the Slum* (1902), and

Children of the Tenement (1903) rounded out a career that honored not only progressivism but the many audiences of the 1890s throughout the country that responded to his favorite theme and learned what to see and do about comparable conditions in their own states and locales. If what they learned and did fell short of standards of pride and decency that would have been preferable, it was in part because American life required a combination of factors and dedications—including those of the immigrants themselves—such as had not yet matured.

One historian put it aptly that "the preoccupation of [John P.] Altgeld's biographers with the governor's famous pardon of the surviving prisoners implicated in the Haymarket Riot and with his telegrams to Cleveland protesting against the use of Federal troops in the Pullman Strike has tended to obscure the more significant state reform inaugurated during his administration."[15] Those reforms included the curbing of shop and factory abuses, exploitation of child labor, demoralizing piecework in the homes of workers, the misuse of charitable organizations in order to recruit workers at wage-cutting rates, industrial arbitration—one of the great formulated ideas of the 1890s—civil-service reform, and antimonopoly legislation. But, in addition, it would have made a false picture to have missed the effect of the personality and idealism of this German immigrant and self-made millionaire—a personality that shone in his *Our Penal Machinery and Its Victims* (1884) and his later essays, which were collected in *Live Questions* (1899).

Altgeld's sense of the duty of society to care for its own took him away from money-making schemes and ultimately left him poor, as businessmen turned cold or malicious toward him. This often-repeated tale warmed many reform annals, which would have been wiser to consider why Altgeld should have become the hero of Vachel Lindsay's poem "Eagle Forgotten," Lindsay himself being fated to dim recollection among the culture-bearers of the land.

Altgeld was the outstanding reform figure of the 1890s on the state level. On the municipal scene, light broke most conspicuously in Detroit where, in 1890, a shoe manufacturer who had scarcely troubled himself with politics in a quarter-century of life in the growing city of two hundred thousand assumed the mayorship. He became a legend of growth in office, which inspired a host of city officials elsewhere; he was a precursor of the wave of reform that transformed the cities before World War I.

Hazen S. Pingree was a Maine boy who worked in a cotton factory, then in Massachusetts as an apprentice leather cutter. He served in the Union army throughout the Civil War. He then followed rumors of great opportunity in Detroit, where he became a successful shoe manufacturer and lived in comfort among its social elite. As an employer, his furthest thrust of progressive thinking was to have become persuaded that the key to industrial peace was arbitration.

The nub of Detroit's city problem was its immigration population; Detroit was a city of immigrants, notably German, Italian, and the least regarded Poles. WASPs were a smaller—some forty thousand—body of people. Differences among the great ethnic bodies prevented the furtherance of measures calculated to help them all. They fought for jobs in ways that often descended to utmost cruelty. Thus, a well-intentioned but ill-conceived attempt to spread limited funds during the 1893 depression through piecework—which threatened full-time jobs and wage levels—caused a savage reaction. Workers used picks and shovels against foremen and others, leaving one dead and more than a dozen wounded, several mortally.

The immigrants also derogated one another. One Polish spokesman criticized Italians as not being true citizens and being only interested in making money to send back to the old country. Another declared that "an Italian can live on black bread and onions, whereas a Pole must have good food."[16] Such divisive attitudes made Detroit a Democratic anchor in a sea of rural Republicans, but it also created a Republican opportunity, which the blunt, egalitarian Pingree was able to turn to shrewd advantage. Asked to run for mayor, he toured the ghetto neighborhoods, drank whisky with the Irish, was cordial to the Poles and their progeny, and fraternized throughout the city. His efforts gained him the mayor's office, where he began his great decade by learning the rough and ready ways of political infighting and discovering in himself a talent for demagoguery. In the course of conflict he refreshed the rundown city streets, resisted corruption, and worked for an equitable tax structure.

When he began his crusade against the power of the traction magnates of the city, Pingree discovered that he had opened not one but a central artery of conflict. Street railways meant franchises that affected the entire life of the city. They were an unqualified necessity to workers and their families, and the fares that were thus charged appeared glaringly in family budgets. Franchise owners could, by the lines and directions they gave their vehicles, determine their availability to entire neighborhoods. They could all but dictate land values, and they could determine political alliances and individual careers through special favors and direct bribes.

Moreover, franchise seekers often created entire networks of public utilities, not only in terms of water, fuel, light, and streetcars, but in many cities. One group of six capitalists combined the street railways of New York, Philadelphia, Chicago, Pittsburgh, and at least a hundred other places from New England to Indiana.[17] Detroit was but one city, but the battle that Pingree undertook became a symbol to the nation, and bread and meat, life itself, to his constituents.

So reactionary were the policies of the Detroit City Railway Company that a strike of its employees in 1891 roused not only embattled unionists but others outraged by a service reluctant to so much as change from horse-drawn to electrically run cars. Riots engaged the respectable as well as would-be unionists. James Couzens, later a mayor of Detroit and a Michigan Senator as well as a maverick associate of Henry Ford, helped stone streetcars sent out on strikebreaking errands by an aggressive police force.[18]

Despite such popular endorsements of a more humane and public service program for street railways, Pingree discovered that a strong portion of Detroit elite society supported the company not so much because it was well served by the company—indeed, the elite used their own horses and carriages—but as a bulwark of social order as against Pingree's disturbing and, as they saw it, dangerous campaign. A now-familiar scene was enacted. Pingree lost his place on the board of directors of a local bank. His financial credit was impugned. Fear and hatred of him took petty forms. He lost his family pew in the Woodward Avenue Baptist Church. Old associates passed him by without speaking.

In efforts to aid the poor who suffered most keenly by the depression of 1893 Pingree again made himself conspicuous by direct efforts to serve them, rather than think in terms of curtailment of services and charity. He resisted the mean-minded thinking that caused the common council of the city to ban the employment of aliens—a prejudice that attracted workers as well as gentlemen. "Chase the Dagos back to Italy" was a slogan offered by an American-born brakeman, while it was an Irish-born engineer who urged restriction on immigration.[19]

Pingree, on the contrary, sought funds for the unemployed. He cursed and denounced the miserly, joined the poor in public demonstrations, and urged lowering of the price of bread. His most enduring idea, which kept his fame alive even after the inundations of progressivism had diminished his achievements, was to apply Henry George tenets to the urban situation and to advocate that patches of unused city lots be gardened by the poor. This offer brought thousands of unemployed to the municipal offices asking for opportunities to give body to his dream.[20]

In retrospect Pingree's battle for a humane society failed in the large sense. His "potato patches" did not inspire a rural flowering within city confines. His struggles with the railway managers did not mature into city-owned transit systems. Nor did his battle for a three-cent fare succeed. In the long run, his influence was mainly inspirational. He enjoyed his fame as a democratic spokesman. His melodramatics before the city council and in the streets roused more hopes than they did results. But Jane Addams in Chicago, building her Hull House settlement and struggling with a deeply corrupt city council, utility fighters in St. Louis, Richard T. Ely conducting his scholarly crusade for responsible municipal government—these and others took courage from Pingree and his friends. Pingree also had a sense of issues and American understanding, which created a bond between needy and anxious people and himself. They responded to such of his summaries of events as:

> Riots are little revolutions and it is always presumed that the troubles bringing them about can be satisfactorily adjusted by the courts. To bring these troubles into the courts, the usual process is to put down the riots with the strong hand and then inquire into the causes. Ordinarily the public is satisfied when the riot is put down. The newspapers are not, because when the excitement is over less newspapers are sold and hum drum court proceedings do not sell so well. This is excellent commercial

> spirit but it is not in line with what people, perhaps foolishly, suppose that newspapers exist for; many, if not all, believing that newspapers are established by philanthropists, like the little city of Pullman, for the benefit of mankind. . . .[21]

Yet, despite the enthusiasm Pingree generated, his program for Detroit was largely voided as Detroit's citizens struggled between their personal dreams of advancement and their true conditions. Pingree himself was far from steady in his campaign. Elected Governor of Michigan in 1897, he attempted to hold on to his office of mayor as well: a plan that muddled reform perspectives. He did not succeed, nor did he dominate his foes in the Michigan legislature—mainly conservative Republicans—who were able to stymie his statewide campaign.

Such battles tested the strength and sincerity of reform forces. A significant chapter in the Pingree saga related to his battle against the traction magnate Tom L. Johnson, who had already proclaimed himself a follower of Henry George yet who fought Pingree in Detroit through the middle 1890s in efforts to obtain a five-cent fare as compared to Pingree's cherished three-cent fare. Johnson himself later, as the enlightened mayor of Cleveland, sought to establish a three-cent fare, but his prior commitment in Detroit illustrated the riptide forces that kept reform from congealing into permanent structures and institutions. The yeasty nature of American society required that it be constantly reexamined for dead spots and realities.

There was still another aspect to reform that persisted in the worst times. Johnson had been on both sides of the transit struggle and pondered Pingree as friend and as foe. In his autobiography, first serialized in ***Hampton's Magazine*** at the crest of the Progressive wave, he summarized his views of Pingree:

> He crusaded because he loved the fight and the cause. And also, he loved to be loved. That is what makes many men "get right" at or beyond middle life. They are men whose ideals have been right from the beginning, but who, engrossed in business, have never felt the great joy of doing for the people. If they get the taste of that happiness they cannot be stopped.[22]

NOTES

1. David Montgomery, *Beyond Equality: Labor and the Radical Republicans, 1862-1872* (New York, 1967), ix.

2. *Ibid.*, 228-229.

3. Robert V. Bruce, *1877: Year of Violence* (Indianapolis, 1959), 173-174.

4. These charges are heaped with "unacademic venom" by Arthur Mann in "Gompers and the of Irony of Racism," *Antioch Review*, 13 (June 1953): 203-214, sharply denounced as false and misleading in Philip Taft, *The A. F. of L. in the Time of Gompers* (New York, 1957), 318.

5. Satirical song that appeared during the 1884 Democratic campaign, directed at James G. Blaine whose Republican candidacy was shadowed by revelations of his official corruption eight years earlier. Also satirized were the candidate, the lawyer, the preacher, and the lover. The farmer was treated gently, and labor not at all.

6. James Bryce, *The American Commonwealth* (New York, 1901), 2: 404-407.

7. For the entire analysis, see Andrew D. White, "The Government of American Cities," *Forum* 10 (December 1890): 365-370.

8. Seymour J. Mandelbaum, *Boss Tweed's New York* (New York, 1965), 70, 112-113; John G. Sproat, "*The Best Man*": *Liberal Reformers in the Gilded Age* (New York, 1965), 58. See, however, pp. 270ff.

9. *New York Times*, October 8, 1872.

10. This fact was hidden by his first biographer, Albert Bigelow Paine, *Th. Nast, His Period and His Pictures* (New York, 1904). Ironically, it was Nast's investment in General Grant's foolish stockmarket endorsements that stripped Nast of his savings. The failure of Grant and Ward helped bring on the Panic of 1884.

11. Louis Filler, ed., *Late Nineteenth-century American Liberalism* (Indianapolis, 1962), 136-137.

12. James Jeffrey Roche, *Life of John Boyle O'Reilly, Together with His Complete Poems and Speeches* (New York, 1891); William G. Schofield, *Seek for a Hero* (New York, 1956).

13. As one of them, John Coleman Adams, put it, in his "The Municipal Threat in National Politics," an article originally published in the *New England Magazine:* "[City] evils . . . are complicated with another. In our great cities are hordes of men who are least fitted for the duties of citizenship . . . who have been in this country but for a short time, who have not yet learned its language, or formed any conception of its institutions. . . . We cannot solve the municipal problem until we have discovered whether we can Americanize these foreigners, and teach them even the rudiments of our system." *Literary Digest* 3 (July 11, 1891): 282.

14. David Graham Phillips, *The Great God Success* (New York, 1901), 172-173. This was Phillips's first novel, written while he was still wholly in

journalism. Although it contains useful materials, and even a section that throws light on his life, to treat it as typical of his style and method automatically stamps the critic as inept.

15. Harvey Wish, "Altgeld and the Progressive Tradition," *American Historical Review*, 46 (July 1941): 814.

16. Melvin G. Holli, *Reform in Detroit* (New York, 1969), 66.

17. Burton J. Hendrick, *The Age of Big Business: A Chronicle of the Captains of Industry* (New Haven, 1919), 121-122.

18. Harry Barnard, *Independent Man: The Life of Senator James Couzens* (New York, 1958), 26.

19. Holli, *Reform in Detroit*, 68.

20. This became an enduring legend of social reform, and of interest because it combined free enterprise, self-employment thinking; see John Chamberlain "Hole in Doughnut Becomes Bigger," *Indianapolis News*, October 9, 1974, a syndicated article on alternative plans for the 1974 economic depression. Chamberlain, author of *Farewell to Reform* (1932), had been a radical camp-follower who later reverted to an ardent advocate of William Graham Sumner free economics.

21. Hazen S. Pingree, *Factors and Opinions; or Dangers That Beset Us* (Detroit, 1895), 25. Needless to say, Pingree was being ironic about George M. Pullman's purposes in building the "model town" of Pullman.

22. Quoted in V. V. McNitt, "Idol of the People," *Michigan Alumnus* 63 (March 2, 1957): 158.

Man of Action, Man of Words

No Progressive flowering could have occurred had there not been a meeting of minds and energies that reached from the bottom of the social order to the top. There had been no national movement that had not done so in the past. That one which was now mounting into view, like earlier ones, needed its articulators, its evangelical figures, its interpreters. It needed also people who could act out its programs and predictions, inspiring others to emulation. N. O. Nelson was one such figure: a businessman who was also a dreamer and more; one who could persuade others that the march toward Progressive enterprise, threatening to neither individual commercial expression nor to larger projects short of monopoly, was feasible, was happening, and could engage businessmen to emulate and legislators to support through law.

Nelson was one of many—not so many that they could change the course of American business but enough so that they could give testimony that the mainstreams of American life had not become frozen and that there was still opportunity for experiment and debate. The Nelsons of his time and after contributed more than an experience that could be recounted in utopian annals. They expressed a faith in human nature, which others of lesser vitality or steadfastness could draw from. Incidentally, they provided actual funds without which the most professedly "proletarian" movement could not function.

Nelson Olson Nelson was born in Norway, but was brought to the United States early. Like Pingree, he served in the Union army, then turned to business in St. Louis. Vigorous, imaginative, and with impressive organizational ability, Nelson succeeded in the manufacture of plumbing fixtures and, in his late thirties found himself a millionaire, but one with a desire for public service.[1]

Nelson began as a man of general goodwill desirous of sharing the goods of the world with others. In 1879 he instituted the Christmas bonus plan in his factory. As a citizen of St. Louis he provided a Fresh Air fund to be used for the well-being of children during the summer months. He gave the city a municipal bathhouse. He set up workmen's self-culture clubs. Such services were later to be treated as trifling, if not worse: mere plasters for the deeper troubles of capitalist enterprise. Finley Peter Dunne was to write sarcastically of Andrew Carnegie's much larger gifts of libraries to communities as an evasion of his duty to pay more ample salaries. This was, however, years before labor was granted the often substantial salaries of good times and developed "TV eyes" in part at the expense of reading.

In any event, Nelson did not offer books in place of good wages. He was widely enough known as a model employer to be chosen in 1886 to be one of three mediators during a strike by the Knights of Labor on Jay Gould's railroad lines. Nelson's experience with the railroad administrators was sufficiently disillusioning to encourage him to seek better ways for closing the gap between wage earners and capitalists.

Basically, he sought to advance the idea of profit sharing, but profit sharing that would not be a product of government intervention. Nelson feared inordinate and irreversible state power. He feared the rise of demagogues who might enter into what should be the amiable terrains of industry and turn them into battlegrounds. His answer to such dangers was voluntarism. Giving and cooperative measures should prove successful and win the loyalty of those who profited from them.

Nelson sought out those who had furthered or who wished to further cooperative plans. He listened to Frenchmen and Englishmen abroad who recalled and who continued to try to activate Fourierite ideas or those that had been initiated in Rochdale, England. He was much impressed by the views of the revered clergyman, Edward Everett Hale, author of "The Man Without a Country," as well as of utopian fiction. Bellamy and Henry George and their followers influenced Nelson's thoughts.

He introduced profit sharing and the nine-hour workday in his plant. Moving as rapidly as he could, Nelson found himself between extremes. Most of his fellow capitalists felt threatened by union organizers and thought it the best strategy to resist all infringements on their authority. They were therefore more fearful than intrigued by Nelson's experiments. Union leaders were no more enthusiastic. Nelson advocated open-shop unionism, which unionists would successfully depict as undercutting true measures for the worker's advance and security, as, indeed, it often was.

Nelson was capable and determined and, in this heyday of his career, was able to carry most of his workers with him, as well as to gain a growing reputation among likeminded reformers in the land. In 1890 he made his most significant move, one that would ensure his place among American experimenters in industrial relations. He purchased a 250-acre tract some twenty miles from St. Louis and there, in Leclaire, set up his factories and homes for those of his workers who chose to live in the vicinity. Workers were free to live elsewhere, if they preferred, as some did in nearby Edwardsville. There in Leclaire the Nelson works, with its profit-sharing schemes, nine-hour day, open shop, and generous employer-employee relations conducted business as usual. Nelson made a profit. So did his employees. Nelson saw himself as a man for all seasons. In 1892 he sought to organize the Association for the Promotion of Profit Sharing but found employers cold to the program. His later effort to create a cooperative store on an ambitious scale and an American cooperative union was no more durable. Yet he felt confident that his principles would succeed.

They were tested by the depression of 1893, which destroyed many commercial houses dedicated to nothing but profits. Nelson himself found it necessary to curb his profit-sharing activities and to reintroduce the ten-hour workday. It was interesting, however, that, as head of his business, he was able to hold the line for forced savings, though many workers would have been glad to lay their hands on all the money available to them. Though this policy caused some discomfort and called forth criticism as interfering with workers' freedom of choice, it seems fair to judge that Nelson, especially in view of his outstanding record as a labor employer, was correct and more farsighted than his workers.[2]

Nelson continued to busy himself with schemes advancing cooperative plans and aiding democratic processes. He involved himself in the efforts to refine governmental procedures through referendums that kept officials up to the mark of enabled voters to unseat them if they stayed: a goo-goo cause to be sure but, as we have seen, a necessary prelude to further efforts to keep administration flexible and capable of change. Nelson also interested himself in various colonies. The Ruskin Cooperative Colony in Tennessee was often noted among libertarians. Less noted was the self-supporting tuberculosis colony in southern California, which Nelson supported. It was one of numerous such quiet philanthropies throughout the land which did merciful work, was carelessly taken for granted, and left no residue of accomplishment for later millennarians—who themselves rarely accomplished more—to acknowledge.

A highpoint of the post-Civil War progressivism materialized in 1898 in Buffalo, bringing together every manner of idealist and would-be activist of the era. Organized by the Christian Socialist W. D. P. Bliss, whose labors are yet properly to be reviewed, it seemed to marshal an army of thinkers and doers, Democrats, Republicans, Populists, prohibitionists, and others deeply concerned about many things—from the single tax and civil service to the Young Man's Christian Association and the Salvation Army. Although in aggregate they appeared to be a tower of babel, they pointed, rather, to the gathering of forces that would inform the Progressive era proper, and, in the meantime, produced such valid results as were to be seen in Detroit, under Altgeld in Illinois, under other reformers in southern and western states, and in Nelson's Leclaire.[3]

Progressives of the 1900s substantially forgot their predecessors, being too busy with new enterprises to pick up the past and build it into its pattern of demands. In general, they were ill advised and suffered themselves a severe revenge of amnesia from the generation that superseded them. However, the Progressive years utilized Nelson in reasonable measure. He was farsighted in rejecting the socialism of the times—excited by Progressive victories, which promised even more victories—as promising more than human nature could sustain. They did cast a shadow upon his work as being composed of half-measures, but the socialist heroes of the Progressive period were to become as forgotten as Nelson. And, meanwhile, he cooperated in kind fashion with the Socialist party of Eugene V. Debs and was recognized as one of the "millionaire socialists" who helped the party with funds.

Leclaire continued to be a loose capitalistic enterprise, which gave promise of further advances in industrial democracy. In 1903 Nelson was able to return his plant to the nine-hour day. Profit sharing was resumed, and a deferred dividend that went back to 1896 was retroactively paid. In 1905 Nelson announced that not only employees but also customers would be able to participate in his program:

> Beginning with the present year [Nelson proudly stated] I . . . have quit taking any profit or interest [on my stock holdings above 6 percent per annum]. I get a living wage for my work; that is all, and it is enough. The profits are divided between the employees, the customers, philanthropy, and the [one-fifth of the] stock held by others. . . .[4]

It was a noble effort and the climax of Nelson's career. It attracted attention as far as England. Nelson's company grew, and he worked to win his employees over to his vision and away from their often curiously compounded individualistic, selfish, and yet also (when it suited their needs) labor-oriented thinking. Nelson was well aware of the conservative component even in the "radicals'" thought, but he had had sufficient control of his own affairs, as a businessman, to work with it, bend with it, argue with it, and thus stay alive in social debates.

He found himself less and less able to do this. His multiplication of plants and increased number of employees multiplied his problems in dealing with them. The unions did not help. Gompers, though a Progressive in comparison with millennarian labor leaders and radicals, was still closer to them than to Nelson. A 1907 strike for a straight 10 percent increase in wages made a dividing line between Nelson and the unions.

He continued to conduct interesting social experiments with such useful theorists and activists as Bolton Hall, who dreamed of a nation that balanced urban and rural living.[5] The times were not with Nelson. His cooperative, mutualistic, and other efforts took him deeper and deeper into business arrangements that represented capitalistic adjustments much more than they did expanding democratic machinery. And with both labor and capital busying themselves with plans that put power first and democracy second, Nelson found himself in classic position between the hammer and the anvil of industrial relations.

Dispossessed by his own company, he ended as a critic of unions and of business, cantankerously pleased with the Bolshevik triumph in Russia, bitter that his profit-sharing and other programs had been wiped out by his successors in business dynasties.

Nelson was essentially a businessman who dedicated himself to making his work a creative pursuit. Frank Parsons was one of the group of Christian Socialists who—like W. D. P. Bliss, like George D. Herron, first minister, then lay socialist lost in the whirlpools of World War I, like Walter Rauschenbusch of Rochester Theological Seminary, and numerous others—was determined to prove life to be a meaningful round for great and small. It was ironical that the one full study of Parsons should have fastened on him as first of all the "founder of vocational guidance."[6] Founder he was, but this achievement represented no more than a trifle of his ambition, which was to give himself totally to mankind and, if necessary, to die in its behalf. Die Parsons did; in this as in other respects he was most like Sylvester Graham (1794-1851), who revered the body as a temple, bringing humanity close to deity, worked without rest to bring his message to all Americans through speeches and publications, fought drink, gluttony, wrong mental habits, and numerous related issues, died of overwork, and came down to posterity as . . . the inventor of the graham cracker.

Parsons was a brilliant student who entered Cornell University at age fifteen in 1869 and graduated first in his class in three years with a civil engineering degree. After some work and teaching he decided he required a law degree and by overwork not only completed his three years of study in one but injured his health in the process. He required three years to recoup his strength.

Parsons became a lawyer in Boston but found the work unsatisfactory. He was formulating his philosophy, which, like Bellamy's, Bliss's, and others needed other outlets for expression. Parsons prepared legal textbooks for the publisher Little, Brown, lectured on English literature at Boston's Young Men's Christian Association, and in 1889 issued his successful *The World's Best Books*. In 1892 he assumed a lectureship at Boston University, which he maintained until 1905.

In 1894, in his *Our Country's Need*, he formulated his views of "mutualism" in which he tried (as so many others were) to find a mean between individualism and socialism. In essence he plundered learning and examples to advance the idea of taking out of competition such public necessities as the railroad and the telegraph and administering them for the public weal, while leaving to the winds of chance and competition other areas in which the private person might test his skills and capacity. Parsons studied incessantly, and from his efforts came valuable books on widely disparate subjects, all written with exemplary clarity and circumstantial detail and idealistically directed at the expert and general reader alike.

Parsons struck up a warm relationship with B. O. Flower of the *Arena*, which in the 1890s formed a journalistic link between the Populists and genteel reform. The *Arena* manifested weaknesses in the kind of detail that was to create links between Progressives and the widest of publics,[7] but it maintained a line of argument, a receptivity to panaceas, an awareness of the many-faced nature of the American public, which was instructive to the dissatisfied journalists who were to bulk large in progressivism. The *Arena* printed Parsons's articles investigating the nature of money, thoughtful and informative in that era of silver and greenback crusades, and it helped publicize Parsons as a guide to a better America. His findings were published as *Rational Money* (1898), and his views of public ownership he detailed in *The Telegraph Monopoly* (1899).

In 1895 Parsons ran for mayor of Boston, supported by prohibitionists, Populists, and socialists. A friend and supporter, Dr. Charles F. Taylor of Philadelphia, urged Parsons to study questions of municipal ownership. Parsons's subsequent volume *The City for the People, or, the Municipalization of the City Government and of Local Franchises* (1899), uncopyrighted and issued in a revised edition in 1901, was in many ways Parsons's gift to the future: his assessment of the city—any city—as a pivot of civilization and of the ways by which it had to be governed.

Like Nelson, Parsons brooded over the rights of the individual as contrasted with those of the community. Public ownership was a key to expeditious service, but it could not care for itself. Home rule for cities, direct legislation and the variant means for overcoming public inertia, private deals between legislators, and other realities of practical politics required refinements of proportional representation, preferential voting, the automatic ballot, and above all an alert and alerted electorate to see that its will remained in constant operation. Parsons not only quoted endlessly from experiments at home and abroad, he made it clear that there was a growing army of men and women to whom questions of government and public service were normal and regular concerns. Parsons's list of members of the National League for Promoting the Public Ownership of Monopolies was so formidable as to raise questions as to what impeded their success. His list included such elder statesmen and stateswomen as Elizabeth Cady Stanton and the well-intentioned though ineffective William Dean Howells. But it also included Nelson, Pingree, the scholar-activist John R. Commons, Charlotte Perkins Stetson, whose *Women and Economics* (1898) was an instant classic, and Robert A. Woods, who was revolutionizing social and settlement work in Boston.

If there was any one element that was not yet ready for extensive operation in the public field it was the public itself, which lacked the unifying forces that would be provided nationally by leaders of the stature of Roosevelt and La Follette.

From 1897 to 1899, while Parsons continued his lectureship at Boston University, he also served as professor at Kansas State Agricultural College, in its glory as a "radical" institution, thanks to the temporary success of the state's Populist party. The more conservative faction on campus finally succeeded in ridding itself of the liberals, and Parsons and his friends, let go, went on to found Ruskin College of Social Science at Trenton, Missouri. Despite sympathy and encouragement, the school failed, and Parsons went on to fructify leaders and projects elsewhere. He traveled across country and to Europe seeking ideas and information, his work taking him directly into the Progressive era. For the National Civic Federation, set up by a combination of employers and unionists and featuring Marcus A. Hanna and Samuel Gompers, he studied municipal trading in England. He became one of E. A. Filene's distinguished advisors on how to help move the great Filene's Department Store in Boston closer to the cooperative ideal. Parsons joined others—philanthropists, professors, social workers—in building the Civic Service Home, a Boston settlement that helped immigrants to find themselves in alien surroundings.

What gave stature to Parsons's all too brief life was his capacity for dealing with vast topics, as in his *The Story of New Zealand* (1904), which dealt extensively with that nation's experiments in cooperative and other social measures. At the same time he busied himself with the details of what came to be called guidance counseling and which would find posthumous expression in his *Choosing a Vocation* (1909), the pioneer work in the field. Like so much else that was conceived in an idealistic matrix, it would be commercialized into mere routine operations. In a sense, this was quite just; much of life required adjustment, modernization, routine. The tragedy was that the living root of the development, Parsons's vision and social aims, was permitted to become lost and inactive.

In 1905, though suffering from Bright's disease and having endured a serious operation, Parsons pressed on to found with friends the Breadwinner's Institute, which gave educational opportunities and a diploma to the poor and inspired philanthropists and intellectuals to join Parsons in this work.

Parsons fixed on the railroad issue as a major test of the cooperative world he envisioned as on its way. As the railroads went, so would go America. The future complicated this formula, but it contained elements of truth. The railroads *could* be watched as one thermometer of the nation's administration of business and social service. Parsons's *The Trusts, the Railroads, and the People* (1906) and *The Heart of the Railroad Problem* (1906), filled as usual with Parsons's awesome array of facts and materials, in high organization, contributed their share to developments, which included passage of the Hepburn Act in that year of 1906.[8] The millennium was far less close than Parsons realized, but his achievements were of a nature to serve his fellow citizens in their least hopeful years. In succeeding years they turned pages of his books to plagiarize data from them respecting municipal government, railroads, utilities, and, of course, vocational education. They would have been wiser to look beyond those passages for inspiration to the earnest and gracious man who could not rest from seeking to inform them, to arouse them to their human opportunities.

NOTES

1. In the following account, I largely follow Mr. Kim McQuaid, currently associated with Northwestern University. Mr. McQuaid's studies of Nelson, "Golden Rule" Samuel M. Jones of Toledo, E. A. Filene of Boston, and other businessmen who contributed to social thought and action bid fair to affect not only general knowledge of the contours of their lives but to influence scholarly and other understanding of their roles in American life.

2. In 1974, when Americans struggled with their complex "depression," Nelson's scheme of mandatory savings was recalled, though not directly attributed to him. Wrote one correspondent to the financial section of the *New York Times*: "Since inflation is caused by too many people spending too much of their income on items which are in short supply . . . the real solution . . . is enforced savings and investment." *New York Times*, October 20, 1974. Although the problem here was inflation rather than scarce money, the need for individual security and responsible financing was common to both eras.

3. There is an interesting contrast between the Buffalo convention and the Free Convention of 1858, which brought together the various proponents of reform of the pre-Civil War era, from spiritualists to land reformers, and which truly represented the end of an era; see Louis Filler, *The Crusade against Slavery, 1830-1860* (New York, 1960), 263-264.

4. Nelson C. Nelson, "Profit Sharing with the Customer," *Independent* 58 (May 25, 1905): 1180.

5. Hall (1854-1938) was one of Henry George's most dynamic followers. He was a successful real-estate operator and critic of inequitable taxes and monopoly. His most successful book, *Three Acres and Liberty* (1907), was printed and reprinted and began a "back to the land" movement. In 1909, Hall began Free Acres in New Jersey, a cooperative colony.

6. Howard V. Davis, *Frank Parsons, Prophet, Innovator, Counselor* (Carbondale, Ill, 1969).

7. For details, see Louis Filler, *The Muckrakers: Crusaders for American Liberalism,* (State College, Pa., 1976 ed.), 39-42, *et seq.*

8. *Ibid.*, 203 ff.

The Old Populism

> Fellow Citizens. . . . as we love our state and our country we cannot ignore the events which mark these degenerate days. Recall if you can the session of a legislature in any state in the Union last winter which escaped charges of scandalous corruption. It will not do to say such charges have always been made—because it would not be true. Such charges twenty five years ago accompanied by legislative investigation retired the man to private life no matter what report the committee made. . . .
>
> Within a few months you have seen our neighboring state almost in a condition of revolution,—an army of indignant citizens marching in a body on their capital to save the great city of Chicago from the tyranny of a Street Railway Corporation—and you saw the legislature indifferent to their appeals. . . .
>
> Why were these supposed servants of the people so arrogant and insulting to their constituents? . . . It was because the machine has supplanted representative government.[1]

Populism stirred friends and foes in its own time, but its disintegration into Democratic and Republican Progressive politics generally roused appreciative interpretations and an awareness that much that had once seemed wildly radical in the Populist platform of 1892 was being institutionalized by legislators of both major parties. The Populist convention of 1912 in St. Louis brought together only eight delegates. The *Chicago Tribune* sympathetically commented that "causes sometimes live by dying," and other papers were equally gentle in treatment and reminiscence.[2]

In time, the Populists were less recalled as legitimate spokesmen for a beset farming citizenry than as fanatical proponents of "free silver." It needed over and over again to be said that William Jennings Bryan had not been a Populist but a Democrat; but that, moreover, many with Populist-style political views had been Democrats and Republicans. Populists had not threatened the fluid nature of American two-party politics but augmented it. The vision of Populists as small minded, dreaming of a past utopia, joyless and authoritarian in their hatred of the demon rum, demanded a reinvestigation, which is yet to be completed.

As a movement, populism carried echoes of Civil War goals, of westward movement and propaganda—as represented by "Kansas and Freedom" slogans. It fed on striking contrasts: the farmers' isolation among their acres, their memories of what home had been in the eastern states. They and their people had inhabited a world that included town folk, workers, even industrialists who shared some of their complaints about weather and railroads but who had alternatives in roads, canals, and banks, which competed with one another as well as with depositors.

The farmers' dissatisfaction found expression in the Greenback party of 1880, which delivered some 300,000 votes to General James Baird Weaver of Iowa, to be sure as against the 4,454,433 votes that were given General James A. Garfield and the 4,444,976 votes that General Winfield S. Hancock received in the closest election in American history.[3] Thereafter, farmers' unrest was diffused among Republicans and Democrats until 1890 when a Democratic Congress triumphantly exchanged the McKinley tariff—the highest tariff in history—for the Silver Purchase Act, which put the government in the business of buying silver without, however, making it the legal equivalent of gold. The purpose of all such maneuvers, as of earlier efforts, was to depreciate the value of money and make farmers' loans easier to repay. If those efforts did nothing of the sort, they at least furnished tests of their potency.

They did not distinguish "radicals" from conservatives. Farmers were, after all, conservative. And no one could have been more conservative than Robert Ellis Thompson, a Philadelphian who helped found the Wharton School of Finance and Commerce at the University of Pennsylvania. He deplored the Democratic victories of

1890. He was a protectionist with faith in the American system; one of his books was *The Hand of God in American History* (1902). He despised the free-silver cause, which he thought would destroy American credit. Yet his solution to farmers' troubles did not differ from that of the Populists who would soon inspire the ridicule and fear of such tribunes as the *New York Times*:

> The revolt of the Farmers' Alliance [wrote Thompson] is an inarticulate and blundering protest against the real mischiefs of a money system which is centralized in the National Treasury and in the banks of the richer States. The Southern farmers showed their sense of this when they devised their plan which requires the Government to establish agricultural sub-treasuries. In these the farmer or planter is to deposit his crop and obtain such an advance on its value as will enable him to go on with his operations until he finds the market favorable for a sale. A local bank . . . would accomplish all that is hoped for from an agricultural sub-treasury, and it would involve no semi-socialist extension of the sphere of government.[4]

Thompson argued that his scheme was no more than was practiced by bankers in Scotland who had made their poor and thriftless fellow citizens the prosperous Scots of the present day. Populists were not crackpots. Nor did they make circles in their fields with Conestoga wagons to protect their homes from maraudering urbanites. Knights of Labor delegates were present at their 1890 national convention, and arguments for a farmer-labor party were seriously bruited there. Final decisions did indeed keep the two great interests of farm and labor separate, but there was cordiality as the one moved toward formation of a People's party and the other struggled between the major parties for recognition and patronage.[5]

Marked cordiality persisted not only between labor and the western farmer but between eastern and western farmers. Farmers' cooperatives were early praised, and with no hint that they constituted a bridge to socialism. Indeed, a writer for the genteel *Forum*, in its September 1891 issue, "whose early life was spent as an agriculturist"—presumably a farmer—argued for "community living groupies" as a relief from the isolation that made western living hard and disheartening.

The *Rural New Yorker* asked why so many papers were fearful of farmers' plans to hold on to their land, "while many of them are loud in their praises of Balfour's Land Act now before the British Parliament, and supported by the whole Conservative party, though it provides for the loan of money by the English Government to Irish tenant farmers . . . to enable them to buy the land they now cultivate?"[6]

Nevertheless, there was fear of the resurgent farmers in many conservative centers, some in the farmers' own terrain. Part derived from fear of the currency schemes, which frightened bankers and their supporters. The Democratic *New York Times* first scorned the Farmers Alliance activities as "a mere recrudescence of the old Greenback party and the old Silver party" dangerous not because of foolish appeals to the "debtor class" but because it could affect the fortunes of both major parties. Populist victories in Kansas roused the paper to a frenzy of fear. A long dispatch to the *Times* from Kansas was reminiscent of correspondence that had been urgently flashed over telegraph wires during the border war of 1855. The *Times* reporter now predicted that a bloody revolution would soon take place in Kansas. The Populists there intended to lead eastern capitalists to invest among them and then to expropriate their holdings. The new Populist-Democratic governor, Lorenzo D. Lewelling, was reorganizing the state militia and dismissing officers who were not Populists. He was encouraging new recruits who were. It was difficult for the *Times* not to agree with those who foresaw a rebellion of some kind "if the present leaders retain their control of the masses."[7]

That the primary goals of populism diverged from those of labor cannot be doubted. Laborers sought jobs. They had little interest in monopolies as such, not being engaged in bulk buying or selling. Moreover, they desired a monopoly of their own in the area of labor. Too, they were ethnically dissimilar to the Populists though the illusion of a native white front opposed to eastern minority groups was to be fostered by historians unacquainted with the troubles of some western farmers who were perceived by some of their Anglo-

Saxon neighbors as "Dutch," "Polack," or some such other designation invidious under American conditions.

Many such responses were good natured, and many of these ethnic associations were kindly and familiar or admiring, as in Willa Cather's fiction. It took a San Franciscan Republican paper to remark unctuously that "the People's Party, in New York at least, is showing that it is not the party of the American people. Of its thirty-six candidates in nomination for Presidential Electors, but one is of American nativity. Thirty-five are of alien birth. . . . Let the American people beware of them." This criticism underscored the fact—too little recalled—that the Populist impulse was national rather than confined to the West and that the strongest and most serious Populist party was to be found in the South, ceaselessly fighting to bring itself out of the economic pit that military defeat had dug for it.[8] The more prestigious West was able to make the greatest impact on the politics of the time, united with other farmers struggling in urban dilemmas.

The *New York Evening Post*, then independent Democrat, even identified rural irresponsibility with urban, equating the Kansas uprising with the dangers threatening the cities, all of which "shows at least that it is not only in the cities, where the foreign-born swarm, that demagogues may thrive and the doctrine of revolution be preached."[9]

That the Populists should have seemed to the Republican *Brooklyn Standard-Union* an "irruption [*sic*] of cranks charging like Cossacks coming out of the Far West as the Tartars of old from the Far East, and swarming to possess the land" said something more of differences between conservatives and liberals of the time than of easterners and westerners. The latter's spokesman, General James B. Weaver, was a man of mind and dignity. His book, *A Call to Action: An Interpretation of the Great Uprising, Its Source and Causes* (1892) deserved better of history than it received. Its calm review of "the decline of the Senate" and "the decadence of the [Supreme] Court," of the "improvident disposal of public lands," and of tariff, monopoly, and debt policies was accurate and judicious. Weaver clasped hands with labor in concern over the increasing role of private police in labor disputes.

Yet though Weaver's program was the program of his party—a program long considered the most prophetic in political history, since most of it was ultimately written into law[10]—Weaver himself swiftly receded into the past once the presidential campaign of 1892 ended and Grover Cleveland resumed the office he had lost four years earlier. It is difficult to say just what intonation of opinion contributed to Weaver's loss of image. He was seen as a traitor by full-bodied Populists in 1896 who protested that he had sacrificed their total program to the Bryan "Silverites." But quite evidently a Bryan administrator would have dealt with much more than money. It would have fought for nationalization of the railroads, for farmers' loans, for a less partisan Supreme Court, and for all the other demands of the time.

Ignatius Donnelly, distinguished Populist and author of the preamble to the Populist platform of 1892, raged that "the Democracy raped our convention while our own leaders held the struggling victim."[11] But Donnelly's was a more vivid than accurate metaphor. Populists in 1896 captured the Democracy and put their cause before the country. The bolt from the party of "Gold Democrats," including President Cleveland, who could vote for neither Bryan nor McKinley, no more than underscored the Populist triumph. Although the "Pops" lost the national election decisively, they preached principles that were to emerge in fresh and more national terms in Progressive causes.

Yet they were in the 1950s to be violently attacked, not from conservative but from liberal-radical standpoints as anti-Catholic, anti-Negro, anti-Semitic, prohibitionist, and withal "fascistic." Whatever the reasons for this strange and unqualified attack, it suffices that it was revealed as badly based in scholarship, though its proponents sometimes held university chairs. Certainly there were intemperate Populists and Populists capable of hazy thinking. Ignatius Donnelly had, in 1896, denounced the Republican party, which, he said, had "a Jewish rabbi to open the convention [and] a milllionaire attorney for the Union Pacific Railroad to act as permanent chairman." But no more hazy than the brilliant Donnelly were those who saw the Populists as somehow huddled in western states and frenzied in hatred of their neighbors elsewhere. One refutation of the abuse they endured speaks for many:

The charge of anti-Semitism that various writers have recent-

> ly leveled against the Populists is one for which absolutely no evidence can be found in the private letters that poured into [Marion] Butler's office from Populists in virtually every state of the union. North Carolina's leading Populist newspaper, the Raleigh *Caucasian*, contained the usual stereotyped references to the Rothschilds but the emphasis clearly was to the fact that they were prominent world, and especially British, bankers rather than on their Jewishness.[12]

The identification of the prohibition movement with populism and even with progressivism[13] made for confusion in assessing the actual course and content of the movement and its potential for good or ill. In essence, temperance—the root idea involving liquor—had as much or little potential for doing harm as any other single-minded cause. The abolitionist movement, too, had received strange scholarly blows from persons supposedly sympathetic to the concept of equality.[14] The key fact was that, normally, one-idea causes were so surrounded with qualifying and opposed forces that their capacity for making trouble was limited.

The victory of the prohibitionists in the 1920s, on the other hand, was of so sweeping a nature as to raise questions about the source of its improbable power. The American tendency to seek scapegoats fastened, in some scholarly alcoves, upon populism-progressivism, to the harm not only of their good repute but of the more legitimate search for necessary liquor controls. This, any sense of the national dilemma—its tender regard for freedom, its need to limit alcoholism—required.

In earlier decades, temperance had once done much for moral reform. It had helped give a shadow of respectability to "extremists" irritating to local audiences, who might otherwise have handled them more roughly than they sometimes did. It had provided an entrée into public view to women suffragists, whose presence angered conservatives who cherished particular images of woman's "proper" role. Temperance had been one of the distinguishing features among moral reformers who, unlike Andrew Jackson's followers, held to a steady, materialistic outlook on life and were indulgent of drink.

Temperance became intemperate fanaticism in the crusade of a Neal Dow of Maine. But in the post-Civil War decades, temperance continued to offer reasonable propositions regarding social needs. Many temperance advocates did contribute to reform on a larger scale, so much so as to upset members of the firmly prohibitionist wing, which drew apart from them. In 1895 a national conference met in Staten Island, New York, and looked toward a union of reform forces. The conference attracted prohibitionists and populists, "with a sprinkling of Single Taxers, State Socialists, and Direct Legislationists." It drew up a set of resolutions that included new methods of direct citizen control of social affairs. The resolutions approved the direct election of United States senators, curbs on monopoly, and the free and unlimited coinage of silver and gold at the ratio of 16 to 1, as well as the prohibition of the liquor traffic except for medicinal and other nonpersonal uses. The *Independent Citizen* of Providence, Rhode Island, a hard-line prohibitionist newspaper, responded tartly to this effort.[15]

Prohibition did not unite reformers; it even divided Populists of the countryside from Populists in the cities. Women were a mighty force in prohibition, but they were far from agreed on approaches to it. Frances Willard was one of the time's greatest educators and suffragists, author of the "Do Everything" slogan that roused women to a sense of their heightened role in society. Almost nothing related Willard to Carry A. Nation, whose life work bore no relation of any sort to populism, education, the vote, or any reform short of saloon-smashing. That Carry Nation was a fateful force in the prohibition movement there can be no doubt. She taught direct action to grass-roots militants like herself and enabled drunkards to feel self-righteous in their reverence for freedom. But Nation no more exemplified the forces of reform in her field than the Ku Klux Klan exemplified those elements in society that yearned for a more stable life. Like Anthony Comstock, she was no more than a stick employed by antireformers, usually of the abstractly utopian persuasion, with which to beat those concerned for important social problems.

Progressives were even more realistic respecting the uses of liquor than were the Populists, who were often closer to the grass-roots than the succeeding Progressives. The muckrakers in particular were likely to have been newspapermen and to have seen liquor flowing freely among their fellow journalists, though the best of the muckrakers were steady workers and controlled their appetites for the most part. They wrote of liquor but mainly in connection with the saloon-politics-prostitution syndrome, which they distinguished not only from the prohibitionist drive but from associated efforts to close businesses on Sunday, increase religious training in the schools, and other interferences with personal attitudes and ways of life.[16]

Lincoln Steffens put the matter for most of his fellow Progressives when he noted that liquor was a greater subject for antireformers than for their opponents. Thus, in New Jersey, when the Everett Colby-Mark Fagan "new idea" movement in government went urderway, which finally brought into politics Woodrow Wilson, then of Princeton University, the antireform corruptionists

> threw into the situation a "moral issue," the liquor traffic. This is an important question [Steffens went on], but it is so important that to drop it into a reform movement with other issues up, is to break up that other movement, and—fail to solve the liquor question. If I were a political boss, in danger of losing my crown, I would get the church to come out against the saloon. That would save me, and it would not cost the saloons very much.[17]

The one outstanding muckraker who made a major crusade of prohibition was Upton Sinclair, and he contributed his main attack after the prohibition crusade had done most of its work.[18] Progressives favored temperance and deplored the uses to which saloons were put, but they did not honor the Anti-Saloon League, which began its momentous career, its step-by-step conquering of towns and districts and states in 1893. League leaders pretended to reform perspectives, and they often identified their cause with labor, the "square deal," and other Progressive tenets. Here and there they captured a Progressive; William Jennings Bryan freely identified with them. But they were essentially a pressure group that played all sides of the social scene in order to influence them all. They gained adherents from all ranks, some Progressive, some anti-Progressive. Non-Progressives like the publisher B. C. Forbes, who impartially admired J. Ogden Armour, Henry Ford, Thomas A. Edison, and Otto H. Kahn, was a prohibitionist.[19] So, speaking for a vital segment of the Socialist Party, was John Spargo. Antimonopolists opposed the

United States Brewers Association for the good reason that concerned them about all such business combines: they acted in restraint of trade. None of such people, as individuals or as groups, could be held responsible for a trend of events that gave an aura of power to those who made prohibition the equivalent of temperance.[20]

Progressives were generally anxious to show rationality about the need for responsible work in the field. As one theologian put it:

> The methods of solving the [liquor] problem demand special attention. In attempting this task, no effort is made to exploit some Utopian scheme for social ills. Any extreme measures based on partisanship and emotionalism, or any academic theory that has not been tested and made effective in the field of action, will fail to meet the present social situation.[21]

The approach he hit upon was rational in the extreme. He broke the problem down into economic, political, social, and criminal aspects. He examined substitutes for the saloon, better work conditions, comfortable restrooms, "the formation of public sentiment," and other relevancies. All of these contributory solutions finally broke down, the result of a concerned series of events that could not be controlled, or prepared against. But it would be the sheerest misreading of history to imagine that those advocating liquor control lost their battle because they had sought to impose authoritarian controls on citizens.

The Progressives did good work in the field, as Populists had done before them, by publicizing clearly defined crime and degradation and contributing information and ideas respecting their roots and relationship to social conditions. A renewed effort at liquor control would require an interwoven program of technical analyses, polls, and reports on American society, which gave a picture of what it was composed of and how it functioned in connection with the liquor traffic. It would also require a set of goals and a good awareness of its own experiences, before, during, and after prohibition. None of this could be accomplished by recourse to scapegoatism and the victimization of Progressives.

NOTES

1. Robert M. La Follette, speech delivered at Mineral Point, Wisconsin, July 1897, La Follette Papers, State Historical Society of Wisconsin.

2. "The Passing of Populism," *Literary Digest* 45 (August 31, 1912): 322.

3. Svend Petersen, comp., *A Statistical History of the American Presidential Elections* (New York, 1963), 48-49.

4. *Literary Digest* 2 (November 29, 1890): 20.

5. Norman Pollack, *The Populist Response to Industrial America* (Cambridge, Mass., 1962), 43ff. spelled out farmer-labor sympathies.

6. *Literary Digest*, 2 (July 18, 1891): 329.

7. *New York Times*, July 7, 1893.

8. C. Vann Woodward, *Origins of the New South, 1877-1913* (Baton Rouge, La., 1951), 235ff.; *San Francisco Argonaut*, in *Literary Digest* 4 (September 3, 1892): 497.

9. *Literary Digest* 6 (January 21, 1893): 328. Venality was a rural as well as urban phenomenon at the polls. A study of fraud in Connecticut politics resulted in the conclusion that "in the country the venal are largely American, in the city of foreign, origin." Professor J. J. McCook, "Alarming Proportion of Venal Voters," *Forum* 14 (September 1892: 1-13. Contributing to election cheats were almshouse inmates, drunkards, tramps, and "shiftless."

10. Louis Filler, ed., *Late Nineteenth-century American Liberalism* (Indianapolis, 1962), 13-19.

11. *Literary Digest*, 13 (August 15, 1896): 481-482.

12. Robert F. Durden, *The Climax of Populism: The Election of 1896* (Lexington, Ky., 1965), 151.

13. James H. Timberlake, *Prohibition and the Progressive Movement, 1900-1920* (Cambridge, Mass., 1963).

14. James R. Gusfield, *Symbolic Crusade* (Urbana, 1963), offered the doctrinaire view that temperance and abolition had been so much one cause that abolition had been able to "stifle completely the organization of the Temperance movement in the South." The inaccuracy of this thesis, the need for more judicious generalization, was indicated in Paul E. Isaac, *Prohibition and Politics: Turbulent Decades in Tennessee, 1885-1920* (Knoxville, 1965), which noted that "the course of events in Tennessee simply does not bear this out."

15. *Literary Digest* 6 (July 27, 1895): 366.

16. Louis Filler, *The Muckrakers: Crusaders for American Liberalism* 142ff., 285ff., on the basis of muckraking publications, treats liquor only in passing in terms of its use in patent medicines, and as an adjunct to the saloon-prostitution connection, that is, as false medicine and as a vice-concomitant.

17. Lincoln Steffens, *Upbuilders* (New York, 1909), xiii-xiv.

18. Upton Sinclair, *The Wet Parade* (New York, 1931), a novel, and one of his autobiographical memoirs, *The Cup of Fury* (Great Neck, N.Y., 1956). The latter had been reprinted nine times by 1960.

19. B. C. Forbes, *Men Who Are Making America* (New York, 1917).

20. Ernest H. Cherrington, *The Evolution of Prohibition in the United States a Chronological History* (Westerville, Ohio, 1920), provides almost no evidence of any kind, even fortuitous, linking prohibition with Progressives or progressivism.

21. John Marshall Barker, *The Saloon Problem and Social Reform* (Boston, 1905), vi.

part III
PROGRESSIVISM

Imperialism

The problem with imperialism was not with its limits or definition but with the total forgetfulness that attended the careers of the anti-imperialists who accompanied their antagonists on their journey as Americans. Later anti-imperialists displayed their emotional sentiments in a total vacuum of experience, in most cases asserting the view that Americans—all Americans, from their very beginnings, from their original preemption of Indian lands—had been and were continuing to be imperialists. There was nothing for the new generation to remember but imperialism.

Yet anti-imperialists had always been vital to qualifying the will of the imperialists and giving an American definition to the nation's foreign relations. Vital to all such discussion, moreover, was a distinction between expansion and imperialism, between the westward movement of Arabs across northern Africa and the proud, hard movement of Roman legions into Greek and Egyptian civilizations.

Necessary, too, was a grasp of the changing principle of nationalism. On the walls of Bristol Cathedral in England hung the shining armor of Admiral Sir William Penn, sea hero and father of the Quaker pacifist William Penn. Both Penns had been instruments in furthering British expansion and national goals. The later Penn's Philadelphia enshrined Independence Hall where revolutionaries had planned civil war in order to enhance their own vision of a new nation.

Both the War of 1812 and the Mexican war had divided the country, and they featured not only peace advocates of great stature—the United States was the birthplace of the first peace movement—but whole sections of the country that had praised peace and international generosity at the expense of expansionist and frankly imperialistic drives. Their efforts, their arguments, their very failures, it would have seemed, ought to have forced memory of the anti-imperialists on their putative successors. William Ellery Channing, however, was best known, if he was known, to the religionists he had fathered. Charles Sumner was probably best recalled as the quarrelsome congressional opponent of slavery and the prostrate South rather than for his peace advocacies. Elihu Burritt, supreme worker for peace, was recalled not at all, possibly because his deep religious feelings conflicted with the principled atheism of later crusaders.

The determining factor in the imperialism of the 1890s was the modernized shipping of major western nations, which enabled them to speed up the process of acquiring choice colonies around the world for development of natural resources useful in industry or for coaling stations. With ships then wholly dependent upon coal, the fuel became central to the lifelines of empire expansion. The United States could either enter into the race for colonies or be left out of world relations. And since not a few Americans recalled that their revolution had been a torch to France and to the world, recalled, too, their long prejudice in favor of republicanism everywhere, they could not conceive that the interventionist impulse in some of their countrymen could do any ultimate harm to the people whose lives they touched.[1]

For the most part, the American public found it difficult to concentrate on underdeveloped places and areas abroad, and its responses to their problems and claims to attention ranged from naive to contemptuous. Thus the word "Yap" in the Island of Yap, one of the Caroline Islands in the Pacific, struck the American public as extraordinarily funny, and its slangy lift gave it a place in the American language. Policy toward foreign affairs, therefore, was confined to small groups of interested or knowledgeable people. Opinion on policy was far from uniform on the subject, as the variety of polled editorial opinion in newspapers showed.

In 1890 a serious crisis developed between Chile and the United States as a result of Chilean politics, which Americans appear to have made some effort to affect. A Chilean street attack by a mob, which was aided by police, left dead in Valparaiso two American sailors from the ship *Baltimore* and nearly a score wounded. It is quite possible that President Benjamin Harrison wanted a war with Chile as an aid to his uninspiring administration.[2] Preparations for war actually accompanied an ultimatum, which the Chilean Government accepted though not without bitterness or the capacity to remember in later years.

Democrats were not thrilled by the President's exploits, and one Republican ex-President, also a former Civil War general, was wholly negative. Wrote Hayes in his personal diary: "Chili consents to do all we can reasonably demand. My regret is that our Government blustered and bullied. President Harrison in his message [to Congress] argued like a prosecutor—made the most of the case against our weak sister. Forbearance, charity, friendship, arbitration should have been in our words and thoughts." Others sought less than a middle ground. The Reform Club of New York invited a Chilean emissary to address it and applauded his violent attack on the United States.[3]

No aspect of the event escaped searching attention: the supercilious and presumptuous attitude of the British press; Irish-American hatred of the American minister to Chile, Patrick Egan, for being both an Irishman and a Republican; the Chileans as "snarling" whelps of the Pacific; American socialist suspicion of a plot to strengthen the armed forces; and simple antagonism based on party, which gave anti-imperialist leanings to political outs.[4]

Much of American opinion on such matters required sorting out. A mob lynching of Italians in New Orleans, which brought a protest from Italy—startling to Americans who had not realized there *was* an Italian government—constituted a species of American affairs at home that took on different weight with various ethnic American components. The situation was complicated by being related to the Mafia, which the general public understood full well to be a criminal organization not meriting high regard or the complete process of legal justice. The Department of State, acting with semi-independence for lack of pressure from outside social interests, finally concluded to award a small sum to the Italian government in comity, that is, in perfunctory diplomatic settlement of differences. Said the New York organ *Cristoforo Colombo* sarcastically:

> We have reached a point at which we can sing hosannahs on Easter Day. Italy presses the United States to her heart and weeps with tenderness; the United States hugs Italy to her bosom and weeps—with joy, at having got out of a scrape so cheaply, what more can be desired? . . . We suspect that if the question were put to them directly, why they hit on the sum paid, they would answer in chorus: "we are not so crazy as to place a higher value on eleven d——d dagoes."[5]

Anti-imperialism took various forms during the 1890s but added up to doubts about the value of foreign accessions and their inhabitants, or concern about their constitutional or economic viability to Americans. Businessmen used the armed forces to unseat the government of Hawaii and ripened the islands for formal American acquisition. Democrats were jealous of the possibility of lame-duck Benjamin Harrison and the Republicans taking credit for additions to American terrain. American farmers feared the competition of Hawaiian products if granted free entry to the United States.

The first report of the coup that dethroned the Hawaiian Queen Liliuokalani caused Democratic and Republican newspapers alike to approve annexation. Only such organs as the old-mugwump *New York Times,* though hard line on Chile, and the conservative *Boston Advertiser*—better informed than the more popular press—questioned annexation. But even the expansionists feared Harrison's "unseemly haste" to win the consent of the Senate. Grover Cleveland, inheriting the situation, read the country a well-regarded lecture on the responsibility of large nations to small nations and deferred approval of the treaty presented to his administration.[6]

As clear a statement of anti-imperialist views as the strong anti-imperialist press presented was that in the *New York Evening Post* in its March 13, 1893, article, then in the hands of mugwumps E. L. Godkin and Horace White. Though they feared labor, despised socialism, and grimly supported law and order above everything else, they were rigid on Free Trade and the open shores they thought it would create. They added little to progressivism with its complex armies of pushing and arguing people, but they made torchflares for anti-imperialism:

> As a friend of the Indian, as one who does not contemn the Chinese, and who does have an honest respect for solemn treaty obligations even with an "inferior" civilization, and who could not personally do a mean act to the humblest of Hawaiian aborigines, we hope President Cleveland will study the [annexation] proposal in the light of American republican principles and of the nature of peace and war. Is it consistent to incorporate another people without a plebiscite, or, having taken a plebiscite, straightway to disenfranchise the majority of those who participated in it? Is it lawful to go to war for this purpose? On the general policy of extra-continental aggrandizement we should also hope that he would ponder well, and fix a salutory precedent.[7]

Some anti-imperialist attitudes were of such complexity as to require the kind of understanding that was due imperialists who could not foresee developments that would change the rules governing their outward thrusts, if they were to avoid the wholesale destruction of civilization. Even in the 1890s the power of new guns and explosives frightened pacifists and near-pacifists and caused them to raise questions and voice concern over technological advances and their effect on nations. Carl Schurz was a Republican emigrant from Germany, leader of the German-American community and its spokesman from Lincoln to Greeley. He was also a literary figure, and, as Hayes's Secretary of the Interior, he was ardent for civil-service reform, conservation, and justice for the Indian. As a *Nation* and *Post* editor he opposed imperialistic adventures in "tropical" accessions like Mexico or Hawaii. He believed such nations could never be "absorbed." Hawaii, he predicted, could never be a state because of its distance from the mainland. Schurz thought Canada might unite with its neighbor because their people and climate were quite similar.[8]

Such was the background for a crisis precipitated by the controversy between Great Britain and Venezuela, which pitted an underdeveloped nation against a giant and brought into militant stance Cleveland's administration, including the too-little-remembered Richard Olney, principal of two crises in the 1890s.

Olney had intervened fatefully in the Pullman strike of 1894, saddling a legal injunction on Eugene V. Debs's American Railway Union—a major effort to bring together the several powerful railway unions of engineers, firemen, and others. That injunction had stopped the strike leaders in their effort to unionize George T. Pullman's kingdom of luxury cars. Olney, a former attorney and railroad man, had persuaded Cleveland to bring in federal troops, who had broken the strike. For these services, Olney had been made Secretary of State and became a close associate of Cleveland's.

Venezuela and British Guiana had nudged one another for more than a century, claiming much of the other's territory, before Great Britain tired of negotiations and concluded to settle the matter forthwith. Venezuela then called on the United States to rescue it. Olney now came forth with a declaration that compromised the government for the future far beyond its deserts. He demanded that Great Britain submit to arbitration and coupled this with the statement: "Today the United States is practically sovereign on this continent, and its fiat is law upon the subjects to which it confines its interposition." This was the case because "its infinite resources combined with its isolated position render it master of the situation and practically invulnerable as against any and all other powers."

The world registered shock at this interpretation of the Monroe doctrine and the threat of war it implied. Fear was heightened when President Cleveland on December 17, 1895, sent Congress a special message asking authorization to appoint a commission to determine the true Venezuela-British Guiana boundary line. The President added: "In making these recommendations I am fully alive to the responsibility incurred, and keenly realize all the consequences that may follow."

"Brinkmanship" may well have been justified since it resulted in a mixed commission, which brought up the rule of reason rather than force. After all, Venezuela itself had appealed to America "as the oldest of the republics of the new continent." Popular sentiment approved Cleveland's boldness. Criticism came mainly from business; the *Journal of Commerce* saw Cleveland's policy as "madness itself,"[9] and Godkin's *Evening Post* was horrified at the idea of war between advanced nations. Godkin compared Cleveland to none other than Eugene V. Debs who, Godkin thought, had also defied law during the Pullman strike. Godkin also execrated Congress as "a body of idle, ignorant, lazy, and not very scrupulous men" to have surrendered its war-making power to the President.[10] With such a view of the representatives of the American public, the Godkins of anti-imperialism were only able to accomplish a minimum of general influence.

They did, however, accomplish something. They alerted thoughtful people to the dangers attending American advances into alien terrain. They reminded their countrymen of old slogans of equality and freedom. Moorfield Storey, long-time and persistent anti-imperialist, had an outlook derived from old abolitionist ideals; however, like Godkin he feared an unleashed democracy. To Storey, the Venezuelan crisis was one in which "demagogues go too far in the way of rousing the jingo feeling."[11]

A species of racism could be discerned in many anti-imperialist warnings about untoward expansion. Yet a sincere idealism qualified many such views and was ultimately fulfilled in policies that made Hawaii a self-governing body, took the Philippine Islands through a long series of steps to self-government and ultimately separation, and granted citizenship to citizens of Puerto Rico and Guam.[12]

The basic reality was that all these territories were subject to foreign rule, if not by the United States then by some other power. The one question was whether administration would take a more or less progressive form. "In general, the United States evolved its own methods for governing dependencies. . . . [It demonstrated] the positivist bent of contemporary thinking about colonies, whose people were envisioned as being ruled in their own interest by cooler and wiser heads from the mother country."[13] In this project, anti-imperialists helped.

When the United States Post Office sought to bar the pamphlets of Edward Atkinson, businessman-anti-imperialist, from the mails as subversive, it called attention to his titles, "The Cost of a National Crime," "The Hell of War and Its Penalties," and "Criminal Aggression: by Whom Committed?" Atkinson had already, several years before, joined with others, including Carl Schurz, to sum up the findings of a series of meetings in major cities on how to promote international arbitration. The Anti-Expansion Conference gathered together and presented in forceful fashion the principal criticisms opposing Cleveland's truculent posture "in a fashion which won the approval of newspapers on both sides of the national argument."[14]

In general, Progressives were sufficiently mixed with popular sentiments to find themselves in the imperialist camp, but an honest and intelligent reading of their record shows that they could always be distinguished from such determined imperialists as Captain Alfred T. Mahan of the United States Navy and author of such works as *The Influence of Sea Power upon History* (1890). To Mahan ships meant power, and nothing but power, in a world that recognized nothing else. Some businessmen, ministers, and politicians followed similar lines of thought without Mahan's learning. They could be distinguished from Progressives who, whatever pride they took in their progenitors or in what they saw as the destiny of the United States, were also determined to satisfy their own citizens in the process and, with greater or lesser competence, to improve the lot of those whom their imperialist plans touched.

It was no accident, therefore, that the triumphant Republicans of 1896 should have leaned as a party toward outward enterprises, their platform for that year calling for Hawaiian control, an isthmian canal to join the Atlantic and Pacific oceans, and a navy and naval bases appropriate to such a program.[15] Democratic resistance to it produced a curious adventure in foreign policy, which their young leader William Jennings Bryan pursued.

Bryan's erratic course is not easy to understand. It suggests an American combination of goodwill and good intentions, doubtful expertise in the handling of world problems, responsiveness to midwestern isolationist sentiment, and a Populist fear of the competition of outside agriculture. As Cleveland, the Democrat, had professed a concern for the well-being of the small nation of Hawaii and won the jealous approval of his party, so Bryan took up the flag for international peace and uncompetitive amity. His stunning acceptance of a colonelcy in the Nebraska Third Regiment, in which he had enlisted as a private presumably to express his oneness with national policy once war in Spain had been declared, would have been a high point in political ineptitude had it not also indicated the more serious inadequacy of his Democratic constituency, which failed to write him off as a serious leader of programs. As it was, his grotesque act merely wiped out the substance of all his later essays in depreciation of war, praise of Tolstoi's pacifism, and other pieties.[16]

McKinley, as commander in chief of the armed services, had no intention of putting any shine on Bryan's armor as a palatine knight. The "colonel" was buried in insignificance in Florida training camps while Theodore Roosevelt and others went on to glory in Cuba and the Philippines. Absurd in peace as in war, the anti-imperialist Bryan first spoke of justice to all contestants, then confounded the world by approving the harsh settlement forced on Spain and sent to the Senate for confirmation. Bryan as accepted party leader could have provoked a country-wide debate, which would have clarified national goals. His view that he needed to join the popular demand for territories to direct it in benign and humanistic ways was total self-deception, which, again, should have disqualified him for responsible office.[17]

That it did not was a measure of Progressive anti-imperialism in general. Specifics modified the picture. David Graham Phillips's views have already been noted. His friend Charles Edward Russell was a long-time friend of the Filipinos, in their battle for nationhood and after. Jane Addams, in her Chicago settlement work, developed deep feelings for families and communities, which inspired her work as founder of the Woman's Peace party, useful in the world that was still without ultimate danger of extinction but had many battles to fight in order to contain war.[18]

Henry Demarest Lloyd did well in the Progressive context, though he died early. He lent his prestige as author of *Wealth against Commonwealth* (1894) to the protest against war and expansion. Josephine Shaw Lowell, at her height as institutional reformer and moral force, reprobated war with Spain. Samuel Gompers expressed himself as an internationalist, as did a number of others in Progressive labor. journalism, and politics. William James was to write an essay, "A Moral Equivalent for War" (1910), prophetic of the New Deal, in which he would call for a battle against antagonistic nature rather than men.

But overall the peace movement—even with Andrew Carnegie to approve it and sponsor affluently some of its principles—summed up to an exercise in futility. Speeches, meetings, pamphlets, and seminars carried an air of thinness and unrelatedness, as in Julius Moritzen's *The Peace Movement in America* (1912), which was an endless and unmemorable record of such activities and products. As George F. Kennan was to write:

> The alternative to the establishment of American power in the Philippines . . . was not a nice, free, progressive Philippine Republic: it was Spanish, German, or Japanese domination. Abstention on our part from the taking of the Philippines could have been argued, and was, from the standpoint of *our* interests; it could scarcely have been argued from the interests of the Filipinos themselves.[19]

The ultimate maker of war was the people themselves. McKinley had not pressed for war. Mark Hanna had opposed it. The business interests, not knowing Spain's weakness, doubted the wisdom of it.[20] America's urge for a scapegoat finally hit upon the publisher William Randolph Hearst as the author of atrocities that stirred up an unthinking public to war.[21]

Yet debate concerning the necessity of war continued from 1896, when Cuban insurrectionists began a campaign against their Spanish masters, to February 15, 1898, when the *Maine* blew up in Havana harbor. It continued as discussion of how much sympathy ought to be accorded the rebellious Cubans ranged from fevered approval to scorn of congressional politics and demagoguery. An interesting view had been that Cuba was the business of the Latin American countries rather than of the United States. During the war itself, and in the midst of propaganda portraying Spaniards as cruel and inhuman, the *Literary Digest* judiciously reviewed a play by the contemporary Spanish dramatist José Echegaray, without drawing moralistic lessons in any way.[22]

Thus America was a loose confederation of views. Americans with war fever were free to express their agitation. Those without it could indulge hatred of war without inhibition. If they chose to express an enthusiasm for expansion, it was not because of Hearst but because of their own conviction that the war was just and merited support.

The larger proportion of Progressives was, indeed, to be found not so much in imperialist camps as in those favoring a vigorous program for world relationship. They could not have influenced the public for good or ill—could not have influenced it at all—had they been unwilling to adopt such a policy. It may, however, be doubted that there was a clear "contradiction" between support of democratic measures at home and support of war with Spain. Progressives believed in results. They were persuaded of America's democratic mission, abroad as well as at home. They approved augmented government power.[23] But none of these tenets necessarily added up to cruelty or suppression of native ambitions. Much American thinking with respect to Cuba was kindly and encouraging of the hopes of Cuban rebels. American heroics in the destruction of Spanish power were of high quality, stand up in retrospect, and were fittingly honored by Americans of the time at home. The conquering of yellow fever through American talent and courage in that pest-ridden island was an epic of world magnitude.

The Philippine assault was shadowed by harsh military measures intended to neutralize Filipino nationalists who might have known how to establish a government capable of advancing materially and also fending off ambitious nations seeking expansion. The American military was peremptory and introduced measures that had once been employed by the Spanish. It was important to note that such programs were reprobated in America by Americans. Brigadier General James F. Bell's concentration camps for captured Filipino rebels in Luzon infuriated numerous editors and caused criticism and investigations. Brigadier General Jacob H. Smith's "kill and burn" order in Samar caused newspapers of every political stripe to express revulsion and also caused the general's court-martial.[24]

Precisely how much the United States had to teach its colonial charges is a matter of judgment. But men of sense and sensibility enlisted in the services and performed meritoriously. One problem with assessing their worth lay in a prejudice that sought out human defects in American operations but did not do the same for others. Walter Millis's *The Martial Spirit* (1931) was intended to do good by unveiling the mean and the calculated in American involvement in Cuban and Philippine affairs. Unfortunately, it taught method to thesis writers who built up a mass of formidable events as an American conspiracy by a few men against the will of the majority of Americans and foreigners. To do this it was necessary to pass by the adulation given Theodore Roosevelt, Admiral George Dewey, and a hundred others of lesser stature—an adulation that freely implicated the masses in their strategems—and to ignore the realities of the world in which they operated.[25]

Thus Americans in Cuba were outraged by the cruelty that they encountered as casually accepted among Cubans:

> One day a bull was found in Siboney, and was to be killed for food. The American soldiers wished to shoot it, but the Cubans would not have a bull killed in that way. The creature was stabbed and stabbed with their knives till it fell, and the incident sank more deeply than one would have supposed into the minds of the soldiers. . . .
>
> "Why," [the Americans] asked in effect, "should we fight for men like these? They are no better than the Spaniards." And it escaped the notice of nearly all, that mean and savage ways were to be expected in those who had long been treated with meanness and savagery.[26]

Thus apologies were invented for Cubans and totally escaped Millis and his followers, as did the following:

> Follansbee . . . took a detachment of soldiers and searched the town for stray Spaniards. . . . The Americans were now closing in on Santiago. Next day, Hearst met his rebel correspondent, Colonel Honoré Laine, who told him how his Cuban forces had been given forty Spanish prisoners taken by the Americans at El Caney.
>
> "And what did you do with them?" Hearst inquired.
>
> "We cut their heads off, of course," Laine replied.[27]

All of this, too, missed the drama of American courage, American chivalry, and, for that matter, that of the Spanish who died in fulfillment of their patriotic promises. One passage from a message sent by Theodore Roosevelt from the field to Henry Cabot Lodge in Washington could stand for innumerable messages not indicated in theses dedicated to demeaning American troops in furtherance of anti-imperialist arguments and gestures:

> Tell the President for Heaven's sake to send us every

> regiment and above all every battery possible. We have won so far at a heavy cost, but the Spaniards fight very hard and charging these intrenchments against modern rifles is terrible. . . . we *must* have help—thousands of men, batteries, and *food* and ammunition.[28]

Passed over, too, were the reminiscences of numerous men who were hardly models of truculence and pride. Lincoln Steffens was excited by the American adventure and would have enlisted had his wife permitted. Sherwood Anderson enjoyed the war, read dime novels and historical romances while on patrol duty at Cienfuegos, Cuba, early in 1899, and was admired by his comrades for his way with the girls. Alvin Johnson, later distinguished as a founder of the New School in New York, as editor of the *Encyclopedia of the Social Sciences*, and as organizer of the University in Exile, which rescued numerous intellectuals from Nazi Germany, did not get beyond Tennessee in his army service as a volunteer (the entire army was composed of volunteers) but he suffered the fevers that attended bad sanitation and doubtful food. But he was spirited and undeterred by military regulations and met good people as well as bad in his camp.[29]

Carl Sandburg was firmest in his faith and most angry with those who mocked their own:

> What I still believe to be established fact is that Weyler herded more than one hundred thousand people in concentration camps where more than half of them died of starvation and fever. I was going along with millions of other Americans who were about ready for a war to throw the Spanish government out of Cuba and let the people of Cuba have their republic. If a war did come and men were called to fight it, I knew what I would do. . . .
>
> When Peter Finley Dunne had Mr. Dooley referring to "Gin-'ral Miles' gran' picnic and moonlight excursion to Porthy Ricky," he had probably had a tenderloin steak garnished with onions before he took up his writing for the day. When Richard Harding Davis wrote that for the troops under General Miles "Porto Rico was a picnic" he was remembering the dry corners

> he slept in, the roads where he never walked carrying fifty pounds in a baking sun, the mosquitoes that never bled him nor closed an eye for him, the graybacks he never picked from an inhabited shirt. . . . [T]he war in Porto Rico, while not bloody, was a dirty and lousy affair while it lasted.[30]

Finley Peter Dunne meant well by his comic stances, treading lightly between objective appreciation of war and admiration for individuals who fought with courage and commitment. It did not occur to him or others that a later generation, untrained in historical reminiscence and capable of handling life and death as materials for shallow wit, would quote him to ridicule American exploits of high and often mortal dignity.

Most telling in the long run was the view of the colonials proper. The Filipino nationalists had suffered the most by American unwillingness to permit them to set up their own government, presumably with American protection, since it was unlikely that it could have endured without it. The role of American interests in the Philippines was thoroughly investigated.[31] Idealism and self-interest compelled the thinking and actions of concerned parties in both the United States and the Philippine Islands. As the insurrectionary leader, Aguinaldo, himself wrote though long after the war:

> And yet, in retrospect, I cannot help but be glad that the expansionists won over McKinley completely. For the alternative to annexing the Philippines entirely might have been partition. The Philippines might have become another Poland with Japan annexing the Batanes group in the north, the United States keeping Luzon, Germany grabbing the Visayan Islands, and perhaps Great Britain taking over Mindanao which is proximate to its territory of Borneo. Had the Philippines been dismembered in this or a similar manner, we should have lost all chances of becoming a free and independent nation.[32]

Events subsequent to the American-Filipino war—a war of painful harshness on both sides—proved sufficiently satisfactory to bring the two nations to no more than controversies over commercial and diplomatic preferences. A substantial portion of Filipino opinion opposed independence of the United States. An imperialist party of military and business interests in America was reluctant to give up ultimate controls in the islands. In 1933 the Philippine legislature refused to accept independence, feeling its national security and commercial and immigration prospects were endangered.

The promise of independence, originally set down in 1916, was consummated in 1935. In June 1941 the Filipino President Manuel Quezon promised that if the United States entered what was then the European war, his nation would be on the American side.[33]

Charles Evans Hughes observed in 1923 that the Monroe doctrine rested "upon the right of every sovereign state to protect itself by preventing a condition of affairs in which it will be too late to protect itself."[34] Although reform implicated itself in imperialism beyond the limits of its Progressive tenets, on occasion it could in an imperfect world point to patent achievements worth candid review.

NOTES

1. In recollection was American sympathy for and aid to the Greek revolution against the Turks, which left a residue in history of pro-Greek feeling based on no evidence and possibly sustained by the fact that there were many more Greeks in America than Turks. See, however, the stunning novel, *The Ashes of Smyrna*, by Richard Reinhardt (New York, 1971), which, for a later period of Greek-Turkish warfare, makes it clear that atrocities were equitably divided between Turks and Greeks and, in addition, that Balkan warfare had long been eminent for its peremptory nature.

American sympathy for Latin American revolutions could be reasonably interpreted as clearing the area of the Spanish and thus making it ripe for American exploitation. But more realistic assessment of the revolution's "leaders" would have made them more responsible than it did for the long, malignant, irreversible disparity between the rich and the poor in almost all the "republics" involved.

2. This David Graham Phillips, an ardent anti-imperialist, indirectly referred to in his novel *The Plum Tree* (Indianapolis, 1905), 378, though the nation he named was Germany. Harrison had served as a general in the Civil War, and as commander in chief of the army and navy might well have gained charisma by organizing and directing an expeditionary force.

3. Charles Richard Williams, *Diary and Letters of Rutherford Birchard Hayes* (Columbus, Ohio, 1926), 5: 51; Louis Filler, ed., *Democrats and Republicans, Ten Years of the Republic,* by Harry Thurston Peck (New York, 1964), 213.

4. *Literary Digest* 4 (November 7, 1891): 20-22; (January 23, 1892): 328-329; (January 30, 1892): 356-357; (February 6, 1892); 384-385.

5. *Ibid.* 4 (April 23, 1892); 693.

6. *Ibid.*, 6 (February 4, 1893): 389-390; (February 11, 1893): 412-413; (February 25, 1893): 468; (March 4, 1893): 500. A clear case of an American interest obtruding upon policy was the California view that Hawaiian accession would degrade American labor by opening the gates to contract labor. *Ibid.* 6 (March 11, 1893): 511.

7. See also Joseph Logsdon, *Horace White, Nineteenth Century Liberal* (Westport, Conn., 1971), 357ff., and Oswald Garrison Villard, *Fighting Years* (New York, 1939), 117ff. The latter deals with *Post* anti-imperialism and the beginning of Villard's liberal-Progressive career.

8. Carl Schurz, "Manifest Destiny," *Harper's Magazine* 87 (October 1893): 737-746. George F. Pearce, "Assessing Public Opinion: Editorial Comment and the Annexation of Hawaii—a Case Study." *Pacific Historical Quarterly,* 43 (August 1974): 324ff. attempts to "[put] to rest the historical myth" that there was a popular groundswell favoring expansion, but no more than demonstrates that there were no strong forces interrupting the normal party processes, interested commercial and intellectual elements, and armed services in which an absentminded citizenry could take pride.

9. *Literary Digest,* 12 (December 28, 1895): 243.

10. William M. Armstrong, *E. L. Godkin and American Foreign Policy, 1865-1900* (New York, 1957), 182.

11. William B. Hixson, Jr., *Moorfield Storey and the Abolitionist Tradition* (New York, 1972), 49.

12. David Healy, *US Expansionism: The Imperialist Urge in the 1890's,* (Madison, 1970), 249.

13. *Ibid.*, 252.

14. *Literary Digest,* 13 (May 2, 1896): 5; 17 (May 13, 1899): 541; 19 (October 28, 1899): 515.

15. Julius W. Pratt, *Expansionists of 1898* (Baltimore, 1936), 213-214.

16. *William Jennings Bryan, The Commoner Condensed* (New York, 1902), *passim.*

17. Paolo E. Coletta, *William Jennings Bryan,* vol. I: *Political Evangelist, 1860-1908* (Lincoln, Neb., 1964), 234-237.

18. John C. Farrell, *Beloved Lady* (Baltimore, 1967), 85.

19. Quoted in Robert L. Beiser, *Twelve against Empire, The Anti-Imperialists, 1898-1900* (New York, 1968), 231. See also C. Roland Marchand, *The American Peace Movement and Social Reform, 1898-1918* (Princeton, 1972), which notes the "second-class" character of the peace crusade it memorializes.

20. For a skeptical view of popular opinion, see Thomas A. Bailey, "Was the Presidential Election of 1900 a Mandate on Imperialism?" *Mississippi Valley Historical Review* 24 (June 1937): 43-52. See also Daniel B. Schirmer,

Republic or Empire: American Resistance to the Philippine War (Cambridge, Mass., 1972), 205ff ("The Victory of Imperialism").

21. This legend is perpetuated in W. A. Swanberg, *Citizen Hearst* (New York, 1961), which puts it: "It was an unnecessary war. It was the newspapers' war. Above all, it was Hearst's war. It is safe to say that had not Hearst, with his magnificently tawdry flair for publicity and agitation, enlisted the women of America in a crusade they misunderstood, made a national heroine of the jail-breaking Miss Cisneros, made a national abomination of Dupuy de Lome, made the *Maine* a mistaken symbol of Spanish treachery, caused thousands of citizens to write their Congressmen, and dragged the powerful *World* along with him into journalistic ill-fame, the public would have kept its sanity, McKinley would have shown more spunk, at least four more senators would have taken counsel with reason, and there would have been no war."

22. *Literary Digest*, 12 (April 18, 1896): 727-728; 13 (May 9, 1896): 54; (May 14, 1898): 581.

23. William E. Leuchtenberg, "Progressivism and Imperialism: The Progressive Movement and American Foreign Policy, 1898-1916," *Mississippi Valley Historical Review*, 39 (December 1952): 500.

24. During William Calley's My Lai trial in 1971-1972, it was noted that Smith was the only high-ranking officer in American military history to have been convicted of war crimes.

25. Millis's later career was of interest in illustrating the dymanics that attended careers of scholarly philanthropy. His *The Martial Spirit* and *The Road to War* (1935), which judged American involvement in World War I as wholly reprehensible, made his reputation. However, his isolationism was dealt a shock by the advent of Nazism. He clung to his pacifist views as late as 1937 when *Viewed Without Alarm, Europe Today* took a moderate approach to international events. In June 1940, however, he urged a declaration of war against Germany. Later he blamed the tragedy of Pearl Harbor on an inept military; by then he had become a military expert for the *New York Herald Tribune*. Millis became a favorite of the Center for the Study of Democratic Institutions in California, favored arbitration, and died in 1968 convinced that major war had become too unthinkable to recur.

26. *Manchester Guardian* correspondent quoted in Frank Freidel, *The Splendid Little War* (New York, 1958), 95.

27. Swanberg, *Citizen Hearst*, 156.

28. Freidel, *Splendid Little War*, 186.

29. Justin Kaplan, *Lincoln Steffens* (New York, 1974), 87; Irving Howe, *Sherwood Anderson* (New York, 1951), 28-29; Alvin Johnson, *Pioneer's Progress* (New.Yorik 1952), 101ff.

30. Carl Sandburg, *Always the Young Strangers* (New York, 1953), 404, 417-418.

31. Henry F. Graff, ed., *American Imperialism and the Philippine Insur-*

rection: Testimony Taken from Hearings on Affairs in the Philippine Islands before the Senate Committee on the Philippines—1902 (Boston, 1969).

32. General Emilio Aguinaldo, with Vicente Albano Pacis, *A Second Look at America* (New York, 1957), 66.

33. Garel A. Grunder and William E. Livezey, *The Philippines and the United States* (Norman, Okla., 1951), passim. See also William Harold Muggleston, "The Sentiment in the United States for and against the Retention of the Philippine Islands" (Master's thesis, University of Vermont, 1941).

34. Donald M. Dozer, ed., *The Monroe Doctrine* (New York, 1965), 37.

Theo

Theodore Roosevelt's changed image from that of a model of American distinction to that of a shifting beach-portrait in sand took place in such a swirl of academic and reference books and perfunctory essays as not to leave a clear trace for study. One of America's greatest men had been degraded to the status of a passing joke, a shallow extrovert. A play, *Arsenic and Old Lace* (1941), identified him to rounds of laughter with a lunatic character who charged aimlessly up the stairs, presumably as Roosevelt had at San Juan Hill. In Clifford Odets's well-esteemed *Awake and Sing!* (1935), an ineffectual father continuously cited banalities he imputed to Roosevelt, at one point suggesting to his moody son that the two of them ought to be closer than they were. "Who said that," the son retorted, "T.R.?"

The 1930s were a period that saw the total collapse of a reputation that had seemed founded in nature and was indeed hewn into the rocks of Mt. Rushmore in the Black Hills of South Dakota. The most startling fact was the manner in which a new Roosevelt absorbed all the attention, public and private, that could be given to the old. There had once been only Theodore Roosevelt; there was now only Franklin D. Roosevelt. Moreover, the issues of importance—the New Deal, the fate of capitalism, the challenge of international communism, and fascism—seemed to thin and wither whatever had once contributed to the earlier Roosevelt's significance.

And yet the end was signaled before F. D. R. began his presidency. In 1931, Henry F. Pringle published his *Theodore Roosevelt*, a lengthy, well-written essay in derogation of an overblown opportunist, long in brashness, short in brains and humanity. That year was issued also Lincoln Steffens's *Autobiography,* which portrayed Theodore Roosevelt as an ambitious, hyperactive, and self-righteous exhibitionist: a portrait done with some affection, no doubt, but also directed by anxiety. Steffens's own career seemed itself in the twilight, and he sought ways to catch the attention of an absentminded and disrespectful new generation.

John Chamberlain for that new generation, in his *Farewell to Reform* (1932), which seemed to hint at revolution, seized on Steffens's view that Roosevelt "thought with his hips" and added to ridicule a note of patronage and contempt. The worst, however, was yet to come, as still newer aspirants reminded themselves of Roosevelt's unqualified patriotism, his belief in the virtues of war and imperialism, and his need to front the universe without fear and in his own person. All of this added up, in one influential interpretation, not to tragic courage. It did not add up, in an open democracy, to a nourishing contributor by one of a social class that had earlier been accused of insufficient concern for the state, insufficient energy, insufficient relationship to life. It added up to insanity: " 'Get action, do things; be sane,' [Roosevelt] once raved, 'don't fritter away your time; create, act, take a place wherever you are and be somebody: get action.' "[1] Such "ravings" presumably were to be avoided by modern Americans.

Yet the popular name "Teddy" persisted for this lunatic doer, attention not even being accorded his arresting "get action" as a reminder that he had once been famed for his phrase-making. The name "Teddy" marked the confusion of a nation that had begun its relationship with Roosevelt on a note of high affection and regard, which had retreated in post-World War I years into aimless laughter at his not-well-remembered activities and which had settled into contempt and anger over his attitudes that a world he could not have recognized termed racist and worse. The "Teddy" was inherited from an old tradition of democratic familiarity intended to express the admiration of the masses for their leader. In too many cases the diminutives were intended to bring the leader down from his high place and (in the case of Roosevelt) to demean him.[2]

The plain fact was that Roosevelt, among his own people, had never been "Teddy." In childhood, he had been "Teedie." After that he had been Theodore, the colonel, the President, and, among intimates, Theo. Those who Teddy-ed him while expressing hatred for his ethics and attitudes needed to take thought about their own attitudes and the implications they carried. Whatever Roosevelt was, he was not amusing, he was not ineffectual, he was not insane. His program had been designed to shape the world and could not be exorcised by careless, empty gestures.

It was interesting that despite the passage of years, despite the snipping of threads that had once connected pre-World War I times to the times following, despite the overpowering presence of a new and T. R.-obliterating Franklin D. Roosevelt, certain recollections persisted of the earlier Roosevelt, picked up in the schools, or passed from mouth to mouth in anecdotes. Children wholly uninterested in war or progressivism or history generally heard somewhere that Theodore Roosevelt had been a sickly child and had, by sheer will-power, made himself an athlete. They were aware that he had actually been a cowboy, that he had been an enthusiast, had charged San Juan Hill, and "shaken a big stick." "Teddy" had been a trustbuster, a conservationist, a Bull Mooser. He had been a candidate of the Progressive party. He had also, in the time of Woodrow Wilson, favored preparedness and had agitated for the United States to join in World War I.

It made a complicated record, complicated further by modern issues that seemed to limit his uses to the future. His phrase "I took the [Panama] Canal" was made notorious by modern American historians as the very model of an imperialist statement, presumably different in kind from any that could have been elicited from a Khrushchev, a Mao, a Sadat, or whoever else the scholar might have approved. Roosevelt's parade of the American fleet around the world in 1907-1908 could be, and was, construed as an arrogant challenge to lesser nations, which rightfully demanded their place in the sun.

What was involved in such assessments was a point of view that needed to be aired, for the past as for the future. But to cope with it adequately, in terms that did not make a mockery of higher education, required a steady view of Roosevelt, a view that saw him whole, in the time he adorned and after. The youthful Roosevelt, scion of Claes Martenssen van Rosenvelt, who migrated to Manhattan from Zeeland, Holland, in 1649, was very conscious of his background. He revered his mother and father. Theodore Roosevelt, Sr., was a New York businessman and philanthropist who served the Union well during the Civil War, setting up a system to persuade federal troops to send their pay home instead of squandering it. The boy "Teedie" loved him but was ashamed that his father had not served in the armed forces during the war; he either did not know or did not care that his father had avoided upsetting his mother, who had been a Georgia belle and whose relatives had fought and died wearing Confederate gray.

Teedie did indeed suffer ill health most of his youth, though he judged it overall a happy youth. He fought incessantly for strength, endurance, and fortitude, as late as December 1904, when he was President, losing the sight of one eye as a result of a boxing match with a professional in the White House, a fact that was carefully hidden from the public. Roosevelt was a product of the Darwinian revelation. He had learned that one must fight to survive, and he was determined that what he loved and revered must survive, if he could help it. For that faith he was ready to die at any moment.

The marvel was that he did survive to record his faith for the ages. There were numerous occasions, from the most ultimate to the most casual—involving no more than a dangerous walk in Rock Creek Park in Washington—when news would have had to go around the world that the President of the United States had died in an accident.

Roosevelt would not have been admired by women's lib partisans. He viewed women as meriting reverence within their realm, adored his mother and young wife Alice Lee, and bought land in western Dakota without consulting either. His phenomenally active memory had him reading and writing books on humanistic as well as military and other topics, but he needed at all times to assert the role of the male—or, rather, the role of his class of male. Roosevelt early noted that members of his landed and financially dominant class were content to leave politics to the pushers and contrivers of the big cities and in state houses while they either enjoyed travel and amusement, or, like Henry James, Jr., took one art or another seriously. Roosevelt was determined to be part of the true ruling class, to challenge the worker interest on the one hand and the capitalistic interest on the other.[3]

Accordingly, he entered Republican politics at age twenty-three and quickly emerged as leader of the Republican faction in Albany. He learned politics. He learned life. Appointed to a committee to investigate tenement-house conditions, he let Samuel Gompers apprise him of the piecework in cigar-making done in homes by the immigrant poor, work filling their rooms with cigar dust that settled in their lungs and darkened their lives. In concluding to favor a bill to control such practices, Roosevelt early transgressed the philosophy that made government more responsible for the property of citizens than for their lives.[4] In 1884 Roosevelt led his group to the Republican convention that nominated James G. Blaine for President.

That year he was all but shattered by the death of both his mother and his wife on February 14, 1884, the former by typhus, the latter by Bright's disease while delivering her child Alice. Nothing held the young man together in this crisis but the bleak determination "to try so to live as not to dishonor the memory of those I loved who have gone before me."[5] He plunged deeper into politics, into writing, into the cowboy saga that saw him winning the admiration of rough men who had begun by doubting the "dude" but who found him ready to fight, with hands or guns. For years Roosevelt performed in public as author, goo-goo reformer, and administrator, winning honors rather than advancement. What the public noted was not so much his work as United States Civil Service Commissioner and police commissioner of New York City as the energy and motivating force that he gave the work. There were more learned civil-service reformers, more sophisticated New York police officers and commissioners. But Roosevelt's tenacious memory and clarity of goals enabled him to pose issues of public service that galvanized other young men and heightened reform perspectives. Skulduggery persisted after Roosevelt retired from the civil-service field, crime and degradation did not abandon New York after his departure for Washington and the office of Assistant Secretary of the Navy. But later workers in those fields found their labors easier because of Roosevelt's dramatizations of their tasks.

Roosevelt had no more qualms respecting the values of imperialism than Andrew Jackson had had before him, yet Jackson was later to enjoy a revival with liberals, which was more than withheld from Roosevelt. To be sure, Jackson had been a Democrat, a political friend of the Irish, and a putative friend of labor. All of this aided

February 25, 1898.

Dewey, Hong Kong.

~~Secret and Confidential~~

Order the Squadron except Monocacy to Hong Kong. Keep full of coal. In the event of declaration war Spain, your duty will be to see that the Spanish squadron does not leave the Asiatic coast and then offensive operations in Philippine Islands. Keep Olympia until further orders.

Roosevelt

Roosevelt alerts Commodore Dewey for action in the Pacific.

partisans to forget his clear-cut record as an Indian killer, a vigorous proslavery partisan, a duellist, an imperialist, a hot-tempered and unpredictable activist, and a dubious economist. What was strange was that those who sneered at Roosevelt while referring to him as "Teddy" and who welcomed malice respecting his motives and policies were slow to put on him the responsibility for the expansionism involved in the Spanish-American War, though a huge portion belonged to him.

The reason was practical. Roosevelt had plotted a role for a big navy. He had conferred exhaustively with Captain Mahan about extending American sea power. Acting on his own, over the head of his superior, Secretary of the Navy John D. Long, and before war with Spain had been declared, he by cable instructed then-Commodore George Dewey, commanding the United States Asiatic squadron, to sail for Hong Kong, making it clear to Dewey that war was near. That Roosevelt did not share with Hearst scapegoat responsibility for the advent of war was a function of their different time-positions in American society. Roosevelt died in 1919. Hearst continued as a force in American affairs. His earlier, negatively regarded reputation for having encouraged hostilities with Spain, therefore, continued to serve Hearst's foes.

The would-be destroyers of Roosevelt's reputation let grow the impression that Roosevelt had his mind hypnotically set on fame and glory in his Cuban service. Forgotten was his passionate love of family and that family's anguish at his decision to enlist in the war. That his second wife was seriously ill and his friends disappointed that he would leave Washington where opportunities beckoned did not enter into this image of the bustling Roosevelt.

"My heart aches for him," his sister Anna wrote their friend Henry Cabot Lodge after Roosevelt's last visit to New York to say goodbye to her and others. She begged Lodge not to withdraw his personal support for Roosevelt as seeming quixotic. He was being warned that entering the army would put an end to his political hopes. Anna—or Bamie as she was called—hoped that New York State, "unpatriotic as it always is," would realize that Roosevelt's decision would be appreciated as unselfish in its primary concern for country.[6]

That Roosevelt yearned to experience war has long been established. He would have as readily prepared to lead a regiment in an assault on Santago in Chile eight years earlier as in Cuba. What was thought-provoking was that this fact was brought up to his discredit in an era that glorified Ernest Hemingway for the mystique that he built around killing and death. To be sure, it was possible in some small measure to hold Hemingway's World War I tales to be an indirect criticism of war's undoing of people. But there could be no doubting Hemingway's admiration for fighters and for killing. Like Roosevelt, he boxed, and boxed to win. Like him, he volunteered for military action and sought out fighting at the front. Like him, he made much of big-game hunting and indeed made much more about the "moments of truth" it was supposed to bring out. Roosevelt concerned himself little with such profundities.

There can be little doubt that it was not for Roosevelt's love of hunting or fighting that he was first ridiculed, then hated. Like Hemingway after him, Roosevelt saw life as a mystery, sought to live it to the full, and spent little time pondering its meaning. But Hemingway had no goals, little social curiosity or social competence, and so entertained a "disillusioned" generation with tales that focused on individuals rather than on society. Roosevelt, by contrast, adhered to family and to nation. He thrilled to life's variety, as in his fascination with the variety of flowers and the world's creatures. And in a time when such qualities of enthusiasm were seen with lacklustre eyes, he stirred resentment and fear among intellectuals.

The ways of public opinion with respect to Roosevelt were wonderful to behold. Finley Peter Dunne was just then, in the late 1890s, making his own reputation as an ironist and philosopher by using the brogue and commentary of his "Mr. Dooley" as a vehicle. Dunne wrote humorously of Roosevelt's exploits in Cuba as head of his Rough Riders, satirizing the strong ego that overflowed through all the chapters of war preparation and attacks in Roosevelt's *The Rough Riders* (1899). Roosevelt had taken Dunne's wit well. "I regret to state," he wrote him, in soliciting his acquaintanceship, "that my family and intimate friends are delighted with your review of my book."[7]

What none could imagine was that Dunne's wit and lightly antiwar skepticism could be taken as wholesale derogation of the high heroics of battle. In fact, Dunne admired men of courage, and he said so. Roosevelt had been as unadulterated a hero at San Juan Hill as American annals had produced, as essential to that crucial battle's triumph as any soldier imaginable. Army military mobilization had been grossly inadequate, and many soldiers suffered and died by that fact. The Spanish had taken poor advantage of their superiority in numbers, materiel, and positions, but they carried live ammunition and used it to deadly advantage. They had fortified positions all the way from Daiquiri to Santiago which could be taken only through searing fire. Of the relatively small American force that landed on the Cuban coast hundreds died and more suffered dreadful wounds, as battle lines were improvised, fire exchanged, murderous advances made.

The Spaniards were more gracious to the desperate Americans than some of their own academic descendants would be in honoring their conquerors:

> I have never seen anything [said a Spanish staff officer] to equal the courage and dash of those Americans, who, stripped to the waist, offered their naked breasts to our murderous fire,

> literally threw themselves on our trenches—on the very muzzles of our guns. We had the advantage of position, and mowed them down by the hundreds; but they never retreated or fell back an inch. As one man fell, shot through the heart, another would take his place. . . .[8]

The camaraderie between Negro troops and white was total; only later would there be partisan accounts concocted by writers who had suffered nothing, been nowhere. Then-Lieutenant John J. Pershing spoke for many who were there when he praised their unity of purpose: "White regiments, black regiments, regulars and Rough Riders, representing the young manhood of the North and the South, fought shoulder to shoulder, unmindful of race or color, unmindful of whether commanded by an ex-Confederate or not, and mindful only of their common duty as Americans."[9]

Roosevelt himself was without peer, wholly ready, wholly alert to circumstances, to the place and condition of his men, and to his own mission. That he was not killed made no sense; he paraded openly on horseback marshaling his Rough Riders. He noted as curious the death of one of his men who had been lying behind a bush and whom he had attempted to rouse by pointing out that he himself was in the open on horseback. The mixture of regiments, Roosevelt's efforts to move them forward in effective array, his constant exposure on horse and on foot finally put him in full command of the critical San Juan Hill assault, which continued under deadly fire. Some 6,600 American troops went into action; the killed and wounded numbered 1,071.[10]

Roosevelt's memoir of the Cuban campaign merited modern rereading. Dunne's humor had been blindly misunderstood by a succeeding generation. Indeed, Roosevelt recounted dreadful things, but with a reverence for his comrades, an intensive concern for their personal qualities, their lives, their precise wounds, which bespoke the dignity of the serviceman. Roosevelt prefaced his account with a poem by Bret Harte, which stoically emphasized duty.[11] And in his relations with officers and soldiers, he asked nothing but service and refused anything less, at one point facing possible retreaters with a revolver in his hand, though retreat was

The assault on San Juan Hill as seen by William J. Glackens.

one of the strategies being considered by his superiors. Throughout Roosevelt's life, he gave full loyalty and aid to ex-soldiers, though some had descended to disreputable depths.

Roosevelt-haters would not leave his Cuban services alone. Millis remarked upon his savage exultation over the dead bodies of defeated Spaniards. Hofstadter was sickened by Roosevelt's pride in having killed a Spaniard with his own hand "like a Jack-rabbit." A more conscientious student of Roosevelt concluded that Roosevelt's last gloating actions would "forever bar him from attaining the immortality of Jefferson, Lincoln, and Wilson."[12] Aside from other debatable points, it seemed strange that historians would prove queasy about Roosevelt's painfully earned hour of triumph in a world that had honored and concluded to continue to honor (if only in part) the character of a Joseph Stalin.

But in addition there was a lack of insight manifested into Roosevelt's life, the materials of which lay generously at hand. He had already shown compassion in the cigar-makers' case. He would continue to give ample evidence of kindliness and goodwill in many directions. His will to victory, however, was philosophical. He would not lie down and die, nor would he treat war as a gentleman's sport. The man who had given his mother and wife to rot in the earth cared little for fleshly habiliments, though he could regret the desecration of his own and nearest:

> That afternoon we made camp and dined, subsisting chiefly on a load of beans which we found on one of the Spanish mules which had been shot. We also looked after the wounded. Dr. Church had himself gone out to the firing-line during the fight, and carried to the rear some of the worst wounded on his back or in his arms. Those who could walk had walked in to where the little field-hospital of the regiment was established on the trail. We found all our dead and all the badly wounded. Around one of the latter the big, hideous land-crabs had gathered in a grew-some ring, waiting for life to be extinct. One of our own men and most of the Spanish dead had been found by the vultures before we got to them; and their bodies were mangled, the eyes and wounds being torn.

The Rough Rider who had been thus treated was in Bucky

> O'Neill's troop; and as we looked at the body, O'Neill turned to me and asked, "Colonel, isn't it Whitman who says of the vultures that 'they pluck the eyes of princes and tear the flesh of kings'?" I answered that I could not place the quotation. Just a week later we were shielding his own body from the birds of prey.[13]

It was time to give up the grotesque "Teddy." The patronizing quotation from Cecil Spring Rice in 1904 that one had always to remember that the President was about six years old also demanded retirement as grossly inaccurate and, essentially, meaningless. Roosevelt knew very well what he was about, and his aims were not too far from those that had been projected by such of his predecessors as Jefferson and Lincoln. They, too, were liable to misconstruance as racists, partisans of special interest (one agrarian, the other industrial), and compromisers.

What they had all sought was a nation capable of eliciting service from those who benefited from its opportunities. It was unlikely that any of these would be able to shake off their special regard for one or another sector of society. All had been born of women, in a particular place, and subject to distinguishing tendencies of one sort of another. All had, in some special way, transcended their direct influences to create larger equations covering friends and even respected foes. After all, Hamilton had given his suffrage to Jefferson in the 1800 election. Stephen Douglas had held Lincoln's hat at the latter's first inauguration. This was the essence of their progressivism: that Jefferson's and Lincoln's nationalism had aspired to go beyond nationalism to humanity at large.

In Roosevelt's case his detractors seized upon his pride in his heritage to hold him unfit for modern regard and to find every reason except graciousness—patronage, expedience, Republican tradition—to explain his famous reception of the Negro leader Booker T. Washington in the White House. Such explanations did not take into account Roosevelt's national perspective or his rigid delimitation of prejudice even when it came from such a well-esteemed friend as Owen Wister, whom Roosevelt especially enjoyed because he helped him keep his interest in literature fresh and current.

So distinguished a leader in the Negro community as Carter G.

Woodson, weighing Roosevelt's services to his people and balancing them against the doubtful Brownsville affair of 1906, concluded that "eloquent defenders of Roosevelt . . . assert that he did so much for the social and civic recognition of the race in dining with Booker T. Washington and forcing upon the Senate and the Southerners the appointment of Dr. William D. Crum as collector of the port of Charleston, that [an anti-Negro] . . . motive could not have thus actuated him [in his dishonorable dismissal of the accused Negro soldiers].[14]

Roosevelt's feelings about Negroes went deeper than Woodson realized. "Why goodness me!" the President exclaimed, when Wister protested Crum's appointment, "Why don't you see—why you *must* see that I can't close the door of hope upon a whole race!"[15] Roosevelt went on to honor the Wister arguments as, in numerous homes throughout the land, reflecting important American viewpoints. But he did not let them deter him from his commitments to the entire nation. He denounced southern unwillingness to give the vote to Negroes while being "equally clamorous . . . that his votes must be counted when it comes to comparing . . . representation with the representation of the white men of the North." And he went on:

> I may add that my own personal belief is that the talk about the negro having become worse since the Civil war is the veriest nonsense. He has on the whole become better. You say you would not like to take orders from a negro yourself. If you had played football in Harvard at any time during the last fifteen years you would have had to do so, and you would not have minded it in the least; for during that time Lewis has been field captain and a coach. . . .
>
> I know no people in the North so slavishly conventional . . . [as] the Charleston aristocrats, on all vital questions. They shriek in public about miscegenation, but they leer as they talk to me privately of the colored mistresses and colored children of the white men whom they know. . . . Too many . . . repeat like parrots the statement that these "educated darkies" are "a deal worse than the old darkies." As a matter of fact almost all the Tuskegee students do well. . . .

> The best people in the south I firmly believe are with me in what I have done. In Trinity College in North Carolina, in Roanoke College, Virginia, here and there elsewhere, they have stood up manfully for *just what I have done. . . .*[16]

Roosevelt would not join the front rank of reformers; had he done so, he would have lost his place in the front rank of politicians. It was as his successor Franklin D. Roosevelt put it: he must first be elected to be able to do anything. But in expanding and intensifying his national views the first Roosevelt not only drew a line between himself and Wister. He drew a line between himself and his old goo-goo associates who had once held the line for responsible government but could no longer stay abreast of the popular upsurge that marked progressivism.

One facet of the President's career deserves special notice. Both Jefferson and Lincoln had been accorded informal literary attention, Jefferson for his phrasings in the Declaration of Independence and his first inaugural address, Lincoln for numerous phrases, passages, and unforgettable speeches. As early as 1899, on his return from Cuba, Roosevelt, with his announcement that he felt like a bull moose, had begun to contribute phrases to the language. His "Bully!" had become stereotyped but helped define his enthusiasm. His concept of "nature fakirs" was always useful in a world that gave opportunities to fakers of various kinds. "Malefactors of great wealth," "muck-rakers," "lunatic fringe," "big stick"—all added color and suggestion to the thinking of his time, and not a little of both promised to serve the future as well.

Roosevelt's services to literature were very special, aside from his own humanistic writing and book interests, which helped give credibility to both in a nation that tended—even on the cultural level—to hold thought a bit lower than action. But for Roosevelt to have lifted the poet Edwin Arlington Robinson out of the trough of failure and given him a place among other Americans of his time was an act unprecedented in political lore.

Since 1896 Robinson had been struggling hopelessly to make an impression with his verse. He had no other competence, and in the process he used up such funds as he had an opportunity for securing himself in trade or elsewhere. His books, *The Torrent and the Night Before* (1896) and *The Children of the Night* (1897), both subsidized, had done nothing for his reputation. Friends had given the Maine dreamer strength to endure and helped him with funds as his family inheritance dwindled.

The very qualities that were Robinson's genius—a forthright questioning of life expressed without the conventional lilts of happy expectation—ensured his failure. Friends helped Robinson acquire a more respectable publication with Houghton Mifflin Company in Boston, which issued *Captain Craig* (1902). It was fairly well reviewed and excited a few readers. But the poetaster Clinton Scollard in *The Critic* spoke for dominant opinion when he recognized that Robinson had substance, but "owed it to his readers, if not to himself, to dress his thought in attractive attire, and not let it go slovenly clad."[17]

Robinson had reached the end of his resources. He had no heart for poetry and nothing to look forward to. Friends got him a timekeeper's job in the subway then being built in New York. In his old-maidish way, Robinson took to drink. An added humiliation was kindly intended: an article in the *New York Sunday World* in May 1904: "A Poet in the Subway: Hailed as a Genius by Men of Letters. Edwin Arlington Robinson Has to Earn His Living as a Timekeeper."

Kermit, a son of the President, attended Groton School in Connecticut. His hall master was a friend of Robinson's. Kermit, hunting for books to read in the master's library, came on *The Children of the Night.* It excited him sufficiently to write for copies from the publisher. He sent one copy to his father, to whom ballads, lyrics, heroic plays, and sagas had been a constant inspiration since childhood. Roosevelt's recognition of Robinson as a poet of stature was an event comparable only to Emerson's artless cordiality to Walt Whitman, who had sent him a copy of his first printing of *Leaves of Grass.* The President, no more than Emerson, feared to be embarrassed by an eccentric, someone, a stranger, who might have been guilty of tasteless or foolish activities. Robinson had been in New York long enough to have convinced its editors that he was too minor to matter.

It was to such a poet that Roosevelt addressed a letter on White House stationary which read: "My dear Mr. Robinson: I have enjoyed your poems, especially 'The Children of the Night' so much that I must write to tell you so. Will you permit me to ask what you are doing and how you are getting along? I wish I could see you."[18]

Meanwhile, friends had learned of Roosevelt's interest through the editor Richard Watson Gilder, whom Roosevelt had queried about Robinson. They immediately thought that a job should be found for Robinson, who had lost his subway place. Gilder made proposals that the President answered with his usual extraordinary pertinacity. He did not think Robinson should go abroad; our literary men were always hurt by going abroad. "If Bret Harte had stayed in the West, if he had not even come East, he might have kept on doing productive work." Roosevelt made little errors; he apparently did not know Harte had come from the East. But he was a man of endless responsibilities and more than handled with due competence a matter that the New York literary establishment had not handled at all.

Roosevelt offered Robinson jobs which he refused out of combinations of hurt pride and reluctance to work at anything but poetry. (He had already turned down a White House invitation to visit for lack of proper clothing.) The two settled finally on a Treasury Department job in New York at two thousand dollars a year: Roosevelt later remarked that he had for once gone back on his civil-service principles, it being understood that Robinson was to concentrate on his poetry. Roosevelt also persuaded the publishers Scribner's to take over publication of *The Children of the Night* from the vanity press that had first issued it.

Finally, in the August 12, 1905, issue of *Outlook*, there appeared Roosevelt's article in appreciation of the book, with full quotations of "Richard Cory" and other poems. The article caused a furor among the professional New York critics who thought it improper for the President to affect literary enterprises they administered. The *Bookman* committed itself to the belief that three-quarters of the volumes of minor verse issued every year contained the "certain sad mysticism" Roosevelt discerned in Robinson's work, to no poetic end. The *New York Times* writer imagined, on no evidence, that there were "numerous poems of religious feeling" in Robinson's collection, which derived from a "wholesome faith." Neither Robinson nor his books were yet in the clear of criticism and assessment, but he now had a foothold in society.

That year of 1905, William James thought over the negative views of Roosevelt held by some of his friends, and wrote one of them:

> Think of the mighty good-will of him, of his enjoyment of his post, of his power as a preacher, of the number of things to which he gives his attention, of the safety of his second thoughts, of the increased courage he is showing, and above all of the fact that he is an open, instead of an underground leader, whom the voters can control once in four years, when he runs away, whose heart is in the right place, who is an enemy of red tape and quibbling and everything that in general the word "politician" stands for. The significance of him in the popular mind is a great national asset, and it would be a shame to let it run to waste until it has done a lot more work for us.[19]

NOTES

1. Richard Hofstadter, *The American Political Tradition* (New York, 1948), 207.

2. An incident in the lives of the Doctors Mayo, while one of them attended the University of Michigan medical school in 1880, is interesting in distinguishing the public status of three notable Americans: "One of the seniors asked to be excused from the next clinic to go into Detroit to hear a lecture by the noted agnostic, Bob Ingersoll. Before giving his permission [Professor George E.] Frothingham began a little lecture on the bad taste of calling a distinguished man like Ingersoll by the nickname Bob. Why, he asked, should Thomas Paine, one of the great constructive forces in the United States after the Revolution, always be called Tom, while Jefferson is never anything but Thomas?" Helen Clapesattle, *The Doctors Mayo* (Minneapolis, 1941), 189. A religious student furiously denounced Frothingham for speaking with respect of Paine and Ingersoll, and the incident caused campus excitement. Since 1880, Jefferson has been accorded the familiar "Tom," sometimes, as with Roosevelt, along with scorn of his "racism." Ingersoll has been largely forgotten.

3. Charles A. and Mary R. Beard, *The Rise of American Civilization* (New York, 1934), 2:425-426, 593ff., is a classic overview of Roosevelt's traditions and purposes.

4. Theodore Roosevelt, *Autobiography* (New York, 1913), 78-80.

5. Elting E. Morison, et al., eds., *The Letters of Theodore Roosevelt: The Years of Preparation, 1868-1898* (Cambridge, Mass., 1951), 1: 65-66.

6. Lilian Rixey, *Bamie*, (New York, 1963), 126-127.

7. Morison, *Letters of Theodore Roosevelt*, 2: 1099; see also Louis Filler, ed., *Mr. Dooley: Now and Forever* (Stanford, 1954), "A Book Review," 103-109.

8. Frank Freidel, *The Splendid Little War* (New York, 1958), 139.

9. *Ibid.*, 173.

10. Theodore Roosevelt, *The Rough Riders* (New York, 1899), 156-157.

11. . . . "But when won the coming battle,
What of profit springs therefrom?
What if conquest, subjugation,
Even greater ills become?"
But the drum
Answered, "Come!
You must do the sum to prove it," said the
Yankee-answering drum.

12. William Henry Harbaugh, *Power and Responsibility: The Life and Times of Theodore Roosevelt* (New York, 1961), 105.

13. Roosevelt, *Rough Riders*, 104-105.

14. Carter G. Woodson and Charles H. Wesley, *The Negro in Our History* (Washington, 1962), 481.

15. Owen Wister, *Roosevelt: The Story of a Friendship* (New York, 1930), 117.

16. *Ibid.*, 254-256.

17. Hermann Hagedorn, *Edwin Arlington Robinson* (New York, 1938), 190.

18. *Ibid.*, 213.

19. William James to Henry L. Higginson, July 18, 1905, in Henry James [his son], ed., *The Letters of William James* (Boston, 1920), 232.

The New Time

The revelation that the twentieth century offered something new—new in the sense that the American and French revolutions had changed perspectives a hundred and more years earlier—became apparent only with time. New types of revolution, affirming different premises, made new philosophical approaches necessary. Technologies that threatened to control other technologies created problems such as Thomas Henry Huxley, who shifted his faith courageously from Christianity to science, did not have to cope with.

Responses to ultimate weapons, final solutions, and dictatorial rule ran all the way from despairing individuality to the adoration of dictators. Nevertheless the need for means to examine conditions in terms of their possibilities for human fulfillment continued to be the last hope for sentient beings. (Some latter-day philosophers, such as B. F. Skinner, boldly declared that this was a vain and unnecessary hope.) Several species of commentator arose who attacked the problem from different vantage points.

Henry Fitz Gerald Heard (1890-1971) won fame under several rubrics, for the most part as H. F. Heard, author of remarkable tales mixing scientific materials or possibilities with moral questions, and as Gerald Heard who wrote more directly on establishing religious values through mystic and substantive data. In older age he became the center of a cult, the most famous member of which was Aldous Huxley, who had moved from science and skepticism to mysticism. But as a young Englishman, a Cambridge graduate concerned for history and science, Heard had begun as a latter-day Christian Socialist, working in Ireland with Sir Horace Plunkett to start agricultural cooperatives. His vision wrecked by Irish freedom fighters who blew up Plunkett's house, he turned to writing and sought to probe the essence and direction of events unleashed by World War I.

He wrote from hindsight; but so did others who surveyed the destruction in human lives and societies and nevertheless justified the massive, world-wide struggles that had just been completed. Others came to conclusions that ranged from sour cynicism to a cheerful readiness to pick up from where they had been in 1912. Heard's approach was different. He sought to read national character as matured by long experience and passed on to descendants, sometimes fatefully. Thus the Boxer rebellion against foreign intruders into China in 1900 cost the lives of a number of them, including the German minister Baron von Ketteler. Kaiser Wilhelm's bitter message to the other German nationals under duress that they behave like the Huns of old "stuck to the Germans and . . . was of incalculable value in that propaganda war which did so much to decide the war of 1914-1918."[1]

Heard went on to examine the intertwining developments in Great Britain and Europe. He noted, for example, the "poor press" that the English received in their efforts to quell the Boers of South Africa. (He could not foresee that where the liberal stance of 1900 supported the Boers as little people fighting the war for freedom, later unfoldings would limn them as racist villains in a world of emerging nations.)

British imperial dreams had ground to a stop. An era of intrigue and jockeying for position had taken its place. The Pacific Ocean, Heard saw, was about to belie its name. And in the Balkans, the killing of the king of Serbia in 1903 by an army junta cast shadows of further disruption in such unpredictable areas. The Russo-Japanese war (1904-1905) demonstrated that war was getting too big for clear national strategy. The Japanese drew closer to British diplomats. The Czar conceded a duma—a parliament without power—following bloody Sunday (January 22, 1905) when a protest of workers proceeding to the palace was fired upon by government troops, who left 70 killed and 240 wounded.

An insurrection was put down in Russia, and atrocities against minorities went unpunished, but there were worldwide protests that promised to maintain the humanistic dreams of labor and its friends and give sanctuary to its activists. In Spain in 1909, the educator Francisco Ferrer was executed on false grounds of treason, but so intense was subsequent resentment that the government drew back, exonerated the dead man, and had his sequestered property restored.

In addition, there was conspicuous liberalism on both sides of the Atlantic. It had built up out of the colleges and churches, and in England created the landmark of Toynbee Hall, dedicated to defining ways and means for building a progressive social order. English efforts inspired American examples. Benjamin Orange Flower published a variety of books that sought to profit from British experience, including *How England Averted a Revolution by Force* (1903). Robert A. Woods, whose Boston labors in settlement work influenced settlements throughout the country, published his *English Social Movements* as early as 1891.

Britain's liberal politics, too, affected American progressive thought, though the latter was so closely bound with its muckraking element as to give a different cast of events from that which took shape in England or, for that matter, anywhere else. Indeed, some midwestern prejudice against the British as such can be found—for example in the writings of Charles Edward Russell and David Graham Phillips, who held Britain to be infested by malignant snobs—which prevented them from close identification with British liberal movements. It would take a later species of Progressive, including Herbert Croly and Woodrow Wilson, with anti-Populist attitudes, to find similarities between the two nations more important than their differences.

Liberalism in Great Britain—there was no Liberal party in the United States and no liberal program to which adherents could comfortably turn—produced a series of measures that were intended both to secure the British empire around the world and also to augment the well-being of the British people. Heard observed the coming to England of old-age pensions and minimum-wage laws for sweated industries. This was the time, however, that also produced the Dreadnought:

> This battleship was undoubtedly both a triumph and a

> problem of specialization. . . . But it has to be mentioned because of its immense political repercussions. It undoubtedly inflamed shipbuilding competition, perhaps unavoidably, and as certainly, what seemed then its almost prohibitive cost (between one and two millions) caused money to be stinted in social reform. The Liberal Imperialists were as clear as any Conservative that national defence came first, and that that defence necessitated that Germany must be kept for ever behind England in her shipbuilding programme. Admiral Tirpitz, in consequence of the *Dreadnought*, increased the Germany naval building plan, according to plan, by adding "Dreadnoughts" to his High Seas Fleet, and the expected and prepared war was a step nearer.[2]

Heard staked his anticipation of advancement and hope in human life on a combination of concern for the life of the individual as well as the life of the human species. He was impressed by—or, rather, found support in—the views of one of the seminal thinkers of his time, Graham Wallas, a founder of the London School of Economics, who argued in his *Human Nature in Politics* (1908) that an approach that sought to influence people solely in terms of their "rational" needs was inadequate. People were indeed "rational" but only as perceived in their deeper sentient strivings.

Heard perceived better than Wallas that people might, unfortunately, be appealed to in terms of speciously rational or patently irrational factors, so that, ultimately, right and wrong might seem interchangeable. He moved increasingly away from social reform, at least in the classical terms with which he had once approached it when religion had been an accepted part of a social reform program. But in this middle period of his life, he still labored to understand the human destiny, not to manipulate it for political purposes but to free it from possibilities of manipulation. In effect, he gave up neither the individual nor the social order but held both subservient to the search for meaning in life. To that extent, there was a "pessimistic" element in his thought, if a reader saw Heard's ideas as to be wholly accepted or wholly rejected. Even if the latter, there was substance to his thought:

> The belief in the Economic Man and his reasonable direct wish to get physical comfort had blinded reformers to the fact that this man was an abstraction. People voted patriotically clean contrary to their own interests. If you were to serve them you must realize their nature. You cannot feed a calf, however much you and it feel it needs, if you offer it the milk in a bowl. Instinct drives its mouth and neck up. Unless you get a bottle and so meet the calf's emotional demand, it will starve to death. You cannot feed an animal on artificial food though it may seem to possess all that the body should require. The body requires much the use of which is obscure. So too with the body politic; economics and reason have to be supplemented with psychology and emotion.[3]

Heard was a Progressive only in the sense that he believed in benevolence as one path toward human assurance and fulfillment. Hence his abortive early labors in cooperatives. Mark Sullivan was the complete Progressive, to whom democratic decisions and the defense of the individual's gains in competition were one and the same. To him, World War I was not a trauma shattering old expectations and forcing a reconsideration of old dreams, old joys. He saw the end of the war as Americans (certainly in the North) generally saw the Civil War: as a triumph of right, a victory over barbarism. He could therefore look retrospectively at a time of progress, of patent advance, technologically, in government operations, city growth, rural renewal, and interesting cultural manifestations from those of magazines—Sullivan had been a strong arm of *Collier's Magazine*—to radio.

Sullivan was a realist but of a type Heard would have found uncomfortable. To Heard, the realist was one who acknowledged the priority of society over self. Sullivan honored society but as a congeries of laws, opportunities, preferences, amusements, and enough tradition to keep them in pleasant balance. Though he did not comment upon that point and differed temperamentally from him, Sullivan could have accepted H. L. Mencken's statement (without making so public a display of his appreciation) that he would stand by his principles all the way to Calvary . . . but no further.

Sullivan's career as journalist and editor could be characterized first and foremost as *useful.* Sullivan had been trained as a lawyer. He had become a top magazine investigator. His high sense of law and material well-being, coupled with a sympathy for the leeway Americans demanded for their personal decisions in and out of government, made him a natural candidate for president of the People's Lobby, which, in 1906, attempted to set up a kind of combination information and legislative service.[4]

Sullivan's greatest achievement as a journalist in the Progressive period was as a leader in the fight against Joseph G. Cannon's dictatorial power in the House of Representatives. Cannon, because of his sanctioned capacity to appoint its working committees, especially its Committee on Rules, which interpreted the legal aspects of the House's operations, had been able to frustrate much Progressive legislation at its source. The end of "Cannonism" in 1910 was a signal achievement of progressivism. In general, it also ended Sullivan's career as an active Progressive.

Sullivan was twenty-five years old when the twentieth century, and his journalistic career, began. He was thus no more than fifty years old when he issued volume one of his panoramic view of *Our Times*, purporting to be the history of the nation from the point of view of the average man. Sullivan worked arduously to make his a true account of all matters ranging from fads and mindless but popular jokes to such major matters as the rise and careers of Theodore Roosevelt and William Jennings Bryan. Writing in the era of the flapper, Sullivan went back twenty-five years to remind the reader of the shirtwaist worn by females of the time, of the street-long skirts and dresses that they fancied and manipulated (photographs illustrated correct and incorrect ways of lifting skirts, as for street-crossing purposes), of men's and boy' fashions, and innumerable other matters having to do with all the tangibles—houses, clothing, transportation, eating, the momentous advent of the automobile. And beyond such matters came theater, opera, books, and songs, both of the season and more or less enduring.

America, as Sullivan depicted it in illustration and text, had in 1900 been a relatively simple if vigorous land. He made it clear that changes had been of staggering dimensions, which were unarguably for the better. Meat that had once been sold in the streets, accompanied by dirt and flies, was now refrigerated. Typewriters had done away with the old maid aunt and created the independent bachelor girl. Popular literature had given the nation such masters as Finley Peter Dunne and Booth Tarkington, the one for political guidance, the other for a detailed and accurate account of the life and works of the average American. Life was not only better. It was richer, and richer for more people.

Nor would Sullivan concede that the nation had advanced only in material terms. It had produced a freedom of opportunity, which had brought forth the talents of such native Americans and immigrants as Thomas A. Edison, Michael Pupin, Joseph Pulitzer, and Charles P. Steinmetz; and these had created wonders not merely within their ethnic groups but for the growing nation at large.

Sullivan wrote at great length of Major William Crawford Gorgas, born in deep poverty, who would not follow ordinary medical ambitions but became an army surgeon, thus honoring two worlds of honest labor. Gorgas became a central figure in the cleaning up of Havana following military victory in Cuba, and one of the central figures in the conquering of yellow fever, first in Cuba, then in the Panama Canal Zone.

There Sullivan introduced another of his peacetime heroes, Lieutenant Colonel George W. Goethals, whose firm, authoritarian management of the canal construction enabled engineers and their workers to overcome its tropical difficulties and create a world's wonder of the time. Gorgas not only eliminated yellow fever there, he fought malaria, quarreling with the economy-minded Goethals all the way. Gorgas went on to fight pneumonia in the gold and diamond mines of South Africa and yellow fever on a worldwide basis. During World War I he served as the masterful head of the Army Medical Corps.

With such a record to point to, Sullivan felt little need to defend America's international or domestic policies. America was a proud land of manifest achievement, which rightly demanded the best of its own and of others who wished to become part of its life. He did not hesitate to express values, some more controversial than others. Thus it may have been true that the discovery of a remedy for diabetes did, as Sullivan asserted, more for human happiness than Henry Cabot Lodge's thirty-one years of service in the Senate accomplished. But whether the vacuum cleaner and the electric flat-iron did more for the average woman than the coming of woman suffrage could be argued.

The problem with Sullivan's dicta was that he was very strong on the benefits to the individual and society from health, good nourishment, and other such gains. What he was less clear about was what could be or ought to be done with the individual after he had been fattened, or lengthened, or whatever he physically required for rehabilitation. Progressivism—Sullivan progressivism—premised a sensible person, judicious in his or her pleasures and concerns and untroubled by psychological or eternal problems. Indeed, Sullivan noted that in his account of changes in American affairs, he had dealt only with material enrichment:

> Whether he was spiritually enriched also, what use man made of his increased years upon the earth, his increased leisure, the energies released by machinery from the need of getting a livelihood—the whole question of the spiritual experiences of man during this period is one about which it is not possible to speak so broadly or so confidently.[5]

Sullivan did not, in his six volumes, find need for defining spiritual experiences too closely. He found something of them in McGuffey's readers, in the spirit of the American Revolution, which he saw as feeding continuing nourishment to the American psyche, and in Christian standards, which sustained as they had in the past the average person. Sullivan did not pursue the topic in depth. Nor did many other Progressives; this was a limitation that could be found in many of their goals and achievements, though far from all.[6]

Sullivan's own version of the causes of social and political discontent in the Progressive era included a number of factors, all material ones. He listed as first the ending of free land and the limiting of natural resources, which would read strangely in an era that discovered fantastic means of intensive farming and new resources that made the very desert useful to government. He listed next the increase in population, "out of proportion to the increase in gold supply," and added as implementing the difficulty the cutting in half of the volume of currency and the increase in silver production.

There followed the Supreme Court decision of 1895 invalidating the income-tax law of that time. In order thereafter came factors of "oppressive" railroad practices, trusts, and monopolies, the growth of factories, the plight of factory workers, the protective tariff, the influence of wealth in politics, and immigration.[7]

Sullivan continued his pursuit of realistic thinking—a species of thinking that defined anticipations bound to be confounded. He was writing after World War I, after the rise and stabilization of the Russian revolution, and in the midst of an unseemly social flippancy, considering the rotund pieties accompanying American intervention in the war. Yet in reporting a last, moving roll call of Grand Army of the Republic veterans, he could not resist adding:

> The reaction of . . . a travelling salesman from Chicago, who spoke with the accent of very recent Americanization, was expressed in a naive question: "Who are them old guys?" In observing that unfamiliarity with our traditions, that unresponsiveness to sentiment about them, one had a glimpse of understanding of that anti-alien feeling which arose in America soon after the Great War, expressing itself in the immigration restriction laws and in some other ways.[8]

Those other ways had included Ku Klux Klan activity, discrimination in schools and civic opportunities, and still other unpleasant, undemocratic ways, which had hurt more than the Chicago salesman. What Sullivan failed to appreciate was that native Americans too had become quite blunted toward and unseeking of their heritage.[9] An unctuous division made between them and newer Americans could only build further the pile of historical rubble on the true history of progressivism. There were Sullivans. There were also Charles Edward Russells, Jane Addamses, and Norman Hapgoods who would sweep away vigorously the artificial intellectual and social barriers set up by shorter-sighted Progressives, however talented, and leave entrances for more helpful understandings.[10]

Sullivan's prideful sense of American accomplishment and of its Anglo-Saxon base enabled him to write things that could in time carry traces of offensiveness and yet could be read as realistic and essentially accurate. The white minorities—and all ethnic groups were minority groups somewhere, somehow—did in aggregate make up the "dominant" race in the nation, even as Sullivan said. Justice Oliver Wendell Holmes, Jr., though he had been wounded in the Civil War and would later receive honors as a Supreme Court liberal, did hand down the decision sustaining an Alabaman constitutional decision in 1901 that deprived Negroes in the state of their vote, thus transgressing the Fourteenth and Fifteenth amendments to the Constitution. Liberals who in the 1940s and 1950s would honor Andrew Jackson as an indispensable friend of democracy, despite his unswerving proslavery policy, would in the 1960s scorn the Progressives for accepting equal but separate doctrine.[11]

This was undiscriminating criticism, which first failed to distinguish Sullivan from some of his ardent, egalitarian colleagues: social workers, founders of the NAACP, and others. Second, it failed to assess American developments as in a state of competition, more than of repression. Alabama laid a heavy hand on its Negro population in the interests of prejudice, which the Supreme Court sustained in the name of states' rights. But other minority groups suffered acutely in mills and sweatshops while finding it all but impossible to get their human rights recognized. As one authority observed:

> There have been few attempts in this country similar to those made in Australia to do away with "sweating," as it is called, either by providing for the placing of labels upon all goods manufactured, *e.g.*, in tenement houses, or, by prohibiting work therein. . . . We have not as yet had any decisions on any of these questions in the United States Supreme Court because of the fact that, in the cases mentioned, state laws of this character have usually been declared unconstitutional, or because the matter would appear to be within the prohibition of a decision of the Supreme Court made with regard to some other matter.[12]

In due course, means would be found to bring strategic cases before the Court and exact rulings that recognized the cruel and unusual results resulting from an outmoded system of labor in twentieth-century America. In due course, too, Alabama law regarding Negroes would move toward reversal. The Progressives worked with popular forces to attain living law. Some was unadventurous, and with no keen sense of human trouble. But even such remained open and vulnerable. Sullivan accepted without protest the Alabama ruling, noting "an increased feeling in the North that it had been unwise judgment to try to force Negro suffrage on the South so quickly after the [Civil] war." But he too was stunned by the outburst of feeling when Edwin Markham's "The Man with the Hoe" was given to the world, and reported the sensation at length.[13]

Finally, there were foreign affairs. Sullivan had no difficulty with them. His long, circumstantial account of the heroic medical work done in Cuba, the Panama Canal Zone, and South America, where deep-seated malignancies were treated by teams of American medical practitioners, ensured that he would have no trouble in justifying American intervention in such ineptly governed areas, or elsewhere.

In 1900 John Hay, once a western poet and secretary to Abraham Lincoln, now Secretary of State, looked at the Chinese situation, saw powers preparing to dismember China into spheres of influence, and proposed his open-door policy. It recognized whatever concessions had been granted by the "stranded whale" and asked assurances from a half-dozen powers, including Japan and Great Britain, that they would recognize the rights of others, including the United States, to trade in China. As Sullivan said, it was like asking every man who believes in the truth to stand up—the liars are obliged to rise first. China's integrity was assured by the agreeing nations.

As Henry Adams, who revered few things or people but who revered Hay, put it: "Nothing so meteoric had ever been done in American diplomacy. . . . For a moment, indeed, the world had been struck dumb at seeing Hay put Europe aside and set the Washington Government at the head of civilization so quietly that civilization submitted. . . . Instantly the diplomacy of the nineteenth century, with all its painful scuffles and struggles, was forgotten, and the American blushed to be told of his submissions in the past."[14]

Shortly after, an explosion of feeling on the part of the Chinese nationalists threatened missionaries and other foreigners at work in China. This was the Boxer rebellion, a feeble effort to drive western powers into the sea. It was crushed without compunction. The Chinese authorities submitted to the overwhelming power of the foreigners and agreed to pay an indemnity for acts of violence committed against the nation's representatives. Of the $315 million that the Chinese paid as an indemnity, $24 million was allotted to the United States. Following some consultations and representations. the money was placed into a special fund to be used to educate Chinese youth in American schools, as Sullivan proudly recounted.

Little honor accrued to Americans for these and other gracious acts of mercy or regard. With time a tradition of scorn for American largesse developed, not only abroad but among elements at home critical of official shipments of food, medical supplies, credits to foreign nations. Some clownish elements both at home and abroad screamed abuse while themselves seizing whatever they could.

Isolationists were enraged at grants of money or supplies to governments committed to anti-American policies. Internationalists, intellectuals, and others interpreted American aid and technological skill as cunningly intended to serve reactionary purposes of one sort or another.

In such an atmosphere Mark Sullivan's display of old news in fresh guise became less and less useful in keeping alive the conservative Progressive view of twentieth-century unfoldings, with more liberal progressivism being accorded lip service at best. Sullivan took his tone from memories of what progressivism had meant to readers and doers in his youth. He lived into another Roosevelt's administration, which he found frustrating when not contemptible. He recalled a Roosevelt, now dead, who had expressed picturesquely personal views and who had fought for measures intended to preserve the individual in a world increasingly centralized. He now at news conferences found all but intolerable a cheerful, smiling Roosevelt who waved a cigarette holder about and pushed for laws that enabled the government to curb competition, create jobs, give and lend money in ways not subject to popular control. This was not the preservation of freedom of opportunity, Sullivan thought; it was the destruction of freedom.

Sullivan's views of Franklin D. Roosevelt tallied in 1935 with those fearful conservatives had expressed in 1915 in reaction to Woodrow Wilson's legislative program. Yet Wilson and the young F. D. R. had both been critical of the energetic activities of Theodore Roosevelt as President. Times changed, and postures toward them as well. In addition it had to be remembered—it was a key stumbling block ever to lose sight of the fact—that all Progressives were not Sullivans. Others were of the legion of Charles Edward Russell, Benjamin C. Marsh, Louis D. Brandeis, Clarence Darrow, Gifford Pinchot, Harold L. Ickes, Upton Sinclair, Lincoln Steffens, Lillian D. Wald, Carrie Chapman Catt, and too many others to mention who survived and bestrode the decades to give advice and some guidance to the new time.

NOTES

1. Gerald Heard, *These Hurrying Years* (New York, 1934), 14.
2. *Ibid.*, 51-52.
3. *Ibid.*, 72. See also Heard's *Morals Since 1900* (New York, 1950), which seeks with high subtlety and example to find relations between national policies and social attitudes.
4. The idea of a People's Lobby continued to attract reformers beyond the Progressive era proper and resulted in the distinguished career of Benjamin C. Marsh, as told in his *Lobbyist for the People* (Washington, D.C., 1953). Among his many achievements was organizing the bloc of reformers who testified before Congress and dissuaded it from selling Muscle Shoals to Henry Ford.
5. Mark Sullivan, *Our Times* (New York, 1925), 1:64.
6. Louis Filler, *The Muckrakers: Crusaders for American Liberalism* (State College, Pa., 1976), "The Spiritual Unrest," 296ff.
7. Sullivan, *Our Times,* 149.
8. *Ibid.*, 27.
9. See preface to Charles A. Beard. *Contemporary American History* (New York, 1914).
10. A sound Progressive statement may be found in Samuel P. Orth, *Our Foreigners* (New Haven, 1921), which deals with the various strands of American ethnic life with candor and disinterestedness.
11. Robert C. Bannister, Jr., "Race Relations and the Muckrakers," in John M. Harrison and Harry Stein, eds., *Muckraking, Past, Present and Future* (University Park, Pa., 1973), 45ff.
12. Frank J. Goodnow, *Social Reform and the Constitution* (New York, 1911), 247.
13. Sullivan, *Our Times* 2:236ff.; cf., Louis Filler, *The Unknown Edwin Markham* (Yellow Springs, Ohio, 1966), 97ff.
14. Henry Adams, *The Education of Henry Adams* (Boston, 1918), 392.

The New Journalism

> And what I was, other American journalists are, and must be, in greater or lesser degree. I was a Paul Pry, a tattler, a crime- and scandal-monger, a daily Boswell to anyone and everyone—all to promote the business interests of others. I realize, now, though I could only occasionally, and vaguely, realize it then, that at times I was worse than all this—in politics I was a veritable Hessian of the press, even a hired assassin of character, striking from the dark, or from behind the mask of journalistic zeal for public welfare—all to promote the political interests of others. At other times . . . I was an aid to piracy, helping to hold up commercial enterprises, and firing broadsides of abuse until the booty was won. Often I had to attack men and measures that I secretly longed to champion. On occasions, however, when it was not unprofitable to my masters, I favored good laws and good men.[1]

The penny press had done much to democratize American communication and, as always, in so doing, had inevitably dragged filth as well as rich soil in its wake. But its day was done. The war, new industry and transportation, the closing of the territorial gap between the Mississippi River and the Pacific Ocean, the growth of cities with new, exotic populations had created new communication needs.

The old journalism had been headed by editors and proprietors of Anglo-Saxon derivation. They had advocated reforms but reforms designed to augment freeholds for farmers and free enterprise for energetic youth. The new industry fulfilled their prophecies but while doing so raised questions respecting the awesome power that had accumulated in relatively few hands. The erstwhile reform journalists, themselves well established in great buildings devoted to publishing their papers, found themselves in greater fear of the restless and insecure laborers than of their economic masters. Their major premise was a need for law and order, whether the emergency was one of hard times or freezing weather.

These editors of an older tradition were often distinguished and intelligent, and they drew young men and women of talent and distinction to their offices. Stephen Crane was a reporter for the *New York Herald* and *New York Tribune* before issuing his sensational *The Red Badge of Courage* (1895). Though of patently artistic flare, he continued to write journalism, some notable as during the Spanish-American War. It is unlikely that had he lived, he, any more than Theodore Dreiser, would have greeted the Progressive era with pleasure. Pessimists of Crane's stamp endured progressivism rather than contributed to it. They lacked its faith in human nature and the meaning of life.

Lafcadio Hearn, though sensitive to the point of neurosis and dreaming of strange settings in which a man of his shyness and lack of self-esteem could live Poesque fantasies, was able to earn bread on the *Cincinnati Enquirer* and then the *Commercial*, and in New Orleans on the *Item* and then the *Times-Democrat*. But such personalities only made colorful hardening journalistic properties. Charles A. Dana of the *New York Sun* symbolized it. He fought the "whisky ring," and made his phrase "Throw the Rascals Out" famous. But he had forgotten the dreams that had made Brook Farm a community of generous anticipations for all society. Surviving Henry J. Raymond of the *New York Times* and Bennett and Greeley of the *Herald* and *Tribune*, respectively, Dana stood high among the giants of the postwar period as grimly representative of older ideals and evidence of what had happened to them.

They did not suffice for the new time. Brilliant, cynical, and suspicious of workingmen and aliens as Dana was, he could speak neither to them nor help them define their relations to the older populations. With new editors coming into the field, he would neither welcome them nor learn from them. Joseph Pulitzer was one of the most notable of the new breed. Himself a young immigrant from Hungary who served briefly in the Union army and became a reporter and political figure in St. Louis, Pulitzer became part owner of the *Westliche Post* in that city, then in 1878 purchased and combined its *Post* and *Dispatch* into his first successful venture.

In 1883 he moved upon New York City where he acquired the *World*, later establishing the *Evening World*. His politics were Democratic, his journalism enterprising. Before his eyesight began palpably to fade he interested himself in political campaigns. It was symbolic of the contrast between the old journalism and the new that Dana's *Sun* maliciously reported Pulitzer's public speeches, which still carried traces of his Old world heritage, in dialect, hinting also, not too subtly, at his half-Jewish background.

Nothing better illustrated Pulitzer's energy and resourcefulness than the welcome he gave to Elizabeth Cochrane, a young girl who had built a reputation with the *Pittsburgh Dispatch* as "Nellie Bly" with fearless reporting of poverty and need, giving special concern to the lot of the working woman. In 1887 she persuaded Pulitzer to hire her to pretend insanity so that she could be committed to Blackwell's Island and observe conditions under which its mentally ill patients lived. Her reports made a sensation and brought reforms. As a regular *World* reporter, Nellie Bly turned again to her investigations of the poor and the working girls, whom she joined on jobs in sweatshops. She detailed her experiences to *World* readers. Such exploits, coupled with such others in a lighter vein as her experiences with "mashers," intrigued and enlightened her newspaper following. They helped raise circulation, as Pulitzer and others explored formulas for catching and holding attention.

Their working-class readers and "petit-bourgeois" readers of several sorts had vital concerns about their very place in society: their jobs and businesses, their housing, their transportation, their taxes, and their general power to affect customs and laws. Yet they also hungered for excitement and what would later be called human interest. So it was that Nellie Bly would be remembered not for her *Ten Days in a Mad-House* (1887), interesting and evocative as it was, not for her accounts of the tragic lot of working-class girls and bewildered family men and women, but for her 1889 trip around the world in emulation of Jules Verne's fictional hero, whose feat she topped by eight days.[2] Pulitzer provided his readers with all the details. They were, to a degree, educational, as were other, numerous details Pulitzer provided in local reform and political developments. Their major quality, and the quality that made Pulitzer a power in society, was that they revealed a sense of the human nature underneath the facade of social concern.

Others built the new journalism, notably William Randolph Hearst, whose murky career ranged from plans of the highest danger to the Republic to campaigns of patent distinction, engrossing both the doubtful and admirable aspects of democratic hopes.[3] There was a striking contrast between the muckraker Hearst and the proto-muckraker William T. Stead who in the 1880s, created a sensation in London by excoriating it as "the modern Babylon." Stead was not alone. Others abroad, notably Henry W. Massingham, editor of the *Star*, the *Daily Chronicle*, and later the *Nation*, contributed attention-seizing journalistic techniques on serious issues that affected popular opinion.[4] But Stead's peculiar approach made him as effective and ultimately ineffective in America as at home. That his journalese affected the future there can be no doubt. But there were differences between American muckraking and British sensationalism, which were essentially the result of national differences.

Great Britain in the 1880s and 1890s proliferated movements designed to aid victims of its industry and urbanization, and intellectuals and philanthropists with plans for society's reconstruction. It also created the Salvation Army, whose evangelical leader, General William Booth, thirsted to lead the dregs of society back to moral and religious paths.

It was no accident that Stead should have helped Booth prepare his *In Darkest England and the Way Out* (1890). Though Stead, in his *Pall Mall Gazette*, appealed to a more respectable readership than Booth, both sought Christian action, a civic church, a religious fellowship. Stead made charges that exposed him to a libel suit. He introduced the interview to British journalism. His most memorable campaign involved prostitution, which he dramatized by personally "purchasing" a young girl to show it could be done.[5]

Such doings created a sensation on both sides of the water and inspired other journalists. Stead's personal campaign in Chicago, in

1893-1894, intended to foster "an alliance between labour and religion," was astonishing; he brought together hordes of reform-minded people who hoped to persuade saloon keepers, labor leaders, and philanthropists to build civic centers in which hearts could be softened, religious feelings renewed, and Chicago transformed. Stead's book, *If Christ Came to Chicago* (1893), was one of many that presumed to imagine Christ's program for their times. Such books linked their authors with Christian Socialists but much less with the Progressives who related vice more realistically to religion, when at all.

Certainly a licentious public nerve was touched by revelations of the vice-liquor-prostitution connections and, at best, they tended to become lurid. Progressives couched their investigations in terms of causes, legal conditions, experts, and commissions. Muckrakers of the Stead persuasion were the equivalent of revivalists who stirred their audiences to a frenzy but left them little as a residue.

Most thoughtful of the new American journalists and among the most influential was E. W. Scripps, creator of the first newspaper chain and of many innovations identified with the popular press. Outstanding in the era was his search not for sensationally attractive journalistic devices but for homely and enduring policies that would capture readers and keep them loyal.

Scripps dreamed dreams but he was neither a rebel nor a utopian. "Once I was a poor man and hated the capitalists," he recalled, "and now I am a capitalist and see the other side of the question."[6] He sought realism, and, though he continuously assessed himself and others, his true genius lay in reflecting the attitudes and impulses of the general public. Thus he coldly calculated that one native white was a better prospect for readership than two or three Negroes or "recent" immigrants. On the other hand he attacked "dirty businesses and department stores deliberately to reduce the volume of their advertising and the pressure they put on his editors. Scripps would have been glad to publish a newspaper without advertising but this would have required a circulation of unparalleled magnitude. And he never ventured far from profit-making policies.

was survival. Therefore, "whether the people of the nation desire it or not, the United States must be a warlike nation; it must fight and conquer or be conquered." He conceded that he was a snob and aristocrat who "did not love my workingmen for whom I loved to work." He deemed it necessary for "superior" races to win in their worldwide struggles with inferiors. Yet he was skeptical of elite classes and of all humanity and privately imagined that miscegenation might prove the best alternative to catastrophic world wars between peoples of various colors.

The paramount fact was that Scripps's views were a mixture of those of his readers, for whom uncomfortable days were ahead as "inferior" breeds boldly appealed to other principles and won adherents from among the smug and bigoted classes. The NAACP was practically created by muckrakers and Progressives. Their services to immigrant groups went on throughout their era and beyond in personal patronage, friendships, and relationships, as well as in settlement, literary, and political work. As late as 1928, such Progressives as Norman Hapgood and Henry Moskowitz made their brave if hopeless stand for the "Lincoln of the City Streets," Alfred E. Smith.

In his time, Scripps's defense of labor unions, of the rights of the poor and the defrauded, and his editorial emphasis on the dignity of the workers and their wives and children constituted benign and valuable social policies, which laid the groundwork for reform. The rebels and the malcontents could not so much as breathe without the tolerance and support of such entrepreneurs as Scripps.

Newspapers did not suffice for the new time. Had there been only newspapers populism would have stumbled into some species of progressivism no doubt, but as hard, separate interests unblended by the positive values of nationalism, of intraethnic sympathies and appreciation, of the admiration for achievement that gave poor youth of talent and ambition like Upton Sinclair and Ben B. Lindsey national forums.

Newspapers were necessarily written in haste; their contents had almost to be read at a glance. Although they were seedbeds for writers and statesmen, they could mature few of them. Magazines were another matter. Their contents could be deliberated and projected. One issue of a magazine could bring together the contents of a number of issues of newspapers, boiled down and perhaps refined. It could expound philosophical principles and political science.

Magazines thus constituted a second chance for judgments and decisions, for taking the long view, for combining public issues with human interests in a manner that influenced the reader with more than information. They could appeal to the psychology of readers as well as their thirst for details and analysis.

Pamphlets had once constituted a forum of deliberation, but for the new mass audience of readers they could not suffice. Little people could not build up pamphlet collections, as such reformers as Wendell Phillips and William Henry Seward had in the 1830s and the 1840s. Audiences and voters could not mentally sustain close-knit, interwoven arguments. Serious reformers had to look beyond circles of intellectuals and social equals. Even problems of good taste in phrasing, in the citing of acceptable examples of points made, could be controlled only to a degree, since the various sectors of society stood unequally in respect to the public figures they honored, the social issues they understood.

Yet the magazines could not be everything to everyone; they had to meet the challenge of the readers' spontaneous response. Purchasers did not range thoughtfully among publications to determine which would profit them the most. They responded to the shouts of magazine butchers, proclaiming headlines. They glanced at magazine covers and were caught by an illustration, a title, a name. Thus, the shrewdest editor had to trust his instincts as much as his experience and principles if he was not to be confounded by failures not explained by logic.

The popular magazine revolution of the 1890s, therefore, spoke well for the time's reading public. It had broad interests, ranging from Queen Victoria's court to the battle for reaching the North Pole. It demanded entertainment, including light, romantic tales and mainly trifling verse, but it gave in return literacy, concentration, and a sense of society. The 1890s publications did not emphasize social issues; had they done so, troubled women, businessmen, and workers would have looked elsewhere for diversion. What they sought from magazines in that era was a sense of relationship to others. They still saw social dilemmas as subject to solutions by practical people.

The new magazines needed new writers. The late Victorian years had grown a species of raconteur who lacked the intellectual power of Dickens and Thackeray but who could spin lengthy yarns to no end; George Gissing described the unhappy lot of such in his *The New Grub Street* (1891). Now, especially in America, came new scribes who struggled with the life of the cities and populations: writers trained on newspapers to study police blotters and walk the streets looking for "stories" and burning to write fiction that would capture the reality of the new America of urban living, technology, Darwinian thinking, and democratic literacy.

David Graham Phillips was the prototype of such writers, though he was to be preceded by such others, successful in journalism and fiction, as Crane, Harold Frederic, and Richard Harding Davis. Phillips's early fiction exploited his newspaper experience with point, though it was later misused by imperceptive scribblers who could not concentrate on the problem of Phillips's growth as a writer. In one novel, Phillips had a newspaper editor advising a woman journalist—Phillips was an early proponent of woman's place in industry—on how to approach a story:

> Send us what you see—what you really see. If you see misery, send it. If not, for heaven's sake, don't "fake" it. Put humour in your stuff—all the humour you possibly can—"fake" that, if necessary. But it won't be necessary, if you have real eyes. Go to the workmen's houses. Look all through them—parlours, bedrooms, kitchen. Look at the grocer's bills and butcher's. Tell what their clothes cost. Describe their children. Talk to their children. Make us see just what kind of people these are that are making such a stir. You've a great opportunity. Don't miss it. And don't, don't, do "fine writing." No "literature"—just life—men, women, children. . . .[7]

During the birth and consolidation of the new democratic magazines of the 1890s—of *Munsey's*, *McClure's*, and *Collier's* among others, their individualism underscored by their names—the new journalists did not presume to lecture readers on social problems. They worked to instruct and entertain them. Nor did they talk down to their readers. Their words were as carefully chosen as though for submission to *Harper's* or *Century Magazine.* Messageless, they were creating an instrument for communication, uncommitted in purpose. What message they might ultimately carry would depend in part on the will of the readers themselves.

Important in this opening of cultural vistas was the idea of fiction. S. S. McClure highlighted fiction in his thought when he conceived his vision of a "syndicate"—an agency to circulate writings to many papers at a small charge rather than to single publications at a large one. His authors ranged from Helen Hunt Jackson to H. C. Bunner, an entertainer. Both types of fiction writer proved satisfying to his readers.

The concept of a syndicate was in the air; McClure was not the first to imagine it, though he fought for it hardest. It became one of the sagas of the new journalism to recount his trials in establishing first his syndicate, next his magazine, which should have involved little risk since McClure had his own backlog of syndicated material to draw from.[8]

Yet success came hard. Established editors were cold to the mercurial young entrepreneur who offered to save them money. They were well to do and in no need of his advice on money getting. Less pompous newspapermen were skeptical of his editorial wisdom and preferred to depend on the great magazines for news about good storytellers. McClure won over customers by persistence, by the support of such sound literary properties as Bret Harte, Sarah Orne Jewett, and the humorist Bill Nye. Still, when McClure established his magazine in 1893 it moved sluggishly. The economic crash of that year did it no good. Money was tight. But it was tight for everyone. McClure, visiting in Chicago, tried to collect syndicate money from the editor of the *Chicago Inter-Ocean,* but the editor smiled. "Money? Oh, no! We can't give you any money. Look out there!" McClure looked out of a window at a crowd pressing against the doors of a bank. It was his first realization of what the panic had done to the public finances.[9]

The heart of the question of the magazine's growth lay in what people wished to read. Once again, the people's choice—a choice that spelled out tenets vital to *McClure's* success—spoke well for them. Ida M. Tarbell had been wooed away from Paris by McClure and set to retrace the life of Abraham Lincoln. McClure had been impressed by Tarbell's clear style of writing, her care with detail, but he had been most impressed by the calm and maturity with which she had set about studying French biography.

Lincoln had already been canonized when Tarbell began her work on his life. Yet he was but thirty years dead. Numerous friends and relatives of his still lived. His earliest scenes were still much as they had been. Tarbell, by visiting them, talking to erstwhile neighbors, collecting old letters, photographs, and homely recollections of his actions and responses brought him to life as the official records, the cabinet-level accounts, the awestruck interpretations could not. Tarbell gave Lincoln himself back to his countrymen to love as well as revere.

McClure's outgoing approach and his eagerness to meet subscribers halfway opened vistas for writers as well as readers. McClure's educational perspective resulted in a search for balance in presentation, which was to influence the form of articles on business, labor, municipal government, and other sensitive topics. Radicals would be impatient with McClure's evenhandedness and insist that in effect it aided the patently wrong position. McClure, they charged, evaded the need for taking a stand and determining due action. What McClure certainly achieved was a democratic forum, one that would reveal as never before the genuine wants of the many-faceted reading public.

NOTES

1. William Salisbury, *The Career of a Journalist* (New York, 1908), 522.
2. *Nellie Bly's Book: Around the World in Seventy-two Days* (New York, 1890).
3. Louis Filler, *The Muckrakers: Crusaders for American Liberalism* (State College, Pa., 1976), 127ff. Pulitzer's and Hearst's methods merit closer comparative study. Thus Hearst's envy of the Nellie Bly exploit caused him to send *three* boys around the world in a race to beat her record. There was suspicion that the race was "fixed" for a favorite boy, a Chicagoan, to win. "The circulation of Mr. Hearst's new Chicago paper was increased.

Advertising rates were advanced." Salisbury, *Career of a Journalist,* 193.

4. Alfred F. Havighurst, *Radical Journalist: H. W. Massingham* (New York, 1974).

5. Raymond L. Schults, *Crusader in Babylon: W. T. Stead and the Pall Mall Gazette* (Lincoln, Neb., 1972). 128ff.

6. Oliver Knight, ed., *I Protest: Selected Disquisitions of E. W. Scripps* (Madison, Wis., 1966), 149. The title is a misnomer. For Scripp's further views, *passim.*

7. David Graham Phillips, *A Woman Ventures* (New York, 1902), 87.

8. Louis Filler, introduction to *My Autobiography,* by S. S. McClure (New York, 1963). This work was given much of its literary finish by Willa Cather, who was a McClure editor.

9. Peter Lyon, *Success Story: The Life and Times of S. S. McClure* (New York, 1963), 125.

Writer-Reformers

That a reform era was in the making was not at first widely recognized, and it would not be conspicuously noticed until about 1905. The reading public was accustomed to sensationalism. The gaudy journalism of the Spanish-American War period had inured it to desperate headlines and imaginative illustrations. The fervor of the Populist crusade was vivid in memory. The excitement of public affairs continued to be reflected in the mayoralty triumphs of Tom Johnson in Cleveland, of Carter H. Harrison in Chicago, and of Samuel M. Jones—"Golden Rule" Jones—in Toledo. Jones added a fillip to reform by printing for his workmen in the highly successful Acme Sucker Rod Company disarming *Letters of Love and Labor.*

Although the reform era displayed genuinely startling sensations of both civic dedication and also civic corruption, it built upon all that had been earlier attempted and gained. Hoyt King, secretary of the Legislative Voters' League in Chicago, reported on his work in the academic *Annals of the American Academy,*[1] which, in addition, displayed reform talents in other fields. The distinguished New York tenement house deputy commissioner, Lawrence Veiller, discussed his problems in the same pages. Lillian Wald reviewed medical inspection facilities in the public schools. And there were articles on the functioning of municipalities; Professor John A. Fairlie of the University of Michigan was just then beginning his career in administration and contributed an article.

The death of Hazen S. Pingree in 1901 brought out a remarkable quantity of appreciation of his bold measures and stubborn egalitarianism, even from his recent enemies. Altgeld, too, was dead, and "there is scarcely one [paper] that does not have some good words" for the man who had not too long before been vilified for having freed from prison the still-living survivors of the 1886 Haymarket bombing in Chicago.[2]

The papers reflected generous opinions and actions of many kinds. Clarence Darrow, already a veteran of labor court cases, published a book, *Resist Not Evil*, which sweepingly repudiated not only capital punishment for murder but even imprisonment. He would have done away with the courts. The Christian socialist of the 1890s, Reverend George D. Herron of Iowa, had emerged as a wholly committed socialist, and, to the horror of his church, divorced and remarried. For this he was roundly denounced by the Reverend Josiah Strong, who believed himself, as author of *The New Era* (1893) and *Religious Movements for Social Betterment* (1900), a reformer. His reform meant carrying the gospel of Christianity to inferior peoples. Academic derogators of religion would later remember Strong and forget Herron. Herron entered into activities that led from the Rand School of Social Science in New York, which he founded with his wife's money, to a relationship with President Woodrow Wilson, before disillusionment darkened Herron's vision of life.[3]

Wilson himself in 1902 caused wide comment as the new president of Princeton University. His qualifications for the post were acknowledged. He was, however, the first nontheologian in an "unbroken" line of theologians to head the institution.[4]

The writing and intellectual world was self-conscious of its role in the unfolding of new social attitudes and preferences. Edward A. Ross's separation from Stanford University because of Mrs. Leland Stanford's dislike of his enthusiasm for municipal ownership and the ending of Asiatic immigration, stirred indignation in both conservative and radical papers. It roused talk of founding a "reformist" college where free thought would be permitted. Yellow journalism was decried by Abram S. Hewitt as well as by both conservative papers like the *New York Press* and liberal papers like the *Independent*; the "Yellies's" editorial abandon—Hearst's especially—seemed to critics to trigger or encourage such events as the recent assassination of McKinley. One journalist loyally defended his profession for its honesty and financial incorruptibility. By 1906, however, Julian Hawthorne, the son of Nathaniel, who capped a hectic literary career as sports editor of the *New York American*, attacked journalism as the great destroyer of literature.[5]

Hawthorne's viewpoint was indirectly contradicted by articles that assessed the humor of Finley Peter Dunne and George Ade, published in the regular press, as literature and by Upton Sinclair's young, pre-*Jungle* complaint that critics were impressed by affluence and the prestige of publishers rather than by quality. Sinclair cited himself as a victim of the system. The *New York Times Saturday Review* saw Sinclair as a pot calling the kettle black. Frank Norris, soon tragically dead of a burst appendix at thirty-two years of age, in *World's Work* argued that novels must prove something—an opinion that received curious endorsement from Reverend Charles M. Sheldon, author of *In His Steps* (1896), a shabby novel in the if-Christ-came-to-Chicago tradition, which for many years enjoyed the reputation of having sold more copies than any other book in the United States after the Bible.

The search for realism went beyond the immediate present. Norman Hapgood's biography of George Washington was noticed not in the traditional way as furnishing an occasion for reverence but for showing that moral conditions of Washington's time "were decidedly not superior to those in which we live today."

The explosion of muckraking, then, came within a context of writing that was yet to grasp fully its readers' potential:

> Gradually . . . publishers . . . came to learn the practical disadvantages of servility and slowly the fawning clipsheet gave way to the paper that stood on its own independent feet. It was seen that success depended upon bona fide circulation, which in turn rested with favoring the reader in terms of progressive and fearless news-gathering methods.[6]

The great advertisers expanded their campaigns as their market grew and were an inevitable factor in the careers of the magazines as they in turn expanded their functions during the Progressive era. Although advertisers concerned themselves with every aspect of their public relations, they were able to control only portions of them as public interest focused on the entire field of communication and picked and chose topics and treatments within it.[7]

A striking development within advertising was the public relations counselor, and most successful in its first stage of development was young Ivy Lee, who emerged from Princeton University and journalism to win over corporation executives to his views. Lee argued they had more to gain from exposing their affairs to public scrutiny than in trying to hide their secrets behind doors. This provided outsiders with a chance to conjecture and to ferret out embarrassing secrets. Lee's great discovery was that a posture of candor gave the company room for presenting its version of events.

Lee began by winning over none other than George F. Baer, president of the Philadelphia and Reading Railway and leader of the coal-mine operators who were in 1902 resisting the United Mine Workers' demands in the Pennsylvania anthracite regions. Baer was memorable for believing that workers were best protected by those to whom "God in His Infinite Wisdom has given control of the property interests of the country." Lee persuaded Baer among others that good public relations would neutralize the criticism and satire such views had inspired.

Thus, when an accident occurred in 1906 on the Pennsylvania Railroad line at Gap, Pennsylvania, instead of "the customary machinery of news suppression" being thrown into gear, Lee had reporters invited to the scene at the railroad's expense; facilities for reporting set up; "facts which reporters had not thought to ask about were offered." The Pennsylvania "found itself basking in one of the few good presses it had enjoyed since the turn-of-the-century."[8]

Lee's biographer, then of Princeton University, did not notice that Lee's activities were viewed with suspicion by embattled reform elements, which saw the work of railroads in terms drastically different from what Lee and his clients did. Nor did he peruse Upton Sinclair's later chapter on "Poison Ivy" Lee, which saw him as a fatal figure in American communication.[9] Certainly the great corporations had to formulate a public image and, in doing so, to counterpose their views to those of their detractors. But how much the direct lie legitimately served them in the long run would be mooted by public opinion pollsters.

In the new time, writers who became conspicuous worked with

facts and personalities but merged with others who studied human nature and human need, and still others, activists, who sought tangibly to create a better life. This was the difference between the new breed of muckrakers and their predecessors.[10] Although the latter could perceive sorrow and human waste in American life, they lacked information that could direct readers to action or the art that could stir those readers to creative understanding of social conditions and their victims. As late as April 1902, "Appalling Corruption" could be detailed in St. Louis with no serious suggestion for combatting it.[11] Not until a year later, when Lincoln Steffens's article, "The Shamelessness of St. Louis" appeared in *McClure's*, was action instigated and then not only in that embroiled city, but in the state, and to a degree in the nation.[12]

Steffens developed an approach to his new work slowly. In May 1902 he was no more than traveling about looking for subjects and writers for *McClure's* and trying "to educate myself in the way the world is wagging, so as to bring the magazine up to date." He was thinking—with Sam McClure's encouragement—of writing articles on "Actual Municipal Government," at home and abroad. His quite vague project seems to have derived from goo-goo sources; Albert Shaw of the American *Review of Reviews* had impressed thoughtful people with his well-researched *Municipal Government of Great Britain* (1894). Steffens jotted down informally that he would like to "take in some of the interesting places I have seen, places and men. The bosses especially interest me."[13]

Plans for a new approach to readers were no more clear to others on *McClure's*. Ida M. Tarbell's round, accurate prose had won readers, satisfied or diverted by her biographies of Lincoln and others. Her history of the Standard Oil Company implicitly—but only implicitly—defined attributes proper to legitimate business in modern times. Ray Stannard Baker was more general in his interests, ready, it seemed, to research carefully almost anything. However, a close student of his writings on the state of the nation's economy, labor racketeering, and his most famous title, *Following the Color Line*, would have been able to sense tension behind Baker's steady balancing of pros and cons, a tension that added interest to his work. Baker's reputation became such that Woodrow Wilson as President would later, incredibly, commission him to visit England and bring back a personal report on the condition of that war-locked nation.[14] That one man could have been so delegated in some ways defined the difference between the democratic controversies of the 1900s and the higher and dangerous degree of specialization that developed in the decade following.

Muckraking, as it unfolded, confusedly suggested, on one side, accurate and penetrating reportage, on the other side irresponsible sensationalism. This was because both elements were precipitated by the public clamor for information. Hearst influenced writers to emphasize the lurid aspects of the facts. McClure, at the other extreme, leaned backward to appear disinterested in his articles' presentation. The two categories of muckraking could be emotionally and even maliciously confused. Mark Sullivan identified David Graham Phillips as a "Hearst writer," though the bald facts should have forced Sullivan to write Phillips down—or up—as a "Lorimer writer." Phillips had little to do with Hearst, aside from his "Treason of the Senate" series, and he had much to do with George Horace Lorimer of the *Saturday Evening Post.*

In point of fact, Phillips was his own writer, as the full canon of his writings showed. However, it was true that the two major promontories of sensationalism and fact-finding were so hazily defined that whole legions of writers could be indiscriminately seen as committed to one or the other.

Most of them were neither, having the temperament of artists or litterateurs, rather than researchers. Phillips had gone deliberately into journalism to overcome his tendency toward dreaming and aloofness. Lincoln Steffens's *New York Commercial Advertiser* had attracted artistic types more than fact-finders. Norman Hapgood, then of Steffens's staff, before editing *Collier's,* was fascinated by the theater and literary criticism. His brother Hutchins Hapgood had on the *Commercial Advertiser* begun his search for human interest writing, which was to be his contribution to muckraking literature.

Abraham Cahan, before editing the *Jewish Forward,* was interested in writing fiction about his people. Steffens himself, and Ray Stannard Baker, dreamed of writing novels. Brand Whitlock actually wrote a then-esteemed novel, *The Turn of the Balance* (1907), and others in the midst of his careers as mayor of Toledo and ambassador to Belgium. Upton Sinclair was never a journalist as such, but critics of his fiction saw it as journalistic in method.

Social perspectives were involved in such judgments. Woodrow Wilson in the 1890s, a highly esteemed speaker on the academic circuit, had in his essay "Mere Literature" defended literature from the scorn of practical men for impractical writing. Though supposedly a historian, Wilson took pride in his style and was critical of historians who were constricted by mere "facts." Others defended "literature" even more vehemently and were suspicious of mere journalism, especially when it challenged the status quo; Phillips probably suffered more at the hands of criticism for that reason than any other writer of the time. There was an interesting contrast between Phillips and Theodore Dreiser, both journalists, both from the Midwest, one from a liberal, well-to-do home, the other from a demoralized home. Dreiser as a novelist was better received than legend later recounted. His work was the reverse of that of the muckrakers'. As a contributor to the premuckraking *Success Magazine* and other publications, Dreiser wrote with envy and adoration of successful people, and saved his artistic gloom for his tales.

As they grappled with the will of their readers, muckrakers developed a variety of characteristics. Their work tended to be local but with national implications. Steffens, for example, seems not only to reveal a particular civic condition but to influence its workings and to generalize beyond it. His St. Louis article alerted not only the city's reformers, but reformers everywhere. It threw a national spotlight on what had previously been a parochial affair. Steffens later thought he had discovered the roots of corruption: the businessmen who gained by the biggest franchises and contracts. But this revelation, if it was one, blinded him to the dynamics of reform. St. Louis politicians could dampen local unrest through court-politics-press control. They had less power outside the city. Steffens noted that Joseph W. Folk, the young circuit attorney who exposed municipal bribery there, became governor at a time he could not have been elected circuit attorney. Steffens thought this was because Missourians still imagined they favored justice. He failed to notice that it was because Missourians outside St. Louis could vote for Folk without being socially or physically harmed.[15]

Steffens's analytical tone was one that most top muckrakers worked to achieve, in addition to other characteristics that gave them their individual image. There tended also to be a note of hope in the darkest reports. Thus Steffens in his Chicago story ("Half Free") reported: "December, 1903.—Chicago has taken up since administrative graft. The Council is conducting an investigation which is showing the city government to have been a second Minneapolis. Mayor Harrison is helping, and the citizens are interested. There is little doubt that Chicago will be cleaned up."[16]

Secretly, Steffens had little faith in the people. His search was for key men—among reformers but also among corruptionists—who would agree to abide by the golden rule. Steffens's obsession with this idea led him into utopian efforts to make a reformer not only of Boston boss Martin Lomasney but also of the truculent *Los Angeles Times* publisher General Harrison Gray Otis, a hater of unions who was determined to exact revenge for the dreadful bombing by unionists of his plant in 1910.

Steffens later advised the communist agent Whittaker Chambers to pay no attention to reformers of his generation.[17] But since Chambers himself repudiated communism, this judgment left open the question of what there was left to respect. For working purposes it could be held that whatever else Steffens and his Progressive associates did or did not accomplish, they did end the old, cumbersome city rings and set up new civic machinery for a new time. It creaked, and was preempted by new bosses. But along with bossism came reform and public participation. Reform was not a matter of a day's work. It was a building process, or it was nothing.

The public did more than support or repudiate reform; it responded to images that gave it a sense of relationship to personalities and events. People were ethnic as well as economic. They were interested in entertainment as well as education. Creative writers and editors took such facts into consideration, as did Hamilton Holt in the volume he culled from pages of the *Independent*, comprising *The Life Stories of Undistinguished Americans as Told by Themselves* (1906). These included a variety of ethnic men and women, as well as the memoirs of a "Negro peon," a Japanese servant, and a "Chinaman."

Magazines like William Jennings Bryan's *The Commoner* and La

Follette's magazine named for himself were too predictable to have a broad readership. The challenge to circulation was to locate themes and treatments that "anyone" could find of interest. No elements in the Progressive era did this better than the muckrakers. *McClure's* did not gain significantly in circulation as a result of muckraking.[18] However, its effectiveness as an organ of public consequence is not probed by this fact. *McClure's* was a national organ, affecting public and political opinion.

Its significance can be best grasped when it is compared with the *New Republic*, as it operated in the following decade. Under Herbert Croly, the *New Republic* forged policy that helped bring the United States into World War I. Yet its circulation was meager compared to *McClure's*. Indeed, it was subsidized by Willard Straight who, in Croly's summary, had "served successively as an employee of the Chinese government, a war correspondent, a member of the American consular service, a financial diplomat [during which he worked to influence the building of American railroads in China], a businessman and a soldier."[19] Straight was rich and interested in a publication that would apply to American life the ideas Croly had expanded in his elitist *The Promise of American Life* (1909). The result was the *New Republic*, which was directed to intellectuals, but also read by bureaucrats in Washington who helped to determine fateful programs.

By contrast, *McClure's* was a tribune of splendor and dimensions, offering stories, verse—to be sure, of little moment—personality sketches, as well as social commentary. So competent were its key writers on social themes that a hiatus was briefly created between their first muckraking articles and comparable work in other publications. It was the public, fed by the sensations of Scripps, Hearst, and other enterprising newspaper editors, that demanded McClure-type writings and found them in authors like Jack London, Upton Sinclair, Edwin Markham, and David Graham Phillips, who had been working between tales and articles in an effort to grasp their times. Charles Edward Russell had even abandoned journalism for poetry but found himself pulled back into the orbit of interests the public helped to create.

That public demand contained many subtleties. The same readers who hungered for civic revelations were also intensely interested in the memoirs of opera singers, suitably expurgated, and exotic accounts of places around the world. They followed expeditions to the North Pole and the careers of European nobility. They made the *Saturday Evening Post* the most successful of magazines; and since it included not only light fiction but the fiction of Frank Norris, H. G. Wells, Edith Wharton, and Joseph Conrad, it obviously merited regular patronage.

Lorimer, as editor, was very clear about his magazine wants, which would not tolerate pessimistic viewpoints. Although this infuriated more sensitive artistic types, it was true that all publications had basic policies, including the socialist *Appeal to Reason*, and they were intolerant of writings that did not comport with theirs. Distinguished authors could write for Lorimer because part of them agreed with his positive view of life. When something of theirs did not, they sent their articles and stories elsewhere. Phillips and Lorimer became good friends, worrying about each other's health, and visiting between Lorimer's Philadelphia office and home and Phillips's New York apartment and club.

Lorimer was well aware of Phillips's intemperate hatred of sham and corruption in politics and business and his advanced views of man-woman relations, and he was neither offended or impressed by them. He calmly accepted or rejected Phillips's tale or article as it suited him.[20] What they agreed upon was the need for people to be strong and deserving.

In some ways Lorimer took human frailties less seriously than did Phillips. In any event, he did not let Phillips's hard-hitting fiction and journalism prejudice him in any way. As he said, with something of a touch of patronage, following Phillips's famous or notorious blast against the United States Senate:

> Some of Phillips's friends are saying of him that he has a "message" to deliver, and that is pretty tough, for when an author gets an idea he has a message to deliver, usually he finds the wires are crossed. Phillips is sane and level-headed—barring a tendency now and then to enthusiasms that have not so many piles driven under them as would be well—and it is quite likely that he will get over the message business, and will continue as a novelist.[21]

Phillips's compromises with Lorimer, though real enough, were in behalf of his larger faith in popular education. The people, he thought, were better aware than formerly, more literate, directed toward civic betterment. In one of his surveys of current writing, he compared the magazines of the day with those of twenty years earlier. Editors were responding to change; for example, they were shunning long essays remote from current concerns:

> In place of the essay we find in our up-to-date magazines educational articles on applied science, industry, industrial development, and success in life as illustrated correctly and helpfully by successful men and institutions. . . .
>
> The other great change in the contents of magazines is in the matter of fiction. . . . That the popular imagination is developing, or rather is unimpaired upon the romantic side, is shown by the great amount of space the magazines now give to fiction.[22]

Fiction in the Progressive era was a fact of life. Progressives took pride in James Hopper, who turned realism into human interest and whose *9009* (1908) (written with Fred R. Bechdolt), the tragic tale of a convict viciously handled by California prison officials, actually aroused sentiment against police brutality and caused changes in law. This was an instance in which fiction served better than direct fact (though a preface indicated it was based on fact) because it generalized cruelty and did not have to cope with the embarrassments of personal controversy.

Frank Norris's *The Octopus*, though not strictly a Progressive novel, could also be identified with the period's purposes and psychology, and it survived as a staple of reading. So did Edith Wharton's *The House of Mirth* (1905). Jack London's fiction struck many notes, but his masterpiece, *Martin Eden* (1909)—with its sad conflict between the main character's name and his, and his author's, despairing death—did touch Progressive attitudes. Several of O. Henry's stories reflected the humanistic ideals of the time. This compulsion to fiction also gave drama and tension to interviews and accounts by Steffens and others and helped investigators focus upon the personalities of their "stories."

None made more of a sensation through fiction than Upton

Sinclair, with his novel *The Jungle* and its grim criticism of social Darwinian ethics. Its theme was suggested by the editor of the socialist *Appeal to Reason*, and it was run in the publication's pages before being issued in book form. The novel's message became so deeply imbedded in American lore as a cry favoring the dispossessed that it attracted practically no aesthetic or even social criticism.

The primary fact about Sinclair was that he was a southerner, and thus one of the post-Civil War generation who, like Tom Watson and Woodrow Wilson, were helping to shape new national attitudes. Sinclair was raised in New York, but his roots were in genteel Virginia families that had long provided officers for the United States Navy. His uncle had served on the *Monitor* in its famous battle with the *Merrimac.* His father was a salesman, a gentle, ineffectual man who kept Sinclair and his mother in poverty and humiliation because of his weakness for liquor. The young Sinclair's life was bewilderingly varied with visits to wealthy relatives in Baltimore. Sinclair was later accused by "aesthetic" critics of muckraking the rich in his fiction on the basis of fantasy. Sinclair, who had a phenomenal memory, countered that he knew the lives of the wealthy only too well and that it was his critics who imagined romantic scenes of grandeur, which took place nowhere.

Sinclair's southernness gave him an outsider's objectivity on life in the North, which he implemented with the socialist principles he accepted during the Progressive era. Hence he was able to report cruel business practices, the oppression of the workers, the horrors of poverty, and persecution of idealists by police and strikebreakers with a clear sense of being in the right, and to impart this vision to radical-minded readers at home and abroad. Radical sympathies around the world and simple antagonism and malice toward the United States combined to give him one of the greatest of world book circulations. Sinclair's long-time dubious status with reviewers and critics helped endorse his socialist view that there were rudiments of a conspiracy in the stature accorded him among American authors.

In fact, readers made a distinction in their minds—which criticism reflected—between what they read in acknowledgment of social concern and what fed their individualistic psyches. Sinclair's works, published by both himself and by "regular" publishers, sold well. He had a species of good humor that enabled him to reveal the paradoxes of American life under capitalism and to suggest that under "the industrial republic"—as he termed the anticipated socialism—they would disappear. With them would disappear the evils of drink and unchastity. Sinclair's novels were much less contrived than some critics tended to suggest, and they included a monument of observations photographically recorded, which Sinclair at least thought the future would hold valuable. At the same time he passed by another monument of human nature with which his writings had to compete for attention.

Sinclair failed to notice that his rigid antiliquor stand, for example, put him in the category of a large class of people whose opinions he did not otherwise share. Carry Nation had hated liquor, too, and, like Sinclair, suffered in family and spirit because of it. She was kindly, and with the money her notoriety earned, subsidized widows and others who had been harmed by drunkenness. Sinclair did not close ranks with such crusaders. He acted as a conscience for his radical-minded contemporaries but with nuances of a double standard; for though he denounced the "kept" press for withholding information that would have illuminated aspects of the news, he himself withheld from public knowledge that the much-admired and sentimentalized-over Eugene V. Debs had a weakness for liquor, which his comrades had to help Debs resist, sometimes quite firmly.[24]

How much the socialists contributed to congealing muckraking into Progressive tenets is difficult to judge. In general, they acted as whippets to Progressives, as the abolitionists before them had to northern antislavery Whigs and Republicans and some Democrats. There were many muckrakers among the socialists; there were all but no Progressive politicians, outside of municipalities, who claimed socialist goals. The leading socialists were varied and enlightened. John Spargo was an English transplant from Fabianism, and he added a reasonable note to American social arguments and recriminations. Morris Hillquit contributed a lawyer's reasoning and planning to socialist perspectives. Victor Berger of Milwaukee, among other socialists of that city, was a firm evolutionist who was dramatically proving to a nation still suspicious of the very word "socialism" that its members could deal with practical matters in moderate, democratic terms.

The prosocialist enthusiasm of the era has to be realized in detail to be fully appreciated. The *Appeal to Reason* claimed eighty thousand salesman-"soldiers" who were selling the paper. One of them rode about the country on a bicycle selling *Appeal* credit cards, good for socialist "literature" and a subscription to the *Appeal* when mailed to its Girard, Kansas, office. He was said to have himself sold over a hundred thousand subscriptions to the paper and thousands of socialist pamphlets.[25]

The intellectuals in their own way were even more spectacular, drawing together and influencing the elite of the colleges, popular magazines, and publishers' lists. Typical of their creations was the X Club, an informal gathering in New York City organized in 1903 by W. J. Ghent, a highly regarded socialist theoretician. His *Our Benevolent Feudalism* (1902), as Jack London noted, depicted a class domination by capitalists:

> Labor will take its definite place as a dependent class, living in a condition of machine servitude fairly analogous to the land servitude of the Middle Ages. That is to say, labor will be bound to the machine, though harshly, in fashion somewhat similar to that in which the earlier serf was bound to the soil.[26]

London lived in California, which boasted intellectuals and civic figures of various stripes. But Ghent, in New York, was able to bring together informally for periodical meetings, following brief dinners, such figures of the time as Steffens, Hamilton Holt, whose major cause was peace, Charles Edward Russell, J. G. Phelps Stokes, of old New York family who married the immigrant girl Rose Pastor, and William English Walling, also of old family who similarly married a spirited girl of no social standing. The historian Charles A. Beard, Owen R. Lovejoy of the National Child Labor Committee, and Walter E. Weyl (who was to help found the *New Republic*) were others among the faithful of the X Club.

It was indeed a golden age of socialism,[26] interlaced with hope and creativity. Left wings and right jockeyed for positions that should ultimately have gained them all suitable roles in American life. In reality, the differences in goals between socialist left and right were acute. The one sought confrontations intended to change the nature

THE WHITE MAN'S BURDEN.

The radical Robert Minor in 1912 before his conversion.

of American society, some elements like the Industrial Workers of the World (IWW) through desperate warfare. The other, as events demonstrated, no more than helped create transition scenes for progressivism. Once more like the political abolitionists, Progressives were to reach a crescendo of passionate affirmation that would make them hard to distinguish from socialists. The more sophisticated socialists knew they were beset by antagonistic legions:

> Berger's reformist comrades shared his fear of the twofold Wobbly threat to attract potential socialists and to frighten the American public into reaction. Adolph Germer and Robert Hunter, for example, discussed the possibility of a national conference to debate political action. They recoiled, however, from the possibility of inviting progressive trade unionists on the one hand, and from programming the general strike for debate on the other. They felt too threatened to move in either direction.[27]

The socialist movement had within it contradictory aims and interests that would obliterate the golden years. But during the Progressive period apparently it could operate only for good. Its international peace crusade seemed to supplement that of the less radical peace advocates like Andrew Carnegie and to create a kind of competition as to who could do the most for peace and progress. One benign analyst of the social impulse toward change in 1903 was struck by the fact that the international socialist movement in the past twenty-five years had moved from revolutionary to evolutionary premises. In France, the socialist movement was in the government itself, and thus Jean Jaurès, leader of the party and an intransigent pacifist, had the highest forum in the land from which to preach his gospel of peace. "In this holiest of all crusades Jaurès and his followers are at the front."[28]

NOTES

1. *Annals of the American Academy* 25 (March 1903): 235-247.
2. *Literary Digest* 21 (August 4, 1900: 139; 22 (April 13, 1901): 436-437; 22 (June 29, 1901): 778; 24 (March 22, 1902): 384-385.
3. George D. Herron, *The Defeat in the Victory* (London 1924). See also *Literary Digest* 22 (May 4, 1901): 529-530; 26 (March 7, 1903): 334-335.
4. *Literary Digest* 24 (June 21, 1902): 834-835.
5. *Ibid.*, 21 December 1, 1900): 641-642; 23 (September 28, 1901): 363-365; 25 (August 2, 1902): 132; 32 (February 10, 1906): 199-200; 24 (January 18, 1902), 1903, (February 22, 1902): 253; (May 10, 1902): 644 (March 1, 1902): 282.
6. P. H. Erbes, Jr., "Fifty Years, 1888-1938," *Printers Ink, A Journal for Advertisers* (July 28, 1938): 49.

7. That there was a public hunger for information was shown in the response to Pennsylvania Governor Samuel W. Pennypacker's effort to enforce stiff libel laws to muzzle newspapers in his state. The "chorus of disapproval and denunciation" which greeted this act "seldom . . . [had] been heard from the American press" (*Literary Digest* 26 (May 23, 1903): 742. Lengthy excerpts from newspapers substantiate this comment.

8. Eric F. Goldman, *Two-Way Street: The Emergence of the Public Relations Counsel* (Boston, 1948), 7-8.

9. Upton Sinclair, *The Brass Check* (Pasadena, Calif., 1931), chap. 47. This book, first published in 1920, was in its tenth edition, having sold more than 150,000 copies.

10. Lisle A. Rose, "Shortcomings of 'Muckraking in the Gilded Age' [by Edward Cassady]," *American Literature* 14 (May 1942): 161-164, lists numerous works of the premuckraking era.

11. *Literary Digest* 24 (April 19, 1902): 527-528.

12. Claude H. Wetmore, Steffens's collaborator, wrote his own account in *The Battle against Bribery* (St. Louis, 1904). An Ohioan, he had attended Western Reserve University and the Ecole Polytechnique in Lausanne. Following his early muckraking effort, he wrote children's books, traveled, and disappeared about 1926; see W. Coyle, *Ohio Authors and Their Books* (Cleveland, 1962), 678.

13. Steffens to his father, May 18, 1902, in Ella Winter and Granville Hicks, *Letters of Lincoln Steffens* (New York, 1938), 1:156.

14. Ray Stannard Baker, *American Chronicle* (New York, 1945), 305ff.

15. Lincoln Steffens, *Autobiography*, (New York, 1931), 385ff. See also Louis G. Geiger, *Joseph W. Folk of Missouri* (Columbia, Mo., 1953).

16. Lincoln Steffens, *Shame of the Cities* (New York, 1905), 275-276.

17. Steffens to Chambers, June 18, 1933, in Winter and Hicks, *Letters of Lincoln Steffens*, 2:961.

18. Edwin H. Lundberg, "The Decline of the American Muckrakers: A New Interpretation," (Masters thesis, University of Vermont, 1966), 45. *McClure's* circulation stood at 369,265 in 1900; by 1906, and following Steffens, Tarbell, and Baker major writings, it rose to 375,000. Unfortunately, there are no estimates of actual *readership* of this and other muckraking publications.

19. Herbert Croly, *Willard Straight* (New York, 1924), xii.

20. "I am sorry, but under a recent ruling of the Department of Agriculture, the Saturday Evening Post is forbidden to put out products in which benzoate of soda is used as a preservative.

"The stories are all good, and all intensely interesting to me personally, but I doubt strongly whether they are Post stories.

"The article is exceedingly good. Whether we can use it or not depends on whether you care to make some changes in it. . . . If you are of an open mind, we can talk it over when I see you next. If not, you can bang the fron[t] door of your soul in my face and be ——." Lorimer to Phillips, n.d. (c. 1909), Historical Society of Pennsylvania.

21. "Who's Who—and Why," *Saturday Evening Post* (August 27, 1907): 17.

22. David Graham Phillips, "Great Magazines and Their Editors," *Success* 6 (May 1903): 309.

23. Upton Sinclair, *The Autobiography of Upton Sinclair* (New York, 1962), 252-253. See also Sinclair's *The Cup of Fury* (Great Neck, N.Y., 1956), which details some of his friends' careers and ignominious deaths by suicide.

24. David Shannon, *The Socialist Party of America* (New York, 1955), 29.

25. Jack London, *War of the Classes* (New York, 1905), 199. This volume of London's "socialist" essays received nine printings by 1912.

26. Morris Hillquit, *Loose Leaves from a Busy Life* (New York, 1934), 55ff.

27. Sally M. Miller, *Victor Berger and the Promise of Constructive Socialism, 1910-1920* (Westport, Conn., 1973), 100.

28. John Graham Brooks, *The Social Unrest: Studies in Labor and Socialist Movements* (New York, 1903), 297. By 1907 it had received eight printings.

Issues

Strong, individual reforms were in operation before the reform era. What made the difference, as during the great reform wave of antebellum times, was their interrelatedness in the 1900s, as compared with what they were in the McKinley years. The antebellum reform era had highlighted abolition; indeed, abolition had been accused of having sapped the strength of such other movements as temperance, education, woman's rights, and institutional reform. This was probably not accurate. Abolition had simply become more conspicuous; other movements had proceeded at a good pace. The problem of trusts in the 1900s did not take on color comparable to that which incarnadined slavery, though the operation of some trusts, notably those in steel and mining operations, did produce national sensations, which, if anything, aided other reform causes of the time.

The difference in vigor and content between general perspectives in the 1890s and those of the muckraking and Progressive era could be seen in such a well-meaning production as Charles Richmond Henderson's *The Social Spirit in America,* first issued in 1897 and considered relevant enough for reprint in 1901 and 1904. The author, a University of Chicago professor of sociology, found a "rising spirit of fellowship, patriotism and of service to mankind" enveloping the land. He contributed to it by noting "home-making as a social art" and "friendly circles of women wage-workers," which pointed to the YMCA and the Little Mothers' Aid Association but did not so much as look at the circumstances of immigrants and Negroes. His discussions of housing, roads, education, and recreation problems were remarkable in their blandness; and his look at "what good employers are doing," unions, and political reforms were a judgment on the offerings at his institution.

By contrast, the newer journalism and analysis was hard and specific, and it reached into questions that concerned public personalities and the contents of their pockets. It was also linked to programs for action, and action itself. This last ranged from the organization of civic bodies for influencing elections to the creation of societies, presses, schools, and institutes, which would bring together like-minded philanthropic and socially alive men and women. Such enterprises required money, and, as in all reform eras, interest and concern gave common cause to people of wealth and enthusiasts without it.

An example of the philanthropic impulse was Charles R. Crane of a Chicago family of manufacturers who interested himself in the city's Municipal Voters' League, with its wide, intensive program for Chicago. He contributed to the University of Chicago's work and to that of the Marine Biological Laboratory at Woods Hole in Massachusetts. He provided financial aid for Joseph Folk's 1902 struggles in St. Louis. Crane's philanthropies extended as far as the Woman's College for Girls at Constantinople, but he did not stint domestic needs. He aided organization of the Woman's Trade Union League, vital to formulating programs for the working woman and her problems, and he helped establish the Chicago Commons, outstanding among the hundreds of settlements, which, throughout the country, set down Progressive foundations for civic reform.

That settlements did admirable work was taken for granted in their own time. Viewed retrospectively in post-World War II times they suffered in prestige as having done their work. How well they had done so before being drained of vitality by war, economic depression, and excessive affluence was surlily assessed by academic critics, many of them children of ethnic elements to which the settlements had been a haven and inspiration. The settlements were set up and developed by men and women who could be termed nothing short of magnificent. Jane Addams became symbolic of them to a later generation, but they required individualization.

Robert A. Woods labored earnestly to understand the varied immigrant types whom he sought to instruct and organize for American life in his South End House in Boston, with the aid of social workers and others who achieved distinction in their own right. Both Woods and Albert J. Kennedy attained the presidency of the National Federation of Settlements. Their long services included not only the building up of programs serving every person in the immigrant family, but studies of their qualities and needs, which could enlighten settlement workers everywhere.

The retrospective criticism of their lives and labors was curious, seeming to suggest that anything they did was not enough. Settlement workers often came from well-to-do families, enjoyed higher education, and could have made useful careers not taxing to their sympathies or imagination, among people raised like themselves. Instead. like Theodore Roosevelt, they chose to work in the world rather than seek out easy comfort and familiar conditions. They made acquaintance with the needy, the bewildered, and the bereft. They exemplified and furthered middle-class ideals in their "battery of child groups, night education meetings, art shows, craft and athletic facilities" and in their presentation of "the tools of the middle class morality."[1] It is difficult to see how they could have or should have done more, especially since the struggling immigrant groups agreed with these values and yearned to attain them. Woods was an "outsider," to be sure. What he or society would have gained by his disposing of his heritage and making awkward efforts to assimilate among the immigrants baffles the imagination. The immigrants desperately needed friendly guides to American ways. Whether they could have been helped to make better equations of their Old World ways and new conditions it is impossible to say. Immigrants were subject to stereotyping. It is too often forgotten that native-born Americans were also subject to stereotyping as snobs, "puritans," assexual, pious, hypocritically religious. Such misunderstandings between peoples had to be endured in the interests of such vital needs as economic unionism, housing, equitable police-citizen relations, education, and vice controls.

That the "philosophy" of the social workers was wrong in emphasizing fair play[2]—decent expectations in exchange for a better environment—seems incredible. Certainly, a low income made clean habits more difficult to attain than a high one, though many poor were models of cleanliness and dignity. Later decades proved that slack habits would make impossible the proper use of higher income produced by wartime and boomtime largesse—from any groups, whether of native or immigrant vintage.

In sum, the settlements functioned splendidly and in combination with reform organizations of every type and hue. "So many organizations had their offices in the so-called Charities Building on Twenty-second Street in New York that one day when Charles Spahr of the *Outlook* poked his head in the assembly room on the first floor and saw Edward T. Devine of the Charity Organization Society, Lawrence Veiller, the tenement house reformer, Samuel McCune Lindsay and Owen Lovejoy of the National Child Labor Committee, Florence Kelley of the Consumers' League, and Paul and Arthur Kellogg of *Charities*, he exclaimed, 'Ah, what's this bunch call itself today?' "[3]

There were disillusionments. Enthusiasts persuaded themselves that poor housing incubated evil tendencies and projects. They picked up from Jacob Riis to fight slum landlords in city councils and the courts, and in the end had to conclude that housing alone did not cause malignancies.[4] But such chagrins only emphasized other Progressive views, such as those of Homer Folks. Folks was a theorist, as well as an activist of social welfare, who labored for child welfare, public health, and social security. When Franklin D. Roosevelt left Albany, New York, in 1933 to begin his New Deal in Washington he later took much of Folks's life work as guidance. Folks emphasized the need for family, for social commitment, and for personal initiative. If this was no "radical" program,[5] it needed to be proved that any tangible radicalism had done more than Folks did, or, indeed, anything remotely comparable to it.

Women's work in the Progressive era was of so torrential a nature as hardly to require any note of itself. There was no field that did not formidably use women. As employees, they were to be found in all but nine of the "gainful occupations" recognized by the Census Bureau. An English woman labor organizer who had come to America to preach unionism for women found their condition so satisfactory as to require no need for her services.[6] There were indeed problems that touched women more than men, and they were amenable to public discussion. A woman professor expressed in the *Independent* her antipathy to marriage: she did not care to look up to a man, had no interest in being cared for, and was unwilling to be "looked upon as a mere means of swelling the census report. Stripped of all the fine language, that is what all this prating of the beauty of large families amounts to."[7]

The "Alarming Increase of Divorce"—one in twelve marriages ended in the courts[8]—inspired frank discussion from many quarters, as did the ever-perplexing questions of prostitution. A useful career of the time was that of Anna Garlin Spencer, born in 1851; she served as a Free Church minister, woman's rights advocate, and child labor, and factory inspection proponent, and she was deeply concerned about social evils. In the Progressive era, Anna Spencer sought a sophisticated approach to social vice, arguing that more than the fate of a few prostitutes was at stake. The status of the family and of the economic compulsions that created a class of females for hire had to be mastered. Her campaigns for education and action kept her on a massive round of writing and lectureships at Columbia University, the University of Chicago, and elsewhere. They culminated in the organization of the American Social Hygiene Association, which accomplished useful work in its field.[9]

Women, of course, were most numerous in the temperance and suffrage crusades, which produced leaders of national repute. Their status in the settlement field was overwhelming, involving not only such figures as Lillian Wald of the Henry Street Settlement in New York and Ellen Gates Starr of Hull House, but such residents of Hull House and other settlements as Edith Abbott who interested herself in the lot of immigrants in transition to full citizenship and as requiring aid in gaining all their civil rights. Their work ultimately created the Women's Bureau and the Children's Bureau in the Department of Labor. All such work was aided by the writings of muckrakers who stirred public sentiment and focused attention on the activities of energetic organizations.[10]

The Negro community, because of its better-established place in American society, received less direct attention from social workers than did the new immigrants. It did, however, receive some. There was no uniform policy on this subject. Lillian Wald's settlement in New York received Negroes without discrimination and also had a branch especially for the use of Negroes. A Boston settlement worker feared that too ready a welcome to Negroes would drive their white attendants away. Wendell Phillips Settlement in Chicago worked consciously to bring together white and Negro residents.[11]

What precisely was the best program for black-white relations in the Progressive era was difficult to judge. Kelly Miller, Howard University professor and an outstanding Negro spokesman, spoke of *Race Adjustment* (1909) in his volume of essays explaining his people's viewpoint. He honored Booker T. Washington and deplored the passion and intransigence of William Monroe Trotter, the Boston editor, a graduate of Harvard, and an enemy of Washington. Miller repudiated the vicious canards of a Thomas A. Dixon who asserted that Negroes were inherently inferior. Miller went over statistics that showed the Negro advance in economics and culture, identified himself with Walt Whitman, Jefferson, and others who had apparently spoken positively on the issue—actually, their opinions were controversial—and otherwise held the line for his people's hopes and achievements.

Toward Progressives, Miller was more than generous, searching them out as aids in the battle against aggressive anti-Negroism. This was manifested during the sorrowful Atlanta riots of 1906, which were fanned by racist slurs and by the Georgia editor John Temple Graves. Graves prided himself on his descent from John C. Calhoun's eldest brother, and, for *Who's Who*, considered himself as "generally classed with Henry Grady as orator and leader of progressive and patriotic sentiment in [the] south." Miller sharply distinguished such a "progressive" from others of truer stripe. The Atlanta riot had cost twenty lives and much chaos and destruction. Miller reminded Graves that in Atlanta had lived some of the most illustrious of southern personages, including Henry Grady, "oracle of the New South." Here lived Joel Chandler Harris of the *Atlanta Constitution* and the immortal "Br'er Rabbitt" and Uncle Remus tales. Miller's brilliant inspiration was to rivet relations between all worthy Americans, whether black or white, and to repudiate all Negroes who could be identified as brutes. And he called the roll of good men who could build a new time, as against those who could not:

> There are two voices in the South to-day. While one preaches hatred and strife, another proclaims justice and humanity. The

> late Chancellor Hill, Bishop Galloway, Professor John Spencer Bassett, Joel Chandler Harris, and William H. Fleming, and a host of others represent the erstwhile silent South, which has remained tongue-tied under the threat of political and social calamity. . . . George W. Cable was banished, Louis H. Blair ignored, J. L. M. Curry was listened to with courtesy, and Dr. Atticus G. Haygood was made a bishop.
>
> But of late this voice has become "something louder than before," and can no longer be ignored as an important, if not a controlling factor in the Southern situation. The fundamental question to-day is which of these voices shall prevail. . . .[12]

It was just as well that passages in Upton Sinclair's *The Jungle* were finally noticed, decades after its first publication, as referring among many other subjects to Negroes. Since the book had been read without criticism by whole generations of radicals, as well as ordinary schoolchildren and adults, it is difficult to pin the label of white racism on the Progressives alone. The value of such new attention given the novel was that it turned concern on its aesthetics as well as the tribulations of its main character, Jurgis. It could then be observed that Jurgis, though harried and driven by cruel agents of capitalism, did, for a time, join them and act as one of its acolytes. Sinclair manifested a certain disinterestedness, which could be identified with art, as he changed roles and observed events from opposite points of view.

His passages about Negroes dealt with a category that had been noticed in labor literature, but not closely and not with focus on individuals. Strikebreakers had an evil reputation among radicals and their sympathizers, and, when white, could be invidiously described, usually with the pretentious "lumpen-proletariat" label. As such, they could be described as corrupt, stupid, and generally degraded. Negroes were, on the other hand, remarked as industrial pawns, cruelly employed to undermine valid workers' demands. They were not otherwise critically examined. There is no evidence that Sinclair seized an opportunity to express southern venom toward Negroes in general in his *Jungle* passages. If anything, his North-South mentality gave him an ease with the subject, which doctrinaire radicals, especially those in northern cities, could not understand.

Sinclair described the strikebreakers, Negro and white toughs, as lazy and incompetent in their manning of the packing houses. His prose concentrated upon the tide of events that went from strike to negotiations to a more intense level of strike, which brought in more than a thousand new strikebreakers, a vast majority of whom were "green" Negroes from the cotton districts of the far South:

> Just at this time the mayor was boasting that he had put an end to gambling and prize-fighting in the city; but here a swarm of professional gamblers had leagued themselves with the police to fleece the strike-breakers; and any night, in the big open space in front of Brown's, one might see brawny negroes stripped to the waist and pounding each other for money, while a howling mob of three or four thousand surged about, men and women, young white girls from the country rubbing elbows with big buck negroes with daggers in their boots, while rows of wooly heads peered down from every window of the surrounding factories. The ancestors of these black people had been savages in Africa; and since then they had been chattel slaves, or had been held down by a community ruled by the traditions of slavery. Now for the first time they were free,—free to gratify every passion, free to wreck themselves. They were wanted to break a strike, and when it was broken they would be shipped away, and their present masters would never see them again; and so whisky and women were brought in by the car-load and sold to them, and hell was let loose in the yards. Every night there were stabbings and shootings; it was said that the packers had blank permits, which enabled them to ship dead bodies from the city without troubling the authorities. They lodged men and women on the same floor; and with the night there began a saturnalia of debauchery—scenes such as never before had been witnessed in America. And as the women were the dregs from the brothels of Chicago, and the men were for the most part ignorant country negroes, the nameless diseases of vice were soon rife; and this where food was being handled which was sent out to every corner of the civilized world.[13]

Sinclair went on to describe other nighttime activities, though the daytime mixtures of sweat, refuse, and animal cadavers in the sweltering processing rooms were in themselves not inviting. Whether the activities or even persons of such characters merited description and in what way became a hidden question among avant-garde and radical circles. It produced social problems for the Negro communities, since they had to cope with the results of such policies. Random and destructive elements, which found themselves unchallenged by public opinion, were encouraged to continue their limited range of activities, shielded by leaders and white sympathizers who found profit in terming Upton Sinclair a "racist." From time to time, when the results of such tolerance became intolerable. they were required to lie low or backtrack in their policies.[14]

Meanwhile, it appeared an accurate long-term judgment that Sinclair had written with high accuracy and that that fact had been recognized and acknowledged by a well-based Progressive readership.

By Sinclair's time, it had been long appreciated that at the base of the struggle for an equitable social establishment, so far as the Negroes and other ethnic elements were concerned, was their political weight. In 1890 the "Bourbons" of South Carolina had attempted to marshal the Negro vote as part of their effort to overcome the popularity of Ben Tillman.[15] They did not succeed, but they did, at least, present the issue: did Negro politicians prefer to work on an anti-Populist premise, in hopes of a state leadership that would encourage gracious Negro-white relations, or did they prefer to dream of a Negro uprising, which would somehow change the rules of American life? In either case, Negro politicos worked for themselves, as well as their constituents. Their choice was a hard one, for there were worthy white southerners whose feelings toward Negroes could only be called loving; and there were southern "crackers" who had worked their way out of poverty who were passionate in their love of, poor whites and hatred of others and who nevertheless hungered to be remembered as builders of hospitals, schools, and roads, for which their own kind would bless them.[16]

Progressives could be linked to social issues, but this by no means —it was a canard to say otherwise—linked them to the bosses. Progressives had to live like everybody else, but their approach to social issues came from another part of the social forest. Bosses concentrated on administering vice, contracts, patronage, and what amounted to neighborly charity—Thanksgiving turkey, pails of coal, Christmas camaraderie, and keeping petty thieves from having to serve jail sentences—and all in the interests of "delivering the vote." Progressivism began from the other end of social rights and responsibilities as embodied in law.[17]

Ward politics were a daily round of visits, acquaintanceships, the passing of cash from hand to hand, the pleas of mothers whose children had been nabbed by the police for fraud, soliciting, the use of fists, and other transgressions. Progressives could—and did—seem less immediately useful to a humble voter. Nevertheless, it was not because of the reformers that political machines became subject to reform. It was because of the results of machine operation. A book that became a species of bible to the antireformers and their academic apologists illuminated this fact. *Plunkitt of Tammany Hall, A Series of Very Plain Talks on Very Practical Politics* (1948), as set down by a reporter, William L. Riordan, was summed up in the philosopher's statement: "I seen my opportunities and I took 'em."

These opportunities consisted of learning enough of the city's business to convert some of it to personal profit, which made this ignorant wardheeler a millionaire. George Washington Plunkitt had no competence other than a mind for selling the city's assets. This he termed "honest graft." Dishonest graft he defined in areas of vice. Others of the Tammany machine were not so nice, but they were able to rationalize the fortunes they made from pimp, prostitute, gambling, theft, liquor and drug operations as satisfying human needs, or however they pleased. Their work was implemented by gangs of the "Plug Ugly" and "Dead Rats" variety, such as besmirched all cities.[18]

Whether "honest" or plainly dishonest, the city graft cost its inhabitants in funds, services, and health; and it was this condition that roused reformers, some of them of the foolish and incompetent variety, others of the kind that we have seen. For businessmen, the Progressive era was doubtless a relatively "easy" time, thanks to the sun of prosperity: an era of controls and requiring no serious civic soul-searching.[19] For the city inhabitant, its political machines had produced a shambles of arson-prone houses, poor, expensive communication and transportation services, exorbitant utilities, inadequate protection from criminals, unrestrained vice, and taxes that served the machine before they did those taxed. Tammany in New York might be composed of "patriots," in Plunkitt's sense of the word, but their patriotism did nothing for the basic city.

All bosses built up facades of love and loyalty to their constituents, fostered their hatred of Americans who had been here before them, and reminded the poor of their wrongs as domestic servants, pick-and-shovel men, and would-be job holders. Many of the bosses were in fact kindhearted and good-natured and unwilling to be close to the uglier elements of their party: cruel, senseless fighters who enjoyed roughing up antimachine voters at the polls and who were capable of the most obscene actions as side perquisites of their strong-arm role in politics. But there were many, many politicians who were less nice in their associations, but just as important to the machine as the friendly ones, the good neighbors. In Jersey City, in a timeless incident, an antimachine worker came into contact with its very chief:

> Burkitt attended the meeting [of the city commission] to have the limits of his police permit to speak at certain corners defined by the commission. Mayor Frank Hague, who presided, was clearly amused by the sight of Burkitt as the latter approached the assembly rostrum to speak.
>
> "What's the matter with your face?" asked the Mayor.
>
> "Some of your thugs beat me up," Burkitt replied.
>
> The Mayor laughed heartily.
>
> "Don't laugh, Mr. Mayor," Burkitt said, irritated.
>
> "I'm not laughing at you, but your face looks so funny," cried Hague.[2]

In Boston, a young Irishman displayed such an intelligent sense of his constituency, spoke with such venom of the city's brahmin leaders, their indifference to the problems of the Irish, their insufferable pride, that by 1900 he was not only a dispenser of turkeys, favors, and the like but was a member of the common council. It bears notice that neither James M. Curley nor his prototypes in the other cities of the land had anything to do with the work of the settlements. Curley became a member of the Massachusetts General Court, the state's legislature, and during that time was sentenced to ninety days in jail for taking a civil-service examination for a less erudite applicant for letter carrier. Curley ran for alderman from his jail cell and was elected.

Curley went on to serve in Congress and to become mayor of Boston, where he built hospitals and other facilities, though at astronomical cost: a detail that his apologists would also cover up with humanistic and other phrases, as they would for all metropolitan centers.[21] Curley also built a mansion for himself from unknown money reserves. He not only appealed to prejudice against non-Catholic Americans and "bluebloods"; he appears also to have created prejudice as an adjunct to his campaigns, having aides burn fiery crosses at sites of his campaign speeches in order to conjure up an imaginary Ku Klux Klan.

Curley went on to further honors, which included the governorship of the state and a second term as mayor; during the latter era he also served time in prison for mail fraud. Although his popularity declined, he was not disgraced and continued formidable until the end. One commentator put the matter succinctly, following a Curley victory: "Bostonians have again disproved the charge that they are narrow-minded people. They can see merits in James M. Curley not visible to anyone else."[22]

The reform era shook up the city machines, in 1905 sensationally shelving a number of conspicuous ones from coast to coast.[23] Such successes roused even greater Progressive ambitions to change the rules of municipal government. In 1909 E. A. Filene, the department store owner, brought Steffens to Boston to draw up a plan for improving the city as a human as well as municipal organization. Steffens's "Boston 1915" project solicited the cooperation of "the people's attorney," Louis D. Brandeis, as well as of Martin Lomasny, Boston's Democratic boss. Steffens's effort to bring together the influential people of the city without regard to their social status was commendable. His problem, and that of his sponsors, was that they thought there was, somewhere, *a* plan that would raise the people of Boston above their mundane concerns.

Steffens's final "plan" was no plan at all: a mere appeal to people and leaders to think socially and to work together.[24]

Brandeis wrote his name into labor and banking law. Filene not only created democratic business institutions, such as the bargain basement; he created a host of social institutions, including the chamber of commerce, the American cooperative union and credit union, and the Twentieth Century Fund for analyzing the work of a civilization. What Martin Lomasny did to merit remembrance is less clear. Steffens, whose experiences constituted a democratic heritage, was at his best in displaying his vivid encounters with civic personages, rather than seeking a foolproof control apparatus to prevent chicanery.

Steffens's tale of the dying boss made more profitable reading than a hundred rationalizations for the boss's career.[25]

He portrayed Israel W. Durham, the Philadelphia boss, as a worthy man fired by Steffens's search for a better municipal government, aware that corruption was somehow wrong but unclear on what he might have done that was essentially bad. He recited the litany of his good deeds, help to neighbors, kindness to outcasts—but he forbade Steffens to criticize him, since he had to continue his work. However, he had a serious disease. He asked Steffens to promise to come, should it take a severe turn, since he would want to hear Steffens's views before the end. And so finally, according to Steffens, the message arrived: "Come; you promised to." Steffens went to Philadelphia to talk with Durham on his death bed and to answer the question: "Just what do I do that's so rotten wrong?"

Steffens told him that his sin had been disloyalty, something Durham had never imagined, for his creed had been first and foremost loyalty. But Steffens went on to explain that he had been a born leader of the common people. They had admired and trusted him.

> And he, the good fellow, had taken his neighbors' faith and sovereignty and turned it into franchises and other grants of the common wealth, which he and his gang had sold to rich business men and other enemies of the people. He was a traitor to his own. He had asked for it straight, I gave it to him—straight, and he got it. Not one word of evasion or excuse. He took it lying

> down, and all he said after a long, wan silence was: "Say, I sure ought to go to hell for that, and what'll they do to me? Do you think they'll set me on fire for—for what you said—disloyalty?"

Steffens hastened, he said, to suggest that as he had been a compassionate boss, there might well be in afterlife a higher Boss to take his human frailties into account. But Steffens was always more the artist than the analyst, and he needed to be read for connotation as well as fact. The Progressive era did not settle the problem of business-bosses-and-public. It wiped out some of the patent abuses, some old-fashioned methods of theft accounting and conspiracy. It substituted such modern inventions as commission government and the referendum, thus creating new circumstances for exploitation and control.

The reform era seethed with issues that ran from local situations to national, and back again. All of them had long careers in social politics. The peculiar strength of muckraking was in dramatizing the issues in ways that took them out of the ephemeral category of sensationalism and impelled action. For example, there were many men and women in and out of the court system who were disturbed by the lot of children who found themselves in the hands of jailers and police, with no future but in accumulating psychic scars and antisocial careers. Judges, social workers, and others struggled to establish the principle that no child should be considered a criminal, and from there to debate probationary and other systems that might rescue the child for individual growth within the community.[26]

It remained, however, for one who had himself sustained a bleak and despairing childhood to dramatize the lot of unfortunate children who fell into the hands of insensitive or cruel officials. Ben B. Lindsey's work as a juvenile judge became part of the lore of the Progressive era, and led him in and out of politics. He was one of Lincoln Steffens's *Upbuilders* (1909), the "just judge" to whom children and troubled parents could turn for aid and comfort. Lindsey dramatized himself, as well as his charges, and some of his performances were bound to gather dust with time. But they contributed to a work that had to be done and that had no end. Lindsey himself went on to make vital contributions to problems in marriage (in his "companionate marriage" idea)[27] in America, which stirred the nation in the 1920s.

A related work made Thomas Mott Osborne a controversial figure in prison reform. Osborne came from a wealthy upstate New York family, and as a well-favored youth showed few traits that singled him out from others of good circumstance. His one oddity, which seems to have had no source except a need for theatricals, was a penchant for masquerades and disguises, which he satisfied not only at costume balls but in lone trips around the countryside when he dressed often as a tramp. Osborne broke family traditions by becoming a Democrat, antagonized his social equals with dissident opinions, and by his solitary rambles acquired a sense of the seamier side of life, which was not otherwise readily available to one of his social caste.

His wife's death during childbirth in 1896 turned Osborne to civic affairs, which included the needs of delinquent children. He served on state commissions on prison reform. His turning point came in 1913 when he had himself incarcerated in Auburn Prison for a week under the name of "Tom Brown." He shared the inmates' experiences, including solitary confinement, and emerged dedicated to prison reform. His prominence made him front-page news, which was underscored by his book *Within Prison Walls* (1914).

Osborne's subsequent career as warden of Sing Sing Prison was stormy and helped keep attention focused on prison conditions, even after the Progressive wave had fallen.[28] Much of the controversy was inevitably partisan and inaccurate, but the very debate nourished the work of reform. Such was also the case with child labor, which called forth writings stirring to readers. The National Child Labor Committee, committed to patient work with friends in the legislatures, was embarrassed, for example, by Edwin Markham's *Cosmopolitan* article, "Child at the Loom," which claimed that fifty thousand youthful workers were so employed in the mills. In fact, protested the NCLC, most of the children were spinners, doffers, and sweepers, and such errors angered the mill owners the NCLC hoped to reach.[29] Yet not a few of the tales Markham recounted were true, and the problem of child rearing in changing industrial times could not be engrossed in simple formulas. The marvel of muckraking was not its errors but its high percentage of truth, considering that it was being directed at general readers.

Such questions as prison reform and child labor were not inferior issues to those that created sustained national sensations. Such a problem of food for example—its sanitary aspects, legitimate prices, honest advertising—involved local conditions, particular industries, critical situations. The problem surfaced from time to time and brought into one pattern disparate personalities. Undoubtedly the troubles created tempted the usual American penchant for scapegoats. The meat packers' friendly biographers complained of this fact and termed the "embalmed meat" rubric an "immortal lie." They received curious endorsement from one highly identified with reform in the area, Dr. Harvey W. Wiley, chemist of the Department of Agriculture, who was convinced that at least nine-tenths of the reports condemning the meat supplied soldiers in Cuba were "purely sensational and without foundation." The question, however, was not whether the meat was poor or dangerous but who or what was responsible for the condition. As Roosevelt, then governor of New York, testified:

> The cans when opened would show usually on top what looked like a layer of slime, a very disagreeable looking substance. The beef inside was stringy and coarse. It looked like a bundle of fibers. Sometimes we could stew it. If you could stew it with potatoes and onions, which was done there when we got some potatoes and onions, you could eat it; but I think I could have eaten my hat with potatoes and onions at that time. I think the men would have eaten anything with potatoes and onions in a stew. . . . There were some others who could not eat it at all.[30]

Rumor continued to plague the food controversy, one apparently maintaining the legend that Germany had prohibited the sending of canned meats and sausages from America—a report that Consul General Richard Guenther, writing from Frankfort, denied. The Imperial Germany Navy, for example, had used these articles for years, had only recently sent large purchases of American salt pork to troops in East Africa, and all without finding cause for restrictions.[31]

Such details fed conservative protest against popular agitation, but did not take into account the need for better outside regulation of vital social concerns. Food packers were as jealous of their prerogatives as Upton Sinclair was of his sudden fame. But whereas Sinclair gave too little credit to the work of highly competent official examiners of the stockyards he had muckraked,[32] the stockyard managers moved with inexcusable laxness, first to try to smother all investigation, then to strip the legislative bills drawn up of as many protective clauses as possible. Sinclair's human indignation was as vital to results as the dispassionate, if revolting, Neill-Reynolds report.

Any study of the spectrum of reforms that excited the era would discover that they did not receive even-handed attention. Vital reforms dragged in legislative fulfillment; some received no fulfillment at all. The drive to end child labor came legislatively to nothing. There were too many familial and social hurdles in the way to move enough social indignation fast and far enough to influence the event. What finally "ended" child labor was the economic depression of the 1930s, which saw grown men competing with children for opportunities to make a dollar. Still later doubts arose in society as to whether some children might not be better off working than dawdling in schools and confusing class circumstances for more ready scholars.

Similarly, the overweighing labor problem was not amenable to easy solution. For one thing, labor was at odds with itself with panaceas that ranged from accommodations with industry to revolutionary solutions calculated to turn over industry into the hands of those it employed. E. A. Filene actually hoped to so arrange affairs that his great Boston department store would finally be entirely owned and operated by his employees. He had finally to conclude that the majority of them had no such ambition—an ambition that would have required them to learn more of the business and of each other's business than they desired, to give more time to the company than they cared to give, to save money they preferred to spend, and to take other steps that would have in essence have given them administrative responsibilities.[33]

The jagged edges of industry-labor relations arrested public interest and resulted in varied decisions. Thus, the crucial unanswered question of whether murder was as fair a weapon for labor as for capital in effect remained undetermined as a result of the trial for the killing of ex-Governor Frank Steunenberg of Idaho—a trial that brought in newly elected Senator William E. Borah as state prosecutor and Clarence Darrow for the defense of several Western Federation of Miners unionists, including the famous "Big Bill" Haywood.[34] The unionists were acquitted essentially on the basis of the Scots Law of not proven. But the haunting question of how much power and support a social segment of society merited remained undetermined.

Roosevelt's demand that the miners' strike of 1902 be negotiated was generally approved, but the problem of the Danbury Hatters of Connecticut had to be absorbed by the workers themselves in that generation. In 1901 the United Hatters of North America decided to organize the workers of the Dietrich E. Loewe shops. They declared a strike and boycott, and their challenge was taken up by Loewe, financed by other hat manufacturers, and supported in a test court case by the Anti-Boycott Association. Loewe charged that the hatters were engaged in a common law conspiracy, for which he asked $100,000 in damages, and, in the United States Circuit Court, $240,000 for violation of the Sherman Anti-Trust Act. The homes and bank accounts of 248 members of the union were attached by legal process.

On February 8, 1908, the United States Supreme Court ruled against the unions on grounds of transgression of the Sherman Act, a decision that stunned not only the hatters but all organized labor. Although the Clayton Anti-Trust Act of 1914 was passed to lift the threat of antitrust suits from labor, its wording did not save the hatters. The organized laborers of the nation taxed themselves an hour's pay to help the Danbury workers.[35]

Had a chart been made of public interests about 1906, it would have shown striking peaks and valleys. Little pressure was put upon Roosevelt to choose vigorous representatives favoring farmers, laborers, and a maintenance of standards in the administration of reform measures in railroads, pure food, and other fields. Roosevelt's Secretary of War, William E. Taft, was an excellent liaison man for paternalistic and diplomatic missions. He was not responsive to popular opinion. His most notorious acts identified him as an "injunction judge" who intervened in strikes in ways that prostrated labor rather than permitted social movement toward negotiation. Yet not only did Taft not lose Roosevelt credibility with the public but Roosevelt was able to carry Taft forward in its regard.

Elihu Root, as Secretary of War before Taft and after him Secretary of State, was a lawyer whose acts justified the military services and the corporations without qualification. Root dreamed of accommodations between government and the industries he had counseled in ways that infuriated David Graham Phillips, who saw in them a cunning plot to tie government to the Machiavellian program of monopolists.[36] In fact they no more than created a new level of relations between private and public business on which various interests—labor, consumers, the nation's sections—could do battle for their own. The point was that the general public was less fearful of centralization processes than Phillips was.

The public read articles about child labor, about skulduggery on the stock exchange, about labor's sorrows, about the less distinguished aspects of race relations, about saber-rattling on the Continent, but it refused to become intensively concerned for such topics. Europe and Japan were far, far away; it was impossible to make vivid the likelihood that America might become involved seriously in their affairs. Stock exchange frauds were revealed from time to time, but the anguish was private, and the public was reluctant to give up its dreams of an unexpected fortune by concentrating on safety in investments. The dimensions of security for labor—the very definitions of labor—were difficult to determine.

The public did become passionate about food purity, and the Food and Drug Administration came into being in 1906. The public was alarmed to learn, as a result of the Armstrong investigation of 1905, that its insurance policies—a major safeguard for widows and children—were administered irresponsibly and gave far less protection than imagined. A rapid turnover of officers and ordinances governing insurance modernized insurance operations, though they required a watchful eye from time to time.

Municipal administration continued to make its presence known to the citizen through taxes, services—or nonservices—and conditions of life. Social anxiety had resulted in a revolution of sorts, as has been seen, by no means ridding the country of bosses but making them more amenable to social pressures. The problem of trust was brought up to date, the nation agreeing with Roosevelt that it desired the economy and efficiency that "good" trusts could give but that it wanted also a proper sense of regulation to ensure that trusts could not get beyond themselves at the expense of the public's resources and rights.

So the great Progressive upswell was essentially a middle-class revolution, reaffirming the nation's willingness to take its chances on competition in business, so long as it could be reassured that no one and no business could become so powerful as to render the ordinary citizen, the "little man," powerless. Muckraking displayed the workings of twentieth-century American society; the Progressive movement carried those revelations to the polling places for popular adjudication.

NOTES

1. Sam Bass Warner, Jr., ed., *The Zone of Emergence: Observations of the Lower Middle and Upper Working Class Communities of Boston, 1905-1914,* by Robert A. Woods and Albert J. Kennedy (Cambridge, Mass., 1962), 10.

2. *Ibid.*, 17.

3. Allen F. Davis, *Spearheads for Reform: The Social Settlements and the Progressive Movement, 1890-1914* (New York, 1967), 25.

4. Roy Lubove, *The Progressives and the Slums: Tenement House Reform in New York City, 1890-1917* (Pittsburgh, 1962), 255. Progressives were interested in Trinity Church, revealed disgracefully as a slum landlord. The church's antisocial policy went back as early as 1857. The agitation now successfully directed at the church corporation highlighted the new power which reform could muster; cf. Louis Filler, *The Muckrakers: Crusaders for American Liberalism* (State College, Pa., 1976), 300, and *Literary Digest* 10 (January 5, 1895): 274-275, (March 9, 1895): 545-546.

5. Walter I. Trattner, *Homer Folks, Pioneer in Social Welfare* (New York, 1968), 145ff.

6. *Literary Digest* 34 (June 8, 1907): 904.

7. *Ibid.*, 29 (July 30, 1904): 130-131.

8. *Ibid.*, 37 (December 12, 1908): 882.

9. Louis Filler, "Anna Carpenter Garlin Spencer," in *Notable American Women*, ed. E. T. and J. W. James (Cambridge, Mass., 1971), 3:331-333.

10. See, for example, Walter Trattner, *Crusade for the Children*

(Chicago, 1970), 48, which notices the increase and effectiveness of popular writing on this movement.

11. Davis, *Spearheads for Reform*, 94-95.

12. Kelly Miller, *Race Adjustment* (New York, 1909), 67. Compare with Jack Temple Kirby, *Darkness at the Dawning: Race and Reform in the Progressive South* (Philadelphia, 1972), which sees southern progressivism, especially as it related to Negroes, as a shambles of self-interest and futility.

13. Upton Sinclair, *The Jungle* (Pasadena, 1942), 327.

14. "To many blacks, the terms 'law and order' and 'crime in the streets' have long been racist code words uttered by white politicians to attract white votes. . . . But now, with crime taking on new proportions in black communities across the country, a dramatic shift is occurring, and blacks in greater numbers are involving themselves in the war on crime. A black who is for 'law and order' and against 'crime in the streets' is no longer chastised by other blacks. . . ." *New York Times*, November 13, 1974.

15. *Literary Digest* 1 (November 1, 1890): 22.

16. A curious campaign work, though out of time, underscores such neopopulist dreams. It is by a governor and United States Senator from Mississippi, Theodore G. Bilbo, *Take Your Choice: Separation or Mongrelization* (Poplarville, 1947), filled with fanatical fancies—it was appropriate that he should have named his home "The Dream House." Bilbo also proudly detailed his services to the state, which included the erection of hospitals, an industrial and training school, a tax commission to equalize taxes, a legal board of examiners, abolition of public hanging, the initiative and referendum, among other modernizing and civilizing laws. Reinhard H. Luthin, *American Demagogues: Twentieth Century* (Boston, 1954), correctly noted that Bilbo would be remembered most clearly as a "victim" of racial bigotry.

17. An interesting difference between Republican and Democratic nascent Progressives involved their attitude toward ward favors. Woodrow Wilson, while still president of Princeton University and scarcely thinking of the presidency as possible, nevertheless sent out signals to the New Jersey Democrats in 1905 of his availability. He decried "amateurs who . . . don't understand the game," though he himself had never served in any capacity in practical politics. He took Folk as an example of one who had pricked the bubble of the "boss's" omnipotence. The boss was no more than a man. He did, however, serve human purposes. The Tammany politician "wins the true love of his constituency and illustrates that private welfare is somewhat involved in public welfare." Arthur Link et al., *The Papers of Woodrow Wilson*, (Princeton, 1973), 16:218.

18. Herbert Asbury, *The Gangs of New York* (New York, 1928), describes one such adjunct of city politics.

19. Robert H. Wiebe, *Businessmen and Reform* (Cambridge, Mass., 1962), 42ff.

20. Quoted in Dayton David McKean, *The Boss: The Hague Machine in*

Action (Boston, 1940), 11. See also the interesting *The Statesman and the Boss*, by George C. Rapport (New York, 1961), which relates Hague to Woodrow Wilson, especially chap. 9, "Woodrow Wilson—Politician," which sees Wilson as having fought bossism in behalf of reform and then reform—which could compete with him—in behalf of bossism. In effect, Wilson resuscitated Hague.

21. For example, they would argue that Central Park in New York was a "great bargain" at the cost Boss Tweed inflicted on New York: an argument worth explicating in economic as well as Plunkittian terms.

22. Luthin, *American Demagogues*, 17. A notable work, showing the interrelatedness of municipal and national politics and also the academic community, is James H. Guilfoyle, *On the Trail of the Forgotten Man: A Journal of the Roosevelt Presidential Campaign*, with an introduction by Professor Robert E. Rogers (Boston, 1933). In effect, the book credited Curley with Roosevelt's victorious fight for the Democratic candidacy in 1932. The purpose of the work, which appears to have been subsidized, was evidently to serve Curley's campaign for governor, no cabinet post having materialized.

23. "Slaughter of the Bosses," *Literary Digest* 31 (November 18, 1905): 734-735.

24. What there is of Steffens's "Boston 1915" analysis appears in three issues of *Metropolitan Magazine*, under the general heading of "A Cure for Corruption": "Failure of Government by Good People" (March 1912): 12; "The Fruits of Good Government in New England" (April 1912): 18; "The Way Out" (May 1912): 33.

25. Lincoln Steffens, *Autobiography* (New York, 1931) 416ff.

26. Samuel J. Barrows, *Children's Courts in the United States, Their Origin, Development and Results*, 58th Cong., 2d sess., 1904, Doc. 701 (Washington, D.C., 1904).

27. Charles Larsen, *The Good Fight: The Life and Times of Ben B. Lindsey* (Chicago, 1972), 162ff.

28. See Rudolph W. Chamberlain, *There Is No Truce* (New York, 1935).

29. Trattner, *Crusade for the Children*, 99. See also the influential *Children in Bondage* (New York, 1914), composed of articles by Markham, Lindsey, and the Denver journalist and reformer George Creel.

30. U.S., Congress, Senate, Document 270, pt. II, 56th Cong., 1st sess., 1900, 1102, 1681-1689. See also Oscar E. Anderson, Jr., *The Health of a Nation* (Chicago, 1958), 128, and Harper Leech and John Charles Carroll, *Armour and His Times* (New York, 1938), 321ff.

31. *Consular Reports* 65, no. 247 (Washington, D.C., 1901). 496.

32. "Conditions in Chicago Stock Yards, "*Report of James Bronson Reynolds and Commissioner Charles P. Neill*, 59th Cong., 1906, H. Doc. 873.

33. For an outstanding effort to make "industrial democracy" a reality, see Louis Filler, "William Powers Hapgood and American Options,"

introduction to Hapgood, *The Columbia Conserve Company* (Philadelphia, 1975).

34. Filler, *Crusaders*, 217ff.

35. Bernard Mandel, *Samuel Gompers* (Yellow Springs, Ohio, 1963), 289-291.

36. David Graham Phillips, "Secretary Root and His Plea for Centralization," *Arena* 37 (February 1907): 120ff.

Romance and Reality

The wind was a torrent of darkness among the gusty trees,
The moon was a ghostly galleon tossed upon cloudy seas,
The road was a ribbon of moonlight over the purple moor,
And the highwayman came riding—
  Riding—riding—
The highwayman came riding, up to the old inn-door.[1]

It was a time of deep optimism, helped along by a sense of the changes in life being unfolded by invention and science and by the spectacular demands of Progressives who were insisting on a leveling up of American life in all its aspects. Yet interlaced with the ebullience of the time was a deep vein of pessimism, made darker by grim winters and the lot of the unemployed. A book like Sinclair's *The Jungle* horrified in part because it suggested that life was indeed a jungle, that Darwin was right, and that it was foolish for man to hold on to the fantasy that he was a special creation and of any particular consequence in an impersonal world.

Such gloomy thoughts made romance doubly precious, and it enjoyed a remarkable flush of success in the pre-World War I years. At the lowest level it offered the *Graustark* version of never-never land, being a tale about an imaginary kingdom in Europe that enabled idlers to escape the real world for a few futile hours. William Vaughn Moody, a University of Chicago literature professor, interested his generation because he seemed, in his verses and plays, to be seeking a modern equation between the old nobilities of an Emerson and the embattled world of current people and nature. His poem "Ode in Time of Hesitation" struggled, not too successfully, with "thees" and "doths," to denounce American war actions in the Philippines. More successful as an effort, though perhaps not as poetry, was Moody's "The Menagerie"; he was one of a number of poets who tried to discern the dignity of man in evolution. He saw such circus creatures as monkeys and giraffes as "botch-work" in nature's efforts to create a better form of life. His poem pondered the uses of pantheism: "there's soul in everything that squirms." And he left his thoughts open-ended for readers to finger and reflect upon:

> If you're a sweet thing in a flower-bed hat.
> Or her best fellow with your tie tucked in,
> Don't squander love's bright springtime girding at
> An old chimpanzee with an Irish chin:
> *There may be hidden meaning in his grin.*[2]

Others frankly sought a past romantic glory. The phenomenon of the time was Stephen Phillips (1864-1915), an Englishman who poured out tender rhymes in verse and in blank verse, which, at the turn of the century, dazzled his readers and theater goers. His *Poems* (1897) were in their thirteenth edition by 1902. His play *Herod* (1900) had sold twenty-one thousand copies by 1902 and was a crashing success on stage. Even more so was his *Paolo and Francesca* (1899), which admirers accounted his masterpiece, ranking its author with Shakespeare and Milton. Critics were dazed by such lines from *Paolo and Francesca* as:

> She takes away my breath.
> I did not know the dead could have such hair.
> Hide them. They look like children fast asleep.

Stephen Phillips who at this time was receiving as much as £500 a week was unable to hold on to his good fortune. He drank and squandered his money. By the middle of the 1900s his reputation was on the decline. And though he continued to pour out plays and new poems, they brought in less and less income, all of which he dissipated in drink and increased rhetoric.

Essentially such poets could not master the language and material contours of the new time. They were bound to be challenged by a newer breed of storyteller and bard. Yet it was not only poets who insisted on a romantic vision of life, one which demanded that human beings and their emotions keep the center of the stage. Many of the public yearned for the old stabilities, as did not a few of their Progressive mentors, sometimes in patently conservative ways. Upton Sinclair overrated his friend George Sterling, another of the poets of the Progressive era who was handcuffed by traditional rhythms and rhymes. Newton D. Baker, Tom Johnson's successor as mayor of Cleveland and the distinguished Secretary of War in Woodrow Wilson's cabinet, later glanced at Thomas Beer's impressionistic *The Mauve Decade* (1926) and found it meaningless. Charles Edward Russell was awed by the "music" of Swinburne and thought Walt Whitman no poet at all.[3]

America produced its equivalents of Stephen Phillips who sought to fend off the cold touch of an industrial civilization. If Phillips's thoughts turned to ancient and Renaissance eras, Ernest Lacy, though he lived and taught in Philadelphia, expended much feeling and imagination on Thomas Chatterton, who died a martyr of poetry in England in the eighteenth century. Poets like Lacy, and their sympathizers, felt harassed by a round of life that deprived them of their dreams; as Lacy wrote, in a five-act tragedy centered around the boy who, though dead by his own hand at seventeen, gave spark to the romantic movement of the late eighteenth, early nineteenth centuries:

> *Song Man.* *[From the street.]*
> Songs! Songs! Songs! Beautiful songs!
> Love songs, new songs, old songs—all for a penny!
> *Chatterton.* The price is up, and poets now can
> nibble
> At hopes and biscuit in Tom's Coffee House.[4]

It was against such a background of romantic aspirations and classical models that David Graham Phillips's search for reality can be best comprehended. Phillips was the meteor of the 1900s, a "fiction factory" of unexampled production, which successive generations of writers and associated critics derogated or ignored in ways calculated to remind the thoughtful of the unsubstantial nature of fame. Phillips took shape for critics in succeeding decades as a muckraker—indeed, the original muckraker—who had scourged the rich and flayed the improvident in words more bitter than penetrating.

One critic deplored his industry; presumably a more leisurely and spasmodic production might have given more profound import to his thoughts. Another scribe thought Phillips confused in criticizing capitalist values while also expressing admiration for them. Still another critic found hypocrisy in Phillips's work, which pretended scorn for a worldly success he actually himself adored. A standard formula that relieved academics wishing to comment on Phillips of the need for reading his writings narrowed them down to his 1906 series of *Cosmopolitan* articles, "The Treason of the Senate," and his posthumous *Susan Lenox: Her Fall and Rise*, which treated at length and with respect the tale of a woman driven by social convention to prostitution and male patronage.[5]

Instructive was the fact that such criticism was impotent to respond to positive views of Phillips, which had been expressed by H. L. Mencken, Ludwig Lewisohn, and Frank Harris, among others. More important, the negative approach to Phillips revealed no method or ability to cope with differences in Phillips's novels, tales, and articles. Phillips had in 1901 cut himself adrift from the liberal journalism of Pulitzer's *New York World* to make a career as a novelist. He had supported those efforts in part with magazine articles that ranged from political analyses to personal tirades against snobbery and waste, some of which were ephemeral or period pieces. His novels had broadened from relatively hasty sketches to others of three hundred and four hundred printed pages, which Phillips wrote by hand and rewrote three and four times before delivering to his publishers. His novel *Susan Lenox* had been conceived in the late 1880s, and it engaged him throughout his life as a novelist.

Criticism merited only part of the responsibility for the casual review given Phillips's life and work. For a while, following his assassination in 1911, he continued to be read as his unpublished fiction was released, his posthumous high point being 1915 when *Susan Lenox* was serialized, and 1917, when it was issued in book

OTHER BOOKS BY

DAVID GRAHAM PHILLIPS

THE extraordinary position which David Grahan. Phillips' novels have taken in the community has its cause and reason.

Mr. Phillips is an Indiana man in the early forties. He graduated from De Pauw University and then from Princeton. He has had a career giving him unusual opportunities to observe the life of all kinds of people, high and low, rich and poor, town and country, here and abroad. As he watched the struggle of humanity to live—the concealment and subterfuge, the extraordinary mixture of good and bad in everyone—all the conflict in the jungle which we call life impressed itself

Back matter for one of Phillips' novels, when he was perceived as a creative writer.

form, challenged by the Society for the Prevention of Vice, and reissued with a hundred pages omitted. During the 1920s, Phillips's fiction persisted in reprints, but for practical purposes, their lives ended then.[6]

Most confusing in Phillips's contemporary, or later, reputation was his identification with "muckraking." Legend had him muckraking not only capitalists and politicians but women, marriage, love. Ludwig Lewisohn's defense of Phillips's later works largely resulted from Lewisohn's own grim experiences with marriage, of a sort, he thought, which had been suppressed in even the most distinguished American fiction. Phillips's view of man-woman relations as requiring natural, rather than mystic or jewel-encrusted, treatment was at least a change from previous handlings, and it made him appear fresh when not shocking to readers in the 1900s.

No effort of any kind was made to separate the "muckraking" Phillips from the chronicler he mainly was, who steadily moved away from muckraking of any kind and who was by the time of his death totally absorbed in the problem of the relations in a democracy of men and women. During his era Phillips contributed excitingly to a field H. L. Mencken disgustedly saw as served by shallow optimists like the American Winston Churchill, "with music by Victor Herbert." Mencken therefore honored Phillips's efforts to put the challenge of American life on a more realistic plane.

Even while Mencken wrote, however, another phenomenon competed for attention, and with some measure of success. Theodore Dreiser was, like Phillips, from Indiana, and like him out of journalism and magazine writing. But Dreiser saw life not as something to be mastered and controlled. He saw it as meaningless drift and compulsion, inevitably defeated. The American public eagerly sought health protecting laws, laws controlling the chicanery of municipal bosses and political party generalissimos. It wanted to write compassion and equality into legislation and constitutional amendments serving women, children, aliens, immigrants . . . yet it also wondered in the recesses of its mind about the validity of life in the first place. A thoughtful minority of critics weighed Dreiser and Phillips in the balance and found the stylistic awkwardness of Dreiser truer to life than Phillips's fighting and determinedly optimistic view that man was not a fallen angel but a rising animal—and that weakness might be mourned but ought not to be honored.[7]

In 1909 was to be published a book which no one wanted, including Viola Roseboro of *McClure's*, Roseboro then being their chief manuscript reader.[8] In that year of 1909 it would be published by subsidy. *Three Lives* by Gertrude Stein was composed of three stories about two servant girls and an unhappy Negress, all vastly less significant than any of Dreiser's drifting nonentities and purposeless executives—flotsam with whom few literate readers would care to relate. Stein had studied psychology with William James at Harvard, but she had drawn different conclusions from her studies. James thought psychology gave modern man a new weapon with which to master fate, as he pointed out in his August 1910 article for *McClure's*, "A Moral Equivalent for War." In it he argued that instead of man fighting man, both could join to conquer nature, disease, and all the other horrors that made life a doubtful experience rather than an inspiring adventure.

Stein was not so sure, and even more than Dreiser, her's was the voice of the future. She tried to treat not only unpretentious lives. By implication she impugned the value of dignity and prestige, of planning and self-control. Stein's prose questioned the reality of civilization itself and clearly held that the most primitive of human impulses, the least intellectual of social efforts, rated equal with the most prideful heritages of art and invention.

Her revolutionary instrument was not analysis but rhythm, the rhythm of words and sentences. which she keyed to her protagonists' careless and unmomentous movements and actions:

> Melanctha was all ready now to find new ways to be in trouble. And yet Melanctha Herbert never wanted not to do right. Always Melanctha Herbert wanted peace and quiet, and always she could only find new ways to get excited.
>
> "Melanctha," Rose would say to her, "Melanctha, I certainly have got to tell you, you ain't right to act so with that kind of feller. You better just had stick to black men now, Melanctha, you hear me what I tell you, just the way you always see me do it. They're real bad men, now I tell you Melanctha true, and you

> better had hear to me. I been raised by real nice kind of white folks, Melanctha, and I certainly knows awful well, soon as ever I can see 'em acting, what is a white man will act decent to you and the kind it ain't ever no good to a colored girl to ever go with. Now you know real Melanctha how I always mean right good to you, and you ain't got no way like me Melanctha, what was raised by white folks to know right what is the way you should be acting with men. . . ."[9]

All this was meaningless to an exasperated publisher who spoke for his generation, in parodying Stein's style:

> *I am only one, only one, only one. Only one being, one at the same time. Not two, not three, only one. Only one life to live, only sixty minutes in one hour. Only one pair of eyes. Only one brain. Only one being. Being only one, having only one pair of eyes, having only one time, having only one life, I cannot read your M.S. three or four times. Not even one time. . . .*[10]

Three Lives was, however, meaningful to those who, like Stein, sought individual expression that was not, like the older individualisms, geared to social experiences and societal hopes. Stein and her friends moved in classical bohemian stances between cosmopolitan sexual and personal liaisons and the delights of upper-class satisfactions. They pursued aesthetic goals suitable to such preferences. Theirs was a program that western society, demoralized by the wastes of World War I and forced to grant democratic privileges to a lower class it had armed and bled, would honor.

It was the democratic decision to embrace further reaches of antinationalism and personal euphoria rather than the jusifications for war. This was seen when World War II, presumably a just war, was followed by continued indifference among wide sections of Americans to traditional American ideals. They manifested an even greater regard for individual catharsis as an end in itself than had the bohemians of Stein's generation.

By the 1940s, the Progressives had sunk out of sight, and Stein and associated writers were established as of classic stature, in and out of the schools. Their individual reputations fluctuated. Out of the Progressive era had come James Branch Cabell, then little read, but in the 1920s welcomed as a subtle leader in emancipated sexual innuendo: a distinction he lost during the rough-edged 1930s. Dreiser, though "classic" for his dark vision of human destiny, was written down by an influential critic in terms that could have been applied to David Graham Phillips: as writing in an inept, journalistic style about worthless characters.[11]

New crises in society relegated some of the latest literary successes to history or academic usefulness, for the most part of little consequence to immediate events. Catastrophic had been the fate of those who, in the 1930s, put their faith in "social significance," who ended up for the most part scorned as merely naturalistic in technique and boringly adept in following the communist "line." The larger scene from the 1930s onward belonged to those who seized on the symbolic, the irrational, the starkly individualistic. Stein was one of their sources of inspiration, but their giant became Ernest Hemingway, whose well-spring of responses was appropriately Spain rather than his native United States. Henry Miller, a favorite of these expatriate talents, imagined himself in one of his fictions as standing at a New York City crossroads and machine gunning the ugly crowds passing him in all directions.

In such a scene of disillusionment, there could be no place for Progressive art. However, as disillusionment succeeded disillusionment, the room available for the irrational dwindled as well. By 1975 the world had become not only gloomy but intensely dangerous. It seemed quite possible that the easy attitudes of experimenters, those who were deliberately obscure, perverse, insulting to readers, might become less a challenge than dull. Readers might ask for "social significance" again but of a more native quality than had been manufactured in the 1930s.

They might wish to read about a spectrum of Americans rather than of a number of formalized types of whatever kind, such as had attracted voyeurs of avante-garde publications—to know better working men and women, farmers, seamen, and civic-minded men and women. How much such a new reading public would wish to repudiate the explorations of a Gertrude Stein it was difficult to say. But in any case, they might wish to draw from some aspects of

Progressivist attitudes: large-minded, materialistic, but with a touch of regard for American habits of thought and expectation. They might then, among other things, feel inclined to consult some of the more attractive cultural relics of progressivism.[12]

NOTES

1. Alfred Noyes, *Collected Poems* (New York, 1920), 1:192.
2. *The Poems and Plays of William Vaughn Moody* (Boston, 1912), 1:67, 15ff.
3. Willis Thornton, *Newton D. Baker and His Books* (Cleveland, 1954), 50. The conflict of generations can be seen in Robert Frost's comment on a 1920 invitation to join a war-weary colony in the South Seas, which was to have included Charles Edward Russell, Clarence Darrow, the literary adventurer Frank Harris, and others. Frost, in declining, noted gratuitously: "I should bar Charles Edward Russell if it were my funeral." Louis Untermeyer, *From Another World* (New York, 1939), 213.
4. Ernest Lacy, *The Bard of Mary Redcliffe* (Philadelphia, 1910), 192. By coincidence, Charles Edward Russell's first biography was *Thomas Chatterton, the Marvelous Boy* (New York, 1908).
5. For an overview, see Louis Filler, "The Reputation of David Graham Phillips," *Antioch Review* 11 (December 1951): 475ff. It treats among others the influential article by Granville Hicks, then a communist, "David Graham Phillips: Journalist," *Bookman* 73 (May 1931): 257ff. See also Louis Filler, "Dreamers and the American Dream," *Southwest Review* 40 (Autumn 1955): 359ff., an article-review of Kenneth S. Lynn, *The Dream of Success* (Boston, 1955), which includes a more modern critique of Phillips.
6. The largesse of President Lyndon B. Johnson gave libraries unprecedented funds for book purchases, creating reprint houses dedicated to tapping those new library resources. As a result, all Phillips's books were reprinted in small editions as a "library service" and sold at absurd prices. It is doubtful that these reprints did anything for Phillips's readership or for that of other reprinted authors.
7. Louis Filler, "A Tale of Two Authors: Theodore Dreiser and David Graham Phillips," in Ray B. Browne and others, *New Voices in American Studies* (West Lafayette, Ind., 1966), 35ff. See also Walter T. K. Nugent, "Carter H. Harrison and Dreiser's 'Walden Lucas,'" *Newberry Library Bulletin*, 6 (September 1966): 222ff., which sees Dreiser's *The Titan* (1914) as "muckraking" plus pessimism.
8. Donald Gallup, ed., *The Flowers of Friendship: Letters Written to Gertrude Stein* (New York, 1953), 42.
9. Gertrude Stein, *Three Lives* (New York, 1927), 207-208.

10. Gallup, ed., *Flowers of Friendship*, 58.

11. James Branch Cabell, "They Buried Me Alive," *American Mercury* 73 (December 1951): 96ff.; see Lionel Trilling, "Reality in America," in *The Stature of Theodore Dreiser*, ed. Alfred Kazin and Charles Shapiro (Bloomington, Ind., 1955), 132ff.

12. They would, however, have to leap over or neutralize some attitudes of their literary caryatids, their informers respecting the true and the beautiful, the good and the bad. Thus, one reconsideration of Booth Tarkington's *Alice Adams*, one of his most challenging works, admitted its virtues of accuracy, control, effectiveness. However: "By the end of the novel the Adamses downfall is complete, completely explained, and to Tarkington completely justified; for he *nowhere considers the injustices inherent in capitalism's inequalities.*" (Italics added.) Adam J. Sorkin, " 'She Doesn't Last, Apparently': A Reconsideration of Booth Tarkington's *Alice Adams*," *American Literature* 46 (May 1974): 197. For another academic example of a jaundiced view of capitalist "injustice," rarely accompanied by an anticapitalist lifestyle, see note 14, pp. 314-315.

Progressives

Progressivism differed from goo gooism, populism, and routine reform by being an amalgam of all of these, plus the more probing aspects of regular party politics. Progressivism in its apparently brief candle of time produced a scenario of drama and passion brilliant in its possibilities for American life. Whether blown out by the gusts of World War I or not, a reaction to progressivism took place that made its career seem futile, if not contrived. Several figures survived the general ruin. Upton Sinclair continued to be useful to would-be radicals, indeed, more so than to would-be reformers. Robert M. La Follette became a legend of a man of the people who had risen from their ranks to voice their discontents and try, against the armies of monopoly, to minister to their wants.

All politicians had to find their way to the fore—and often through the most ordinary channels of political life. Some had no problem in doing so. Joseph L. Bristow of Kansas was a regular Republican who found little to criticize in society—or to recommend.[1] He urged irrigation for the Great Plains, improvements in the administration of forests, and, having served as fourth assistant United States Postmaster General, investigation of frauds in the postal service. Elected as a United States Senator in 1908, Bristow was involved in tariff questions, conservation of resources, and the direct election of senators—all of which was intended to give a modern cast to old ways. In 1910 he became one of the senators who convened to refine a declaration of principles, which became the basis for the Progressive party.

George W. Norris earned a far greater national fame than Bristow, yet as a new congressman he conferred amicably with Speaker of the House Joseph G. Cannon of Illinois, who ruled the House through his command of the Committee on Rules. This was not only because Norris was a fledgling politician. All politicians had to determine their relations to others and to consider how those relations affected issues that concerned them in Congress or at home. By 1910, when Norris became conspicuous as leader of the congressional junta that unseated the Illinois "tyrant" from the Rules Committee and made it independent of him, he had learned more about tariffs, trusts, and other matters vital to the electorate. Nevertheless he was still unwilling or unable, thanks to his own Nebraska alignments, to come out forthright for the Progressive party in his fight for a Senate seat. An anecdote he liked to tell revealed his view not only of regular Republican and Progressive affairs but of the voters whom he had to reach:

> "Mr. Norris [said one of his auditors], I am so anxious to have you succeed that every night before I retire on my bended knees I ask God to see that you are elected to the Senate. Why, I sometimes get so anxious to see you elected that I almost feel as if I ought to vote for you myself."
>
> "My friend," said Norris, "if you feel that way about it, why don't you vote for me?"
>
> "Oh," he replied, "I could not do that. I am a Democrat."[2]

Norris no doubt couched the tale in self-serving verbiage; still, it contained some gritty sense of what Americans were. They could be as cheerful and unsearching as the *Saturday Evening Post* staff writer who thought a "boss is frequently a reformer who has finally grown up, got on to the rules of the game and is willing to play it square."[3] Or Americans could be as cutting as was Deputy Police Commissioner of New York "Bill" Devery who commented scornfully on the efforts of the Tammany boss, Charles Francis Murphy, who had learned to eat peas with a fork and was now looking for higher things. Murphy was seeking a more respectable image by, in 1903, running for mayor George B. McClellan, son of the Civil War general. Said Devery, "He's goin' through the bluff of being decent but look at his record on the old Dock Board" (Murphy's one official job, as dock commissioner). "Does that look as if he's dying for his feller man? He's for Murphy, and he ain't satisfied to use his hands. He wants to get in and use a steam shovel."[4]

McClellan won, and won again, but his second victory consolidated Murphy's reign in Tammany rather than McClellan's, and Murphy rid himself of the gentleman at the next election. Murphy's style might be judged by his insistence that McClellan retain one of his creatures as commissioner of water supply, gas, and electricity on grounds that since he had tuberculosis and was unable to work, it would be an outrage to deprive him of his job.[5]

All administrations did not carry distinctive Progressive or anti-Progressive labels, nor were they either regularly Republican or Democrat. Typical of administrations that ranged within the spectrum of progressivism was that of Judson Harmon, elected governor of Ohio in 1908. Ohio was a key state in the Union, which, a dozen years later, would nominate presidential candidates for both major parties, neither Cox nor Harding being Progressives.

Harmon was an outstanding Cincinnati lawyer who had tended toward Republicanism but found its Reconstruction policy too harsh, and so affiliated with the Democrats. He was Cleveland's Attorney General in 1895. In 1905 Roosevelt appointed him one of two commissioners to look into illegal rebates granted by the Santa Fe Railroad. The investigation implicated Roosevelt's Secretary of the Navy, Paul Morton. The President refused to accede to the commissioners' request that Morton be indicted for contempt, holding that only the corporation could be held responsible. Harmon and his associate resigned in protest, declaring that "the evils with which we are now confronted are corporate in name, but individual in fact."[6]

Such was the man who in 1908 became the gubernatorial candidate of a Democratic party that included "Boss" George B. Cox of Cincinnati, as well as Tom Johnson and his reform junta at the other end of the state in Cleveland. The party platform included proposals for the initiative and referendum in state and local government, home rule for cities, municipal ownership of utilities, and a franchise tax. Harmon was known to be tepid on several of these proposals, and his Wall Street railroad connections outraged the reformers. His administration, however, was vigorous in exposing frauds and waste, and the reformers found him willing to go part way with them in tax reform. Most significant was the fact that both Republican and Democratic factions, representing different sets of reformers and standpatters, made it difficult for the reformers to pass a full package of reform measures.

Most Progressives were not glamorous and were often not even progressive in a deep and committed sense. John W. Davis of West Virginia in 1897 made himself popular as a lawyer with striking miners who defied an injunction of so sweeping a nature that almost any lawyer could have protested its application. Davis spoke for miners arrested under its mandate, in court mustering eloquence to say no more than that "these men had simply marched along the public highway, peaceably and quietly; they had made no threat and offered no abuse."[7]

Davis never represented labor again in an important matter. Yet he went to the House of Representatives in 1911 with an aura of renown as a lawyer of distinction and public interest. His stand there on tariff reform was like the stand he proposed on injunctions: a protested against glaring, incontrovertible inequities. His case for workingmen's compensation was, again, less progressive than inevitable in the new industrial situation created by modern machinery. The American Bar Association—no radical body—had drawn up a model bill covering compensation's constitutional aspects. Davis added little to the argument but legalistic skill and a certain surprise that he would be on the modern side of the argument at all. As Solicitor General of the United States (1913-1915), he supported Progressive measures but as no more than a legal instrument of the Wilson administration. As he himself said, he approached the courts only so that the law might be declared and enforced.

Louis D. Brandeis was a lawyer of different stripe. His cause was security for the common man. His problem was to resist a working law that defended free and unlimited competition at any cost. Brandeis engaged in public-service causes that included campaigns for equitable taxes, for leasing of municipal utilities at fair return to the city, for life insurance and savings banks that would secure the citizens' holdings, and other civic-supportive causes. Brandeis feared bigness. He feared poor social contracts. He was no automatic liberal. A Boston gas situation he called "a source of infinite disgrace to us" was adjusted by consolidation, and the cost of gas decreased. It was an adjustment that pleased Brandeis, who feared that Boston, unappeased, might chose municipal ownership, "for which we are by no means ready."[8] A legislative proposal that would have barred the issuance of injunctions except upon due notice to both parties in the dispute—an aid to labor, since injunctions had often harmed it when granted to employers—struck Brandeis as "objectionable as improperly abridging the power of the Federal courts. . . . Working men who have very properly protested in the past against class legislation in the interest of capital ought not to set the bad example themselves of seeking class legislation."[9]

Brandeis's turning point was 1907, when he agreed to act as attorney for the state of Oregon defending a law it had passed establishing a ten-hour workday for women. The law was challenged through an earlier decision, *Lochner* v. *New York* (1905), which held the legalization of a ten-hour day for bakers unconstitutional. Although the case made Brandeis a national figure, honors for the victory signaled by *Muller* v. *Oregon* had to be shared with others. In one sense, the "Brandeis brief," which became identified with the case and many cases thereafter, could as properly have been termed, as will be seen, the "Kelley brief."

Brandeis was not the first to amass evidence and turn it into an arsenal for affecting judicial opinion. Charles Evans Hughes had, two short years earlier, broken open the private doors of the insurance executives and shown their dark operations by his strong marshaling and organization of evidence.[10] A brief before the Supreme Court was not quite the same as an investigation such as Hughes had conducted, but both required a grasp of enormous detail and the utmost clarity of presentation. Neither would have been available to Brandeis without the work of Florence Kelley.

She was the daughter of William Darrah Kelley who, in Congress, became known as "Pig Iron" Kelley because of his strong protectionist stand. A brilliant student, she entered Cornell University in 1876 where she attained Phi Beta Kappa honors. Her thesis, "Law and the Child," foreshadowed two of her major concerns. Since no law school would accept women, she studied law at the University of Zurich and was influenced by Marxist thought. In 1887 she published a translation of Friedrich Engels's *The Condition of the Working-Class in England in 1844*, for which Engels himself wrote a preface in 1892.

Her marriage to a Polish-Russian physician, Lazare Wischnetsky, did not flourish, and she left him in 1889, taking her three children with her to Chicago. There she plunged deeply into social questions and relations. In 1891 she joined Jane Addams and her associates in Hull House, which became headquarters for various vital campaigns. Kelley's analysis of sweatshops and slum housing, developed under United States Commissioner of Labor Carroll D. Wright, a pioneer in fact finding, resulted in a new state child-labor law. Governor Altgeld appointed her chief factory inspector. Her work being frustrated by languid Chicago attorneys, she entered law school at Northwestern University, which granted her an LL.B. in 1894. Such reports of hers as *Hull-House Maps and Papers* (1895) were milestones in social investigation.

In 1899 she moved to New York City to be secretary of the National Consumers' League, largely a woman's organization. She lived at the Henry Street Settlement and helped build a distinguished pattern of reforms, which took in minimum wage laws, woman suffrage, and federal aid to mothers and babies. Her *Some Ethical Gains through Legislation* (1905) was itself a high point in progressivism in indicating directions for social change.

The National Consumers' League was no paper organization, no New York office with threads of correspondence elsewhere. The Consumers' League of Oregon had been formed in 1903, had observed closely the progress of the state's ten-hour law, and had informed the New York office of its coming test before the Supreme Court. The women in the home office had just been defeated in a New York case, partially because of the weakness of their legal counsel. But they took hope from a passage in the decision. The judge had written: "I find nothing in the language of the section which suggests the purpose of promoting health *except as it might be inferred that for a woman to work during the forbidding hours of the night would be unhealthful*" (italics added).[11]

The women sought a strong attorney. Joseph H. Choate was eminent at the New York bar, and they arranged an appointment with him while Kelley was out of town. But she had set her mind on Brandeis. Both of them admired the late Henry Demarest Lloyd.

Her close associate Josephine Goldmark was the sister of Brandeis's wife. All of them had various interests in common. But they had Choate to bypass. At their appointment Choate boomed: "A law *prohibiting* more than ten hours a day in laundry work. Big, strong, laundry women. Why shouldn't they work longer?" Kelley seized the opportunity to agree with him and cut the interview short.[12]

The women went to Boston, where Brandeis agreed to try the case, provided they supply him with the great amounts of evidence he felt he needed to demonstrate that more than ten hours of labor per day would be detrimental to the lives of women and, as a result, their offspring. It was an approach that Kelley had been working to refine.

The women had a fortnight in which to do their work. They plundered the New York Public Library for materials and received authorization from Professor E. R. A. Seligman, a distinguished economist and, happily, chairman of Columbia University's library committee, to take whatever reference books they needed from the library's stacks. The evidence of women's difference from men they abstracted and rushed to Boston. From it emerged the Brandeis brief. Court hearings and arguments followed. The epoch-making decision was reached that the Oregon law was constitutional. It was a major Progressive achievement affecting legislation all the way into the future—as much an achievement as any act of Congress and inseparable from the drives that found their center there.

The Progressive era is often seen as reaching its high point in 1912 and then sliding toward oblivion. It helps perspective to note that Kelley's last compilation, *The Supreme Court and Minimum Wage Legislation*, appeared in 1925. For those with will and imagination, and principle rather than glib opportunism, progressivism could be found wherever they determinedly looked.

A "consensus" developed among historians in the 1950s and after that progressivism had attracted a particular class of Americans, and largely at the expense of others. Progressives, in such an interpretation, became middle-class business elements, for the most part white, Protestant, and urban centered, well favored in social opportunities but resentful for having been displaced as the dominant power in society by truculent moneyed individuals of no background. According to this interpretation, although Progressives seemed to bespeak the future, they were in reality nostalgic, looking back dreamily to a mythic world of opportunity and egalitarianism.

This hypothesis dovetailed strikingly with another that saw the earlier abolitionist movement as less one that energized idealists sincerely concerned for freedom than as a collection of declassed whites of Anglo-Saxon heritage, women without men, clerical figures and others displaced in society by aggressive entrepreneurs and Democrats, who sought to reinstate themselves by assuming a moral stance toward slavery: a stance basically insincere since it did not intrinsically honor Negroes.[13] Such an interpretation, like that affecting the Progressives, was calculated to demean their crusade as insincere and ineffective.

What was perplexing about such views, which presumably tallied with those of the general public, was that viable alternatives to the crusades of abolitionists or Progressives were not spelled out, when even so much as indicated, and so mirrored a dissatisfaction that could give validity to almost any countercrusade.[14] The Progressives had needed to reach voters if they were to accomplish anything at all, and they had risen from among those voters. The fact that those voters had been of variant components—such as easterners, midwesterners, several species of southerner, and westerner, even New Yorker—should have given reasonable analysts pause. In addition it was fantastic to imagine that Progressives were only political Progressives, thus ruling out of context women, journalists both male and female, minority group figures such as Charles A. Lindbergh, Sr., of Minnesota, Booker T. Washington of Tuskegee Institute, and the Moskowitzes of New York, Belle and Henry, concerned for settlement work, industrial relations, and such enterprises as founding the National Association for the Advancement of Colored People, as well as the furtherance of Progressive political candidates.

Moreover, it was equally fantastic to consider business as somehow separate from Progressive politics and to rule out of the Progressive complex such figures as James Couzens and John Wanamaker. Couzens was busy building up the Ford automobile company in defiance of would-be trusts in the field, Wanamaker was the strong-willed pioneer of the department store, his building in Philadelphia filled with democratic innovations. He cooperated with the Ford partners in their campaign to overcome stifling patent rights in a way that could have cost Wanamaker his fortune.[15]

All of this complicated the Progressive pattern only if one was constrained to discriminate data in terms of a "thesis." It aided reality if one recognized that Progressives were bound or contributed to ideals of individuality, respect for forebears, and a desire to maintain a direct relationship to the sources of power. Such desires created social dangers, as the Progressives worked to maintain their own characters as well as to respond to the will of their multiethnic neighbors. At the other end of the Progressive rainbow lay the tragedy of World War I. But this no more impugned progressivism than it did any other Americanism, left or right on the political spectrum. A tragedy was not a conspiracy.

The variations possible among Progressives could be indicated in such a contrast as that afforded by Charles A. Lindbergh of Little Falls, Minnesota, and Edward P. Costigan of Denver, Colorado. Lindbergh, whose family name had been Mansson when his father emigrated from Sweden, was a Republican nominee who ran successfully for Congress in 1906. His opinions were closer to populism than to regular Republicanism, as a quotation from his election pamphlet indicated:

> Labor gives the main wealth of the world. The so-called capital of the world is mostly the past product of labor and its use and service depend entirely on labor. . . . The day is near when those who furnish the energy of the world's progress will govern.[16]

In Congress Lindbergh fought for the graduated income tax, the eight-hour day, against high tariffs, and against intervention in Mexico in 1916. He offered a bill of his own in opposition to the Federal Reserve bill.[17] His resolution calling for an investigation of the Catholic church "to clear the air" of allegations surrounding it was interpreted as anti-Catholic, though it probably was not, and hurt his candidacies of 1916 and 1918.

Lindbergh lost his bid for the United States Senate to Frank B. Kellogg in 1916 and all but gained the Republican nomination for governor in 1918. The mounting antipacifism, anti-"foreigner" assaults—with its new view of what constituted the "100% American"—hurt Lindbergh during the war years. In one town he was fired upon while urging his son, who was driving their car, not to speed up since this might be interpreted as from fear. Lindbergh made other attempts to regain office, but failed as a Farmer-Labor candidate and died frustrated and embittered.

Costigan's career differed from his in many respects. The son of an Irish lawyer and Spanish mother, Costigan was raised in affluence in Denver, thanks to his father's wise mining investments. Nothing that he did during the Progressive era proper affected national events directly. But his tireless work in favor of democratic processes was exemplary of labors that could not be characterized as backward looking or status seeking. An orator and a lawyer, Costigan fought vice in a locale permissive toward miners' libidinous preferences, and he fought special privileges to utilities when the state's inhabitants were eager to welcome public services on almost any terms. In 1902 Costigan was beaten in his run for the state assembly, through blatant corruption at the polls and his persistent efforts to expose the brutal tactics of the political machine in Denver taught lessons to voters that accumulated results in subsequent elections. Costigan's program of home rule, municipal ownership, and an independent judiciary marshaled Progressive forces, which he implemented with a state voters' league. Costigan worked closely with Ben B. Lindsey, whose fight for the juvenile court had drawn the same fire from special interests and political bosses as had Costigan's crusade. Both went down in the 1906 election, but their continued labors, plus the vital strength they were able to draw from the national Progressive drive, reversed results two years later. By then, Lindsey was a national figure and Costigan a highly practiced fighter who could choose which issues to present to voters.

Lindsey, aided by the journalist Harvey O'Higgins, published in the muckraking *Everybody's* his series "The Beast and the Jungle," which detailed his and the Colorado Progressives' battle with the many-headed corruptionists of their state. The series focused attention on Costigan's fight in 1910 to stop renewal of the franchise of the Denver Union Water Company. Working through the Direct Legislation League and other organizations, the reformers swept the election. Although their mayor proved a disappointment, their new police commissioner, the fighting, assertive George Creel, began a career that was to make him a national and symbolic figure during World War I.

Costigan was the most steadfast of Progressives, holding on when others departed. He supported La Follette's candidacy in 1912 as long as he could, then worked for Roosevelt. In his own state he refused a coalition with the regular Republicans, though it could have made him governor, and he maintained the Progressive principle through 1914, though the signs all stated that as a separate political party progressivism had no immediate future.[18]

Costigan's later career furnished evidence that progressivism was no mere matter of electing a President or of being elected a governor. He served for years with honor and effectiveness on the United States Tariff Commission and in 1930 was finally rewarded with a senatorship. In the Senate he thoroughly supported antidepression measures, from the Reconstruction Finance Corporation to the welfare, public works, and special programs conjured up by the Franklin D. Roosevelt administration. Though he came from a state with few Negroes and many citizens originally from southern states, Costigan sponsored the Costigan-Wagner antilynching bill, which drew the anger of his constituents as well as of southern filibusters.[19]

Lindbergh and Costigan were responsive to the individual voter, the civic organization, the party operating at grass-roots and city street level. William E. Dodd was one of the new southerners, weary of the tales of antebellum grace and eloquence and wartime heroism. He came of small North Carolina farmers and had to bestir himself to attain advanced work as a historian and a position in Virginia's Randolph-Macon College. He was ambitious and believed he had ideas to help the nation. He latched on to the Virginia Progressives, with their hatred of special interests and absentee northern landlords.

As a devotee of the "new history," Dodd sought documents and "scientific" formulations that would separate him from the purveyors of nostalgia. Moreover, he intended to speak for the mass of southerners, as distinguisned from Jefferson Davis and, in Dodd's words, his "ruling, monopolistic class . . . ready for war at any time to avoid a surrender of their privileges."[20] Dodd's idea, calculated to provide a national viewpoint and distinguish him from the sectionalists, was to reprobate oppression in whatever era it might appear. Hence he could deplore monopolies in the South "freely voted by unsuspecting legislatures. The result is a newer and milder form of slavery."

In 1905 Dodd worked feverishly to obtain the election of a candidate for the Virginia Assembly against a stipendiary of the Chesapeake and Ohio Railroad, and his group's victory stimulated his dreams of political advancement. Dinner at the White House in 1907 as a result of Dodd's having sent Roosevelt an inscribed copy of his biography of Jefferson Davis further excited him. Meanwhile he had advanced among his peers in the American Historical Association, and in 1909 he joined the history department of the University of Chicago on pointed invitation to develop southern history studies. Dodd put himself to acquiring the paraphernalia of scientific history: documents, manuscript materials, and the like.

Dodd differed from such other "new" historians as Charles A. Beard, who sought realism through his *An Economic Interpretation of the Constitution* (1913), by being unwilling to serve as just an analyst. Dodd meant to influence contemporary life. He joined other Chicago professors in fighting municipal battles and in 1910 was roused by the advent of Woodrow Wilson, a fellow southerner, to the New Jersey governorship. Maintaining his Virginia connections, Dodd knew Wilson had disturbed some factions in the South because of his "socialistic" schemes. Dodd defended Wilson, and also found himself at odds with historians who clove to Theodore Roosevelt's "new nationalism" program.

Dodd was thus part of a new elite, one mustering opinions to contribute to Progressive thought. It was far from uniform. Dodd, for example, had been unable to cooperate with Ray Stannard Baker when he was accumulating materials for his "Following the Color Line" series for *McClure's.* As Dodd said, he was not sure he, Dodd, had "an intelligent and unprejudiced view of the Negro problem."[21] Baker, possibly more than Dodd, was striving for as unbiased a presentation as possible, or thought he was. Progressivism was made up of both of these views, molded by regional circumstances as well as by efforts to refine national phrasings and perspectives.

It might have seemed grandiloquent and absurd for Robert M. La Follette, in his autobiography, to have characterized himself as having been "alone in the Senate" in 1906. But first it would have served reality to have turned hot and glaring floodlights not on La Follette, who had suffered them for years, but upon those of his modern detractors who might be willing to risk interrogation respecting their own courage and record of sacrifice and philanthropy. "Alone in the Senate" could remind the thoughtful and unpigeonholed student of Dunne's gentle irony respecting Roosevelt's career in Cuba as being properly designated "alone in Cuba." Yet in a real sense, Roosevelt *had* been alone there, as any person was under immediate threat of death or agonized wounding.

La Follette's description of his situation in the Senate raised questions about his earlier situations as a Wisconsinite who claimed to have been fighting the machine during his political rise and even about his very beginnings as a farm boy and student at the state university. That La Follette always had a sense of drama no one would deny. He was, in addition, from student days, an outstanding orator. The question was whether he had falsified his actual status among students or citizens or political organizations in developing his account of his life's journey. In a world in which scholars receive Ford and Guggenheim and Huntingdon Library and even Fulbright money in order to prove that American capitalism and America's leaders were and are intolerable and the national government a danger to world peace, it seems wise to seek perspective on La Follette's version of his rise to national consequence.

That La Follette was poor and constrained to make his way, no one has denied. That he gave good value for his services is also evident. He was a good friend and a good neighbor: sincere in his love of country and loyalty to the well-being of his section of the country. La Follette portrayed himself as fighting the machine in his early (1880) battle for the post of district attorney. Had there been no dissension among Republican regulars, he would have been as thoroughly obliterated as McClellan later was in New York when Boss Murphy turned his malevolent political machine on him. In any case, La Follette would not have gained this foothold without his passion and eloquence and his ability to draw believers to his side.

The year 1885 was a repeat of his earlier campaign: a year of oratory, organization, and resistance to opponents. La Follette was a Republican regular. He accepted the proud party argument that the protectionist tariff protected American living standards from the products of cheap and even slave labor abroad—an argument that was no more true or false than the counterargument of Democratic regulars that free trade meant freedom. The vital question was always what honesty and intelligence a particular proponent gave to his side of the argument—an argument that comprehended national policy and also local conditions.

The program that La Follette developed over the years was as much a product of circumstances as of need. The growing, ever-more complex nation was bound to move toward more regulation, more modern civic techniques, better information. The problem was always with priorities and with conservative reluctance to disturb older habits ard patterns. La Follette was a pioneer, but he was also a beneficiary of a vigorous farmer class in Wisconsin, which perceived its own needs and took steps to satisfy them.

The farmers saw their university as seated no more than a mile away from their capitol in Madison and as early as the middle 1880s demanded that it provide agricultural education. Institutes arose. Charles Dudley Warner of *Harper's Magazine*—and Mark Twain's co-author of *The Gilded Age* (1873)—visited Wisconsin and reported: "I knew of no other State where a like system of popular education or a vital and universal interest of the State . . . is so perfectly organized . . . [and] brought systematically into such direct relations to the University."[22]

Such ideas needed leadership and direction, legislative funds, and the insight and imagination that a La Follette could—and did—provide. It needed the ability to tack and swerve without losing direction, to win and recover from defeat. Steffens later became infatuated with La Follette *because* he perceived that he was no mere idealist who spoke and ran but who held to a line sometimes with aid, sometimes in the face of popular befuddlement or indifference. He discovered in Wisconsin no illusions that La Follette pretended to nonhuman, martyrlike, better-than-thou attributes:

> Mr. LaFollette [*sic]* has ambition. He confessed as much to me, but he is after a job, not an office; Governor LaFollette's

> ambition is higher and harder to achieve than any office in the land.
>
> The first office he sought was that of District Attorney of Dane County, and . . . I gathered . . . that his only idea at this time was to "pose" before juries "and win cases." . . .
>
> "They" say in Wisconsin that the Governor is "selfish, dictatorial, and will not consult." . . . There must be something back of this charge, and a boss should be able to explain it. Boss Keyes cleared it up for me. He said that at the time "Bob" was running for District Attorney, "a few of us here were—well, we were managing the party and we were usually consulted about—about things generally. But LaFollette, he went ahead on his own hook, and never said a word to—well, to me or any of us." So it's not a matter of dictation, but of who dictates, and what.[23]

As governor of Wisconsin from 1901 to 1906, La Follette headed an administration that attracted the country's attention for the broad nature of its reform program. Direct primary legislation, railroad controls, and tax reform headed the list of achievements, but behind them was a battery of university and reference service experts who pondered the often baffling question of what constituted a fair profit. It was also a painful question, since profits were but one item in a schedule of costs, which included depreciated rolling stock, changing economic conditions, and varying details of haulage. A railroad commission helped greatly, but a state was subject to circumstances in adjoining states and in the nation. Finally, the state of public opinion—its interests, its priorities—was a decisive factor.

The La Follette administration kept its reform irons heated. When, early in 1906, La Follette moved on to Washington it was to carry his Midwest crusade to the nation. There were other vital issues beside the railroads and the tariff. The railroads were destined to have to share their importance with other means of transportation; and the tariff was to diminish in consequence with time. In the 1900s, however, they had a heavy responsibility for indicating the direction the country wished to take.

Was La Follette, then, "alone" in the Senate in any material sense?

> [William] Allison and [Nelson W.] Aldrich firmly maintained

> Republican unity; effectively dispensing rewards, they promoted their friends and isolated their enemies. Senators who joined the alliance soon occupied vital committee places while dissidents were excluded from influence. To be sure, anyone could use the chamber as a forum and address the nation. Senators willing to abandon the opportunity to increase their authority could act freely, following their own inclinations. . . . Barring a take-over of the party offices, they could hardly affect the exercise of power. The country might honor their names but the Senate barely felt their presence.[24]

La Follette was not "alone" in the sense that there were not other senators of power and conviction who would affect positive legislation during the Progressive era and after. He was alone in his impatience with the powerful committees and dominating figures able to determine the momentum of change. Moreover, senators, being elected by their state assemblies, were more subject to powerful interests within the state than congressmen who were constrained to appeal to the general electorate. Businessmen were careful to nurture kindly opinion toward their concerns in the Senate. All this helped make the Senate somewhat notorious as "the rich man's club" and a comedown from what it had been in the time of Henry Clay and Daniel Webster.

Fortunately, by the 1900s, businessmen were themselves at odds on law most helpful to their particular functions or industries. The Elkins Act of 1903, for example, sought to eliminate railroad rebates, a practice that had made some railroad men and shippers wealthy at the expense of others. But rebates were now more a trouble than an aid. The Elkins Act was conceived and furthered by businessmen. Similarly, the tariff gave many industrialists added advantages over foreign competitors. They were a nuisance and worse to importers and other businessmen.[25]

La Follette, then, came to the Senate in a situation that had soft spots, except for the party rule which he could either accept or challenge, and the business-senator relations which, with his record, he was hardly prepared to assume. Behind him were a series of hearings that probed aspects of railroad and related public issues but that lacked all drama or a clear road toward consummation in law.

Indeed, there appeared to be, on the surface, as much to say for the railroads as against them as they went about their business granting services and, as occasion suggested, putting their best faces forward. As Theodore Dreiser wrote, with a cheerfulness that belied the somber message of his *Sister Carrie*:

> [I]f the public had nothing save greed and rapacity of its railroads, the sight of the latter adopting a reasonable business policy, whether they seek to educate and make prosperous the public in order that they in turn may be prosperous, is one which, if not inspiring, is at least optimistic. No corporation is soulless, whatever else may be thought of it, which helps all others in helping itself. The philosophy involved in this statement is the enlivening breath of the latest and most successful railroad policy, now being generally adopted.[26]

Dreiser went on to tell joyous tales of railroad agents concerned for the proper shipping of poultry, vegetables, and other commodities and of their efforts to educate their farmers to the best methods of crop raising and preparation. Dreiser was disingenuous, since he cared not a feather for farming or farmers or railroads, despised muckraking, and was engaged in what another generation would call "playing it sincere." As a successful woman's-magazine editor, he urged his staff to adhere rigidly to formulas, admired a Mary Stewart Cutting who wrote "Little Stories of Married Life," and said of the jingler Richard Le Gallienne's "October Vagabonds" series, "Yes, he knows how to write—he knows; and so few do."[27]

So Dreiser, studying the market, reflected many of its impressions and could give testimony that not all Americans were alert to the problems of railroad operation or interested in understanding it in depth.

In Roosevelt's time intense debates went back to 1902, with hearings that brought out all points—specious in the months of attorneys and their clients, sincere to those cautious about committing American choices to government controls. The hearings involved congressmen and senators of high individuality. William Peters Hepburn of Iowa had served as a cavalry officer during the Civil War. He became a long-term member of the House of Representatives and, as chairman of its Committee on Interstate and Foreign Commerce, an expert in transportation. He was opposed to Cannon's autocratic rule of the House but was also an opponent of the civil service and of trades unions. He was to be joint author of the Pure Food and Drug Act of 1906.[28]

Albert J. Beveridge in the Senate was a younger man and differently made. He seemed fated to be made symbolic of not only American imperialists but of all leaders of his time, thanks to his maiden speech as Senator in which he had extolled the American destiny in the twentieth century. And yet not only did enthusiasm for imperialism fade during the Progressive era, and Beveridge's ability to sustain it, but his own concerns, which ran from due transportation regulation to merciful controls on child labor, absorbed his time and diverted him from the issue that academics were later to make notorious.[29] A nationalist was not necessarily an imperialist.

It was in such a combination of circumstances and personalities that La Follette brought to the Senate his passion and experience as Wisconsin's chief executive. Other issues helped. The beef magnates not only handled questionable beef products, they handled railroads and set prices, matters that separately but significantly developed their own careers.[30] Upton Sinclair no more than wrote a novel and La Follette no more than seized the attention of the reading public with his Senate eloquence, but both loosened the flow of legislative action so that leaders in both the House and Senate were forced to act.

The result was the Hepburn Act, which revitalized the Interstate Commerce Act of earlier vintage, giving commissioners the right to judge the validity of railroad rates rather than merely recommend rates to no legal end. The Hepburn Act far from settled all questions. Beveridge, for example, was a forthright Hamiltonian whose meat-inspection act, to his mind, represented the furthest extension of federal power. Yet he continued to be reluctant to extend the powers of the Interstate Commerce Commission to make physical valuations of railroads a basis for rate fixing.[31] In making such a judgment, it is quite likely that Beveridge reflected much of the conservative aspect of the Progressive movement, though newspaper ard magazine agitation seemed to reflect a preponderance of more liberal and even "socialistic" preference. Beveridge himself, struggling to keep his Indiana electorate in line and also to keep options open that might make him President, noted in November 1906 that both the Democrats and Progressive Republicans had made gains in the elections. It was the Old Guard of Republicans that had lost strength. Wrote Beveridge to the conservative publisher Frank A. Munsey, following a cross-country trip: "You have no idea how profound, intense and permanent the feeling among the American people is that this great reform movement shall go on."[32]

The railroads seemed so vital to the day-to-day existence of the nation that it would have been difficult to persuade anyone that the battle for the Hepburn Act was more important for its advancement of the principle of federal regulation than for its specific administration of railroads. In time, the railroads would take second place to other forms of transportation, though the challenge to recapture the uses of the "Iron Horse" would also become one indicator of Americans' ability to master their society. But in their time, the railroads were an imperial instrument of civilization. So powerful were they, so cared for, that one of them in 1905—the Pennsylvania Special—set a record for speed never afterward attained. As such, the railroads became symbolic of the nation's will to modernize its federal-industrial relations, and the Hepburn Act signaled its decision to do so.

In succeeding years, Americans would hold on to both the principle of regulation and the principle of antitrust. Thus, the great John M. Harlan, Associate Justice of the Supreme Court, refused to the end to agree that the "rule of reason," as distinguished from the obliteration of trusts, was good law. The Sherman Anti-Trust Act specified antitrustism as law. A business was therefore a trust or it was not a trust. It was such a hard-bitten viewpoint that caused Felix Frankfurter, as late as 1947, to write Harlan off contemptuously as a mere "eccentric."[33]

Harlan was not so much eccentric as he was unwilling to live with Janus-faced law. And yet the American indecisiveness on this score, the desire to distinguish among the variety of cases—the difference, for example, between telephones as a monopoly and the Du Pont Company—left no alternative to slow and ambivalent action. Socialists who demanded quick yesses and noes to American opinion were polling in the face of history.

Americans were moving toward consolidations. The storm of muckraking views and revelations made it appear that they wished to move more rapidly than they did. Although the Progressive years were filled with new legislation, it was sufficiently qualified to leave options open for forward or backward movement.

NOTES

1. A. Bower Sageser, *Joseph L. Bristow, Kansas Progressive* (Lawrence, 1968).
2. Richard Lowitt, *George W. Norris: The Making of a Progressive, 1861-1912* (Syracuse, 1965), 264.
3. Forrest Crissey, *Tattlings of a Retired Politician* (Chicago, 1904), 90.
4. Allan Franklin, *The Trail of the Tiger* (n.p., 1928), 278.
5. Harold C. Syrett, ed., *The Gentleman and the Tiger: The Autobiography of George B. McClellan, Jr.* (Philadelphia, 1956), 231. Murphy at his death left a fortune in excess of $2 million.
6. Hoyt Landon Warner, *Progressivism in Ohio, 1897-1917* (Columbus, 1964), 214.
7. Harbaugh, *Lawyer's Lawyer, the Life of John W. Davis* (New York, 1973), 40.
8. Melvin I. Urofsky and David W. Levy, eds., *Letters of Louis D. Brandeis,* Vol. 1: 1870-1907: *Urban Reformer* (Albany, N.Y., 1971), 331-332.
9. Brandeis to Samuel Gompers, February 13, 1905, in Urofsky and Levy, eds., *Letters,* 284.
10. Louis Filler, *The Muckrakers: Crusaders for American Liberalism* (State College, Pa., 1976), 190ff., "Insurance on Trial."
11. Josephine Goldmark, *Impatient Crusader: Florence Kelley's Life Story* (Urbana, 1953), 149.
12. *Ibid.*, 154.
13. Although others laid the research background for such a view, Richard Hofstadter, *The Age of Reform* (New York, 1955), was accorded classic stature as summing up such reviews of American experience. It merits notice that this sense of reform movements, which were truly efforts at increasing the "status" of participants, was never applied to the academics themselves. Thus, at a professional meeting, one professor confided of another who was apparently of southern aristocratic origins that he was in fact a "cracker" putting on airs: a southern version of a "Madison Avenue" type who was in origin a small-town Ohio yokel. The critic was himself of southern aristocracy who affected casual clothing and slovenly speech.
14. See, for example, Carl H. Chrislock, *The Progressive Era in Minnesota 1899-1918* (St. Paul, 1971), which, in its first chapter, "The Rise and

Decline of American Progressivism," concludes: "One question of supreme importance remained for the future to answer: . . . [D]id American society have to find new and more radical responses to the revolutionary challenges of the late twentieth century?" See also LeRoy Ashby, *The Spearless Leader: Senator Borah and the Progressive Movement in the 1920's* (Urbana, 1972), which finds the Progressive movement operating in contradiction "between the facts of urban life and the rural sentiments of progressives such as Borah." Cf. Marian C. McKenna, *Borah* (Ann Arbor, 1961), which sees Borah's life as richer than indicated in Ashby and showing much more achievement.

15. Harry Barnard, *Independent Man: The Life of Senator James Couzens* (New York, 1958), 57ff.; Joseph H. Appel, *The Business Biography of John Wanamaker, Founder and Builder* (New York 1930), 154ff. Couzens went on to become an effective post-World War 1 Progressive.

16. James M. Youngdale, *Third Party Footprints: An Anthology from Writings and Speeches of Midwest Radicals* (Minneapolis, 1966), 117.

17. *Public Meetings of Committee on Banking and Currency. Hearings before Subcommittee 3, June 10th, 1913; Statements of Charles A. Lindbergh (and others)* (Washington, D.C., 1913).

18. In that year of 1914, too, Costigan crowned his career as a lawyer by defending in the courts coal miners embroiled in the Ludlow (Colorado) coal strike and accused of murder by the operator-dominated grand juries. Costigan's services included not only gaining acquittal for the defendants but serving as their legal counsel in the congressional investigation of that same year. Fred Greenbaum, *Fighting Progressive* (Washington, D.C., 1971), 58ff.

19. There is an interesting contrast between Costigan and his erstwhile Colorado coworker, Creel; see Frank Annunziata, "The Progressive as Conservative: George Creel's Quarrel with New Deal Liberalism," *Wisconsin Magazine of History* 57 (Spring 1974): 220-233.

20. Robert Dallek, *Democrat and Diplomat: The Life of William E. Dodd* (New York, 1968), 37.

21. *Ibid.* 48.

22. Quoted in V. Carstensen, "The Origin and Early Development of the Wisconsin Idea," *Wisconsin Magazine of History* (Spring 1956): 183.

23. Lincoln Steffens, *The Struggle for Self-Government* (New York, 1906), 82-85.

24. David J. Rothman, *Politics and Power: The United States Senate, 1869-1901* (Cambridge, Mass., 1966), 60.

25. Robert Wiebe, *Businessmen and Reform* (Cambridge, Mass., 1962), 56-57.

26. Theodore Dreiser, "The Railroad and the People," *Harper's Magazine* 100 (February 1900): 479.

27. Charles Hanson Towne, *Adventures in Editing* (New York, 1926), 137.

28. For a summary of House testimony, *Interstate and Foreign Com-*

merce Committee. Hearings . . . on H. 1043; [and others] *to Amend Interstate Commerce Law 1905, 411 p. in H. Doc. 422, 58th Cong., 3d Sess. in Vol. 100; 4879; Adamson, W. C. and Others, Views of Minority of Committee on Interstate and Foreign Commerce, adverse to H. 18588, to Amend . . . H. 10431 in H. Rep. 4093, p. 9-14, 58th Cong. 3d Sess., in Vol. 3, 4762.* See also J. E. Briggs, *William Peters Hepburn* (1919).

29. John Braeman, *Albert J. Beveridge, American Nationalist* (Chicago, 1971), 67. See also *Beveridge Acts and Proposed Acts April 2, 1906, 54 p. S. Doc. 292, 59th Cong., 1st Session in Vol. 6, 4914.*

30. See *HR Resolution March 7, 1904* [to] *Investigate the low prices of beef cattle in the United States since July 1, 1903, and the high prices of fresh beef, . . . in 59th Cong., 1st Sess., Doc. 706, Proceedings against Beef Packers. Message from the President of the United States, April 18, 1906.*

31. Braeman, *Albert J. Beveridge,* 103, 135.

32. *Ibid.*, 111.

33. Richard F. Watt and Richard M. Orlikoff, "The Coming Vindication of Mr. Justice Harlan," *Illinois Law Review* 44 (1949): 13ff.; Edward F. Waite, "How 'Eccentric' Was Mr. Justice Harlan?" *Minnesota Law Review* 37 (1953): 173ff. See also Louis Filler, "John M. Harlan," *Justices of the United States Supreme Court*, ed. L. Friedman and F. L. Israel (New York, 1969), 2:1281ff.

Woodrow Wilson

Theodore Roosevelt was Albany politican, mayoralty aspirant, civil-service commissioner, police commissioner, Assistant Secretary of the Navy, war hero, and governor of New York by the turn of the century. Woodrow Wilson, by that date, had become one of the most influential members of Princeton University but with no place of any sort in political life and no better than a sound status as author and respected spokesman on civic circuits. One was increasingly known to millions, the other to a self-aware elite that set standards in culture and public deportment and took seriously its responsibilities as statesmen, presidents of banks and universities, editors, and industrialists.

The key to Wilson's life was his love of family, his southern heritage, and his Jeffersonian belief in government by the democratic elect. What was remarkable was that Wilson should have risen at all in national affairs. There were scores of distinguished college presidents, many of them shrewd administrators and men of magnetism. None of them attained Wilson's ultimate peak. Nicholas Murray Butler of Columbia University hungered for national honors and for decades maintained intimate relations with Republican movers and shakers. He could reach no higher than, with Taft, the futile vice-presidential candidacy in 1912.

The son of a Presbyterian minister and educator, young Woodrow enjoyed a happy childhood and youth in Staunton, Virginia, and Savannah, Georgia, shadowed by the Confederate defeat and the discomforts of Republican Reconstruction. He was educated at home and at a North Carolina institution, Davidson College. Like so many other southern youth since colonial days, he went on to the College of New Jersey at Princeton, which his father had attended. He then entered the University of Virginia, where he studied law. This proved to be an abortive project; Wilson had no skills for finding clients or furthering their interests. His passions were politics and—a taste he had picked up from his fiancée, Ellen Louise Axson of Rome, Georgia—conventional literature, mainly English. He had few basic sources of inspiration, and he did not augment them. He was awed by Edmund Burke as political analyst and orator and modeled his style on Burke's; and he returned again ard again to the methods and approach of the nineteenth-century English essayist Walter Bagehot, who mixed humanism with public affairs, employing a wit and fancy, a "realizing imagination," a "vivacious sanity," which Wilson also sought to emulate in his writing.

Having no career at age twenty-seven and supported by loving though somewhat anxious parents, he entered the graduate school at Johns Hopkins in 1883. By then he had formulated or privately expressed a wide variety of attitudes, which made sense in the circles he inhabited but did not as yet add up to any professional stance. He was a foe of the protective tariff, slurred Jews, sneered at Omar Khayyam's "miserable philosophy," and patronized both Negroes and George Washington Cable's negative attitude toward secession. Wilson's intensity in connection with politics was extraordinary in view of his remoteness from it. In 1884 he was all but overwrought by the Blaine-Cleveland duel and could not rest until he knew "the right philosophy of practical politics" had won at the polls. His thoughts on the significance of Cleveland's victory were inchoate but revealed an approach the years would mature:

> Overthrow is a much ruder task than achievement; and a party which became crystallized for the purpose of overthrow would not be fit for the execution of great comprehensive plans. We [Democrats] are fortunate in having overcome our enemies *before* we became organized *for that purpose.* Our *sympathy* is thereby established and we are free from the embarrassing task—the impossible task—of converting an army of conquest into a parliament of legislators.[1]

Wilson excitedly saw the Republican party as the "most unscrupulous political 'machine' that ever existed under free institutions." This would have been amusing had Wilson been a comrade-in-arms of Tammany Hall and other northern-city Democrats. In his case, it no more than underscored his profound śense of wrongs foisted on the South under Reconstruction by northern industry.

Wilson had done more than follow elections; he had brooded over national government. He had written several essays, one of which, "Cabinet Government in the United States," was published in 1879 in the *International Review.* In 1885 he carried off a major coup, publishing *Congressional Government*, which was a total success. It won the suffrage of northern and southern scholars and publicists and went into many printings. *Congressional Gcvernment* was really a long essay, offering some pretense to scholarship but being mainly dependent on felicitous expression and the empathy of readers.

Wilson argued that Congress had usurped the powers of government, vitiated the presidency, and so curtailed true democracy—the democracy of the best. Wilson admired the British parliamentary system. He would have had a strong President and responsible cabinet that could be brought down if it failed to meet the expectations of the country. Hidden in his argument was his southern-based hatred of Reconstruction government, which he believed had criminally prostrated his own people. His examination was far from airtight or precise. Senator George F. Hoar went over it conscientiously and pointed out its blatant errors and confusions. Wilson could afford to ignore Hoar's strictures. The approval he received from northern journals and intellectuals was a tribute to his forensic skill and a certain hardheadedness, which saw that North and South had priorities of mutual interest, priorities of commerce and culture that required smoother relations between the sections.

Wilson's curious realism required years for full realization but did not conflict with the image of total rectitude, which he increasingly presented and which in 1912 would be offered as one of his major characteristics. It was so treated by his first campaign publicist, William Bayard Hale, a former clergyman who in 1900 became managing editor of *Cosmopolitan Magazine* and who worked on various journals until 1913. In his *Woodrow Wilson, the Story of His Life* (1912) Hale told his tale, one he could have got only from Wilson himself, which went back to Wilson's Princeton days and illustrated his rectitude.

Wilson had been outstanding in few areas at Princeton, but he had been one of his class's most impressive orators. In 1879 he had been expected to enter the prestigious Lynde competition as a debater and to carry off its prize. Wilson had refused to compete since doing so would have required him to defend the policy of protection. As a dedicated Free Trader—Free Trade was his major cause in 1912—he had been unable to defend, even for debating purposes, a position he held to be reprehensible.

All this was true and admirable, except that in fact the issue offered by the Princeton prize committee had not been protection versus free trade. It had been universal suffrage as opposed to limited suffrage; young Wilson had been opposed to universal suffrage as debasing true democracy. By 1912, however, woman's suffrage had made many successful campaigns. Ten states had already granted women the right to vote, and more were about to do so. It would have been a poor moment for Wilson, running for the presidency, to have clarified the old issue and corrected the record.[2]

Wilson was now married and in need of an academic start. He persuaded his Johns Hopkins mentors to grant him the Ph. D. on the basis of *Congressional Government*, though it did not meet doctoral standards, and he began to teach at the newly founded Bryn Mawr College near Philadelphia. In many areas of outlook Wilson was as firm as he would ever be. He and his wife were both unenthusiastic about Bryn Mawr, Wilson because it housed females who were unlikely to give significant leadership to the nation, or so he thought. In any case, he took steps to advance his professional status. Considering his late start, or because of it, he progressed steadily and without impediment. He maintained contacts with Princeton and Johns Hopkins, in time becoming an esteemed visiting lecturer at the latter institution.

Wilson made the truly original decision to develop the field of administration—something presumably necessary to a responsible government—and scoured the world's literature for works on the subject. He learned German to extend his mastery of sources. An event in his career was Bryce's *American Commonwealth,* with its untidy account of American civic affairs which Wilson later reviewed at length, predicting that in time "America would have to restrict her vagaries, trust her best, not her average members."[3]

Wilson made long lists of titles bearing on administration and government such as an authority should know and impart, and he made other gestures to academe. He had sufficient insight to recognize that he had only a limited interest in scholarship as such, and he actually rejected offers as writer and teacher that would have advanced him as a scholar. Wilson recognized that he was more interested in administration than in the study of administration. John Dos Passos in his cold, unsympathetic portrait in the novel *1919* dubbed him "Dr. Wilson" sardonically, accurately discerning that his was the facade of a scholar rather than the reality.

As important in his development was Wilson's insistence on the importance of literature. The literature esteemed in his community excluded the rugged talents that were creating realism and naturalism in the outer world, the world of Mark Twain, Bret Harte, Hamlin Garland, and E. W. Howe, and thought of Robert Browning as avant-garde. Nevertheless, in the milieu of specialists with whom he consorted, Wilson's humanistic attitude had a refreshing air of novelty, which increased his reputation as a man of warmth as well as responsibility.

It also gave him an advantage in judging the work of others. In reviewing John W. Burgess's two-volume *Political Science and Comparative Constitutional Law* (1890-1891) Wilson took a view that annoyed some academics but won him wide sympathy beyond their control. Burgess was, like himself, a southern transplant in the North, also trained in law, German scholarship and literature, American history, and political science. A scholar would have been grateful for Burgess's scholarship. But not Wilson:

> Mr. Burgess . . . does not write in the language of literature, but in the language of science. . . . A book thus constituted may be read much and consulted often, but can itself never live; it is not made of living tissue. . . . Politics can be successfully studied only as life; as the vital embodiments of opinions, prejudices, sentiments, the product of human endeavor.[4]

Wilson was here more right than Burgess in spelling out an attitude derived partly from his own strangely frustrated political ambitions. But he could use it also in his carefully matured program for linking the South with the rest of the nation. He honored Lincoln on all occasions. A favorite thought of his was the "masterful" nature of the Anglo-Saxon people: indomitable, always advancing, not to be stopped by arms or law alone. Wilson, of course, believed in law, but he distinguished between "lawyers' facts" and "historians' facts" —the latter recognized that life created its own inevitabilities, which were not to be shunted aside by mere established tenets.

In the South, he spoke as a southerner and honored the Confederate war as a necessary fulfillment of convictions and character, a necessary test of national principles. He would later express delight that, as he saw it, Robert E. Lee had been accepted as a national hero and that sectionalism had disappeared.[5] He used his "literary" point of view in another way in order to downgrade, in an unsigned review, James Ford Rhodes's great multivolumed history of the nation since 1850 with its powerful, highly informed analysis of slavery as a way of life in the South. Wilson complimented Rhodes on his studies—he could have done no less—but went on to say: "The truth is that Mr. Rhodes has no insight, at least into complex characters, taking men either individually or in the mass."[6]

In effect, Wilson demanded acceptance of his own view of the South as too "complex" for a northerner to fathom. His remarkable achievement was in succeeding in imposing his view on northerners. Rhodes had, after all, done all the work. Yet he was sufficiently daunted by Wilson's forcefulness to write the journal's editor that he would give "careful consideration" to any errors the reviewer could point out and revise accordingly.

Wilson left Bryn Mawr as soon as he legitimately could. He joined the Wesleyan University faculty in 1888 where he was soon one of the most popular of professors. He not only extended his work in administration but coached the football team. His public image developed. Privately Wilson was as unsmiling and deliberate as any man of serious affairs. But he had had a traumatic speaking experience with Princeton alumni, which had all but made him despair; they had greeted his overearnest call to public service with boredom and over-cigars conviviality. The crisis had taught Wilson that the public wanted to be amused as well as edified. Thereafter he mixed his eloquence with folksy anecdotes and trifling recollections.

In 1890 the call finally came that brought him to Princeton as professor of jurisprudence and political economy. The following decade for him was one of increasing honors untroubled by the depression of 1893, the Populist uprising—which he despised—the tragic strikes that had reformers grasping at mediation principles, or the war with Spain. Wilson wrote for the elite magazines—*Century*, the *Atlantic Monthly*, the *Forum*. He published his conciliatory *Division and Reunion, 1829-1889* (1893)) and his *An Old Master and Other Political Essays* (1893) and *Mere Literature and Other Essays* (1896), all of which sold well, and some essays which had been delivered with charm and profit to civic groups and clubs. Wilson moved his auditors by deploring the "scientific and positivist spirit of the age." He invoked "the great spirits of the past" and called for a revived sense of heart and dedication. At Princeton he continued his earnest attention to football and sang hymns and college songs with its students, who crowded his lecture halls and were awed by his combination of wit and apparently vast learning.

Wilson came into the twentieth century a full conservative who called himself an old-fashioned conservative and who took lightly, for example, the dismissal of Professor E. W. Bemis from the University of Chicago faculty for prolabor attitudes. It was a "family quarrel," Wilson opined, and required no protest or sympathy on his part. Over and over again he cited Burke on law and order and the need for education and culture to support authority. To audiences he made jocund remarks about his own Scotch-Irish people in a kind of fun-competition with the Puritans who, he thought, were less earthy than people of his own "blood." His genteel audiences gave him leeway in comments on immigrant and other less established social elements. He told Negro jokes with hints of dialect, but also with delicacy; he had no intention of being stereotyped as a southern gentleman.

His hero of the 1890s was Grover Cleveland, but as Wilson had thought that the southern cause had needed the effusion of blood to endorse its traditions, so he now accepted the Spanish-American War as necessary: "Whatever our judgments or scruples in these matters, the thing is done; cannot be undone."[7] Fortunately, his views on such matters were not momentous in his daily life, and his references to national events tended to be infrequent and indirect. It was as a dedicated professor and author, one deeply concerned for the nature and role of Princeton—he had in 1896 delivered the principal address at the sesquicentennial celebration of the founding of the college, an address read by leaders in the land—that he was in 1902 unanimously elected president of what had become Princeton University.

His ascendancy was a national, even an international, event, convening trustees, statesmen, scholars, men of the highest affairs. Impressive as was the assembly, it still differed, at least in degree, from that which ruled Washington and the business and journalistic worlds of New York and Chicago. Present were such contemporaries as Grover Cleveland, who lived in Princeton. Among the other important people was J. P. Morgan. The platform could not contain all guests in education and other fields, and many of them, including Booker T. Washington, adorned the first orchestra seats. President Roosevelt was unable to attend though he was understood to admire Wilson's writings. At the luncheon were presidents of other universities, the governor of New Jersey, Mark Twain, Morgan, Henry C. Frick, "Czar" Thomas B. Reed, formerly of the House of Representatives and now a New York lawyer, and Robert T. Lincoln, the late President's son.

Many of those at the ceremonies provided leadership for important financial and political operations in the country, but they did not do so with the public directly in view. In this Wilson agreed. As he said frankly in 1904 to a chapter of the American Institute of Bank Clerks: "No majority ever rules anything. Majorities are manipulated. The discerning minority invariably determines what the majority shall do."[8] What he intended to do as president of Princeton was to produce a keener, more competent, better equipped minority to administer the country beyond the capacities of demagogues and shortsighted conservatives.

As president Wilson did a considerable amount of retooling. He dropped much of his levity, not to be picked up again until he undertook to charm New Jersey voters in 1910, and those of the nation two years later when he offered to respond to the name

"Woody"—a suggestion that was not picked up by the public. Forgotten were football and fripperies. He now defined the object of the university as "simply and entirely intellectual." It would not be long before the students who had once joined him in song would convene to jeer because he had had an iron fence erected around the president's house, which he and his family inhabited.

All of this would have seemed light years away from the progressivism that swirled about the country and agitated Trenton not far from Wilson's campus. Indeed, Wilson paid little direct attention to the issues that absorbed the writer-reformers and Progressives.[9] He deemed himself a conservative of the "less popular" wing of his party, though his principles were to permit him to approve the swift condemnation of insurance skulduggery by the Armstrong committee as a sign of social virility. In the end Wilson was to be made nationally famous by many of the people who took the Progressive issues seriously and, like Wilson, thought his "old-fashioned morals" provided a bulwark against socialism.

Meanwhile, he attended to details of the Princeton scene. He conducted a vendetta against a popular French teacher, Arnold Guyot Cameron, who seemed to him a "mountebank" and who gave lectures "beyond the bonds of decency." Cameron had offered such opinions to his students as that women were good only for raising bread, babies, and hell.[10] Wilson had exalted views of the classroom's function not unrelated to his own experiences, as a place for orientation, stimulation, and example, and though he rid the university of Cameron. he pressed for other goals of seemingly much larger scope.

Basic was his "Quad Plan," borrowed from the English examples, which would divide students into separate colleges. They would be headed by masters who would live with them, study with them as individuals, and eat with them. Thus each college would be a community, interrelated, coordinating social and intellectual life. It would inevitably be democratic. There would be no way for the aristocrats among the youth to avoid contact with their less-favored college mates.

The proposal produced a major shock among alumni, who divided into westerners who found the quad plan attractive and eastern elite businessmen, country gentlemen, and others who were utterly revolted by it. Directly impugned were their well-established student clubs, sentimentally recalled, which had effectively separated the socialites from the plebes. Some of the clubs, with detailed rules for electing new members, had functioned for many years and welcomed father and son.

Wilson could point to administrative successes. In 1905 he brought into the faculty, giving careful attention to their backgrounds and character, some forty-seven young scholars to give individual instruction to students and conduct small groups. Wilson pioneered honors and tutorial work. But his larger schemes were destined to fail. As the *Hartford Times* noted, Hartford being (a Wilson supporter confided) a center of "New England ideas and New Haven prejudices," Wilson's quad plan constituted a blow to individual freedom. The *Hartford Courant* warned the plan would create a "pretty commotion" among Princetonians.[11]

It did precisely that. So much protest came from clubmen, alumni, and older faculty that Wilson's trustees voted to ask him to withdraw his plan, with its dependence on massive funds for buildings, and doubtful alumni support. Wilson bent to their will but contemplated resigning.

The controversy had brought him before the country as a defender of democratic principles on the college level, and his public image was now augmented by a quarrel that divided him less from his alumni than from his own trustees and faculty. Hence, although he acted cautiously and judiciously, when the conservative editor and Democrat, George Harvey of *Harper's Weekly*, spoke February 3, 1906, before the Lotos Club proposing Wilson as a Democratic candidate for President, Wilson was mightily excited. Harvey and he were both conservatives and agreed on Harvey's ironic reference to "the general reformation of the human race now going on by executive decree," meaning Roosevelt's. But, Harvey went on, there would soon have to be a "breathing spell," requiring a leader who combined "the activities of the present with the sober influences of the past." He offered Wilson.[12]

Wilson protested he was in education not politics, but he probed Harvey about influential persons who might have agreed with him. Harvey mentioned Adolph S. Ochs of the *New York Times,* Henry Watterson of the *Louisville Courier-Journal,* Thomas F. Ryan, the financier, and Dumont Clarke, president of the American Exchange bank, among others. Harvey did not rest with words. He negotiated with James Smith, Jr., New Jersey political boss, to groom Wilson for the United States Senate in order to tone down the clamor for reform in Trenton. Wilson, finally, working closely with Harvey, concluded temporarily to bow out of the Senate race in order not to upset delicate alliances affecting the future: a future that would see him first repudiating Smith after his election to the governorship, then repudiating Harvey as his drive for the presidency gathered momentum.

All of this was muted and in the background as Wilson fought his classic battle for the location of a new graduate school: a battle that brought him renewed sympathy from Progressive circles. It was strange that he and Dean Andrew F. West, a classic scholar, and soon to be Wilson's major antagonist, had had no background of differences. They had been cordial since Wilson's accession to the presidency. The actual issue of where to place the graduate school seemed less than momentous to outside viewers, and amenable to compromise. But Wilson was not easy to get along with. He had no equitable temper in the best of times, and his temper was often sharpened by illness and nervous responses. He was even made impatient and intransigent by the best-phrased suggestions of his kindest associates. Later analysts would find in the graduate school controversy a foreview of his mismanaged and confused battle to obtain American participation in the League of Nations.

Wilson's firm demand was that the graduate school must be in the middle of the Princeton campus, with students and others coming and going as part of its daily life. West, dreaming of Parthenons and cloisters, saw the graduate school as removed from the wear and tear of common life. On this issue Wilson chose to stake his authority.

His problem was that West had been the major force in acquiring the gift that was to make the graduate school a reality. And as an executor of the gift he could and did persuade the Princeton trustees to accept his judgment on the proper location. Once again Wilson thought of resigning. He contrived to have the gift refused, but in May 1910 the benefactor, Isaac Wyman of Boston, died and left several million dollars for the graduate school, essentially for West to administer.

Wilson could not refuse the legacy, but the graduate-school duel, coupled with the nagging Quad Plan controversy, roused a new restlessness in Princeton circles over Wilson's stiff-necked attitudes. His credibility as first consul was much depleted. Yet what hurt him with his associates helped him with the general public, respectful of educational mysteries but suspicious of what it saw as an inbred world of snobs.

Following the Harvey pronouncement of 1906, newspaper comment had multiplied about the learned and eloquent champion of democracy. During 1907 Wilson was covered with fair regularity by the press and identified as a presidential "possibility." In a respectful *New York Times* interview he traced tentative lines in the direction of a political program, advocating state regulation of corporate transactions and other controls. He also, having Roosevelt in mind, coupled such suggestions with criticism of too much government; what was needed, he thought, were clearly defined standards of business deportment, with penalties for transgressions.

At the Jamestown exposition in that year of 1907, he sat quietly while the crowd cheered Charles Evans Hughes as the next President of the United States to be. In his own remarks, Wilson informed the assembly that he had not seen much of Roosevelt since he had become President, "but I am told that he no sooner thinks than he talks, which is a miracle not wholly in accord with an educational theory of forming an opinion."[13] Since he repeated this thought a number of times elsewhere, it is evident that he had been polishing it for public use. Wilson continued to refine his thoughts for public display, moving between the pomp of Princeton jargon and "newspaper English," which he approved as "generally terse and clear and right to the point." By 1910 he was ready to leave the rocky academic boat of Princeton and start afresh, this time in politics, taking advantage of the New Jersey "machine's" interest in splitting the reform forces of the state.

NOTES

1. Arthur Link et al., *The Papers of Woodrow Wilson* (Princeton, 1971), 3:410-411.

2. *Ibid.*, 1:480-481. Hale later turned on Wilson who, as President, had

failed to advance him as he thought he deserved. Hale's *The Story of a Style* (New York, 1920) was a bitter, detailed analysis of Wilson's oratorical technique, which emphasized simplistic appeals to emotion, using concepts like "hearth" and "home." Hale was conflicted between the old enthusiasm for Wilson's eloquence and his pride in helping sell Wilson to the public, and his new-found disillusionment. His new book proved little beyond his own mental and moral limitations.

3. Link et al., *Papers of Wilson*, 6:72.
4. *Ibid.*, 7:202.
5. *Selected Literary and Political Papers and Addresses of Woodrow Wilson* (New York, 1925), 1:198ff.
6. Link et al., *Papers of Wilson*, 8:301.
7. *Ibid.*, 10:575.
8. *Ibid.*, 14:329.
9. *Ibid.*, 16:333, 536.
10. *Ibid.*, 15:53.
11. *Ibid.*, 17:245
12. *Ibid.*, 16:300.
13. *Ibid.*, 17:519.

High Noon

Taken as individual crusades, there were no issues of the muckraking period that were wholly novel. Articles, books, and newspaper series had over the previous decades detailed practices of railroads, conservation frauds, Senate highhandedness, municipal corruption. Such publicity efforts had not been futile. The Cleveland administration's work had slowed down land manipulation and even resulted in some returns to the government. Reformers had challenged city machines and never allowed them to sleep at unconscionable length. Railroad issues had been made more sophisticated through constant attention.

What distinguished the muckraking-Progressive drive of the middle 1900s was the writer-action synchronization given social issues covering a wide pattern of needs. Important, too, was the imaginativeness of muckraking. Pallid conservative writing could not compete with it for attention. It was a curious fact that there were more muckrakers than Progressive politicians sympathetic to socialism, just as fifty years before there had been more abolitionists than political abolitionists who were friendly to communitarian idealism. The people as dreamers listened to the hopes and feelings of a Charles Edward Russell, a John Spargo, a Gaylord Wilshire. They responded to Jack London's emotional social sympathies and to Upton Sinclair's overreasoned critique of capitalism. But at the polls they expected greater caution from their politicians.

To many people it seemed that socialism was gaining an important percentage of adherents. It was even electing "socialist" mayors. In fact, this should have suggested the truth: that socialism was no more than providing transitional ideas to enable the more soundly rooted public personalities, such as Roosevelt, to modernize their programs in changing times.

The pure-food drive provided the classic example of writer-action synchronization. It employed the two areas of clean meat and responsible patent medicines as bastions of the campaign. Both areas had received critical attention through newspapers and congressional investigations over the years. Yet it took a combination of factors to force through legislation creating a special agency to deal regularly and expertly with the complex problems of production, packaging, claims, and prices.[1]

Not only the products but the companies handling them helped crystallize public opinion to demand official regulation. The fact that patent medicine manufacturers had organized a powerful lobby, or "trust," as the public called it, added to their ill repute. The fact that Chicago packers were caught in shoddy business practices not directly bearing on the cleanliness of their meat helped mount suspicion of their social conduct generally. Trust charges, railroad abuses, labor policies—all added strength and voices to the demand for radical change. It was one of the distinctions of Sinclair's *The Jungle* that it created a pattern of issues reflecting life as a whole, and so let the reader see that he needed to interrelate his social concerns.

Investigators not infrequently made errors or overreached. Mark Sullivan's own early investigation of patent medicine had involved the advertising of the Lydia E. Pinkham Company and its famous pills for female disorders. The company had urged women to write directly to Mrs. Pinkham about their symptoms. Sullivan had published a devastating photograph that showed that Mrs. Pinkham had died twenty years before. All of this exposed insincerity in advertising. What it did not prove was whether the pill was harmful or useless to women. Mrs. Pinkham had been an earnest, reform-minded person who had worked to make a vegetable compound that might cut the pain and upset in gynecological change. Her formula did contain alcohol, which critics said was the true specific attracting female buyers. The company survived muckraking attacks. What was remarkable was that an inquiry in 1940 not only exonerated the pill of harm, but said it had actually helped women in their menstrual traumas through two of its major drugs, Aletris and Asclepias. The

"The Crusaders" as seen by Puck.

pill appeared to "establish a normal rhythm in a previously arhythmic contractile pattern, and to eliminate superimposed contractions on the normal contractile phase."[2] Practically speaking, the pill cut down pain and "hot flashes" using nontoxic substances.

The Food and Drug Administration had been negative in its findings about the pill, seeing not so much fraud as uselessness. It was a subsequent test by the Federal Trade Commission that brought out the happy tidings for company and buyers. So there were problems in equity in journalistic work, which a simple distinction between truth and falsehood did not cover. There had to be publicity. There had to be skilled writers able to speak with the voice of conscience as well as technical skill. Errors were inevitable. But there was no substitute for an appeal to the public interest.

Such a process of journalistic and legislative appeal could be observed in a dozen fields, which, moreover, impinged one upon another and made the muckraking saga unique in American annals.[3] By 1905 muckraking raged like western fires through social topics, taking some good timber with it, no doubt, but for the most part burning down brush that obscured the vision. Never before had there been so concerted a campaign of popular education to bring the citizen closer to the world he inhabited. The issues were sensational and were so treated in the sensational press. But writers for *McClure's*, and others that followed *McClure's* lead, including *Collier's*, *Success*, the *Arena*, and *Everybody's*, worked carefully to win credibility with the readers and, if necessary, in the courts.

It has already been noted that muckraking did not result in great circulation gains for the most part. What it did was raise its broad-based readership (including the even larger number of nonsubscribers) to unprecedented heights of social awareness, which led to social action. *McClure's* was not even among the top four magazines in circulation.[4] Its readership, however, extended deep into the middle-class home and into influential Washington. This happened also to other publications that entered the battle for light on insurance, on food, and other issues.

The hectic nature of the times, insofar as its reading was concerned, can be shown in many ways but in none more picturesquely than in the career of Colonel William d'Alton Mann, a genuine hero of the Civil War and Gettysburg who appeared in New York as publisher of the notorious *Town Topics.* Mann's major source of revenue was blackmail. His list of donors eager to fend off his charges or sly information boggled the imagination, since the list included such figures as William K. Vanderbilt, J. Pierpont Morgan, Roswell Flower, former governor of New York, and the financiers Charles M. Schwab and Thomas Fortune Ryan.[5]

It was the inspiration of Norman Hapgood, editor of *Collier's,* to denounce Mann in his magazine as a scandalmonger, for which the colonel had the temerity to sue him for libel. The ensuing court case brought forward the "reform" district attorney, William Travers Jerome, who accomplished little reform and who now acted in behalf of Mann. The proceedings were part of the sensations of the decade, filling the courtroom with famous people and circumstantial evidence endless in detail and variety. Mann himself was the best show in town, in his grandiloquent claims of full innocence and good intentions to a skeptical and hilarious audience.

Hapgood was not only acquitted; he was made. "The *Town Topics* suit," wrote his colleague Sullivan, "did for *Collier's* what Collier [the publisher] most desired and needed. The first page stories and heavy headlines . . , the parade of names of the best-known figures in New York yielding to intimidation . . . all combined to give *Collier's* esteem, *éclat, kudos.*"[6] Such were some of the factors that entered into creating one of the chief tribunes of progressivisim.

It remains only to note that *Town Topics,* the blackmail magazine, the rag of innuendo and scurvy intent, was nothing less than distinguished in its cultural profile. It employed James Huneker to cover music and enabled him to develop his impressionistic criticism. It permitted Percival Pollard to write seriously of contemporary American fiction. It published Willard Huntington Wright, who influenced H. L. Mencken. Ludwig Lewisohn contributed to *Town Topics,* as did Ambrose Bierce, Jack London, Israel Zangwill, and Somerset Maugham. Lewisohn put the matter nicely in his *Expression in America* (1932): "One can imagine the scorn with which [Professor] Brander Matthews would have received the information that in 1905 the future of our letters was implicated with nothing that took place in his noble drawing room on West End Avenue and with everything that had its faint but definite beginnings in certain editorial offices, not in the best repute, in the Knox Hat Building at Fifth Avenue and 40th Street."

Collier's was, like *McClure's*, one of the stable forces in muckraking journalism and, as a weekly, was more effective in influencing events than in analyzing them. Its rise in circulation was steady, from 260,000 in 1902 to 528,000 in 1905. The *Town Topics* trial focused attention on *Collier's* but did not do much for its circulation. As Sullivan indicated, it was the quality of public attention *Collier's* precipitated that made the difference, rather than mere numbers.

The one muckraking magazine that did multiply subscribers spectacularly was *Everybody's*. It rose in circulation from 150,000 in 1903 to 250,000 in 1904 to a half-million the next year.[7] The reason was its publication of Thomas W. Lawson's "The Story of Amalgamated," which came to be better known as *Frenzied Finance*. It was indeed a lurid, circumstantial tale that brought into public question and debate the reputations of such figures in finance as Standard Oil chieftains Henry H. Rogers and William Rockefeller and such others as James Stillman of the National City Bank of New York and F. Augustus Heinze of the copper mines of Montana.[8]

Lawson's was an absorbing and in many ways a shocking tale, for he described operations in the sale of stock to the public, which, with high circumstantiality, indicated that men in key financial positions could manipulate public investments—manipulate them in ways that must lose the great army of investors at least part of their investments and with no legal means of indemnification. Lawson portrayed himself as an innocent whose energy and enthusiasm had been used to draw in investors in ways he would have avoided, had he been privy to the financiers' plans.

Yet Lawson had himself been the ballyhoo man for some stocks and enterprises that had not materialized gains except for himself and other "in" people, and in many cases lost the hordes of hopeful investors their all. The basic fact was that stock-market rules were loose and flexible enough to offer a field for every manner of unscrupulous operator.[9] The Lawson sensation derived from the fact that he seemed to describe not a particular piece of financial skulduggery but a system of siphoning money from an unsuspecting and manipulated public—one that dreamed generous dreams of social reform, as well as of gains it had done nothing to deserve.

Lawson's series was of high educational value, even though he undoubtedly told his tale of highly placed associates from a self-serving viewpoint, seeking to protect himself from financial attacks on his Boston and other interests. Americans wished to gamble, and their investment splurges derived some justification from the fact that they gave financial sinews to what were often daring or doomed ventures into unknown industrial terrain. Lawson and others who roused the public to stock-market risks with elaborate full-page advertisements in newspapers were part of a world of losses and gains that could not be fully controlled if it was to function at all, but that needed more and more public knowledge of investment ways and at least a minimal control over reckless claims and false prospectuses.

During the Progressive era, a torrent of articles appeared to warn popular magazine readers of the pitfalls of investment. The articles accomplished little other than underscoring how innumerable were the fraudulent stocks offered and the means by which they appealed to greed, naiveté, and false logic ("Lead and Zinc Most Profitable and Permanent of All Mining"). Most bewildering were the duels the financiers fought among themselves. These resulted in false, planted "information" about industrial developments and contrived interviews in the press designed to draw attention to projects or to divert attention from others. Parties of stockholders or sympathizers, sometimes identified with political parties, whipped up excitement that literally affected stock-market gyrations and could disorient even the most sophisticated insider. Bernard M. Baruch during the Progressive era made himself a millionaire by studying what he called crowd madness, "without due recognition of . . . which . . . our theories of economics leave much to be desired."[10]

Lost in the excitement of Progressive issues and economic ups and downs was a memoir almost as remarkable as Lawson's own *Frenzied Finance* and related to it. Cardenio Flournoy King (or C. F. King as he styled himself) was not so rich as Lawson at his height, but he was a Boston millionaire, evidently with a serene and secure family life, as his son's vacation book clearly indicated,[11] and able to donate a lyceum to St. John's Military School in Manlius, New York. Like Lawson, he was a promoter and advisor. Both issued reports not only on their own enterprises but on the general state of the market, intended to win the trust of the thousands of little people who read such publications and hoped to find advice that would help them to make money.

King came of North Carolina people who, he said, had survived the fall of the confederacy, only to be robbed by a James W. Reid who left the state to become a silver-tongued orator in Idaho. King was highly circumstantial in the memoirs he poured out and published as *The Light of Four Candles* (1908) shortly before he was brought to trial for fraud. These memoirs seem never to have been combed through, endorsed, or controverted. They remain, almost three-quarters of a century after publication, to be tested in the fires of analysis. In 1905 King was held one of the most estimable of Bostonians, and with a large following in the stock market.

Lawson was the fatal figure in King's life. King vowed he had never spoken personally to Lawson; but he had seen him often at a distance and remarked his cold, ruthless eyes. King recounted a tale intended to indicate that Lawson had used a social occasion to confide false stock information pointing to a "bull" affair—one of rising stock values—and then rid himself of stock at inflated prices. King also described Lawson's elaborate estate named "Dreamwold" to draw a picture of a man who lived high on the losses of others.

According to King his war with Lawson was touched off by King's warnings to investors to stay away from the Trinity Copper Company, which he saw as rigged by Lawson and dangerous to investors. In subsequent releases he warned against such other Lawson stock projects as Copper Range and the Arcadian Copper Company and in time cited prices on the stock exchange to substantiate his predictions. The point was that with stock-market agitations it was not always possible to say precisely what had been rigged or not rigged. What was certain was that the two promoters had become deeply opposed. King professed full innocence. He claimed at one point that he could have "destroyed" Lawson by his combination of holdings but withheld his fire having learned that Lawson was sick.

Lawson, on the other hand, he accused of having tried to shake public confidence in his own operations through such false inquiries as:

NOTICE TO HOLDERS OF NORTON OIL, DOUGLAS COPPER OR KING-CROWTHER STOCK

> All persons who had had dealings in any of the above stocks are requested to write to the undersigned, giving the amount and cost of their shares, the person to whom their money was paid, how they were induced to purchase, and particularly if the United States mail in any way entered into the transaction and how.[12]

The implication that fraud had somehow been committed was part of the Lawson campaign that King detailed, naming a variety of well-known Bostonians. He further detailed his public answers and charged that his offices had been invaded, lists stolen, and his customers sent false information. The agent of this deception had been none other than Franklin J. Moses, who had once been governor of South Carolina, had descended to drug addiction and ruin, and been taken in by King. Moses, as "Judas," had been responsible for the panic stories at the order of Lawson. Later, when confronted with his treachery, Moses committed suicide.

King did not display the information that enabled him to know that Lawson had subverted the miserable Moses. Whether then there was indeed a plot to implicate King in forgery and other crimes, and so destroy him, cannot now be known. Lawson does appear to have solicited information respecting Moses's suicide, and King may have persuaded the Post Office of the legitimacy of his dealings. Beyond that, there was much detailed naming of living persons who should have been able to deny his reminiscences but who do not appear to have done so.

King was approached by John F. Fitzgerald, mayor of Boston, to call off his battle with Lawson on grounds that the war was hurting Boston's repute.[13] King stated without qualification that he had been offered a million-dollar bribe to stop questioning Lawson's projects. King's responses, as given, were all couched in phrases of the highest morality. Several campaigns and negotiations later, King claimed to have had "a very Niagara of letters" from investors whom Lawson had victimized. Nevertheless his business in Boston and New York somehow permitted him to lose track of his own responsibilities. Yet he was able to force the "Master Thug" (Lawson) to plead with the mayor to persuade King not to ruin him. King acceded. There was peace, but the panic of 1907 forced King to close his New York office.

It is not possible to say precisely what caused the collapse of the King enterprises. He had entered into the promotion of a mining stock; Lawson reappeared as his foe, working to bring down the stock's price. And now a series of suits and demands surrounded King with immediate demands, for some of which he claimed not to be answerable. King fled—to New York . . . Liverpool . . . the Orient. He returned and expressed a strange surprise to find that all his holdings were gone:

> "Then my Boston offices are closed," I said, early in the conversation with my brother.
>
> "Closed?" he repeated. "They're gone. The business is gone. Everything is gone. . . . Your automobiles have been sold and at this minute an auctioneer is selling your magnificent library, and on next Thursday every piece of furniture—every picture frame and chair in your Brookline home is scheduled to 'go under the hammer.' "[14]

It is impossible to determine the right and wrong of King's jury trial. The prosecutor flayed King as a "hypocrite of the most despicable type," thereby apparently seeking to establish intent to commit larceny rather than larceny itself.[15] Witnesses described transactions, offered testimony on King's character, described his advertisements and business methods. King seemed confident throughout. But he had fled. His accounts were in disarray. He was sentenced to from ten to fourteen years in prison, and died July 21, 1913, at Bridgewater State Farm while awaiting a governor's pardon. Whether he had, as he said, been hounded to defeat by Lawson cannot be known.

It might have given King satisfaction to know that Lawson himself was doomed as a financier. He continued during the Progressive era and after to make lurid charges, which finally eroded all his prestige. In 1909 for example he predicted bloodshed in the streets if a "wheat pool" continued to raise the price of bread. During World War I he made charges of leaks in government policy intended to enrich "big boodle," in one of the phrases he wore out with overuse. In neither case did he produce any evidence of the alleged malfeasance, though in the second instance the House of Representatives had a Washington committee interrogating a wide variety of witnesses, including Bernard M. Baruch, in an effort to track down the charges.[16]

But the great banks and houses never trusted Lawson again, and his fortunes withered. Dreamwold had to be sold down to the ground, as King's home had been. When Lawson died, February 8, 1925, in Boston he had nothing—not a five-cent piece, the court was told. The Progressive era was perhaps right to have used him and discarded him. It gave high moments of relevance to many people who could not sustain their flight.

The "Treason of the Senate" sensation in *Cosmopolitan* (March-November 1906) raised that publication's circulation from 300,000 to 450,000. But, once again, that achievement lay not so much in the new crass readership figure as in the magazine content to which the readers were exposed. By 1906 Phillips was an established article writer, with long practice from his Pulitzer days. As early as Cleveland's second administration, Phillips had prepared a series of articles in which he cited trust after trust to prove that the Sherman Anti-Trust Act was not being enforced. In his "Treason" series he employed the device that had earlier proved effective with readers: of repeating in each article the words of the Sherman Act, following his recital of trust misdeeds, "Such, Mr. Olney, are the facts, and here, sir, is the law," in Phillips's phrase.[17]

Dissatisfaction with the Senate as an impediment to progress and modernization had been long established. The Populists had made the popular election of senators part of their creed. The fact that state assemblies had been thoroughly converted into mercenary bazaars in which United States senatorships could be sold to the highest bidder, representing the most influential and affluent industry, was a notorious truth, casually assumed by men in the street. As the *Outlook*, no muckraking organ, put the matter in 1907: "If a rich man wishes to buy high office for himself, he looks first of all to the Senate. He does so because he knows that whereas a whole State may not be purchasable, a Legislature may be."[18]

An academic essay of 1893 candidly assumed the need for popular elections if the Senate was to regain the reputation it had earned in the days of Daniel Webster and Henry Clay. In 1894 the Senate itself felt constrained to defend itself against charges that it had been subverted by the sugar trust by corruption, in its passage of the grossly protective tariff schedule.[19]

"No: the people don't like the Senate," wrote a citizen to Senator George F. Hoar in 1897. "It grows in disfavor daily."[20] Yet there seemed little that could be done about this powerful arm of government. It could all but stymie reform at will. The reason was that it was firmly integrated in a series of senatorial relations superficially signaled by "senatorial courtesy," but more profoundly by the give and take needed to get railroad, beef packer, raw materials, and manufactured goods industries fully satisfied. So powerful was the interlocking directorate of senators that Roosevelt had to work as best he could through such Senate strong arms as the Old Guard cabal of Nelson A. Aldrich of Rhode Island, William Boyd Allison of Iowa, Orville H. Platt of Connecticut, and John Coit Spooner of Wisconsin.

The heart of their power was the committees they dominated. Roosevelt had to make deals with them and take advantage of changes caused by death or elections. He would work to persuade his friend Senator Henry Cabot Lodge of the validity of measures and urge him to influence other senators. He held innumerable lunches in which he defended measures, using the tariff—so tender to their major constituents—as a threat when appropriate. Roosevelt's whole reform potential was limited by his fixed desire for a great navy, for which he would have all but sacrificed anything else. Many conservative senators were little interested in the navy and could use it as a counterclub to the President's demands. When all else failed, the President would threaten to convene extra sessions, and in the pure food fight he appealed to public support of his legislative demands.[21]

The problem was to reach the citizen who could direct pressure on his state assembly and on the Senate to change or be changed. The idea of the Senate as a "House of Lords" and duly jealous of conservative prerogatives was well established and speciously acceptable. The fact that the nation was in process of modernization and in need of a Senate more responsive to its complex needs required dramatic display.

Phillips had already published in the *Saturday Evening Post* of February 14, 1903, his portrait of Aldrich as "The Real Boss of the United States." It was the sort of title that careless academics would imagine without reading to have been a "muckraking" article, without considering whether the magazine editor Lorimer would have been willing to publish such an article. The article had no muckraking tone or content of any kind. Phillips had agreed with Lorimer—or, at least, understood him sufficiently to meet his criteria—that what Aldrich represented was *power*: something all of the *Post*'s 375,000 subscribers of that year admired.[22]

But Phillips was not content to castigate his readers for weakness or admire industrial and political doers for strength. And when *Cosmopolitan* gave him his opportunity to lash the Senate as a stronghold of reaction, he gave himself to the task with a will. Mark Sullivan in *Our Times* was unimpressed and resentful. Phillips used too many exclamation marks, he claimed: the sure sign of a hasty writer. In fact, an actual reading of Phillips's articles shows careful editorial work—of a partisan nature, true, but effective in what it intended. The portraits of the Senate leaders were fair and representative. Photographs of their homes indicating riches raised legitimate questions about their source. And their precise roles in the Senate—their capacity for usefulness and harm—their long-term services and disservices were appropriate matters for public discussion. The wonder was that there was sufficient public concern to take the matter out of dissident, left-wing politics and make it a matter of public debate.

The word "treason" in "The Treason of the Senate" might have seemed too highly keyed for fair or memorable statement. But when it is realized that at stake were matters of pure food, among other vital issues, a due excitement can be understood, and was. Senator Joseph W. Bailey of Texas, for example, was to be soon disgraced by revelations that he was a stipendiary of the Standard Oil Company, and Phillips's article about him, in the July *Cosmopolitan*, broke ground for the later exposures:

> The Constitution must be *strictly* interpreted; the rights of the states must not be violated! Here is Bailey, denouncing, last March, the bill purporting to check the poison trust:

"I believe that the man who would sell to the women and children of this country articles of food calculated to impair their health is a public enemy, and ought to be sent to prison. No senator here is more earnestly in favor of legislation against adulterated food and drink than I am."

Fully as impassioned as Bailey's protest that he would "fight to the last ditch" against admitting to Texas a monopoly to prey upon his beloved constituents [a reference to Bailey's role in aiding Standard to enter the oil business in Texas]! But—Hear the "tribune of the people" further:

"But I insist that such legislation belongs to the states and not to the general government. When something happens not exactly in accord with public sentiment, the people rush to Congress until it will happen after a while that Congress will have so much to do that it will do nothing well."

Phillips went on to riddle Bailey's reasoning and the intolerable burden it put on government to carry out its functions. His excoriation of Chauncey Depew was given to history as the occasion for Roosevelt's having dubbed Phillips, and writers like Phillips, "muckrakers," as though something unseemly or untoward was inserted into the article. Yet careful rereading of it fails to bring up any point that merits reproof. No subsequent writing on Depew has elicited a single fact to qualify Phillips's portrait of a total machine politician who put his legal training and talent at the beck and call of New York railroad interests and had no other interest or capacity to offer the general public. Thus:

In no one of Depew's own accounts of his career will you find mention that he was a commissioner of the state capital [of New York] from 1871 to 1875. It was during this period that the plans were adopted and the works undertaken which have made the capitol the most expensive building for its size in the world. It ought to have cost about four million dollars. It has cost more than twenty-five million and is not yet finished. The scandal over the doings of Depew and his colleagues was so great that the legislature was forced to appoint a committee to "whitewash" them. The commission in its report complied to the

> extent of saying that it had "found nothing involving the personal integrity of the commissioners." But it went on to say of one part of the work that "if it had been *honestly* done, the commission would have saved at least a million dollars." It cited one building "made entirely of brick, stone and iron," yet against which bills of $59,129.64 were charged for lumber and $100,215.25 for carpenter work! Depew and his colleagues were kicked out of office.

Phillips's other comments upon Depew's career in and out of the Senate were on a comparable level of fact and analysis, as applied to Arthur P. Gorman of Maryland, Spooner of Wisconsin—La Follette's other Senator—Henry Cabot Lodge, and others. Not only did Phillips's readers and editors across the country find his organization and use of facts enlightening, but they responded to the novelistic skill that showed his subjects as having grown into their roles of authority and the conditions that had permitted them to do so. Phillips's pen-portraits, mingled with the public-interest issues which gave them their significance, made them memorable, and more than memorable in the mounting wave of progressivism that carried the demand for popular elections.

How necessary such anchor materials were to popular understanding was revealed in 1909 when, in a tangle of personalities and the most intricate party politics, William Lorimer was elected Senator from Illinois. Subsequent investigation gave evidence of corruption, but so subtle were the relations involved and so much a matter of who might be the greatest liar that Lorimer's election seemed secure. He took his seat comfortably in the Senate, voting with the Old Guard.

The "confession" of a Democratic assemblyman in April 1910, that he had been bribed to vote for Lorimer, opened the case and brought on a Senate investigation. Additional evidence of tainted votes cast shadows on the entire election. In the Senate the issue was posed by Beveridge, who argued that even if one clear case of bribery was shown, the election should be held invalid. Bailey on the other side perceived a clear election even with eleven clouded votes.[23]

Lorimer was acquitted. Attention then turned to the legislature in Springfield, Illinois, where a new investigation dragged the case into further view, with evidence that assembly-directed elections of senators were doubtful at best and with repulsive possibilities at worst. Nothing was truly proved of Lorimer, a fact that oddly operated for good, since the very lengthy process of investigation furnished a case study of the realities of assembly-centered elections. In a sense, the Lorimer case supplemented Phillips's examination of unchallenged senators by revealing the machinery that had produced them. Whether Lorimer was a sacrifice to old ways, he suffered expulsion from the Senate, and the movement toward ratification of the Seventeenth Amendment to the Constitution providing for direct elections was accelerated.[24]

Overstatement often justified itself in muckraking, though it as often resulted in backlashes, which lost crusaders some ground. A curious example of this process involved Gustavus Myers, who gained a reputation for having written a "classic" of investigation in his *History of the Great American Fortunes* (1909-1910). Though it was presumably a monumental exposé of the excesses of capitalism and available to a progressive generation, readers apparently sensed that something was awry in its texture. Its slow route to publication was no result of a capitalist plot. Years passed before even a socialist firm, Charles H. Kerr of Chicago, issued it and decades before its "classic" rubric gave it place in a series.

The reason for this dubious status appears to have been in Myers's method, which exuded an uncomfortable monotony. He turned pages with infinite patience looking for what appeared to him facts for an indictment. Thus his second book, *The History of Tammany Hall* (1901), had to appear by subscription, patently against the will of the Democratic leaders. It appeared an unanswerable bill of indictment of endless mismanagement and corruption, and from one standpoint a just one.

The question of understanding what society was and how it functioned was another matter, and one into which Myers had no insight. He could serve readers looking for one-sided evidence, but such readers hardly needed his book at all once they realized what he was doing. Myers worked with a type of myopia all his life. When the European war came to the United States in 1917, he dropped his socialism and became a convert to President Wilson's vision of life. Myers set out to prove, and proved to his own satisfaction in *The*

German Myth (1918), that Germany oppressed its farmers, drove its underpaid workers, enslaved its women and children, and fostered "mental and social servitude." He drove other themes hard, as in his *History of American Bigotry* (1943), which, as a philosopher and student of freedom was to point out, failed to distinguish "between bigotry and justifiable anxiety, between fanaticism and the indispensible vigilance which is the price of liberty."[25]

Myers's arsenal of capitalistic chicanery, as provided in his *History of Great American Fortunes*, was similarly single-minded in its accumulation of evidence of fraud and inhumanity and in its total inability to fathom the world of competition and of supply and demand.[26] Inadvertently, Myers created a tale that became "classic" to later historians and that passed into popular folklore.

Briefly, and with heavy footnotes, it told that while the federal government was preparing for the defense of the Union, young John Pierpont Morgan had purchased a lot of condemned rifles from the government itself, then turned around and sold them at inflated prices to General John C. Frémont in Missouri. Subsequently the guns exploded or showed other signs of defectiveness in the hands of Union troops.

This account was denounced in a biography of Morgan by his son-in-law Herbert Satterlee in 1939. Undaunted, the then-muckraking John T. Flynn, in his *Men of Wealth*, retorted that Satterlee had apparently not read the record, which clearly and officially spelled out the charges. A cloud of witnesses appeared to endorse the charges in a score of influential books and even in encyclopedias.

A Morgan partner, R. Gordon Wasson, then bestirred himself to look into every detail of the transaction—including the guns, prices, sales office, personalities—and in 1941 issued a private printing of *The Hall-Carbine Affair: A Study in Contemporary Folklore*. It determined, with endless detail from official sources, that not only had Morgan had a small part in the affair as a lender not a principal, but that, barring the initial foolishness of the sale on grounds that the carbines were obsolete, they had been rifled and brought up to standard and sold at a fair market price of the time. All the rest was made-up elaboration by would-be radical or liberal authors.[27]

Wasson's examination of the legend of the condemned rifles was devastating, as was his facsimile reproduction of pages from works by Lewis Corey, Matthew Josephson, and others. It was still not possible to make a hero of the Morgan who had pressed the government hard in interest rates during its Treasury crisis of 1894 when the gold reserve of the nation was dangerously depleted. In 1907 Morgan helped quell a panic that threatened to engulf the entire banking system but not without exacting his own pound of flesh and demonstrating that such "personal leadership" was no firm staff to the country. One biographer even spiritedly refused to exculpate Morgan entirely from the Hall-Carbine dealings, though he made no case for the foolish liberal historians.[28]

What was significant was that Myers's tale made no impression on the Progressive era, which realized that there had to be finance and willy-nilly financiers. If the times did not probe Myers's overdry and contracted historical method, it did not at least take it seriously. Myers did not like the muckrakers and upbraided Lincoln Steffens as a dilletante reformer who was impeding his effort to "do some fundamental work for a better state of society."[29] It was left for a later generation of millennarians to seize the hazy allegations that presumably foretold the end of capitalism, and to treat them as real. Muckraking as such stood up as a valid report on its times and people.

NOTES

1. Louis Filler, *The Muckrakers: Crusaders for American Liberalism* (State College, Pa., 1976), 142ff.
2. Jean Burton, *Lydia Pinkham Is Her Name* (New York, 1949), 274.
3. Despite the towering presence of Watergate, it seems impossible to refer to revelations in the present era as comparable to those of the 1900s. The Watergate exposures seem closer to events in the Grant era than in Roosevelt's. Also, the 1970s scandals are too narrowly political to compare with those of the Progressive era. Drew Pearson and Jack Anderson clearly rate as modern muckrakers, but they hardly constitute a movement. Ralph Nader appears to wish to generate a muckraking movement geared to legal fulfillment. But whether he is an agency or a movement is yet to be determined.
4. Theodore P. Greene, *America's Heroes: The Changing Models of Success in American Magazines* (New York, 1970), 173.
5. Andy Logan, *The Man Who Robbed the Robber Barons* (New York 1965), 165.

6. Sullivan, *The Education of an American* (New York, 1938), 209ff. Hapgood's countersuit against the old rascal failed. See also [Arthur Train] *Yankee Lawyer, The Autobiography of Ephraim Tutt* (New York, 1943), 164ff.

7. Edwin N. Lundberg, "The Decline of the American Muckrakers," (masters thesis, University of Vermont, 1966), 46-47.

8. Louis Filler, *Crusaders*, 171ff.

9. Cedric B. Cowing, "Market Speculation in the Muckraker Era: The Popular Reaction," *Business History Review*, 31 (1957): 403ff.

10. See his introduction to the classic *Extraordinary Popular Delusions*, by Charles Mackay, originally published in 1841 (New York, 1932), xiii. See also introduction by Louis Filler to *The Deluge*, by David Graham Phillips, originally published in 1905 (New York, 1969). This novel was published while Lawson's series still ran in *Everybody's* and included a remarkable prediction of the coming panic of 1907.

11. C. F. King, Jr., *A Boy's Vacation Abroad* (Boston, 1906).

12. C. F. King, *The Light of Four Candles* (Boston, 1908). 116.

13. *Ibid.*, 173ff.

14. *Ibid.*, 492.

15. *Boston Daily Globe*, December 16-19, 22-23, 25, 29-30, 1908, January 14, 1909.

16. "The Crime of Making Bread Dear," *Literary Digest* 38 (April 24, 1909), 673-675; *Alleged Divulgence of President's Note to Belligerent Powers. Hearings before the Committee on Rules. H. R. Sixty-fourth Cong. Second Sess. on H. R. 420* (Washington, 1917).

17. Charles Edward Russell, *Bare Hands and Stone Walls* (New York, 1933), 241.

18. Robert Rienow and Leona Train Rienow, *Of Snuff, Sin and the Senate* (Chicago, 1965), 110.

19. John Haynes, *Popular Election of United States Senators*, Johns Hopkins University Studies in Historical and Political Science, XI (Baltimore, 1893), 547ff.; *Literary Digest* 9 (August 11, 1894), 424.

20. David J. Rothman, *Politics and Power: The United States Senate, 1869-1901* (Cambridge, Mass., 1966), 245.

21. Gerda Elizabeth Weitz, "Theodore Roosevelt and His Relationship to the Senate (masters thesis, University of Vermont, 1963), 60 and passim.

22. By the end of the muckraking era (1912), the *Post's* circulation was 1,739,182, a fact which reflected neither muckraking nor antimuckraking but the rugged middle ground that the *Post* of that generation sought and found.

23. Joel Arthur Tarr, *A Study in Boss Politics: William Lorimer of Chicago* (Urbana, 1971), 255,261. See also *Report of the Committee of the Senate . . . S. Res. 60 Directing a Committee . . . to Investigate whether Corrupt Methods and Practices Were Employed in the Election of William Lorimer. . . . with the Views of the Minority. 62nd Cong. 2d Sess. Report No. 769 Parts 1 and 2* (Washington, 1912).

24. How well it has worked has been debatable. George H. Haynes, *The Senate of the United States* (Boston, 1938), 2:1074ff., spelled out some of the "costs," financial as well as in health and other factors, incurred. All of the caveats fail to add up to a case for a return to state-centered elections.

25. H. M. Kallen, review, *Saturday Review* 26 (July 31, 1943): 6-7.

26. A useful approach to analyzing his method and its implications is Sidney Ratner, ed., *New Light on the History of Great American Fortunes* (New York, 1953), which ponders the meaning and extent of wealth in ways Myers could not fathom. Ratner's introduction precedes a listing and identification of American millionaires compiled in 1892 and 1902.

27. In 1971 Wasson issued a revised and further elaborated version of *The Hall-Carbine Affair.*

28. George Wheeler, *Pierpont Morgan and Friends: The Anatomy of a Myth* (Englewood Cliffs, N.J., 1973), 75-77.

29. Myers to Steffens, March 17, 1911, Special Collections, Columbia University Libraries, New York.

Consolidations

A legend was fomented in the 1950s and given establishment status that progressivism, far from acting to prevent monopoly or monopoly-type business structures, was engaged in wedding business to government and so giving industrial masters a grip not only on business but on government. This hypothesis was remarkable on several counts. It assumed that business influence in government had somehow been suppressed or undesired. There were, indeed those like David Graham Phillips who feared industrialists' machinations. His friend Charles Edward Russell, too, as a socialist treated industry as a foe of public interest, as in his fusillade on its plots and strategems:

> . . . Business usually selects a great part of the national cabinet and all of the nation's judges. Mr. Morgan, representing the iron and steel Interests, may select the Secretary of State; Mr. Harriman's successor, representing the railroad Interests, may pick out the Attorney-General; Mr. Ryan, representing the traction and lighting Interests, may choose the Secretary of War; the gentlemen who control the great oil Interests may choose the Secretary of the Treasury; and by these means a cabinet is assured that will not be hostile to the welfare of the great exponents of Business.[1]

The difficulty with Russell's views was that they assumed a uniformity in business sentiment such as did not exist. There was, of course, always the will to meddle with government; everyone, even traitors, wished to do so. The problem was that businessmen were not agreed on what policy would produce the best results, and for whom. They could unite in freezing a Tom Lawson out of their councils on grounds that he was not responsible or predictable; and his appeals over their heads to the "people" ran out of strength as he had less to offer them in stocks or credibility. Determining due government policy, for example on railroads, was another matter. Roosevelt's break with the railroad magnate E. H. Harriman was a sensation of the time. On the other hand, as early as 1891 a railroad executive with a Granger background but a prime commitment to his railroad held that price schedules were so befuddled that the government ought to regulate the industry.[2]

He was not an eccentric figure among capitalists. Gerard Swope, though of affluent St. Louis family, capped a Massachusetts Institute of Technology education with work as a laborer in the Western Electric Company machine shops and as a teacher of algebra and electricity at Hull House. His subsequent career in the Progressive era and after with General Electric in labor relations and welfare capitalism was impressive enough to make him a close consultant, along with his associate Owen D. Young, to Franklin D. Roosevelt as governor of New York. Young and Roosevelt cooperated to establish the Walter Hines Page School of International Relations at Johns Hopkins University. In 1926, Eleanor Roosevelt, impressed by Young's views of society's needs, publicly expressed her preference for Young over liberal Robert F. Wagner in that year's senatorial primaries.[3]

Dissension among businessmen was produced in 1904 by the proposal to license trusts and corporations engaged in interstate commerce, such words as "unconstitutional," "centralization," and "imperialism" being uttered by worried executives. The railroads themselves abolished free passes, partly because of a sudden upsurge of public irritation with the fact that Roosevelt had been discovered riding free on presidential trips but also because free passes had outlived their usefulness. The government operated with varied measures of control, here pondering an investigation of the Pennsylvania Railroad as possibly moving toward trust arrangements with other lines, there puzzling over law that gave beef trust defendants immunity from prosecution because they had testified freely, leaving only the corporation liable to suit.[4]

The yearning of railroads for government support was far from secret. The panic of 1907 hurt railroads as well as bank depositors and caused its leaders to "astonish the country by a public appeal for cooperation between the government and the railroads."[5] But even before the panic, they had been most active in seeing that the Hepburn Act would service them as well as their passengers and freighters. Here again they produced no united front. George W. Perkins of the Morgan Company championed federal control and modified reform as the best protection for the economic system he supported. James M. Beck, however, as a Harriman lawyer fought the entire way in defense of the legal punctilia that had been the main resource of railroads in their battle, since the 1870s, to limit the power of state and federal commissions to intervene in their affairs. Beck would not so much as concede that the Sherman Anti-Trust Act was good law. He blamed the panic of 1907 on the "impassioned diatribes from men in high places against owners of wealth" and obviously had Roosevelt in mind, though he had earlier been Roosevelt's assistant Attorney General, and received commendations from him.[6] Since Roosevelt had himself made emphatic distinctions between good and bad trusts, it was evident that a Beck, who gathered honors under reform and antireform Presidents, was not so much for or against consolidations or regulation as the spirit in which either program was handled.

Beck expressed over and over again his reverence for the Constitution, which he deemed transgressed by reformers. Needless to say, he read his own interpretations into what the document's generalizations implied, and it would have been fantastic to suppose that any of his interpretations would vary from those of his clients. By the same token, other interests such as organized labor also pored over the Constitution's phrases to note whether any could be seen as partial to their cause. Labor leaders like Gompers thought constantly how they could influence political leaders, especially during election campaigns. What they had in common with industrialists was their belief that the times required new relations between government and special interests.

The movement toward consolidation was not unique to industry; it was also sought by unionists. Gompers denounced the organization in 1905 of the Industrial Workers of the World as schismatic and harmful to labor. He denied that the IWW's goal was industrial unionism, though it obviously challenged the crafts-union structure of the AFL. The Wobblies' real goal, Gompers held, was socialism, and its real purpose to disrupt the organization of labor, and leave it vulnerable to capitalist aggression.[7]

The concept of socialism haunted the Progressive era and woke many fears and defenses. The socialists themselves saw the social possibilities more calmly. As Morris Hillquit, one of their spokesmen, put it:

> Government ownership is often introduced not as a democratic measure for the benefit of the people, but as a fiscal measure to provide revenue for the government or to facilitate its military operations. In such cases government ownership may tend to strengthen rather than to loosen the grip of capitalist governments on the people, and its effect may be decidedly reactionary. Similarly government ownership is often advocated by middle-class "reform" parties, for the main purpose of decreasing the taxes of property owners and reducing the rates of freight, transportation, and communication for the smaller business men.[8]

How much better actual, consummated socialism was to serve its several arms of society remained unknown. Hillquit was in the happy position of being outside responsibility and thus able to live on social promissory notes. But as one scholar was to observe: "The irony of evolutionary socialism [such as Hillquit represented] was that it proved compatible with a political style which systematically undercut its revolutionary message."[9] In due course, both progressivism and socialism were to disappear into the shadows, in the interests of more enigmatic political programs and personalities. But, in the meantime, both contributed to the American debate on how to hold on to individualistic ideals while adjusting society to modern cooperative and regulatory needs.

The public showed something of its true self in its response to the

1908 elections, which once again featured Bryan, this time with a government-ownership-of-railroads proposal.[10] Democratic papers divided on whether it would keep them supine and divided or (like the late silver issue) provide them with a wedge behind which a Progressive program could follow. The Democrats had tried Alton B. Parker, a conservative, in 1904 against Roosevelt and been thoroughly trounced. The defeat had given new strength but no new candidate to the more radical Democratic segments, and Bryan a third try for victory.

The remarkable feature of the 1908 campaign was its Republican presidential candidate, who had been sold to the voters as an amiable but keen-minded administrator—just what the nation needed after the turbulent "Teddy." In effect it was Taft's conservative qualities, the implicit promise that he would not go beyond Roosevelt, and concentrate on jurisdictional formulas, which gave Taft his party's sanction and the nation's. As the *New York World* said:

> [There is Taft's] honorable career as a just and upright judge; a brilliant record as an administrator in the Philippines; a respectable service as Secretary of War; a reputation for great tact, for exceptional ability, for unimpeachable integrity, and for intelligent radical sympathies tempered with a saner judgment than Mr. Roosevelt usually displays.[11]

With such vague generalizations passing for judicious assessment—especially "intelligent radical sympathies," for which no substantial example could be imagined—it is evident that the voters who gave Taft more than twice the electoral votes they gave Bryan, and almost a million and a quarter more votes, had in mind a relationship to government that Taft's victory did not explain.

The Progressive movement continued, and it was evident that Taft could not possibly be its leader. His stiff speeches emphasized law, his references to labor were remote, and labor could not forget that he had made part of his early reputation as the "injunction judge" who had retarded their union drives.[12] Taft's good repute at the beginning of his presidency could be explained only by expectations that he would not reverse the achievements, especially in conservation, of his mentor and sponsor Roosevelt and that he would add a touch of legal and administrative finesse to Progressive measures that were already accumulating in such number as to bewilder the ordinary citizen.

It had been one thing for the citizen to concentrate on the pure food fight. He had followed the insurance investigation to some extent. And the question of railroad regulation. But the Roosevelt era had also thrown up suits against the tobacco trust. The paper trust had by government action been enjoined from unlawful price fixing. The gunpowder trust, the fertilizer trust, the Standard Oil Company, railroads, banking houses, and numerous other areas of business were thrust upon the public's attention as government suits and investigations cried for attention.

Like Filene's employees, the public had had enough of personal responsibility for the common weal. Those who hopefully saw the public as tired of muckraking and excessive legislative and journalistic investigation were to be proved wrong, drastically wrong.[13] But the public had had enough of trying to follow tortuous arguments in a dozen important fields. It longed for competent people of executive ability and social vision who would make decisions for it and see that they were carried out.

Such a man "Bill" Taft, as they tentatively called him during the awkwardly jocund aspects of his campaign, appeared to be: one who, as the *New York World* excitedly put it, would make an end of "Rooseveltism . . . of personal government, of autocratic régime, of militarism, of jingoism, of rough-riderism, of administration by shouting and clamor, tumult and denunciation." Significantly, the *World* distinguished Roosevelt's program, which it generally endorsed, from the methods it expected Taft to apply to it.[14]

The public was receptive to an elite that would administer its affairs for it knowledgably and efficiently; and, public opinion being heavily middle class, it was willing to overlook Taft's patent obtuseness on labor and his view of law as a brake on democracy. His major achievement, for he contributed little to Progressive achievement, was a remodeling of the federal judiciary. "In pursuit of this goal, he demonstrated singleness of purpose, a fertile imagination, and extraordinary dynamism."[15] But the purpose of his work, in direct contrast to Brandeis's, was to retard democracy, to put impediments in its way, not to further it.

American enterprise, linked with progress, had long sought efficiency. It had grown out of "Yankee ingenuity" into the genius that produced interchangeable parts, factories, and the awesome career of Thomas A. Edison. In the Progressive era the movement toward efficiency grew in an atmosphere of excitement, almost passion, attracting numerous talents. It became linked with mass production. The story of Frederick W. Taylor and his refining of the stop-watch technique for determining the most efficient operations in a plant has been many times retold. Taylor's ideas were not his alone, nor new. As Henry R. Towne of the Yale and Towne Manufacturing Company recalled, in his introduction to one of Taylor's books, he had himself as early as May 1886, in the *Proceedings* of the American Society of Mechanical Engineers enunciated the basic principle of efficient management, as follows:

> To ensure the best results, the organization of productive labor must be directed and controlled by persons having not only good executive ability, and possessing the practical familiarity of a mechanic or engineer, with the goods produced and the processes employed, but having also, and equally, a practical knowledge of how to observe, record, analyze, and compare essential facts in relation to wages, supplies, expense accounts, and all else that enters into or affects the economy of production and the cost of the product.[16]

It was a short step from such thinking to the system of thought that became the rage among one order of industrialists and Progressives. The *American Magazine*, organ of Tarbell, Steffens, and others—apostates from the McClure idea—ran a thoroughly persuaded series "The Gospel of Efficiency," from March to May 1911, featuring the ever-dependable Ray Stannard Baker and Taylor himself. One writer referred to the Taylor system as reconciling the impossible selflessness of Tolstoy with the impossible selfishness of Nietzsche.[17] Labor viewed the system with apprehension, seeing it as no more than a cunning industrial gambit with which to exhaust workers through the speed-up system without increasing their wages. Gompers inveighed against Taylorization in the interest of his "three eights" ideal: eight hours of work, eight of sleep, and eight for personal expression. Others, like Ida M. Tarbell, saw efficiency as the golden rule of business, giving workers and employers goals of production in common, from which all gained.

Enthusiasts went further. They sought to answer perplexing problems in civic administration by applying "scientific management" principles to key operations in the life of municipalities. Outstanding in the Progressive era for action and evangelical faith was Morris L. Cooke, whom a reform mayor, Rudolph Blankenburg, made his director of public works in Philadelphia.

Cooke not only made highly touted and highly regarded efforts to define responsibility in the various offices under his control and to measure increases in efficiency and production thanks to superior organization. He became a famous lecturer whom numerous municipal leaders invited to their council chambers to explain his theory and describe his operations. Cooke dilated on how to improve worker-administration relations. He held his auditors with analyses of the work flow of offices.

Efficiency was far from being the equivalent of progressivism, some Progressives emphasizing the "gospel of work," and others, like Edwin Markham, Jack London, Upton Sinclair, and Gompers being concerned for other values as well. When Henry Ford, identified with efficiency as linked with mass production, in 1915 announced his five-dollar a day minimum wage for workers, he created a sensation in line with Progressive thinking and stirred antagonism from the managers of Wall Street concerns. But such controversies no more than demonstrated that there were potentialities in the efficiency crusade which could, or could not, be progressive.

Thus Frank Bunker Gilbreth and his wife Lillian Moller Gilbreth were industrial engineers, interested in efficiency without regard to philosophic principles, yet with a strange flair. Gilbreth, who never wasted a moment, and taught his children to bathe with the fewest motions humanly possible, had a much more joyous family—including twelve children—than might have seemed likely.[18] But, warm and useful as their lives were, their contribution led more directly to computer research and electronics than to the problem of social relations, which true Progressives sought always to further.

Taylorization was like the movement generally toward consolidation, and much like the Constitution to which all ultimately appealed:

no mandate for anyone, but an open field in which the several national interests had to prove their strength and resourcefulness. "Scientific management" did relatively little harm to skilled and organized workers. It was the unskilled, the unorganized, often immigrants who could not unite or study means for resisting mean company standards who suffered most by them and who needed the wit and dedication of reformers in their strivings for a better life.[19]

Elitism and efficiency were related, since both assumed an expertise that democracy could not manage. It was therefore no accident that the central theoretician of elitism should have founded the foremost reform journal of his time and also been an admirer of Mark Hanna, whose biography he wrote in 1912, only two years before his first issue of the *New Republic* came off the press. Herbert Croly despised the muckrakers and their affiliated type of progressivism, and during their entire era served as editor of the *Architectural Record*, architecture being a peculiarly elite field requiring large sums for technical plans for completion. In his milestone work, *The Promise of American Life* (1909), he referred contemptuously to reformers who thought "that reform means at bottom no more than moral and political purification." To Croly the goal had to be a larger program: one of government intervention in crucial aspects of the nation's business, with popular unity achieved around a national ideal.

Croly was the son of interesting parents. His father David Goodman Croly had been a journalist who had coined the concept of "miscegenation." His mother Jane Cunningham Croly was a pioneer woman suffragist, with many achievements to her credit as author and organizer of women's clubs. They passed on to their son the gospel of "positivism," Auguste Comte's view of life as expressing the "solidarity of mankind" but adding scientific understanding to the gospel of Christ: altruism, but with a grasp of human nature.[20]

Croly spent time at Harvard and in Paris and formulated a critique of "Jeffersonianism" as inadequate for the role the United States had to play in the world, if markets and colonies were not to go to other nations and leave his own country helpless to compete and influence events.

The reform component in Croly's thinking was his willingness to give material benefits to those elements of the population that would do their duty to the state; others would suffer condign punishment or be left out of the distribution of goods and honors. Croly was forthright in spelling out aspects of his program. Negroes, he thought, were "a race possessed of moral and intellectual qualities inferior to those of the white men." National unity, he thought, could be attained only by giving the thoughtless masses a patriotic ideal to swallow and follow. He deplored the "recent outbreak of antimilitarism" in France and scorned peace conferences and amicable resolutions. National destinies could be advanced only as Bismarck had advanced them—by deliberately provoking wars and gaining foreign holdings and control for the nation by the "same old means of blood and iron."[21]

It was not surprising that Croly's long and closely knit book was not popularly read, but it did impress Theodore Roosevelt who subsequently built not a few of his "new nationalism" thoughts upon it. Some of Croly's thoughts sank out of sight as a new wave of elitists rose in the 1910s out of the strong currents of muckraking and progressivism—one that could not tolerate the derogation of particular races or ethnic groups, and protested war, though not class war. The basic principle of a new elitism, however, was admitted in fact if not in words in such a book as young Walter Lippmann's, whose *Drift and Mastery* (1914) categorically rejected public appeals and democratic decisions but sought to influence the experts, the intellectuals, those who counted. The *New Republic* itself discounted extensive advertising and mass circulation. It sought leaders, not followers.

Of such was to be the new progressivism that would succeed the old after the elections of 1912: a progressivism that looked for dominating personalities, efficiently binding together in order of priorities the revelations and demands of the preceding decade. Unforeseen was the youth movement of the 1910s which, thanks to the Progressive drive, would walk freely and without hindrance through the woods of censorship, boss-ridden politics, indifference to immigrant travails, moat-defended private business: all leveled or breached by Progressives. This new youth would demand still further freedoms—unlimited freedoms—and unqualified revolutionary goals.[22] During the 1910s their drive for further liberation and the Progressive drive seemed loosely connected. Youth alienation and the erosion of middle-class values would not make its appearance until World War I had come and gone.

The difference between the old progressivism and that in the making could be seen in the excitement crystallizing around the tariff issue. In many ways it was a last hurrah. Free trade and protection arguments had multiplied and filled pamphlets and books at a time when they could literally determine the availability of bread or clothing on their own terms. It was not foreseen that the price of bread might be as readily determined by the availability of jobs, or the value of money, by reciprocity arrangements between nations that were as political as they were economic, or by such other conditions as the later issuance of food stamps or welfare funds in general.

In 1909, the tariff was still a potent factor in its own right and a powerful symbol of the concern of statesmen for people, as distinguished from industry. When, therefore, La Follette and other Republicans set out to fulfill their party's 1908 election promises of tariff revision—which all understood to have meant revision downward—their crusade became one of progressivism against standpattism.

Critics of La Follette, seeking novelty, would later notice that he was for tariff revision in general but for protection of Wisconsin dairy industries against inroads into their market by Canadian farmers. Such irony would have best inspired a rereading of La Follette's own words on the subject, which indicated that he was by no means a follower of new Progressive opinions but a leader who had learned much about the tariff since 1890 and the McKinley era. La Follette and others in the Senate had looked forward to Taft's fulfillment of his campaign promises, though Taft's actual commitments had been general and as brief as possible.[23] Taft had promised a special session on the issue, but when convened it learned nothing from him about a program of revision.

The battle for a new tariff became one of public education: a species of muckraking, this time from the Senate floor. The tone of the proceedings could be judged by La Follette's response to the taunt of a Wyoming Senator who reminded La Follette of his previous diatribes on tariff inequities, especially in wool, and asked him what he had gained from his efforts. La Follette's retort was that once he had stood there alone. "Now there are nearly a dozen men who stand with me. . . . The lines of those who wittingly or unwittingly serve great interests will be further broken. . . ."[24]

To La Follette's side now gathered such senators as Bristow, Beveridge, and others who had come from regular Republican ranks but now intended to break down the tariff into its parts and assess them for usefulness to citizens and industries. Their job was made more complex because Taft had become an advocate of reciprocity with Canada. Much needed to be clarified. As La Follette explained in his retrospect of the tariff fight:

> Republican doctrine, as expounded by Blaine, is based upon the protection of all American industries that can economically be conducted in this country. It then places a high tariff on articles, such as tropical and semi-tropical products, that cannot be produced in this country except at excessive cost. But this tariff is not for the purpose of protection. It is for the purpose of "trading capital." Its object is to enable the President to make a trade with foreign countries by offering to them a reduction of duties on articles which we do not care to protect but which we wish also to export. It is a kind of double protection for American industries—protection of the home market against foreigners, and extension of the foreign market for Americans.
>
> But the Democratic doctrine applied to reciprocity is exactly the opposite. It is based upon the free trade theory. It proposes to make "trading capital," not of the industries which we cannot build up economically, but of the industries which we want to protect. In fact, carried to the extreme, as was done by President Taft in his [proposed in 1911] Canadian pact, it sacrificed the farmers, who, with the laborers, are almost the only interests we want to protect, in favor of the trusts, which are the last interests needing protection. It proposed to reduce our tariffs on farm products if the Canadians would reduce their tariffs on our trust products. No wonder the Canadians rejected it! and I believe the Americans would have rejected it if they could have had a similar campaign of education upon it. . . .[25]

The tariff became a rampart behind which Old Guard Republicans determined to take their stand. They judged it sufficiently complex not to trouble ordinary citizens and sufficiently important for their resistance to uncontrolled democracy. Plainly put, Taft had broken his campaign promises. He could be excused as insufficiently informed on tariff details, but this could hardly redound to his or his party's benefit. The Payne-Aldrich tariff of 1909 paid no attention to the La Follette-junta assaults on it. It raised some tariffs, and it lowered others. But Finley Peter Dunne, in one of his satiric "Mr. Dooley" essays, had already taught the country how to distinguish between luxury items and necessities, between the protection of industries needing protection and those that did not.

All this meant little to the Republican tariff managers, who defied their own insurgents, as well as the Democratic minority, passed their tariff schedule, and left it for their President to defend. This he did with lumbering candor, September 17, 1909, in an address at Winona, Minnesota, while the nation listened grimly:

> In the Senate a new system was introduced attempting to make the duties more specific rather than *ad valorum*, in order to prevent by judicial decision or otherwise a disproportionate and unequal operation of the schedule. Under this schedule it was contended that there had been a general rise of all the duties on cotton. This was vigorously denied by the experts of the Treasury Department. . . . I agree that the method of taking evidence and the determination was made in a general way, and that there ought to be other methods of obtaining evidence, and reaching a conclusion more satisfactory.
>
> Criticism has also been made of the crockery schedule and the failure to reduce that. The question whether it ought to have been reduced or not was a question of evidence which both committees of Congress took up, and both concluded that the present rates on crockery were such as were needed to maintain the business in this country. . . .
>
> On the whole, however, I am bound to say that I think the Payne tariff bill is the best tariff bill that the Republican party ever passed; that in it the party has conceded the necessity for following the changed conditions and reducing the tariff rates

accordingly. This is a substantial achievement in the direction of lower tariffs and downward revision, and it ought to be accepted as such.[26]

The committees concluded. The best tariff bill that the Republican party has ever passed. The party has conceded. The tariff ought to be accepted. Taft's sympathetic biographer Henry R. Pringle insisted that Taft was wholly accurate in his assessment of the new schedule. It *was* the best tariff bill that the Republican party had ever passed. . . . The nation, however, listened to the tone, the specifics, and the outlook and concluded that Taft's version of elite rule was not what it had in mind, not in the Progressive era. This conviction was underscored by the role Taft elected to play in what became known as the Ballinger affair.

There seems no question but that Taft was, to a degree, victimized by the event. For one thing, the chagrin provoked by the tariff imposition lost him great amounts of the sympathy and credit that the public had been ready to give him during their honeymoon period. His pomposity about the sacredness of law also acted against him when it was discovered that he had apparently cooperated with those who transgressed law, however debatably.

Efficiency was, oddly, the dominant feature in the historic happening, though it was so buried in moral strictures as to lose its public features. Circumstances made a wide schism between "conservationists" and others who were not so much against conservation as wanting a balance between conservation and the use of the land. Moral postures continued to confuse questions of policy toward the nation's resources, as in the Teapot Dome scandal of the 1920s. As late as 1943 a historian would denounce Progressive conservation as "hysterical" and then-Secretary of Agriculture Henry A. Wallace's regulatory policies as "un-American."[27]

Progressives did not see their work in conservation as "hysterical." Theodore Roosevelt peremptorily put large tracts of western land into a national reserve as unavailable for private exploitation. Meanwhile would-be exploiters of the public domain, denominated "public land grabbers" by the press and muckrakers, were given national headlines as hundreds of bills of indictment were issued across the country and courtroom disclosures informed readers about assaults on forest reserves, potential water-power sites, and the precious coal deposits. As early as the fall of 1907 there were predictions that "the keenest battle of the coming Congress will be fought between the supporters and the opponents of the Administration's public-land policy."[28]

The battles did not materialize mainly because the issues were too many and interrelated for Congress to resolve, especially since the western public flatly hungered for commercial developments. It could admire a Francis J. Heney, a cowboy turned lawyer and government prosecutor of municipal crime rings and Oregon land frauds, since he had killed a man in gunbattle and been shot at in court. But many of the businessmen were uninteresting and their cases matters of legal interpretation and conjecture about the value of alleged resources buried in out-of-the-way sites.

Gifford Pinchot gained the most attention, as the result of Progressive anxieties about land conservation. As chief of the Division of Forestry in the Department of Agriculture he had begun his work in 1898 with eleven employees. He rapidly, by adroit strategems, especially after Roosevelt came to power, was able to expand his bureau to four hundred men working in six field offices and to augment their work by shrewd transfers of land from the Department of the Interior. In 1898 Pinchot supervised 19 national forests covering 20 million acres. By 1909 he had in his charge 149 national forests covering 193 million acres.

Because of the loose structure of the several offices involved, the good feelings between Pinchot and Roosevelt's Secretary of the Interior James R. Garfield, and the intensely empathetic relations between Pinchot and the President himself, Pinchot became a national figure, "due to his recognized efficiency in the forest service."[29] In fact, Pinchot's efficiency amounted to withdrawing from public settlement and use, through Roosevelt, some sixteen million acres of timber, mineral lands, and other valued terrain. "The magnitude of the withdrawals and of their local importance may be measured by the fact that the forest, coal, phosphate, and water reserves in Idaho alone covered one-half of that state and totaled an area equal to the size of New York State."[30] As important was the spirit which Roosevelt, informed and inspired by Pinchot, though himself squirelike in his love of nature and of "his" domain as President, infused into the conservation issue. Roosevelt very often sponsored research into the nation's holdings. He set up commissions to oversee aspects of conservation and spoke with his regularly recognized vigor in its behalf in speeches, often lucubrated by Pinchot, which infuriated his antagonists. The man who had "taken" the Panama Canal was not to be limited by congressional punctilia, and he undoubtedly transgressed the letter, as well as the spirit, of many of its acts.

Pinchot's activities in creating a powerful conservation movement, as well as a long-armed and muscular forestry service, were marked by high political skill and daring. He set up conferences in furtherance of his drive that brought together scientists and professors who issued resolutions and reports supporting Pinchot's program. They not only reached the public but put pressure on Congress itself to accede to conservationist demands and extend Pinchot's authority to everything above and below ground. He was limited by little more than the vital right of the Interior's land office to issue titles for leasing or sale.

Pinchot was, in his own way, even more vibrantly aggressive than the President himself. He persuaded William Jennings Bryan to write an editorial opposing monopolies and, as was his wont, sent Bryan a torrent of materials along with charges that the General Electric Company and the Westinghouse Company were conspiring to gain control of water and power resources in various parts of the country. Pinchot admitted that he lacked "legal proof" of monopoly—obtainable only through somehow acquiring the companies books—but emphasized that if they waited for unqualified proof, "the monopoly will be riveted upon the people" so firmly that there would be difficulty in undoing it.[33]

It was this kind of arbitrary action and conjecture that the new Taft administration undertook to modify, to be sure with arbitrary action of its own. That it was sympathetic to developers and industrial combines there can be no doubt. Pinchot labored to prevent sales to them and fought for leasing arrangements. He also advocated a direct type of action, which disturbed the legalistic Taft—disturbed, too, his new Secretary of the Interior Richard A. Ballinger, an expert on land law from Seattle, where he had served as a reform mayor. At some financial loss, Ballinger had reluctantly accepted the post of commissioner of the General Land Office. He had reorganized the bureau, made it more efficient, and returned to Seattle, taking with him the praises of Roosevelt and Garfield. Apparently it was his work for Taft during the 1908 election that suggested him for position of Secretary of the Interior, though Taft had promised Roosevelt to keep Garfield on. Ballinger returned to Washington, this time with the entire department in his keep.

It soon became evident that Ballinger and Pinchot had serious disagreements, and it was a sign of the times that a bureau head should have ranked in public esteem with a departmental secretary. Ballinger would have been wise to take note of the fact. He sought, instead, bureaucratic avenues for advancing his program for consolidation of Interior functions and (here the picture blurs) a cohesive approach to policies governing the public domain. Without doubt he agreed with the National Public Domain League, based in Denver, which saw Pinchot's policy as "imperialistic," and with the *Portland Oregonian*, which condemned Pinchot's irrigation plans as "socialistic." He could not have been too far removed from his Acting Secretary Ormsby McHarg's thinking, when that worthy denounced Roosevelt's approach in conservation as "chimerical and impossible," and went on to see Roosevelt as thinking he was the Lord himself: "He acted like it around here for a good many years."[32]

McHarg was dismissed within twenty-four hours but the message was clear that the new efficiency was based elsewhere than in progressivism. Certainly, there was deep sympathy for Ballinger in wide areas of the West. But it would have been wise for an astute analyst of the public temper to distinguish between the public's materialistic interests and the proper face it thought its government should wear. In the Progressive era and even after, the public would demand respect, if only the respect implicit in hypocrisy. The McHarg outburst in its vehemence and crudity suggested that the new administration was less than stable in temperament.

In due course the Ballinger affair unfolded as a classic of Old Guard-Progressive confrontation. Ballinger himself was probably closer to a reform perspective than to an antireform program. He was critical of Roosevelt's flexible attitude toward big business—which Ballinger identified with eastern monopoly—and would have encouraged the adventurer, the westerner, the man on the make. As he said in his first annual report: "The best thought of the day is not that development shall be by national agencies, but that wise utilization shall be secured through private enterprise under national supervision and control."[33]

Precisely, therefore, how he viewed the so-called Cunningham claims to Alaskan land properties believed to be valuable is unclear. Clarence Cunningham was one of a number of adjacent claimants, all of them located in Seattle, Portland, and Spokane. They were almost certainly planning—and against the clear intent of the law—to unite their holdings and possibly sell them to or develop them for a combination of Morgan and Guggenheim interests. Ballinger certainly dealt with those northwestern entrepreneurs. As a government official, he was liable to suspicion as involved in a conflict of interests, though just what he hoped to gain by such maneuvers, if anything, was never spelled out.

Whatever Ballinger's reasoning, he took steps to clear the claims, pressed his agents on the West Coast to hurry up their formal investigation of them so that he could act, and ran up against a persistent young man in his department, Louis R. Glavis, age twenty-four, who insisted that there was evidence that the claims were fraudulent under the law. Glavis transgressed bureaucratic procedure with his pertinacity and went to Washington to present his case in person. He failed to impress Ballinger and turned to Pinchot for support. The plot thickened as Pinchot got Glavis an interview with Taft. The President was even less touched by Glavis's ardor and recommended his dismissal to Ballinger.

The story was to be told many times: how Pinchot took the matter to *Collier's*; how he had Glavis write his report for Norman Hapgood, who made a major campaign of the matter; how Pinchot was first warned by Taft not to interfere in Interior concerns, then dismissed from his post for defying instructions by making the issue public. Unlike Taft, Pinchot had eyes on the press and citizenry, and the dismissal was an occasion for rejoicing in the Pinchot household. "Lots of reporters," wrote his mother. The muckrakers poured out innumerable articles in newspapers and magazines on monopoly, on Alaskan resources, on the conjectural relations between Taft, Ballinger, and interests elsewhere.

Those who derogated the influence of the press included Glavis's associates, who continued to be suspicious of the Cunningham claimants but who also doubted the complicity of Ballinger. Wrote one, Glavis "is suffering from a case of self-poisoning. . . . He has been patted on the back by Pinchot and [A. C.] Shaw [of the Forest Service] and led astray by the Lincoln Steffens brand of muckrakers."

The muckrakers included C. P. Connolly, a lawyer as well as a conservationist, whose legal analysis in the December 18, 1909, issue of *Collier's*, "Can This Be White-Washed Also?" finally forced a congressional investigation. It was important, too, that E. W. Scripps had been personally persuaded of Ballinger's culpability in a meeting arranged by a Progressive lawyer, Hal C. DeRan, who brought Connolly and Glavis to Scripps to state their case. Scripps turned the machinery of his newspaper chain upon the Taft administration.[35]

The Joint Investigating Committee that met in January 1910 to determine the right and wrong of Interior and Forestry affairs became the focus of all eyes, with conservation policy apparently in the balance.[36] Once more Brandeis reached a height of public attention as counsel for Pinchot, Glavis, and *Collier's*, which had reason to fear ruinous suits in court if the investigation went against them. Brandeis's clear, unrelenting, and directed questioning of witnesses brought out not so much the matter of land law as the intentions of the administration. In his demand for documents and more documents, Brandeis managed to suggest a cabal of furtive, mealy-mouthed functionaries, reluctant to cooperate, evasive, and almost certainly lying, and in sharp contrast with the candid and public-spirited Pinchot and Glavis who had no more than sought to defend part of the nation's heritage.

There were strange aspects to the testimony elicited, such as that by Stephen Birch, manager of the Morgan-Guggenheim Alaskan Syndicate, who volunteered the information that his employers expected to realize $25 million dollars from coal lands the government would sell them for $25,000. The syndicate leaders appear to have believed they were contradicting wild charges flung about by the newspapers, but Ballinger, for one, was puzzled that they would freely display information substantiating one of Glavis's charges.[37]

Brandeis's interrogations were masterpieces of undiminished

pertinacity, which had the bureaucrats refusing to answer, denying imputations but without proof, and otherwise looking like culprits. Brandeis's powerful attack was crowned by his discovery that Taft had predated a letter to give the appearance of having consulted materials not available to him. The news that the President had been caught in a lie created a sensation. Its ultimate result was to cost the Republican party its control of the House at the next elections.

Brandeis's admiring biographer conceded that predating was not uncommon and that nothing was clearly proved about the Cunningham claimants and the Interior. Had Ballinger and the President simply stated their position on land policy and attitudes toward subordinates, it is likely that the country would have accepted their views as either realistic or, for better or worse, conservative. After all, as has been seen, a large percentage of the country agreed with Ballinger's general position. In addition, the Alaskans did—they were eager to see industry come to their territory on almost any terms.[38] The public was not so foolish as not to understand that much lying went on in Washington as elsewhere. It did not, at that point, care to carry so gauche a set of bureaucrats over the obstacle course it had itself created. In effect, it abandoned them.

Taft's actual conservation program was every bit as good as Roosevelt's. He did not like trusts and would take pride in having dissolved the Standard Oil and tobacco trusts. "I am in full sympathy," he informed Congress earnestly, "with the concern of reasonable and patriotic men that the valuable resources of Alaska should not be turned over to be exploited for the profit of greedy, absorbing, and monopolistic corporations or syndicates. . . But everyone must know that the resources of Alaska can never become available either to the people of Alaska or to the public of the United States unless reasonable opportunity is granted to those who would invest their money to secure a return proportionate to the risk run in the investment. . . ."[39]

This cold fact would continue to confront the nation into the 1970s when "environmentalists" would pick up from the old conservationists to express willingness to see Alaska brought in closer contact with continental America, while preserving wildlife, ice floes, fit habitats for animals, and other natural conditions. In the 1910s the Ballinger affair separated the Old Guard from the Progressives, though not necessarily on the Alaska issue. Borah, for example, was less interested in conservation of forests than in benefits for settlers. "What does the government have these lands for?" he asked. "Jackrabbits and coyotes, or for men?" Taft in July 1910 ordered forty million acres of public lands withdrawn from public entry.[40] The *New York World* thought that this should silence his critics. But it failed to appreciate the will of the electorate, which was for a more competent elite than the one Taft headed. It approved the fall of "Cannonism" that spring in the House of Representatives that stripped the "czar" of his power to appoint working committees and deemed Cannon's overthrow a Progressive revolution.[41] And in the fall it deprived the Republicans of their House majority.

The public made other striking judgments. For example, it elected to forget its young Galahad, Glavis, whose most notable achievement following his great moment was in the 1920s when he wrote an excellent series for Norman Hapgood on the Ku Klux Klan when Hapgood had, following the war, assumed editorship of *Hearst's International Magazine.* Thereafter, Glavis lived obscurely in Washington at modest chores, undisturbed by newspaper scribes.

Pinchot preserved his flair, as late as the 1930s stirring the fury of his fellow-Progressive Harold L. Ickes for having raised a hue and cry by means of a whirlwind of bulletins and releases alerting Washington correspondents to Pinchot's charge that Ickes, as Secretary of the Interior, was plotting to take Forestry out of the Department of Agriculture and add it to his own department. Pinchot won. Forestry stayed in Agriculture. Ickes, in revenge, penned an article for the May 25, 1940, issue of the *Saturday Evening Post* entitled "Not Guilty! Richard A. Ballinger—an American Dreyfus." Ickes issued a more detailed account of the historic event through the Government Printing Office, also entitled, but without the exclamation mark, *Not Guilty.* It failed to disturb the nation. Indifference was one form—though not one of the best—of registering sophistication.

Samuel Untermyer preempted the headlines as chief counsel of the "money trust" investigation headed by Congressman Arsène Pujo of Louisiana two years after Brandeis had bearded Ballinger and Taft, yet Untermyer received none of the acclaim that finally carried

Brandeis to the Supreme Court. Indeed, Brandeis's little book, *Other People's Money* (1914), based on an analysis of the testimony given during the Pujo committee hearings was remembered long after Untermyer had been put out of public recollection.

Yet Untermyer was one of the important Americans of his time, with at least as much to do with the establishment of the Federal Reserve Bank as anyone else[42] and with great influence on the formulation and passage of both the Federal Trade Commission Act and the Clayton Anti-Trust Act. It is not precisely clear why he missed fame. He was as successful as Bernard M. Baruch, thanks to wise investments and fees; he thought every young lawyer ought to have a "nest egg" of $5 million to ensure independence. He was as much on the side of the angels as Baruch, though Baruch had his role of economic "dictator" during World War I to make him conspicuous.

Untermyer was as sharp a lawyer as Brandeis. The difference may have been that Brandeis became associated with the fortunes of the "little man." Untermyer was known as legal counsellor to vast corporations, having been on James Hazen Hyde's side during the Equitable Life Insurance Company struggle that had ranged Hyde against James W. Alexander (Untermyer's work had helped bring on the great 1905 insurance investigation). Untermyer had been on the side of William Rockefeller and Henry H. Rogers in their struggle, luridly recalled by Lawson, with F. Augustus Heinze. He worked for H. Clay Pierce of the Waters Pierce Company to resist domination by the Standard Oil Company after its 1911 dissolution as a trust.

He was much like James B. Dill, whom Steffens enormously respected: a trust-maker who believed that trusts were inevitable—the people wanted its centralized power and efficiency—but who looked forward to increased government regulation to ensure that trusts could not acquire strength at the expense of democracy and could not jeopardize free enterprise. On December 27, 1911, he gave a talk before a New York forum in which he asserted that eighteen companies constituted a "money trust." Untermyer was invited by Pujo to interrogate the financiers as to their modes of operation.

His work constituted an education in finance. It focused on the clearinghouse aspect of financial business and also the New York

Stock Exchange, both of which were central to key financial dealings and had been at the storm center of the panic of 1907. Indirectly, the hearings added up to a criticism of the emergency Aldrich-Vreeland Act of 1908, designed to protect banks from collapse during a "run" on their deposits, even though they might have assets that were unfortunately not "fluid" and could not be reached. The aim was primarily to protect banks before depositors, but the act was still of so limited a character as to keep uneasy even the proudest of bank presidents.

It did not help their morale to hear a manager of the New York Clearing House Association candidly admit that "the rumor that the clearing house privilege has been withdrawn . . . is sure to cause a run on a bank."[43] With rumors and manipulations used as a major technique in financial duels, the human factor took on mortal features. Untermyer asked a Mr. Sturgis how he justified a pool or syndicate giving out buying and selling orders for no other reason than to raise or depress prices. Sturgis first imputed such actions to individuals, for whom he would take no responsibility, then decided that their actions were not illegitimate. The persistent Untermyer trapped him into saying that what was involved was not a moral question, "sometimes."

You may explain, "if you care to," Untermyer suggested to J. P. Morgan on the stand, why Morgan had bought 51,000 par value of stock from his financial peers Ryan and Harriman that paid only $3,710 a year for $3 million since it could yield no more than one-eighth or one-ninth of 1 percent:

> A. Because I thought it was a desirable thing for the situation to do that. . . .
>
> Q. Where is the good business . . . in buying a security that only pays one-ninth of one percent?
>
> A. Because I thought it was better there than it was where it was. That is all.
>
> Q. Was anything the matter with it at the hands of Mr. Ryan?
>
> A. Nothing.
>
> Q. In what respect would it be better where it is than with him?

A. That is the way it struck me.
Q. Is that all you have to say about it?
A. That is all I have to say about it.[44]

It did not take a far throw of the imagination to realize that what was involved in Morgan's transaction was not money but power. And this fact was underscored by such other witnesses as George F. Baker of the First National Bank who would not agree that the control of credit had reached dangerous proportions but did agree—as the public learned in headlines—that it had "gone about far enough." George F. Perkins, a former Morgan man who now considered himself a "student" of public affairs and who was to be given a more central place in final Progressive flourishes than he merited, avowed, in the name of efficiency, his faith in the concentrations of capital. He did acknowledge to Untermyer that "undue" concentration could be a problem. That, he said, was the problem he was working at on the "outside." Perkins meant the political arena.[45]

It was unlikely that anything Perkins did would be calculated to hurt Morgan, or the New York Life Assurance Company with which Perkins had long been connected. To Judson Harmon in Ohio he wrote, remarking the increasing socialist vote and emphasizing that since regulation of business was inevitable, it should be aided by businessmen who "have had the right sort of experience."[46] It would, of course, have been absurd to expect of Perkins any other view; American businessmen were unlikely to lie down voluntarily on the scrapheap of history. It was interesting that alarm was expressed not only from the suspicious socialist camp, but from that of the defenders of capitalism. The *New York Times,* for example, noted that a government-controlled Federal Reserve Bank could fall, by the fortune of politics, into the hands of the Bryan Silverites.[47]

Untermyer's dream was of an established democratic process that could ensure equitable control of the flow of credit. This could not be entirely done, so long as Americans also wished to preserve their gambling option. It could not be entirely done even when the Wilson Administration had erected a Federal Reserve system with privileges to assess the validity of bank operations. The Federal Reserve was staffed by individuals who, whatever their virtues, were unable to prevent the financial collapse of 1929. It could not be wholly accomplished even after the establishment of the Securities and Exchange Commission in 1933.

Gambling produced difficulties. Indeed, regulation produced difficulties of its own. Crusaders for regulation could not foresee the day when regulation itself could be coldly analyzed as inept, dangerous, and inexcusably costly.[48] Untermyer, working on the principle of regulation, was of service to both the Wilson and the Franklin D. Roosevelt administrations. His type of public servant, essentially progressive, needed better to be appreciated, his ideas better understood, by those who had not fully committed themselves to the dreams of socialism.[49]

NOTES

1. Charles Edward Russell, *Business the Heart of the Nation* (New York, 1911), 128.
2. A. B. Stickney, *The Railroad Problem* (St. Paul, 1891).
3. Kim McQuaid, "Owen D. Young, Gerard Swope, and the New Capitalism of the General Electric Company; a Study in Corporate Liberalism, 1920-1960" (ms.), 8-9, 13-14.
4. *Literary Digest* 30 (January 7, 1904): 6-7; 31 (December 23, 1905): 943; 32 (February 17, 1906): 234; (March 31, 1906): 472.
5. *Ibid.*, 34 (March 23, 1907): 445.
6. Morton Keller, *In Defense of Yesterday, James M. Beck* (New York, 1958), 80ff.
7. Bernard Mandel, *Samuel Gompers* (Yellow Springs, Ohio, 1963), 256ff.
8. William English Walling and Harry W. Laider, *State Socialism Pro and Con, with a Chapter on Municipal Socialism by Evans Clark* (New York, 1917), xxvii. This valuable compilation presents a wide variety of documents "showing the world-wide replacement of private by governmental industry before and during the war."
9. Richard W. Fox, "The Paradox of 'Progressive' Socialism: The Case of Morris Hillquit, 1901-1914," *American Quarterly* 26 (May 1974): 140.
10. "Mr. Bryan's New Ideas," *Literary Digest* 23 (September 8, 1906): 299.
11. *Ibid.*, 34 (January 12, 1907): 39.
12. See, for example, Taft's speech at Cooper Institute in New York City, January 10, 1908 on "Labor and Capital," which argues that both need each other, that an injunction does not make law; the judge "merely interprets the

law and applies it to the circumstances." A sample of Taft's thinking on "Legal Remedies for Abuses" follows; William H. Taft, *Present Day Problems* (New York, 1908), 264.

13. "A Change in the Spirit of Magazine Criticism," *Literary Digest* 32 (May 19, 1906): 750-751

14. *Ibid.*, 36 (June 27, 1908): 915. See also 32 (June 30, 1906): 962 for a *New York Times* summary of Roosevelt's achievements, in response to Bryan's charge that Roosevelt was helping trusts "to make meat" of America.

15. Alpheus T. Mason, "William Howard Taft," in L. Friedman and F. L. Israel, eds., *Justices of the Supreme Court,* (New York, 1969), 3:2103ff.

16. Frederick Winslow Taylor, *Shop Management* (New York, 1911), 6.

17. Samuel Haber, *Efficiency and Uplift: Scientific Management in the Progressive Era, 1890-1920* (Chicago, 1964), 59.

18. Frank B. Gilbreth, Jr., and Ernestine Gilbreth Carey, *Cheaper by the Dozen* (New York, 1948).

19. Haber, *Efficiency and Uplift,* 69.

20. Marilyn Judith Berger, "Herbert Croly: Spokesman for Liberalism" (Masters thesis, Columbia University, 1949), vi.

21. Croly's ideas are assessed in context in Louis Filler, "The Dilemma, So-Called, of the American Liberal," *Antioch Review* 8 (June 1948): 131ff. It is protested by Heinz Eulau in *ibid.* (September 1948): 382, 384, who argues that one must see beyond Croly's "peculiar" language to the larger issues of "collective security" and other desirable international policies.

22. Louis Filler, *Randolph Bourne* (New York, 1966), 57ff.

23. Taft, *Present Day Problems,* 197ff.

24. Bela Case and Fola La Follette, *Robert M. La Follette* (New York, 1953), 1:275.

25. Robert M. La Follette, *Autobiography* (Madison, Wis., 1913), 112-113. Also contributing to Taft's failure was his inept hints that Canada might become part of the United States, which roused Canadian nationalism to its height; Mowry, *op. cit.,* 167. See also Kendrick A. Clements, "Manifest Destiny and Canadian Reciprocity in 1911," *Pacific Historical Review,* 42 (February 1973): 32ff.

26. Louis Filler, ed., *The President Speaks* (New York, 1965), 75.

27. James C. Malin, "Mobility and History," *Agricultural History,* 17 (1943): 177.

28. *Literary Digest* 35 (September 14, 1907): 354-356.

29. *Ibid.*, 39 (August 21, 1909): 255.

30. Paola E. Coletta, *The Presidency of William Howard Taft* (Lawrence, Kan., 1973), 79-80.

31. M. Nelson McGeary, *Gifford Pinchot, Forester-Politician* (Princeton, 1960), 77.

32. *Literary Digest* 39 (August 28, 1909): 291; (September 11, 1909): 373.

33. Coletta, *The Presidency of Taft,* 83.

34. McGeary, *Clifford Pinchot,* 143.

35. Hal C. DeRan to author, February 7, 1952; *cf.*, Oliver Knight, ed. *I Protest* (Madison, Wis., 1966), 442ff. DeRan also figures in Thomas W. Lawson, *Frenzied Finance* (New York, 1905), 427-429.

36. The classic examination is Alpheus T. Mason, *Bureaucracy Convicts Itself* (New York, 1941); see also James Penick, Jr., *Progressive Politics and Conservation* (Chicago, 1968).

37. *Literary Digest* 40 (March 5, 1910): 425-426.

38. Herman Slotnick, "The Ballinger-Pinchot Affair in Alaska," *Journal of the West* 10 (April 1971): 336ff.

39. Louis Filler, *The President Speaks,* 81-82.

40. Marion G. McKenna, *Borah,* ((Ann Arbor, Mich., 1961), 114; *Literary Digest* 41 (July 16, 1910): 86.

41. It was a revolution that suffered a "counter"-revolution in 1974 when a House caucus voted to take the power to assign all House committee members away from the Ways and Means Committee, headed by its then chairman Wilbur Mills of Arkansas, and give it to the Democratic Steering Committee headed by Speaker of the House Carl Albert. This gave him an elective power "not held by a House leader since it was carved away from the autocratic Speaker 'Uncle Joe' Cannon in 1910." *Time* (December 16, 1974): 18. At this point Albert did not seem inclined to take "full advantage of his potential power."

42. Samuel Untermyer, *Who Is Entitled to the Credit for the Federal Reserve Act? An Answer to Senator Carter Glass* (New York? 1927?).

43. *Report of the Committee Appointed Pursuant to House Resolutions 429 and 504 to Investigate the Concentration of Control of Money and Credit. 62d Cong., 3d Sess.* (Washington, 1913), 23, 46-47.

44. *Ibid.*, 83.

45. *Ibid.*, 1614ff.

46. James Weinstein, *The Corporate Ideal in the Liberal State* (Boston, 1968), 153.

47. *Literary Digest* 47 (July 5, 1913): 1-2.

48. "The Regulators: Federal Agencies Draw Fire," *Wall Street Journal,* October 9, 1974.

49. See, also the autobiography of John Moody, *The Long Road Home* (New York, 1933), by another of the financial progressives, to whom many turned in hopes of better understanding the "money trust."

Armageddon

We have been busy with material things, making money, building railroads, sinking mines, occupying land. . . . All this was good. But finally we became so busy with material things that we forgot ideal things; so busy with results that we forgot methods. . . .

Those that cried out that we were wrong when we began to make laws for the moral regeneration of American business . . . now declare that we must not pass any more such laws. But . . . no, the road will be builded to its terminus. . . .

Not many more things need to be done—the road is nearly finished . . . First, we must revise our tariff. . . . We must have a law that will stop the watering of stocks. Ultimately, all interstate railroads . . . must come under exclusive national control. . . . Our forests have been slaughtered—they must be replaced; our streams have been neglected—they must be improved. . . .

All of this is the statesmanship of construction, not of destruction. We are building up, not tearing down; we are working for the whole Nation, instead of for a few individuals, and for the future as well as for to-day.[1]

The Progressive drive in its political phase was of relatively short duration, but it marked an era of national consciousness such as had not been seen before and would not be seen after. Jacksonians and Republicans had worked through political machines and had taken care to satisfy as best they could local prejudices and concerns. But none of their rhetoric and exaltation had attained the moral surface that the Progressives were able to muster. The Populists had matched them in fervor and overmatched them in piety, but their crusade had been so narrowly gauged that despite the wide sympathies to which they could appeal, they had been able to become no more than helmsmen for a season of one of the normal ships of state, the Democratic party.

Progressivism responded to a different condition: a conviction by many people, and some of their statesmen, that America was at a crossroad and about to make a fundamental change in its way of life. Public figures like Beveridge, forgetful of John Jacob Astor's franchises and the spoils system, made every effort to persuade voters that no such change was in prospect; that they were no more than returning government to old ways from which it had been deflected. But with Europe furnishing numerous examples of state ownership, state philanthropy, and radical participation in government it was evident that the national struggle with trusts must force it into some posture that had been unknown to earlier electorates.

Socialists and quasisocialists foresaw a movement that would in effect Europeanize American politics. A London commentator had already concluded that "[in] a government of parties there can be no place for two parties that offer a choice merely of names and not of principles. . . . Great as the United States is, it is not great enough to support two great conservative parties."[2] It suggests how bold were radical perspectives when a leading socialist theoretician, though approving reforms, felt it urgent to explain that "the one great political fact" needing recognition was the unalterable difference between the reform movement and socialism. All societies, he noticed, including the slave societies, contained the "beginnings" of socialism. But the reforms of progressivism, though commendable, differed in kind from those that would—and he thought soon—materialize under true socialism.[3]

Walling perceived that much of progressivism stemmed from the uprising of the "small capitalist," but Walling too little estimated the "little man's" complex passion for free enterprise, however defined: his tendency to release bits of his freedom to government for reasons of expediency or idealism but to commit himself to minimum deeds, however grand the program in prospectus. Steffens was later, bitterly, to decry muckraking; "[it] stretched out the age of honest bunk, and held us back from the French stage of progress: the period of intelligent, cynical self-knowledge and the conscious preference of pleasure and privilege."[4]

Steffens underrated American cynicism and, needing compassion, should have been more compassionate toward error and the harsh, unexpected turnings of social and political fortune. The "little man" admired enthusiasts and appeared half-persuaded by their messages. But his combination of liberalism and conservatism was an equation requiring constant study, for which activists—and Steffens, for all his theories, yearned to affect events—could rarely find time.

The traumas of Republicanism provided the political news of the decade. The Democrats were a congeries of interests, stretching from the South to the northern city machines and still recovering from the wounds inflicted upon their political accommodations by the Populist uprising. The Republicans had remained solid in their own right behind a tradition of government that saw free enterprise in idealistic terms and no more than Daniel Webster saw a conflict of interest between federal authorities and the nation's business. Each year they recalled Lincoln and the saving of the Union, and they participated in reviews of large bodies of Civil War veterans throughout the land, many of them carrying the wounds of war.

Progressives saw themselves as more concerned Republicans: true patriots who would not cover up scandals and maladministration with false rhetoric. It is inaccurate to imagine Progressives attached to "unworkable" antitrust measures.[5] Indeed, even their antagonist Taft was seeking to rehabilitate himself with attacks on trusts, which would, paradoxically, hurt him with his conservative supporters and prove even more "unworkable" than anything any Progressive would fancy.

The Progressives had become a congeries of citizens in and out of government who were exasperated to find their search for regulation and reform frustrated by their own party. Many of them, like Jonathan P. Dolliver of Iowa, had been regular Republicans once persuaded by the high tariff and nationalistic arguments but who now found themselves unable to sit quiet under a monolithic program of unreflective legislative ritual. Others, like Moses E. Clapp of Minnesota, had fought at home for positive railroad legislation and were continuing their fight for regulation in Washington.

Inevitably they found themselves often closer to Democrats than to their own chieftains, even though this meant a weakening of party unity. Champ Clark of the House of Representatives, an outstanding Missouri Democrat, later confessed that though sympathetic to "Czar" Cannon personally, he joined the fight to overthrow "Cannonism" in part because it helped to split the Republican party.[6] Others in the Democratic ranks were more committed to the Progressive premises involved in the action and would build their own cabals to advance progressive reforms in their party.

Numerous clashes persuaded the Progressives that they could not hope for reconciliation with the party regulars. A major issue, especially with midwesterners, was the railroad issue, which, despite the implementation of ICC powers under the Hepburn Act, still needed strengthening in such sectors as stock watering and excessive rates. Progressives found a stubborn opponent in Taft's Attorney General George W. Wickersham and were angered to learn that leading railroad executives were working closely with the administration to shape the railroad bill promised in the Republican platform of 1908, Wickersham not only pointedly ignored the Senate Progressives but withdrew a projected suit to prevent merger into a powerful monopoly of the New York, New Haven & Hartford Railroad with the Boston and Maine Railroad—a plan that Brandeis had steadily fought and would continue to fight.[7] Although Taft proposed railroad measures that were expected to be "soothing" to insurgent sensibilities, his administration's entire course—the Ballinger affair, Wickersham's bluntly reactionary posture, the tariff fiasco, and, not least, the crude effort of House and Senate managers to deprive insurgents of their patronage—drove them to organization.[8]

The Progressive saga created many legends but none more troublesome than that it was mainly a midwestern Republican upheaval. It did, certainly, include significant midwesterners and responded to midwestern interests.[9] It was led by La Follette, at whose Washington home in January 1911 the National Progressive

Republican League was created. But not to realize that the midwesterners were no more than the flying wedge of a national progressive impulse is to misconstrue the entire effort: one that would affect Democrats as well as Republicans.

La Follette's new organization featured elements from city and nation. Jonathan Bourne, Jr., of Oregon was its president. Frederic C. Howe, now famous as an analyst of city and state government, was its secretary. The philanthropic Charles R. Crane served as treasurer. The new organization's declaration of principles bore no taint of sectional parochialism. It advocated more democratic party machinery, a corrupt practices act, reconstruction of banking and other services, and conservation laws. It asked not for the squelching of trusts but for statutes "dealing" with them, "based on sound economic principles," obviously necessary to the whole country.

Moreover, the league rapidly drew in a variety of figures in state and municipal government, including W. S. U'Ren of Oregon, whom Steffens had popularized as the "father of the Initiative and Referendum." Steffens himself, James R. Garfield, Brandeis, and Norman Hapgood were also among the moving spirits. No small factor in their work was E. W. Scripps, whose interest in the formation of a new party—the insurgents originally seeking only to nominate the Republican candidate—helped move Progressives out of party trammels.[10]

The league spread rapidly, in a few weeks showing branches east and west as partisans bestirred themselves. La Follette was their evident candidate, since Roosevelt resisted their call on various grounds. La Follette leagues mushroomed to sustain his candidacy, not, he insisted, so much against Taft as in behalf of principles he had long maintained. It amounted to the same thing. What La Follette could not accept, and was deceived about because of the early enthusiasm he enjoyed from such Roosevelt followers as Gifford Pinchot and his brother Amos and because of kind articles about his life and opinions, was that he was available for Progressives mainly because Roosevelt apparently was not. In October 1911, La Follette's candidacy and eventual election seemed possible to Progressives.[11]

Nevertheless the situation continued fluid, with politicos testing their party strength at home and in national councils. La Follette's

Such Enthusiastic Solicitude!

A pro-La Follette cartoon.

supporters studied their strength in the West, and in the East where it did not grow. They kept weather eyes open to developments in the Democratic party and in Oyster Bay where Roosevelt offered opinions that could be variously interpreted.

Critical to the future of the Progressives was the strengthening role of George W. Perkins and Frank A. Munsey in their affairs. La Follette saw them as insidious forces intent upon creating relations with government that would support their empires in industry and the newspaper world. This, it seems fair to judge, was precisely what they hoped to do, Perkins in rather statesmanlike fashion, Munsey from as coldly commercial a standpoint as any man of his time. They saw more virtue in Roosevelt as chief executive, with his belief in regulation, than in Taft who, for all his conservatism, was prosecuting trusts under the law.

Who would represent the insurgents? In January 1912, Roosevelt assumed the position of a potential candidate and excited Progressives anywhere. Many of them had already committed themselves to La Follette and needed an occasion to get from under their early avowals and public commitments.[12] Their opportunity came, February 2, 1912, in Philadelphia, when La Follette addressed the annual banquet of the Periodical Publishers' Association in words that were intended to be a call to battle but that were interpreted as signaling a "breakdown" on his part.

His actual speech was a reasonable, though not inspired, statement expressing concern that a "mighty power" of monopoly, which was building up in the country, needed to be curbed; and he warned that the free press was being assailed. His actual deportment at the banquet was another matter. He "suddenly began to repeat himself, and talked ramblingly for an hour and a half, despite the efforts of his secretary, John Hannan, sitting immediately behind him, who kept begging him in audible whispers to wind up his address. . . . At the end, La Follette sat down, seemingly in a state of collapse, with closed eyes and his chin sunk on his chest. . . . Hannan and I led La Follette from the room."[13]

La Follette afterwards agreed he was tired from a speaking trip, worried about the health of one of his children, and not up to par. He denied that his health had been impaired and repudiated a statement by his campaign manager that he had withdrawn from the race. He had made no such statement, he said. He later saw the entire development as a conspiracy "so cleverly . . . managed, so rapidly were the scenes shifted . . . that doubt and confusion prevailed everywhere, outside of the little circle of which Roosevelt was the centre."[14]

What La Follette could not face was that the Progressives flatly preferred Roosevelt and felt only he could win the convention away from Taft, and that their shiftiness was not treachery but just the normal maneuvers of politicians.

Yet the high uniformity of journalistic response to the incident also suggested that La Follette's point about the dangers of increasing centralization of newspaper opinion was apposite, if incorrect. Times were changing. The muckraking magazines were rapidly disappearing; and not because of drastic declines in circulation (it has already been seen that national influence was not at all dependent on circulation.)

For one thing, the muckrakers were far from united, as their antagonists paranoidly imagined. It has been noted that Mark Sullivan despised Hearst and David Graham Phillips enough to see their brief and limited relationship in muddled light. Norman Hapgood despised Tom Lawson enough not to appreciate his uses as an informer. The McClure writers had not only looked down on lesser social reporters but had quarreled between themselves so as, in 1906, to split. Some stayed with McClure; others, including Steffens, Tarbell, and William Allen White, created the *American Magazine.*

Above all, the Croly Progressives despised the muckrakers as sentimentalists who stirred the people to no end. They agreed that the people needed stirring but only under the wise guidance of their best, their most competent, their most directed—in short, themselves.

The Progressive era had been outstanding in the quantity of serious, social-minded articles that had been disseminated. But now the magazines were turning popular in a new sense. They mixed entertainment with educational features, some of high quality; but channeled more concentrated public-interest materials into more specialized outlets, such as the *New Republic*, the *Nation*, and, in its way, the socialist *Masses.* Those who wished to read those publications were free to do so. Others could feel their social duty accomplished by enjoying features of the renovated *Collier's, Metropolitan*, and the ubiquitous *Saturday Evening Post.*

Some of the muckraking publications had died of buccaneering and dubious business practices. But they had not risen in the first place because of shrewd business methods. They had been made famous and wealthy by public demand, and, though the public still sentimentally honored and would continue to give lip service to independent editors, bold journalists, and crusaders, it would distribute its favors between sensationalists and steadfast public servants with bewildering, and sometimes exasperating impartiality. This process embittered some former muckrakers and disillusioned others; but, from time to time, new aspirants would arise who would take their inspiration from Upton Sinclair or Lincoln Steffens or both.

La Follette might well have conjectured that a vital muckraking press, such as the 1900s had possessed, might have traced the rumor of his "breakdown" to its source and stilled it. But it is evident that the nation believed it no longer needed such a press. It had, instead, a vital elite that would handle its routine affairs for it, fight out their intergroup battles as they pleased, and present it with the results of its conferences and intrigues for endorsement. Rarely had the nation reached such a height of optimism, such a sense of well-being and confidence as it attained in 1912.[15]

The Perkins-Munsey spectre accompanied the Progressives to Chicago where the Republican National Convention was held. Attention centered on the Roosevelt bandwagon and the cries of "fraud" and "theft" that Progressives accorded the regulars—a chorus that might have given La Follette a moment of entertainment. The Progressives marched off to their own hall to nominate Roosevelt with acclaim, and the great challenge to a major party had been made.

Taft was overshadowed, but what he was and represented warranted understanding. His administration was a shambles, and public judgment on the Ballinger affair had, in the 1910 elections, cost him control of the House of Representatives. But Taft was not only supported by his party managers; the electorate, too, stayed relatively fast. Taft divided the preferential primaries with Roosevelt, taking New York and Massachusetts among the more populous states and also becoming involved in mixed results that caused some of the bitterest recriminations at the Chicago convention. There, his machine held firm, giving 254 contested seats to him and only 19 to Roosevelt. Desperate efforts to find a compromise candidate came to nothing, though they included Supreme Court Justice Charles Evans Hughes and Robert T. Lincoln, son of the President.

In the end, Taft was accorded 561 delegate votes to Roosevelt's 107, many of his supporters not voting in protest. La Follette, because of wholesale desertions, had 41. The regulars could enjoy Warren G. Harding's words, prefiguring 1920s perorations, which placed Taft in nomination. Harding found Taft an example of "lofty patience [unexampled] since the immortal Lincoln bore the scourge of vengeful tongues without a murmur from his noble heart." And, "rejoicing in the gratifying record of things done," Harding looked into the future with assurance, "glad of the new hopes and higher aspirations of our people and their faith in national progress and the harmony of [Taft's] purposes therewith."[16] Taft's nomination was seconded by John Wanamaker.

In sum, much of the nation's Republican following continued conservative by one definition or another, though the Progressive hope had to be that their cause would generate a movement that would grow into a November triumph.

Democratic excitement could not match the historic schism that (some thought) could end with the regular Republicans following the Whigs into political oblivion and a new, Progressive party becoming a standard feature of the two party system. Nevertheless, the Baltimore meeting of the Democrats, though exultant with the Chicago news, had problems of its own. As the *New York World* observed:

> With Woodrow Wilson chasing Colonel Harvey out of the front yard; with Colonel Watterson denouncing Governor Wilson as an ingrate; with Mr. Hearst sobbing hysterically over Governor Wilson's historical references to Chinese labor; with Mayor [William J.] Gaynor having fits over the wickedness of Mr. Hearst; with Mr. Bryan alternately bumping Judson

> Harmon and reading Oscar Underwood out of the party; with Champ Clark chawing Joe Folk and Joe Folk chawing Champ Clark . . . with Mr. Bryan acting as the house of representatives, and with Mr. Underwood defying Mr. Bryan to do his worst—it has been years since we had a Democratic party so full of vigor and action and the joy of living.[17]

Woodrow Wilson's nomination represented a victory for the progressive wing of the Democratic party, which, however, included as hardy a set of principled reactionaries as any the Republicans could show. Although a national consensus could and did bury the fact that Wilson was a southerner born, bred, and complete and represented as true a return of the South as a national power as any that could be identified since 1859, the alliance Wilson headed was so national in another sense that not a few key Roosevelt Progressives would in time become followers of Wilson with no inner conflict.

The electorate had many things to turn over as it prepared to vote, most of them constituting pleasant choices. For with Roosevelt, Wilson, and the socialists urging them on to Progressive and neo-Progressive measures, and with Taft arguing for a "scientific" tariff, enforcement of the antitrust law, and—a novelty in then-current thinking—emphasis on peace treaties and if necessary an international police force,[18] there would have seemed to be an embarrassment of riches for amply endowed Americans.

There was much truth in the current view that little separated Roosevelt from Wilson. Both were responding to inevitabilities forced by the propaganda and activities of a decade of journalists, reformers, and the special labors of woman suffragists, child labor defenders, and unionists. Roosevelt's New Nationalism and Wilson's New Freedom probed one another for implications of tyranny, subservience to special interests, and the like. Fundamentally, however, it was the people who had given priority to the issues and who would judge how they might best be handled. The candidates labored to read the voters' preferences. Thus, obviously, Wilson's concessions on women's suffrage represented less of a change of heart than his respectful awareness than the western states were rolling into the suffrage column. In 1912, four of them—Kansas, Michigan, Oregon, and Arizona—joined six others that had already granted the suffrage to women. Anna Howard Shaw, president of the Woman's Suffrage Association, commented that "in the next presidential election every political party will have a woman suffrage plank in its platform."[19]

Roosevelt may have seemed more high-tariff minded and sympathetic to big business than the firmly stationed free-trade Wilson. And the latter's good-humored but reasoned approach may have seemed a welcome change from that of the tempestuous Rough Rider, especially for a projected efficiency era. Even so dramatic an event as the attempt by a fanatic to kill Roosevelt in Milwaukee, October 14, 1912, and Roosevelt's insistence on delivering his speech though with a bullet in his right breast, fortunately deflected to a degree, may have served Wilson more than it did Roosevelt. Wilson muted his campaign while the country awaited news from the hospital. But Wilson delivered several speeches, in one remarking that he had come "with a great reluctance because my thought is constantly of that gallant gentleman lying in the hospital at Chicago."[20] It occurred to not a few voters that Roosevelt's heroics suited a field commander better than an executive in charge of the whole national enterprise.

Wilson was in time to give rein to an exalted rhetoric, which Roosevelt neither fancied nor could approach. His clearly enunciated "lily white" policy for the South deprived him of votes by Negroes who were totally disillusioned by Republican promises and traditions and who, moving to the northern cities, could hope to gain a larger proportion of city and Democratic patronage. But the major decision was made not in the popular vote but in the electoral college. Wilson's united party gained only 6,301,254 popular votes against the combined Taft-Roosevelt, 7,613,619 votes. Wilson was a minority President as Lincoln, who had faced a disunited Democratic party, had been. The electoral college told a different tale. Wilson had garnered 435 votes against Roosevelt's 88 and Taft's 8—so deeply had the Republican schism cut.

Roosevelt had beaten the Republican candidate, but the record was less promising for progressivism when state and local elections were added up. Progressives had elected only one governor and a baker's dozen of congressmen. At the grass-roots level they had even less to show: some 250 minor offices among thousands. Roosevelt took some satisfaction in having come in second place, but as he wrote Gifford Pinchot: "We must face the fact that our cutting loose from the Republican party was followed by disaster to the Progressive cause in most of the states where it won two years ago."[21]

The nation was now in such a progressive era as it had not savored under Taft, but it was also not the era of Roosevelt. Roosevelt's had been a time of much debate, public involvement, and muckraking exposure, headed by a leader who asserted himself as an individual and who became a model for others to emulate. Wilson was a more withdrawn person, an executive with a program that the nation's leaders did not have to fear. Indeed, it surprised the country to learn that "big business" had no hectic concern about Wilson's program or intentions. In time, it received cordially his message on trusts, for which the long battles of the 1900s had prepared it. This was partly because of the smooth eloquence with which he began to enchant the country and against which the *Wall Street Journal* warned a lulled business community. But in part his trust prospectus contained nothing new and nothing to which special interests could not accommoderate themselves, with superior legal counsel, sound public relations, and the ability to persuade others through authoritative technical knowledge.[22]

Wilson carried through his promised tariff reduction with dispatch, heading personally the fight to scale down the schedule. He saw to the creation of a Federal Reserve Bank, which, in theory, would make the 1907 panic the last one of such events. The Federal Trade Commission Act passed on his recommendation, designed to prevent unfair interstate competition. And the Clayton Act implemented almost with eloquence the earlier Sherman Anti-Trust Act by declaring that "the labor of a human being is not a commodity or article of commerce" and seemed to endorse labor unions, limit the use of injunctions, and approve traditional strike techniques, with inevitable qualifications respecting the injury to property and the need for confining picketing to peaceful picketing.

What was remarkable about many of these and other measures that went to make up a record of reform unexampled in the past was that although they seemed to add up to a torrent of Wilsonian achievements, they were limited on two counts. For one, they were largely a bipartisan program: the voice of the people at least as much as the voice of Wilson. Thus, the famous Seaman's Act of 1915, the

"Magna Carta" of the common seaman, was an American Federation of Labor measure, tirelessly proposed and explained by Andrew Furuseth, a seaman of Norwegian extraction, and sponsored by La Follette in the Senate. It capped a hundred years of effort to give human status to the sailor at sea and curbed much of the tyranny that had earlier ruled vessels.

But in addition, many of these brave measures, though they established rights and privileges on statute books, did less in actual practice. Even the tariff, and despite tariff commissions, functioned scarcely at all in a world at war and with submarines roaming the ocean; and in 1922, with farmers reeling from the effects of the war's end, the Forney-McCumber tariff topped the 1909 rates which had caused so much excitement by 24 percent on manufactured goods and set up walls against foreign farm products.

As for the Clayton Act, labor's "Magna Carta," it failed to serve labor, which had given itself fully to the war effort and, in the great steel strike of 1919, under Wilson, suffered rigors of capitalistic response, which impartial commissions reported with horror.[23] Such events, which repeated themselves in succeeding years, added to the demoralization of Progressives more than the rapid deterioration of the Progressive party proper because of the preemption of its principles by the Wilson administration.[24]

It does not do to derogate Progressive laws too cavalierly. They were gained at far less expense than the long, drawn-out action that brought the nation the Thirteenth Amendment, outlawing slavery, to the Constitution. That hallowed enactment had dug a chasm between the past and present and filled it with Union and Confederate dead. Americans would never return to slavery. Their later debates would involve definitions of freedom that ranged from anarchy to contract labor.

Progressive laws were generally much less fundamental. They were opportunistic yet with a residue of ideals, individual in intent, yet seeking efficiency, and they carried along in their wake prejudices and traditions from campaigns that had rocked the electorate in years past. The one characteristic that all Progressive laws had in common was their effort to stay abreast of the times, to put the conditions attending pure food, railroads, insurance, conservation, finance, and the conduct of municipalities and social institutions on a modern footing.

This neither diehard Republicanism nor Plunkitt-like municipal time-serving was capable of doing. The tragedy of Progressive achievements was that the shock of world events, for which the nation and its leaders had been meagerly schooled, appeared to demean those achievements, and so to increase difficulties for upgrading them for use in late, still more modern times.

NOTES

1. Albert J. Beveridge, *The Meaning of the Times* (Indianapolis, 1908), 423ff., in an address, January 17, 1908, before students at Yale University.
2. A. Maurice Low in *The Monthly Review*, quoted in *Literary Digest* 29 (December 24, 1904): 885.
3. Walling, *Progressivism and After* (New York, 1914), xi. Walling's services to socialist and labor thought were halted by World War I, intervention in which he ardently supported. He did not foresee Bolshevik theory and practice and was shocked by both into silence, after denouncing them as subversions of socialism. For an examination of his own theory, see Jack Stuart, "William English Walling," *Science and Society*, 35 (Summer, 1971): 193ff.
4. Ella Winter and Granville Hicks, *Letters of Lincoln Steffens*, (New York, 1938), 1:519.
5. George E. Mowry, *Theodore Roosevelt and the Progressive Movement* (Madison, Wis., 1946), 145.
6. Kenneth W. Hechler, *Insurgency: Personalities and Politics of the Taft Era* (New York, 1940), 206.
7. Henry Lee Staples and Alpheus T. Mason, *The Fall of a Railroad Empire: Brandeis and the New Haven Merger Battle* (Syracuse, 1947).
8. *Literary Digest* 40 (January 15, 1910): 85-86: Heckler, *Insurgency*, 163ff.
9. Russel B. Nye, *Midwestern Progressive Politics* (East Lansing, 1951).
10. Oliver Knight, ed., *I Protest* (Madison, Wis., 1966), 483ff.
11. Helene Maxwell Hooker, ed., *History of the Progressive Party, 1912-1916*, by Amos R. E. Pinchot (New York, 1958), 24.
12. For a detailed account of the La Follette boom and its undermining in one state, see Mowry, *The California Progressives* (Berkeley, 1951), 160ff.
13. Hooker, ed., *History of the Progressive Party*, 134-135. For his speech, Robert M. La Follette, *Autobiography* (Madison, Wis., 1913), 762ff.
14. La Follette, *Autobiography*, 583.

15. Such was the consensus of the press in its review of the year: *Literary Digest* 46 (January 11, 1913): 62-64.

16. *Great Leaders and National Issues of 1912* (New York, 1912), 210.

17. *Ibid.*, 19.

18. *Ibid.*, 43ff.

19. *Literary Digest* 45 (November 23, 1912): 941-943; see also 51 (October 16, 1915): 827-828.

20. D. H. Elletson, *Roosevelt and Wilson* (London, 1965), 117.

21. Mowry, *Roosevelt and the Progressive Movement,* 283.

22. *Literary Digest* 48 (January 31, 1914): 186-187; (February 7, 1914): 241-244.

23. *The Interchurch World Movement Report on the Steel Strike of 1919 with the Technical Assistance of the Bureau of Industrial Research, New York* (New York, 1920).

24. For a die-hard view of the Progressive party dissolution by one who accompanied it on its downward trek, see Harold L. Ickes, "Who Killed the Progressive Party?" *American Historical Review* 16 (January 1941): 306ff. The culprit was Perkins, according to Ickes.

Shadows Forward

The country seemed, with Wilson's ascendancy, doubly endorsed as the most fortunate and secure of nations. "[His] inauguration marks the beginning of a new political epoch," the *New York World* thought. "The United States has entered on a new phase of popular government." But this seemed no more than dessert for the feast. Wilson had not taken over from a country in trouble. He had inherited an enormous reserve of progressivism, which had already opened all avenues of social life to further enhancement. It had educated a citizenry to examining them and choosing among those who wished to administer their development, and it had created new agencies for the work.

All was well with the Republic, and would be better. No wonder that a positive attitude toward it became one mark of true citizenship and patriotism. William Dean Howells had praised the "smiling" aspects of American life as most representative and therefore most accurate. Those Progressives would survive publicly for the most part, in the 1910s, who accepted this dictum and who discerned the "average" American as grateful for new inventions and open-ended native opportunities, and for a history replete with integrity and good, victorious causes.

The keynote of optimism infected even the critics of progressivism, who saw themselves as enriching and refurbishing the national heritage. Partly they would do this by ridding their minds of worthless American intellectual baggage: in Van Wyck Brooks's phrase, separating the "usable" from its useless portions. Many of these intellectuals emphasized a new view of beauty and the good life. But they did not differ in essence from less aesthetic-minded dissidents and malcontents who demanded sympathetic attitudes toward labor history and critical attitudes toward manifest destiny. They were at one with critics of an education which had once been proud of such humbly born graduates as Henry Clay and Abraham Lincoln.

The new radicals, standing on all the Progressives had accomplished in years of intense effort, believed they could direct national opinion. They could install their new programs, either through popular education and labor organization, or by pushing reform leaders to do more and more, as Furuseth had pushed La Follette and La Follette had pushed Wilson. The new radicals varied in type. Randolph Bourne was college trained, with friends who reached from the Columbia University campus into Greenwich Village. But such an even younger man as Louis C. Fraina, who had not so much as completed high school, put the matter as clearly to his radical readers as Bourne did to his followers in the *New Republic* pages:

> Our agitation, or organizational efforts must recognize this fact: *Common labor dominates industry.* And when common labor in steel revolts, when this basic industry feels the clutch of the Revolution, Capitalism will be shaken to its depths. The revolt of the steel workers will sound the call for the Social Revolution.[2]

All of this was less remote from progressivism than was apparent at first glance, if one recalled Edward P. Costigan, Gompers, settlement workers of the caliber of Jane Addams, and others who worked with the poor and ethnic, and if one kept in mind socialists like William English Walling who probed the potential of their movement for American policy. But it was remote from the expectations of those to whom progressivism was a living faith: one that mounted through the triumphs of Wilson's first administration to those of the second. For dedicated Progressives saw American intervention in World War I as an extension of domestic progressivism: the crusade for democracy carried further.

The great man of this enterprise was, of course, Wilson, whose eloquence seemed a wonder of the age, filled with substance and a moral purpose that lifted it above material things. Yet as vital to Wilson's achievement as his own talents was the work of Edward M. House. He piloted Wilson to victory in the nomination fight. He gave Wilson much of his tangible program. House's importance to Wilson was well recognized in his time. Less studied was House's importance to progressivism, and what it had become.

House was a wealthy Texan able to give full time to acting as campaign manager for such important Texans as James S. Hogg, whose difficult 1892 campaign for governor he brought safely home. House's political, journalistic, and industrial contacts multiplied. They were marked by smooth, temperate relations and by House's obvious disinterestedness; House refused all emoluments except the honorary "colonel" with which Hogg endowed him. House was unhappy with Bryan's free silver campaigns but endured them for party harmony, and he studied alternatives while his party lived as best it could through the Republican era.

As a Texan and a southerner House esteemed his own friends and section, but he concentrated on the national scene. In the late 1900s, he seized on New York reform mayor William J. Gaynor as the man for a revived Democracy. Gaynor proved too independent, did not take seriously House's attempt to introduce him to Texas politicians, and otherwise disappointed House. In November of 1911 House first met Wilson, was impressed by his New Jersey reform program, and taken by him personally.

House undertook to advise Wilson, who dearly needed advice. Wilson was apt to be abrupt with people he needed to win, and his outlook lacked strategy. His attack on big business was in the spirit of the age but without direction, as in his reference to J. P. Morgan's being a menace to democracy. House's mind ran to using what could have been a merely schismatic detail positively by touting Wilson as fearless and dependable. House also persuaded Wilson not to break with Tammany and Boss Murphy on the issue of the conservative governor Murphy wished to sponsor. A break with Murphy would have cost Wilson vital votes at the Democratic convention. House soothed Murphy, assured him of his and Wilson's good opinion, and persuaded him to agree to endorse for governor the more liberal William Sulzer.[3]

There were other crises in Wilson's march to the presidency.

Wilson had been revealed by opponents as opposing Bryan's continued candidacy; but House was able to placate Bryan by adroitly suggesting that such other would-be candidates for the presidential nomination would be more painful to work with. House also persuaded Wilson to speak glowingly in public of Bryan's services to the nation. Later he aided Wilson to realize how necessary Bryan was to his young administration and had him appointed Secretary of State.[4]

"Had I gone into the Cabinet, I could not have lasted eight weeks," said House. It was a remarkable piece of self-analysis but did not help House to see dangers in his new, efficient progressivism. House was a superb conciliator among elite forces. He and Wilson worked to augment southern power in Washington, but House was shrewd enough, for example, to have a northerner made Secretary of the Interior because of his control of the pensions. A southerner in the office would have caused endless confusion and antagonism, with so many former Union troops and their dependents about. But House, and Wilson, had committed themselves to an elite point of view, which made thin their conduits to strangers and principled opponents:

> *December* 18, 1912: Governor Wilson [wrote House in his intimate notebooks] came at half-past one. I talked to him about [Henry] Morganthau [chairman of the Democratic Finance Committee, for whom an appointment had to be found] and suggested him for Turkey. He replied, "There ain't going to be no Turkey," and I said, "Then let him go look for it."[5]

It was a proud, even joyful remark of victors dispensing party patronage—except that there was in fact to be a Turkey, and a different Russia, and a fascist Italy not foreseen by their journalistic sources. Wilson and House not only knew less than they realized. They had fewer facilities for improving their knowledge than they knew. Wilson would later be disturbed by the fact that only the United States, of all major "white" nations, was not at war. The United States was alone, therefore, in defending western civilization from war's effects,[6] and what his generation had been taught to think of as "the yellow peril." Wilson's yearning for peace was real and purposeful. Whether it satisfied the deeper social and psychological needs of the time may be doubted.

Wilson and House appeared to be masterful men in control of their own and others's destiny. In reality they rode a whirlwind, which would deposit them where it willed. This would have been difficult to prove in 1912 when House anonymously published his awkward novel, *Philip Dru: Administrator*, which was later recognized as his work simply because it had materialized in so many of Wilson's administrative programs and public phrases. Dru in the novel was not so much an administrator as a dictator, and one who had been made so by a West Point training and the need for organizing an army to fight a conspiracy of capitalists who planned to destroy the nation. Dru, "God's instrument for good," met the conspirators in bloody battles, dispersed them, and set up a government of equitable laws, commissions, and benefits.

The book was, to a degree, a retroactive psychological triumph of a southerner over what amounted to northern capitalism and featured not only wars but war stances. "The Administrator" Dru had behind him an army of five hundred thousand, which, "considering international conditions," seemed to Dru—and doubtless House—insufficient; he therefore increased it by a hundred thousand, all thoroughly armed and equipped. In time, he was required, "with a heavy heart," to use his troops against an army combination of Mexicans and units from Central American Republics, which were crushed by the Americans at the battle of "La Tuna," as part of a "broadening of the Monroe Doctrine." The victorious general-administrator explained his program to the gallant but defeated peoples below the United States border:

> In the future, our flag is to be your flag, and you are to be directly under the protection of the United States. It is our purpose to give to your people the benefits of the most enlightened educational system, so that they may become fitted for the responsibilities of self-government. . . . Above all things, there shall not be thrust upon the Mexican people a carpet-bag government. Citizens of Mexico are to enforce the

> reconstructed constitution and laws, and maintain order with native troops, although under the protecting arm of the United States.[7]

House's fantasies did not directly influence Wilson's actual policy toward Mexico though Wilson did deliver himself of the determination "to teach the South American republics to elect good men!"[8] The point was that Wilson's unstable policy, which caused him to range from neutrality measures to all but war declarations, reflected the confusion of the American people as well as his own. It constituted a weak preparation for larger decisions common not only to Progressives but to other major elements of the population.

However exultant Wilson and his triumphant Democrats and the nation they headed may have been, it contained numerous social elements lacking full expression, unenlightened and unreached by efficiency techniques, and seeking endlessly for fuller power and vengeance on imagined foes. They made no pattern that could be readily identified and indeed were lost as components in the interventionist crusade that was later inaugurated to end "international anarchy." Better examined, they spelled the decline of progressivism as a dominant American force in that generation.

Even this was not closely perceivable, especially not during the first Wilson administration, which saw major laws enacted deemed helpful to workers, farmers, business people—the major units of society. Such laws, moreover, seemed implemented by professional reformers and agencies able to keep the nation abreast of its changing needs. Such an agency was the great Nonpartisan League: a grassroots organization begun in 1915 in North Dakota, which quickly spread into neighboring states and, with varying success, reached some twelve of them where it fought local battles on current issues, working through established parties.

The league owed much, perhaps most, of its success to an indefatiguable organizer, A. C. Townley, an ex-socialist bankrupted by farmer's troubles, who set out to unite fellow farmers in defiance of bank, elevator, and railroad interests. Townley developed a skilled body of organizers, a careful and persuasive set of campaign techniques, and a powerful journal, the *Leader*. He was so phenomenally successful that he was able to snatch power from the Republican Old Guard in North Dakota. Within two years and in the face of hostile forces, Townley had put Lynn J. Frazier, a farmer with statesmanlike qualities, in the governor's seat.

All of this Townley did with a minimum of democratic procedure and in the spirit of the new, efficient progressivism. Townley was uninterested in personal publicity or public office, so much so that photographs of him are difficult to obtain. He made public accountings of all league expenditures. The confidence that farmers gave him was striking, but explained by his spectacular results. In North Dakota, most successful of league strongholds, but in other states as well, the league wrote laws into statute books that created an industrial commission to manage newly authorized state elevators and banks, made state hail insurance compulsory, fought shortchanging of farmers by private companies, and made loans at reasonable interest rates available. In 1919, a farmer-labor party seemed no dream at all.

The league survived the "patriotic" terror of World War I directed at "aliens" (including those of second and third generation) and "reds." What it could not survive was the postwar deflation of farmers' enterprises. Even more killing was the subsequent prosperity. By 1923 the league was dead and Townley totally forgotten, though he lived on and on among the people who had once gratefully hailed him as their chief.[9] All of which helped to explain in part why a young man like Charles A. Lindbergh would have concluded to absorb himself in airplane mechanics rather than politics.

Labor-capital relations were even more cruel, in the cities and in the mines, as evidence mounted that the refurbished magazines were not able to play the role of mediator they had assumed in the previous decade and that Wilson progressivism could not control the excesses of social prejudice and industrial war.

The struggle for unionism in the garment-making industries of New York made a tragic epic and revealed the dark side of machine politics, which, beneath hearty generosity and tolerance of human foibles, permitted criminal disregard of the safety standards of work plants and malevolence toward unionists. The role of the police and courts was totally in the interests of property owners, who, in their fear and malice toward workers showed some of the basest qualities resulting from the inhuman competition of city life. Their mortal concern was to apprehend thieves and "agitators" within the shop, and to deter these they were prepared to spend any sum and to take any measures.

When in the summer of 1909 two large manufacturers, one the Triangle Waist Company, decided to fire some of their women employees for agitation, their action capped numerous plaguings and exploitations and caused a strike for union recognition. Efforts to divide the girls as Jews and Italians failed, and the brutality of hired ruffians stirred the outrage of ethnic groups and reformers. A unique tactic of the manufacturers to fend off pickets was to hire prostitutes to fight the pickets outside their establishments and also to urge some of the younger girls to join them in their own professional work.[10]

The state of society created by machine politics and needing continuous reform efforts not to become worse was shown by the discriminations practiced by both officers on the street and magistrates. Mary Dreier of the Women's Trade Union League and of social prominence joined the pickets in their efforts to keep the factories closed. Seized along with the other women, she was quickly set free by a policeman who cried, "Why didn't you tell me you was a rich lady? I'd never have arrested you in the world." A New York judge rejected the demand of one of the striking women for a warrant to arrest a man who had attacked her, saying: "You had no right to be picketing. You only got what was coming to you."[11]

Desperation brought the women to the fateful day of November 22, 1909, when a mass meeting in Cooper Union elicited a fiery outcry in behalf of a general strike by a young woman who had been hospitalized by strikebreakers. Violence magnified, beatings, woundings, and arrests multiplied. The women endured injuries—one for life—and degradations that caused the men to marvel at their fortitude. University people helped by gathering the facts for influencing public opinion. Moral support and funds came from such members of the elite as Mrs. O. P. H. Belmont, mother of the Duchess of Marlborough, and Helen Taft, daughter of the President and a charter member of the Bryn Mawr Suffrage Club. Samuel Untermyer and Morris Hillquit protested the judicial bias that refused to honor the state law permitting picketing.

The great effort raised the membership of the International Ladies' Garment Workers's Union (ILGWU) from 800 to 20,000 and inspired men in the cloak and suit division of the garment industry to embark on their own inferno of strikes in behalf of unionism in New York and other cities. Out of their efforts rose the Amalgamated Clothing Workers, which struggled with its own conservative union leaders, as well as the employers. A tragic aspect of the struggle for unions was that activists would be reduced by desperation to using gangsters as mercenaries—gangsters who would not retire from the scene once battles were done but who would hold on as parasites on union funds and, as union "leaders," make unions too scenes of corruption and violence. Big Jack Zelig was employed by the garment workers in the 1909 strike. He was one of many who preyed on the garment workers as "organizers" and business executives. When the gangsters in unions fell out among themselves and took to guns, middlemen had to be called in to prevent unrestricted murder, forcing citizen attention and reform. One of the influentential middlemen was the gambler Arnold Rothstein, whose wide connections with politicians and criminals, and his own judicious if greedy temperament, made him fit for the role.[12]

But such developments were hidden in the tense and often heroic struggles between workers and employers. A major effort by Louis D. Brandeis to break the impasse of the closed shop was his concept of "preferential shops," which would hire a majority of union men. It was scorned by firm closed-shop union spokesmen as "the open shop with honey." Still another Brandeis invention was that of the protocol of peace, intended to settle labor disputes without strikes or lockouts through boards of arbitration, grievance, and sanitary control. Gompers, representing Progressive as opposed to class war ideas, fought for the protocol, which, he thought, taught workers patience, organization, and negotiation. Protocol worked fairly well for several years but broke down into the most severe strike of all in 1916.

So sorrowful as to confound the nation and suggest new laws, if not solutions, was the Triangle Shirtwaist Company's next major appearance in the news, March 25, 1911. On that day fire broke out in the eighth floor of the top three floors the company occupied of a ten-story building near Washington Square Park. The girls there employed were trapped in rooms that were intended to keep them confined; the owners concentrated entirely on controls that would, for example, prevent the workers from slipping out of the work rooms with stolen shirtwaists. When the fire broke out the women made for doors, elevators, and the one fire escape and one stairway as best they could. Forty-six died by plunging from the windows, some with hair and dresses aflame. A hundred burned within the factory, many to skeletons. Seven were never identified.

The building had been declared fireproof in 1900 when it was opened and probably had been for its original purposes. but in the days that followed the fire, a defensive screen of public statements by building inspectors, city officials, state officials, and others established that there was no direct responsibility for the horror unless it lay with the owners of the company, Max Blanck and Isaac Harris.

Blanck and Harris were indicted on April 10, but it was not until eight months later that they went on trial, defended by Max D. Steuer, himself a graduate of the slums and noted, even notorious, for the cunning of his cross-examination and ability to shift lights on issues. By then all the dead had been long buried, the monster parade in their honor long dispersed. There were only parents and relatives to fight the police who protected the defendants against physical violence and screams of "Murderers!"

This Is One of a Hundred Murdered

Is any one to be punished for this?

Steuer was steady, incisive, quick to find humor whenever possible, to divert attention from harrowing details, to underscore the confusion or question the honesty of witnesses. A sad irony of the Steuer interrogation was that the girls had died because of incompetence and inefficiency at the lower rungs of civic operations and that justice could not be obtained because one of their own was capable of obstructing it. The elite, the "best" could do nothing for their charges. Woodrow Wilson was not required to know of their fate or deal with it.

Over the three weeks of testimony Steuer impressed upon the jury that there need not have been any deaths had the employees been calm and marched promptly and in order through the available door and down the stairway.

The judge was punctilious in his charge to the jury, in effect raising doubts on all counts of the indictment as part of the duty he imposed on them. The verdict brought in was "not guilty." As one juror, a shirt manufacturer, put it: "I know I have not done my duty toward the people. But let me tell you I could not do my duty toward them and obey the Judge's charge at the same time, although I did vote once for conviction." Another juror, an importer, thought the fire was an act of God and that the girls, being not too intelligent, had been susceptible to panic.

The horror, however, lingered and affected legislation. Boss Murphy of Tammany, sensing the ravaged feelings of his hard-core constituents, gave free rein to young Robert F. Wagner, Sr., and Alfred E. Smith in Albany to develop their reform impulses. Their Triangle commission investigation was given only $10,000 with which to do their work—which said something for the machine's priorities—but, for example, inspired Henry Morganthau to acquire an excellent lawyer to work without fee. Numerous reformers cooperated as witnesses and investigators to describe conditions and to help create "a golden era in remedial factory legislation."

Nevertheless the Blancks and the Harrises continued to ply their trade and even to transgress labor laws, with no significant loss in money or status—a fact that would not be lost on ironic minds. An effort to reopen the Triangle case in court on the basis of persons other than those named in the first bill of indictment was reproved by

Judge Samuel Seabury—later head of the Seabury investigation into New York corruption[14]—who admonished his jurors that "the court has neither the right nor the power to proceed with the present trial. These men are to be tried for the same offense again and under our constitution and laws this cannot be done. I charge you, gentlemen of the jury, to find a verdict for the defendents."[15]

There were curious similarities and differences between the somber events in New York and the desperate warfare between the miners on one side and company police and state militia on the other. The cause was the same, for the ending of harassment of workers and for unionization in the domain of the Colorado Fuel and Iron Company. The company was rigid in its control of miners' lives. It forced them to live in company shacks and paid them in scrip. Officials did not hesitate to censor their reading matter, proscribing not only socialist writings but Darwin's *Origin of Species* and *The Rubaiyat of Omar Khayyam.* Said a company spokesman, "We wish to protect our people from erroneous ideas."[16]

In 1913 the United Mine Workers sent in organizers to demand a series of changes in company policies, which were actually against existing Colorado laws. Driven from their shacks by intransigent officials, the miners set up tent colonies at mine centers while undertaking a strike that immediately broadened into warfare. A company detective and a union organizer died. At another point, machine-gun fire killed one laborer and put nine bullets into the leg of a boy. At still another location, company police broke into a miners' meeting and killed three workers. Four company men were killed in retaliation.

When the state's governor concluded it was his duty to protect strikebreakers, the final abomination was foreshadowed. At Ludlow, a major coal mining installation, were sheltered some 900 to 1,200 strike sympathizers, including women and children, in close confrontation with National Guardsmen who believed themselves committed to the defense of the mines and their partisans. A hated guardsman who had seized prounionists, under allegations of attempted escape, shot them as they fled. A battle broke out along the whole line of combat, which reached its climax with guardsmen pouring over into the tent colony and, by accident or design—a military commission found for design—set them on fire. In the conflagration died women and children.

With the state Federation of Labor now summoning every miner to arms, open warfare raged for hundreds of miles. Mines were dynamited, buildings burned, strikebreakers and police killed. "Exactly as in war, each belligerent issued communiqués, reported casualties, and boasted of victories." The governor gave up his empty authority and appealed for federal troops to put down "open insurrection against the State." In April 1914 several regiments arrived to police the mines.

As a government commission headed by the Missouri lawyer Frank P. Walsh investigated the Colorado situation, the nation was now given another lesson in labor-capital relations. For a while, even the miners were befuddled by John D. Rockefeller, Jr., owner of the mines, who presented himself to the public as one bewildered by events and eager to understand them and right conditions where possible. However, the commission now saw its chairman, Walsh, emerge as a voice from earlier Progressive days. His researches and interrogations brought out the fact that Rockefeller, far from being remote from western events, had guided them. He had dictated policy to the mine directors. He had persuaded the governor himself of his duty to the company. Rockefeller had had Ivy Lee promote a procompany publicity campaign for the nation and had himself cooperated with Lee in preparing some of the patently false materials that went into the campaign.[17]

The press divided in its estimate of Walsh, some papers setting him down as a demagogue, others as a radical. In fact, Walsh, the son of poor Missourians before he became a famous trial lawyer and Progressive, had risen to what he clearly saw as a test of the nation's policies. The people, he argued, must own the trusts or the trusts own them. He had been known, heretofore, for temperateness and impartiality. But the evidence he had accumulated respecting eastern capitalist domination of western mines had put all his principles into focus.

The miners later set up a stone pillar to memorialize their Ludlow dead, but in the end they had little to show for their effort. Rockefeller claimed to be chastened, a new man to whom much had been revealed. But he offered the Colorado Industrial Plan for settling the situation. This plan had been produced by W. L. Mackenzie King of Canada, then of Rockefeller's industrial relations department, later Canadian Prime Minister. His plan improved some material conditions. It created grievance and other committees. It did not provide for unions or collective bargaining. It was a western version of Brandeis's protocol plan for the New York garment industry and, like it, left a heritage of uncertainty for Progressive hopes.

There were other ominous signs of worms in the Progressive triumph—for it needs always to be recalled that Progressives had been elected in a nation that contained every brand of conservative and patent reactionary, as far separated in kind as from Little Rock, Arkansas, and New Haven, Connecticut. There had been exploitation of ethnic differences in both the New York and Colorado strikes as part of industrial warfare. There were still lower levels of unrest not thoroughly explained by economic frustrations, which threatened the rational order of society. They furnished opportunities for demagogues who could appeal to the fantasies of frustrated or otherwise clouded personalities.

On April 27, 1913, a thirteen-year-old girl, Mary Phagan, an employee in an Atlanta, Georgia, pencil factory was found in its cellar strangled and disfigured. Charged with murder and desecration was twenty-nine-year-old Leo Frank, superintendent of the factory and part owner. He readily admitted that she had visited his office the day before to collect her pay. He did not then realize that no one in ordinary pursuits had seen her alive after she left his office. Nor did it occur to him that anyone could identify him with so crude a murder and body disposal on the premises.

He hired Pinkerton police to seek evidence in connection with her death. The evidence they and the Atlanta detectives and police gathered and failed to gather was not accidentally or maliciously mishandled. They were all puppets of circumstances, who could have done nothing right no matter what they did or intended. As the chief of detectives said, when he arrested Frank two days later and charged him with murder: "The town seems to be very much wrought up over the murder and I think this is the wisest course to take."[18]

The wisest course would have been to have wasted no time on the obviously innocent Negro watchman, Newt Lee, and to have arrested the Negro sweeper of the factory, Jim Conley, a worthless drinker with discovered sexual fantasies who had actually committed the murder. Professor Kelly Miller of Howard University would have approved, for he saw no gain to the Negro people in defending dissolute persons who happened to be black. The problem was not with the Negro community, which had suffered enough in the 1906 arson and killings in Atlanta. It was with the white Georgian community, composed of anxious middle-class families and poor whites who had come from the farms to eke out small livings without honor or decent wages and without support of state regulations in labor, housing, and other conditions.

Neither middle-class nor worker elements of Atlanta knew what could help them to feel more secure. They held on to family, religion, and tradition as best they could, hated northern "capital," of which they knew nothing, and easily conjured up mental images of their economic betters as occasion suggested.

Frank, born in Texas and raised in Brooklyn, had attended Cornell University and received his engineering degree there in 1906. Several jobs and four years later he married an Atlanta belle and settled in its Jewish community, in which he attained some prominence. Mary Phagan was the child of workers who lived humbly and anticipated little social consideration. Atlanta lived with ethnic tensions that needed little to be set free. What form freedom would take depended on the vents offered.

Ten thousand persons came to view the girl's corpse before burial, and emotional words found ready expression from ministers, neighbors, and observers. The newspapers competed for the attention of their readers, with headlines recalling each pathetic detail of the child's brief life and death. They varied in tone, from the *Atlanta Constitution*, which assumed Frank's guilt, to the *Journal* and the *Georgian*, which maintained a more equitable reportage. Such later events as the raising of a monument to the child helped further unite those who fed their hatred on the outrage.

In time, the bases of the psychosis that cost the young businessman his life would be better understood. Atlantans were eager to believe that the Jew was a "pervert," a concept that was never adequately explained or demonstrated because their knowledge was limited and their mentor, Conley, gave vague testimony out of his own, and perhaps suggested, fantasies. What was crucial to the case was that he found a sponsor who was glad to ignore the revealing notes he had written and left near the body, in crude hope of diverting attention from himself to Newt Lee, who was, unlike himself, tall and thin. The sponsor was willing to forget that Conley was black in his search for bigger game. He concocted a tale that he firmly rehearsed with Conley, and kept him away from newspapermen and others who could have picked it to pieces. He also persuaded the grand jury not to indict Conley and so maintained him as a witness—cleaned up, respectable appearing—rather than a defendant.

The sponsor was Atlanta's solicitor-general, Hugh M. Dorsey, an ambitious man with few talents, who had lost cases and needed a court victory. He moved swiftly to his great opportunity, with vast faith in the prejudices of Atlanta's citizens, evidently self-persuaded that in some higher sense the gross lies he sponsored and the subversions of testimony he engineered contained some intrinsic truth. Dorsey's role in court was essentially that of an actor playing to an empathetic audience.

As the pastor of the Baptist church the dead girl's family attended said: "My feelings, upon the arrest of the old negro nightwatchman [Lee], were to the effect that this one old negro would be poor atonement for the life of this innocent girl. But, when on the next day, the police arrested a Jew, and a Yankee Jew at that, all of the inborn prejudice against Jews rose up in a feeling of satisfaction, that here would be a victim worthy to pay for the crime."[19]

Frank was not only Jewish, he was a symbol of industry, which embittered southerners who saw it as penetrating into their homeland from the North and oppressing them. Tom Watson, later whipping himself into a frenzy, would refer to "the indescribable outrage committed upon 'the factory girl' *in the factory*" as symbolic of the factory owner's unfeeling arrogance. The crowd that gathered in the courthouse came to hear a tale indicative of their sorrows and humiliations, and it made no difference that it was a nightmare of legal absurdities.

Conley, an instrument of their purposes, claimed he had acted as watcher while Frank perpetrated obscenities with various females in his office. He had, he said, at Frank's instructions, taken the dead girl

Hugh Dorsey and Jim Conley in close collaboration.

down to the cellar by elevator, though evidence disproved beyond controversy the use of the elevator. The notes found near the body written to divert suspicion to Newt Lee were in his handwriting. He held that Frank had dictated the crude message to him, though the words "night witch" were peculiarly esoteric in Negro lore and unconnotative to others.

Dorsey treated all Conley's claims with deep respect. The distinguished lawyers Frank employed brought out much of the grotesque aspects of the testimony, but their very excellence offended the restless audience, prone to hisses and savage outbursts. The conscientious interrogation of Conley only gave him more time to stir the auditors with his simple accounts of sexual exploits, sly gestures, and offers Frank allegedly made to female employees.

What stayed with Dorsey's audience were the accusations, not the rebuttals. A policeman thought he had caught Frank and a young woman in a park some time back engaged in sex. He later admitted he had confused Frank with someone else. Witnesses in time admitted to having been threatened or bribed to say that Frank had sought rooms for liaisons, but their original statements continued memorable. Over and over again Dorsey asked factory girls on the witness stand whether Frank had touched particular parts of their bodies, fondled their breasts or their nipples, all of which inflamed anguished auditors, even though the witnesses' answers were denials. Dorsey could make no mistakes. He preened himself on not having himself introduced the question of Frank's "race," but used the fact to speak kindly of Disraeli and Judah P. Benjamin, Secretary of State of the Confederacy, and to philosophize that "[the Jews] rise to heights sublime, but they also sink to the lowest depths of degradation."[20]

Frank was found guilty. National efforts to get the verdict reversed only called further attention to northerners and Jews. Progressive opinion to save Frank roused comment from multitudes of notables, informed students of the case, and lawyers of the caliber of C. P. Connolly, leaders ranging from Charles R. Crane to Jane Addams. An upswelling of sympathy brought Frank a hundred thousand letters and storms of pleas and petitions. Editorial comment from coast to coast expressed horror at the jury's verdict. The "demons of malice" were undeterred. Tom Watson found himself bathed in a glow of popularity such as he had never before enjoyed as Populist or even as racist, as he denounced the "lustful Jew" and anticipated his death. Monster rallies in Georgia gave evidence that its masses stood firm and would condemn anyone at home who defied them.[21]

Dorsey was sustained by the Georgia Supreme Court, unshaken

by the fact that the trial judge himself had admitted that perhaps he had shown "undue deference to the opinion of the jury." The United States Supreme Court denied it had jurisdiction, though it later received a similar case and agreed to render judgment.

It would be a gross distortion of history to see as a Progressive Watson, who threatened lynching if the decision against Frank should be reversed, any more than to view the mobs that defied national opinion as the authentic voice of Georgia. They no more than gave evidence of the dangers inherent in appeals to the masses. The Georgia that produced a Dorsey and the Frank tragedy also produced a John M. Slaton, governor of the state and a legislator of many years who spoke for the state's best sentiment and was able to do something for its honor.

Slaton had been a popular governor, and, had he let Frank die legally, would have gone on to the United States Senate. Instead, June 21, 1915, having studied the evidence with care, he destroyed his political career by commuting Frank's sentence. Slaton's life and home were threatened and required police protection. Popular rage, sustained by demagogues but also by educated and respectable community leaders, became wild with frustration. Vigilance committees were organized, Jewish boycotts imposed. Slaton was hanged in effigy.

Frank was taken to the farm prison at Milledgeville where, four weeks later, another convict plunged a butcher knife into him while he slept, then slashed his throat. The hemorrhage was stopped in time, and Frank lived. But a month later, the prison was efficiently stormed, guards overpowered, and Frank kidnapped by some of the "best citizens" of Marietta, Georgia, which had been the dead girl's home town. "Riffraff" was deliberately excluded by the avenging party, which included a clergyman, two former Supreme Court justices, and an ex-sheriff. Frank died a hero, asking no quarter and so shaking one of the posse that he urged that Frank be returned to prison. The majority won. Frank asked that his ring be returned to his wife, a request that was carefully respected.

Before the hanging, the leader, in his role of civilized avenger asked: "Mr. Frank, we are now going to do what the law said to do—hang you by the neck until you are dead. Do you want to make any statement before you die?" The question had a species of dignity such as many reconstructed southerners liked to dream of possessing. In 1916 a popular wave of enthusiasm carried Dorsey into the governor's mansion, from which he retired in 1921. He later served as judge of Atlanta's City Court and of the Fulton County Superior Court.

It was far from an accident that the nation was, at the time, being thrilled by a new motion picture, *The Birth of a Nation*, done from the novel, *The Clansman*, by Woodrow Wilson's friend from Johns Hopkins days, Reverend Thomas Dixon. The film portrayed "villainous Radicals, sinister mulattoes, blameless Southerners, and faithful darkies."[22] The film was so replete with novelties and artistic inventions as to affect the future of the medium. Woodrow Wilson viewed it in the White House. His cabinet saw it. Chief Justice Edward Douglas White of the Supreme Court was first bewildered by the thought of viewing a motion picture, but when told by Dixon that it gave the "true" story of the redemption of the South by the Ku Klux Klan, the Chief Justice slowly removed his glasses, pushed his work aside, and said, "I was a member of the Klan, Sir."[23]

That year, too, after Frank's death, a group of men convened at Stone Mountain near Atlanta to inaugurate another Ku Klux Klan under an Alabama organizer and orator, Colonel William Joseph Simmons. His Klan sought not solely a southern but a national career, and before its race was run its fiery cross had burned not only in southern fields and towns but as far away as Vermont. It was concerned not only for carpetbaggers and Negroes, as the former Klan had been, but for all other "aliens" and immoral people arbitrarily defined. Although none of this had anything to do with progressivism, and was fought by major Progressives, it helped define the challenge to their faith as a living force in American life.[24]

Dorsey was far from being the only demagogue who could appeal to the lower impulses of the people in whom the first wave of twentieth century Progressives had put their faith and whom their administrative-minded Progressive successors had intended to control. Nor were the demagogues by any means confined to the South. New York City in 1912 was a capital of crime and politics, which was moving in directions of organization and efficiency as swiftly and necessarily as conditions required. In that year William Sulzer, a

New York Democrat who was a rugged, Populist type, was elected governor by the largest margin in the state's history. As tried and matured in politics as Slaton had been in Georgia, Sulzer supported social legislation, direct primaries—the issue on which he would be politically ruined—direct election of United States senators, and even recognition of China. His determination to root out corruption, and his public declarations on the subject infuriated Boss Murphy, who called for his head.

Murphy acquired evidence, easily acquired since it was common practice industriously refined by his machine, that campaign funds for Sulzer had been what would later be called "laundered," that is, passed through banks to separate donor from receiver. In 1913 the impeachment of Sulzer charged him with having failed to report contributions totalling $9,000, among them, $2,500 from the financier Jacob Schiff and $1,000 from Henry Morganthau. Sulzer protested that his failure to report had been an oversight, but the Democrats voted for conviction and won handily. Voting with the Murphy followers were Robert Wagner, Senate majority leader, and Alfred E. Smith, speaker of the Senate.[25]

The public reaction to this political execution elected John Purroy Mitchel to be the youngest mayor in the history of New York. Mitchel fought for and won positive reforms, but Sulzer's career was ended, and the demonstrated strength of the political machine gave evidence that the nature of "progressive" civic achievements needed continuing review.

In 1912 occurred a minor event which, however, was of greater consequence than the destruction of Sulzer and his program. The new sensation not only arrested the attention of the country but would continue to do so. It was like certain other events that seemed of passing moment, being only one of many, but that contained elements that gave them precedence over all similar events. The shootout at the O. K. Corral, the St. Valentine Day massacre in Chicago—such episodes became all but legendary, memorializing eras and drawing scholars and fiction writers again and again to tell once more the classic tale.

Such an episode was the killing of Herman Rosenthal on the night of July 15, 1912, outside the Hotel Metropole in mid-Manhattan by a group of gunmen who sped away in a car. Rosenthal was a gambler who had had some good years, but for the past several years had been quarreling with police over "protection." Associates had urged him to pay and be quiet. Rosenthal, stubborn, confused, and not over-bright, was being persuaded by a newspaperman to reveal to the district attorney some of the secrets known to him about police-gambler relations. Much of what Rosenthal was preparing to tell was no secret at all to great numbers of people engaged in or related to politics, graft, and, of course, gambling. But a loose federation of bribe-takers and bribe-givers maintained a system that was, after all, supported by great numbers who enjoyed gambling, vice, drinking, and related activities. These caused keen competition and deaths among antagonists. As was repeatedly noticed by sophisticated reporters, gamblers and others in the vice industry killed each other regularly.

What was striking about the Rosenthal killing was that it brought about the electrocution of the police officer, Lieutenant Charles Becker, responsible for controlling gambling in the city. It raised his prosecutor, District Attorney Charles S. Whitman, on a wave of popular approval to the governorship of the state and possible candidacy for president.

Those involved in the actual Rosenthal killing were not memorable in any way, and those who were executed for the crime or served time in prison for the killing would have left no traces by themselves. What was impressive was the public reaction to the incident, the role played by the press, and the attitude of both to the strong-minded mayor William J. Gaynor, to Whitman, and to Becker representing the old social control system of local vice.[26]

That Becker was a hard man no one has denied. As a police officer he was ruthless not only to men but to women. In his early days Stephen Crane, then reporting on the local journal, observed him being unnecessarily rough with a young prostitute, Dora Clark, whom he accused of soliciting. He ignored Crane's protests and hauled her off to Magistrate's Court. Crane appeared as a witness in her behalf, and the entire newspaper fraternity was exercised over the fact that Becker was avenging a policeman whom she had refused services under the impression that he was a Negro (there then being no Negroes on the force). The prostitute later claimed that Becker on next meeting her seized her by the throat and knocked her down.

Once again Crane appeared, this time at a departmental trial that captured headlines up and down the coast, to speak in her behalf. The trial judge tried to establish that Crane himself was disreputable, an effort the journalists sourly received. Becker was eventually cleared for having made an honest mistake in line of duty, but his misadventure was one of a number of such over the years that later came up to haunt him.

A rumor took shape that Crane based his *Maggie: A Girl of the Streets* on Dora Clark. In fact, the novelette was already in print. But such misapprehensions, including one fatal one, would have made no difference in the long run, whatever they might have done for Becker personally. The fact that he was in a car that passed the site of the Rosenthal murder about an hour after it occurred and that he checked into the nearby police station to inquire what was known about it, suggested to Whitman the plan that he triumphantly pursued. But Manhattan, after all, though a maze of streets in some districts, was relatively small. Becker had been heading elsewhere and normally would have been far from the scene of the crime. A change of plan seemed vaguely to connect him with it. Thereafter he was doomed—not by the evidence but by the will of the people to reach the police by any means.

The response of both public and press to Mayor Gaynor's view of the killing was one of fury. Gaynor, a blunt, unpretentious man, saw only what appeared to the naked eye: a gang vengeance for some undisclosed purpose. Rosenthal had been talking to the press and was about to talk further to the district attorney. But as one disreputable witness giving state's evidence against his associates, he was liable to retaliation by anyone. Arnold Rothstein, already an arbiter among vice lords in close touch with Tammany leaders, had urged Rosenthal personally to get out of town until his treason to their kind had been forgotten. Rosenthal's foolish refusal to do so had cost him his life.

Gaynor's surprise that Becker would have socialized with such a person as Rosenthal showed naiveté. Had he read Josiah Flynt's decade-old *The World of Graft*, or, indeed, any of Flynt's books,[27] he would have known that police-criminal relations were vital to any control of crime. Gaynor did realize that graft was inevitable and that it was the task of those concerned for law and order to keep it in check rather than to hope to obliterate it. But his criticism of "the clamor

GAYNOR TO BOY SCOUT

Everything is all right, you're all right, I'm all right. There is no gambling, Rosenthal isn't even dead. Everything is all right except blackleg newspapers.

Muckraking as sensationalism.

and false statements of vicious persons and newspapers" affronted the newspapermen, and his sufficient target for the police of upholding "outward order and decency" raised a hypocritical cry of horror, which boded ill for candor and good reason. With the power of the reform magazines depleted, irresponsible journalism decked itself with the honors of muckraking. The issue was seen nationally, and as a besmirched police being protected by an incompetent mayor. As the *Atlanta Constitution* said: "Thank God Woodrow Wilson was nominated for the Presidency, and not Gaynor!"[28]

Gaynor could do nothing right. District Attorney Whitman could do no wrong. Whitman was a straight organization man ambitious to rise and determined at all odds to rise. His response to the Triangle Shirtwaist Company fire revealed, as later events would reveal in detail, his cold-hearted ambition. He came excitedly into the office several days following the Triangle catastrophe demanding to know of his head of the homicide division what was being done. The man demurred; they were investigating, and there was no evidence as yet.

> "Well, get an indictment! We can always *nol pros* it." [That is, decide later not to prosecute on the ground that there wasn't enough evidence after all.] "Here, look at it!" and he held up an editorial in the Hearst New York *American*. "You go and get an indictment. We can *nol pros* if we can't maintain it. You can always *nol pros.*"[29]

Whitman's reckless charges against Gaynor as a do-nothing mayor brought him praise and private funds from wealthy citizens to dig out the truth. He moved uptown to a luxuriant suite of rooms and sent investigators upstate and about the country to find witnesses, meanwhile making daily charges against the police and mayor as hiding evidence or refusing to help find it. Whitman publicly highlighted Becker as a major suspect, hinting at incontrovertible evidence. Gaynor had asked for a police investigation of Becker but noted that he was not to be condemned, certainly beforehand, on the word of criminals and degenerates. Becker had certainly been involved in graft. He had received protection money and distributed it, though how much would never be determined. Wild guesses and detailed journalistic snooping, with Becker futilely denying and explaining, gave a degraded "muckraking" tone to the reportage. In any case, all this was irrelevant to the issue. Becker was a grafter as were many, perhaps almost all, police in small or large measure. The question was whether he had ordered a murder.

Whitman's method was to feed accusations satisfying to the wishful thinking of reporters and their readers, and, when patently, glaringly proved wrong to explain that the newspapers had printed errors. And since the case he was constructing to send Becker to the electric chair was based entirely on the word of criminals, he had to labor strenuously to keep them in line, prevent them from committing too many discrepancies and above all to be assured that the public was behind him and the judge cooperative.

Long practice at public forums had taught Whitman what the crowds wished to hear, and they responded with enthusiasm to his demands for action. At a rally at Cooper Union dedicated in curiously goo-goo fashion to "municipal righteousness" his appearance caused a five-minute demonstration.

> "Three cheers for our next governor," someone cried in the audience, and at the words, according to the *Times*, "a bedlam of sound shook the hall."
>
> "We need you in New York," another voice cried.
>
> "Yes, and we need you in Albany, too," cried someone at the rear of the platform.
>
> "You don't need me half as much as I need you," Whitman shouted back. The killing of Herman Rosenthal, he went on to tell them, "was a murder, an awful murder, but it was more than that. In the light of all the circumstances connected with it, it was 'a challenge to our very civilization itself.' " When the applause died down, he concluded: "I appreciate tonight, ladies and gentlemen, that you have accepted that challenge. I knew you would."[30]

Whitman was more than fortunate in his trial judge, John W. Goff, who had made his reputation baiting the police during the Lexow investigation of 1894. It had had reform overtones but little sense of purpose or goals. Goff was a strangely cold man whose main quality was contempt for people and, residually, hatred of police. Less famous than it should have been was Goff's sweeping injunction in 1910 against the striking ILGWU, which had crippled their mortal efforts. Goff denounced their seeking the closed shop as a "common law and civil conspiracy." Even the manufacturers, fearing some strong public reaction, had been taken aback by an injunction that permanently restrained peaceful picketing. If Goff had done nothing else he had faced workers and reformers with the dilemma of a next step.[31]

Goff did respond to flattery, and Whitman worked assiduously to win him to his viewpoint; and so successfully that Becker's first trial was notorious for the prejudice shown by its presiding judge. The trial featured a succession of criminals, including Bald Jack Rose, Bridgey Webber, and Harry Vallon, who had turned state's evidence on promise of immunity. They were in court to say they had made arrangements with the gangster Big Jack Zelig, on Becker's orders, to hire four gunmen, Gyp the Blood, Lefty Louie, Dago Frank, and Whitey Lewis to kill Rosenthal. It was typical of Whitman's methods that when Zelig was killed, two days before Becker's trial began, that Whitman immediately declared Zelig would have been the principal witness against Becker, though Becker protested he had never seen Zelig. Since Becker was in custody, the trial thus became a trial of the police—who presumably wanted Zelig dead—rather than Becker.

The trial itself was a "shambles of justice," with Goff harassing the defense counsel openly, at one point forcing him to question a witness beyond exhaustion and advising another witness of his right to take the Fifth Amendment: a device not yet generally available to known or suspected criminals. The Court of Appeals, 6 to 1, following Becker's conviction set down an opinion devastating to Whitman and Goff.[32]

As startling, however, as the bill of particulars was the public and press reaction, which amounted to a lynching spirit. The charges made at the second Becker trial, and endorsed in the press, hinted darkly at a conspiracy between the police and Becker to suborn witnesses by threats or money, though this was exactly the tactic of the prosecutor. Another cooperative judge, Samuel Seabury, sat on the bench for Whitman's second appearance. The verdict of death to Becker gave satisfaction to the city.

Had Sulzer been governor of New York, he would have commuted

Becker's sentence. But Whitman was governor in July 1915, and though he did not stay Becker's execution, he did pardon a friend of Bald Jack Rose who had tried to kill a gambler, and a notorious gunman and swindler who had testified for his case but who was in Sing Sing on a twenty-year sentence. Whitman had aspired to the presidency, but a variety of factors, including the rise of Alfred E. Smith and his own propensity for liquor, not only caused this hope to wither but, in 1924, even lost him his bid for the old district attorney post.

All of this was vastly less important than the adjustment of relations that, on Becker's death, made Arnold Rothstein the successor to Becker as arranger of protection money and political liaisons in New York, with national connections. There were, of course, numerous smaller Rothsteins throughout the land, arranging bets, and all gained by the demonstrated weakness of the police to protect their own. Heretofore, gangsters had been little people who needed the protection of the police. In succeeding years protection would turn the other way. A long saga of labor racketeering, of political appointments and nominations, of expansion of the narcotics racket, and, following the victory of prohibitionists, of the great liquor trade began, to much of which Rothstein was a central or associated figure.

As such he transacted business with such rising figures as Lucky Luciano, Jimmy Hines, a machine man who became mayor of New York, and the various machine judges. Fights were fixed. It was likely that the famous "long count," which kept Gene Tunney heavyweight champion of the world, was fixed.

> Yes, all kinds of people made their way to Rothstein's table. A cop who wondered if Rothstein would help him get a promotion to detective. A garment manufacturer who was a friend of Abraham Rothstein [Rothstein's distinguished and religious father, to whom his son was lost] . . . who needed help in a union dispute. A bookmaker who wondered if Rothstein would help get him an "okay" to operate in New Jersey.[33]

Progressivism was not killed by crime or even by "muckraking"—that is, irresponsible—journalism. The public was a sea of interests, which was affected as much by things that fed the spirit as fed the body politic. Lincoln Steffens had made a major revelation of the fact that municipal corruption was supported by respectable businessmen who made deals with bosses at the expense of society. His reports, in one sense, flattered a public that gave inadequate attention to its own complicity in the process and that veered between throwing the rascals out and expressing gratitude to them for favors received.

It merits notice that the Chicago "Black Sox" baseball scandal of 1919 took place on the heels of the "war to end all wars"; it was the first major sporting event to follow the great crusade. The irony would not be lost on a public that had been whipped up to patriotic frenzies with lurid accounts of German villainy. Keen-eyed children would be among crowds that cheered parading troops of the American Expeditionary Forces, and they would contrast the high-minded rhetoric of the welcoming committees with the revelations of fraud and demagoguery highlighted in the newspapers. Such spectacles would test the children's faith in all they were part of and help form their attitudes.

The baseball scandal was to become a national legend, revived and embellished over the years in every detail. As the ball players and others passed on, their roles in the tragedy were recounted for new generations of readers. All other sports would have to go through their own Gehennas of treachery, exposure, and retribution, but it was significant that the thorough sifting of argument and recrimination over the fixed World Series of 1919 after a while—though not before a number of painful scenes had been enacted—allowed baseball to settle down with some sense of security. Something was accomplished, though not with justice and not with full comprehension.

A later generation made much of a chapter in F. Scott Fitzgerald's *The Great Gatsby* that saw American corruption in the event. The novel told something about the American character—not overmuch, but something—and less about the shadows through which progressivism was passing, into an uncertain future.

Those highlighted by the scandals were in themselves no more memorable than the principals in other sensations. They reflected their times more than they molded them. Arnold Rothstein was remembered, wrongly, since he played almost no role in the actions. Commissioner of Baseball Kenesaw Mountain Landis was remembered and made a confusing link with the Progressive era, which he no more represented than had Tom Watson. Best remembered was "Shoeless" Joe Jackson, and not so much as himself, the illiterate Georgian who many believed the greatest natural ball player of all time. It was rather the appeal of a boy, which rang in memory, when Jackson emerged from his grand jury investigation in September 1920: "Say it ain't so, Joe." Jackson's sad answer was said to have been: "Yes, kid, I'm afraid it is."[34]

Strangely, Jackson could have answered firmly that it wasn't so. Jackson was the star of the series, outbatting and outplaying everybody. But he knew in a muddled way that he had gone along with friends, accepted money, and not told. None of the involved players was very deep, and one had initiated the plot. The "fix," what there was of it, was more complicated than anyone was able or willing to believe. Americans were at their old game of scapegoating. But it made the genius-sportswriter and humorist Ring Lardner a bitter cynic and so indirectly contributed to the writing of several great American short stories. It probably also killed Lardner young with bad 1920s liquor, as it certainly did others. Baseball was only a game, but it took its toll.

How much the game had come to mean to the public was shown by the incredulity that greeted the news that a World Series could be "thrown." The revelations (or apparent revelations) caused outbursts of indignation and despair that anyone could tamper with the nation's fun. Yet baseball, in its fifty-year history, had been far from pure. Brutal wars between owners, exploitation of players without thought to their needs or futures, had in 1889-1890 caused a players' revolt and their setting up of a new league to compete with the old for patronage. The players' league failed, and the continuing struggle for power and privileges on clubs and over players showed how much the public had to endure of greed and dishonesty in order to enjoy its athletes' prowess. As the *Sporting News* of April 8, 1889, had protested:

> What's the matter with these . . . magnates? What a shame it is

> that the greatest of sports . . . should be in the hands of such a mal-odorous gang . . . [with their] mud slinging, brawling, corruption, breaches of confidence, dishonorable conspiracies, [and] threats of personal violence.[35]

Betting early became part of baseball as of other sports, outstandingly horseracing. Thereafter, gamblers were much a part of the game, looking for tips, getting to know ball players, and, whenever they could, influencing games. Since there were thousands of games, a species of submorality developed among special interests in baseball, as in other businesses. Aging pitchers, for example, losing their cunning and strength and needing money, could be persuaded to pitch a shade off their usual performance for bribes or betting against themselves. And since the best of pitchers lost often, despite their best efforts, detection of deliberate losing was difficult. Game-throwing was a minor art, though there were also players, the pride of their profession, who could not be remotely connected with such arts.

Players and even clubs were occasionally caught, or half-caught, in shaky exploits, with managers or public willing to forgive or avert eyes in order to enjoy their further company. Hal Chase of the Cincinnati Reds, then of the New York Giants, was persistently shifty, though a fine first-baseman and hitter. Chase was unabashed in trying to tempt others to join him in his betting schemes. Yet he not only survived exposure, he survived the White Sox he helped disgrace, thanks to his good relations with gamblers and officials.[36] Sincerity was no guarantee of compassion, or even justice.

The wonder was that such doings could come to the World Series and to the White Sox, who were admittedly the best team in baseball, one of the best ever. In time, the source of the involved players' discontent would be evident: their incredibly low salaries, their bondage to their owner Charles Comiskey who feted newspapermen but kept his players on meager allowances. His pitching ace Eddie Cicotte actually needed money for a mortgage payment. Comiskey, "the Old Roman," himself a star player in the past, was unimpressed by players and held them in line as in a stable. So bad had been their condition that the players had been threatening a strike. It was

The second inning of the opening game. Chick Gandil is tagged out while apparently trying to steal second. (Courtesy of the Chicago Historical Society)

symptomatic of the state of things that the conspiring players made only casual efforts at secrecy: so reasonable seemed their purposes to themselves.

The plot was instituted not by gamblers but by one of the players, first-baseman Chick Gandil, come up from poverty and resentful that his power in the field brought him so little. He resented, too, the "lily white" attitudes of second-baseman Eddie Collins, who had attended Columbia University, and Ray Schalk, the White Sox fiery catcher, proud of his craft. Gandil won over the two key pitchers, Eddie Cicotte and Claude "Lefty" Williams, and then enough of the rest of the team to ensure the series' loss.

The setting up of the "fix," accomplished only several weeks before the series' start, was indicative of the choices the nation was making in crime-society relations. Rothstein was approached by gamblers for money, did not believe the "fix" could be arranged, and put forth nothing. It was one of his entourage, Abe Attell, a formerly brilliant featherweight boxing champion who, with no authority, told the conspiring players that Rothstein was behind the deal and held them in line with promises and false telegrams indicating that money would be forthcoming after they had proved the deal was on. It was Hal Chase who kept the fix active when it seemed to lag. In the end, $10,000 in cash was put under starting pitcher Cicotte's pillow.

Cicotte hit the first batter squarely on the back, and the fix was underway. Even so, it was far from consummated. "Buck" Weaver, the great third baseman for the White Sox, soon made it evident that he had changed his mind. Joe Jackson did not know how to cheat, and though he later imagined he could have moved faster during several games of the series, the scorecards could find little he had done in left field to help the Cincinnati Reds and nothing he had done at bat. In the crucial fourth inning of the first game, Edd Roush, star Cincinnati Red, hit a tremendous blow to centerfield marked for extra bases which "Happy" Felsch miraculously caught, in his try proving that he could not, after all, go along with the plot.

Cicotte himself had been in torment, unable to sleep, uncertain what to do. He had indeed given the signal for the fix, but, in the same fourth inning, he made two outs with clear legitimacy. It was his shortstop Swede Risberg, working with the committed Gandil, who unnerved Cicotte to give the Reds the four runs that meant the game.

It was the poor morale behind an uncertain pitcher, rather than plotted error, that lost the White Sox their first game, 9 to 1. It was deliberately bad pitching by Lefty Williams, lowering morale further, that lost the White Sox their second game 4 to 2. Low morale continued into the third game, which the White Sox won behind the superb pitching of second-string Dickie Kerr. The White Sox, a power team, were not hitting. Cicotte's second effort was a pitching duel won by Cincinnati, 2 to 0, as was the game after, pitched by Williams, until the White Sox blew up as a result of a close and, they thought, a wrong umpire's call. In the 5 to 0 loss, Williams may have been trying to pitch legitimately; he had after all a career to continue. Kerr once again came through for a White Sox victory, but the 5 to 4 triumph could not wipe out the fact that the White Sox had gone until then 26 innings without a run. Their "lily whites" had, of course, done their best—and done almost nothing at bat—and been joined by the regained conspirators. But the rhythm that had made them a great and resourceful team had been destroyed.[37]

Cicotte's third performances was brilliant. Humiliated by Dickie Kerr's two victories and by his own need to recover prestige for the future. he dominated the Reds and won 4 to 1. Another victory would tie the White Sox in numbers of games to the Reds and enable the Chicagoans to go ahead. An oddity of the situation was that the rumor was now rife that it was the Reds who were about to throw the series, under pressure of gangsters. Americans were beginning to accept the view that their protection from gangsters' wiles was limited. The police were no recourse. This belief directly affected Lefty Williams's third try. His family had been threatened by phone if he should give a true accounting of his arts. In his eagerness to appease the criminals, Williams gave up five runs in the first inning and left the game. The series ended in ignominy.[38]

The scandal would not down, and not because of Comiskey, who had learned enough of the fix to have stopped it after the first game. The scandal burst forth because of three of the least tainted of those involved. Joe Jackson had been given $5,000 and felt guilty enough to sign a "confession," as did Happy Felsch and Buck Weaver. And now baseball had a "commissioner," Landis, who stipulated that he was to have absolute authority to rule on any and all matters involving the game and the clubs and was given that dictatorial power.

Landis was the legal equivalent of the sensational press, wholly interested in self-serving sensations, without regard to law or democracy. He had been an ambitious boy as Ben Lindsey had been an ambitious boy, and he reached for publicity as Lindsey had. But whereas Lindsey had substantial causes and reasonable solutions, Landis sought only to hit the headlines. He did so in ways that demeaned his office and his cause. In 1907 he caused excitement with his absurd $29,240,000 fine on Standard Oil of Indiana in an antitrust suit that was quickly overthrown by the Supreme Court. His melodramatic demand that Kaiser Wilhelm II of Germany come to his court and stand trial for the sinking of the *Lusitania* made a travesty of human tragedy, which suggested that Landis was of that coldhearted fraternity that could exploit others' sorrows with self-deceiving emotionalism. Landis's superpatriotism during World War I was of so blatant a variety as to recommend him only to the most self-righteous of those who were digging graves for free speech and conscience.[39]

Yet the shock of the series scandal was such as to seem to require a drastic operation, burning out, if necessary, infected elements in baseball. Landis in his career had been drastic, if nothing else. Unfortunately, he was a demagogue rather than a crusader, and the operation he performed was distinguished by violence rather than by character or intelligence. Had Landis shown either of the latter, he would have penalized Gandil, Risberg, Cicotte, and Williams, and warned them to take care thereafter. And he would have exonerated Jackson, Weaver, Felsch, and a utility player who had had little opportunity to do anything and drifted early out of the connection. A civil court had acquitted *all* of the players, who had enjoyed a brief moment of happiness in the sensation of a return to status.

But so gracious and greathearted an action was beyond Landis. He lacked the courage to touch the implicated Comiskey or to debar the truly infectious Hal Chase from baseball. Landis needed to demonstrate his power and importance. He issued a pompous statement sweepingly condemning all players past and present who might have had so much as had traffic with gamblers. And he read out of baseball forever all eight of the White Sox suspects. He pursued Joe Jackson into the minor leagues, where Jackson was unable to hide his identity due to his irrepressible excellence. Public opinion continued to be wiser than Landis, though slow to cope with his draconian decisions. And when Landis had evidence that the public would find it intolerable for him to run out of baseball the superstars Ty Cobb and Tris Speaker, who had been seriously compromised in games of the same year of 1919, he retreated to kind interpretations, which won him popular approval.

Landis maintained his fierce demeanor of integrity until the end, and so illustrated an aspect of the native dilemma of democracy. It tended toward serious and sometimes character-testing competitiveness but with an appreciation of high competence. The urge to win created dangers to quality, and given undue conditions of temptation, inequity, and disharmony could deteriorate the social fabric. A public aware of what it had permitted or accepted could seek an apparently strong person to act for it, and try to right its wrongs.

Not even the elite Progressives had foreseen that a nation having numerous trained intellectuals, executives, journalists, and others necessary to a national dialogue covering all fields would have had to fight a war in which one half the population was substantially suppressed, so that the other half could conduct it efficiently, unfettered by debate. The World Series was enlightening because it was apolitical, and should therefore have required the least ugly manifestations of ego and authority. The course of the scandal suggested that Americans had a dark forest to traverse before they could hope to capture once more that sense of power and control they had experienced in 1912.

NOTES

1. Alan Valentine, *1913: America between Two Worlds* (New York, 1962), 2.

2. Louis C. Fraina, *Revolutionary Socialism: A Study in Socialist Reconstruction* (New York, 1918), 246. Fraina soon gave himself a new name, Lewis Corey, as better suited to one who then intended to be the "American Lenin."

3. Charles Seymour, ed., *The Intimate Papers of Colonel House* (Boston, 1926), 1:75.

4. *Ibid.*, 1:52 *et passim.*

5. *Ibid.*, 1:96.

6. Alexander C. George and Juliette C. George, *Woodrow Wilson and Colonel House* (New York, 1956), 175.

7. [E. M. House] *Philip Dru: Administrator* (New York, 1912), 290.

8. John A. Garraty, *Woodrow Wilson* (New York, 1956), 90.

9. Robert L. Morlan, *Political Prairie Fire: The Nonpartisan League* (Minneapolis, 1955).

10. Graham Adams, Jr., *Age of Industrial Violence 1910-1915: The Activities and Findings of the United States Commission on Industrial Relations* (New York, 1966), 105.

11. *Ibid.*, 105, 107, *et seq.* for following details.

12. Leo Katcher, *The Big Bankroll: The Life and Times of Arnold Rothstein* (New York, 1959), 266ff.

13. Leon Stein, *The Triangle Fire* (New York, 1962), 199.

14. William B. Northrop and John B. Northrop, *The Insolence of Office: The Story of the Seabury Investigations* (New York, 1932).

15. Stein, *The Triangle Fire*, 205.

16. Adams, Jr., *Age of Industrial Violence*, 149 *et seq.* for further details.

17. For the Rockefeller-Walsh confrontation, see *Industrial Relations Final Report and Testimony Submitted to Congress by the Commission on Industrial Relations Created by the Act of August 23, 1912 64th Congress 1st Session Senate Document No. 415* (Washington, 1916), 8:7763ff. Others testifying included Ben B. Lindsey, Ida M. Tarbell, and Edward P. Costigan, Samuel Untermyer spoke for reform as a brake on socialism, Henry Ford for his industrial relations system, which was intriguing the country.

18. Leonard Dinnerstein, *The Leo Frank Case* (New York, 1968), 5ff., for details of the case's unfolding. This is the definitive work among such others as Harry Golden, *A Little Girl Is Dead* (Cleveland, 1963), and Charles and Louise Samuels, *Night Fell on Georgia* (New York, 1956), in addition to numerous important memoirs.

19. Dinnerstein, *The Leo Frank Case*, 33.

20. *Ibid.*, 53.

21. George Brown Tindall, *The Emergence of the New South, 1913-1945* (Baton Rouge, 1967), 185.

22. *Ibid.*, 186.

23. Raymond Allen Cook, *Fire from the Flint: The Amazing Career of Thomas Dixon* (Winston-Salem, 1968), 172.

24. Notable people found it necessary to make peace with the Klan to function in society at all. So liberal journalists explained when, in 1937, Hugo Black of Alabama was proposed for the Supreme Court. Black had been a member of the Klan from 1923 to 1925. As United States Senator, 1927-1937, he was consistently liberal, and his work on the Supreme Court was so

perceived. Golden, *A Little Girl Is Dead*, was "dedicated to the city of Atlanta, Georgia, which suffered the most of all Southern cities in the 1860's. In the 1950's Atlanta led the South in the resolution of the desegregation crisis, and in the 1960's it led the nation in the reapportionment process."

25. Nancy J. Weiss, "Sulzer, William," in *Dictionary of American Biography,* ed. E. T. James, Supp. 3 (New York, 1973), 751-752.

26. The best account is Andy Logan, *Against the Evidence: The Becker-Rosenthal Affair* (New York, 1970), but see also Jonathan Root, *One Night in July: The True Story of the Rosenthal-Becker Murder Case* (New York, 1961). The latter book assumes Becker's guilt, but both books agree that the basic change created by the event was from a political machine-police-vice relationship to a political machine-criminal caste relationship, with the police stepping back into second place.

27. Louis Filler, *The Muckrakers: Crusaders for American Liberalism* (State College, Pa., 1976), 68ff.

28. Lately Thomas, *The Mayor Who Mastered New York: The Life and Opinions of William J. Gaynor* (New York, 1960), 411ff.

29. Logan, *Against the Evidence,* 149.

30. *Ibid.*, 134.

31. Adams, Jr., *Age of Industrial Violence,* 115-116.

32. Logan, *Against the Evidence,* 240-241.

33. Katcher, *The Big Bankroll,* 306.

34. James T. Farrell, who appears to have been present, reported the boy's remark as, "It ain't true, Joe," with Jackson and another of the accused not answering. James T. Farrell, *My Baseball Diary* (New York, 1957), 106.

35. Quoted in Harold Seymour, *Baseball: The Early Years* (New York, 1960), 304.

36. Eliot Asinof, *Eight Men Out: The Black Sox and the 1919 World Series* (New York, 1963), 14-15 *et seq.*

37. For a controversial play-by-play analysis of the team's performance as a whole, and the critical plays revealing players's intentions, see Victor Luhrs, *The Great Baseball Mystery, the 1919 World Series* (New York, 1966), 243ff. For an overview, see Seymour, "Baseball's Darkest Hour," in *Baseball the Golden Age* (New York, 1971), 294ff.

38. Asinof, *Eight Men Out,* 112ff.

39. J. G. Taylor Spink, *Judge Landis and Twenty-Five Years of Baseball* (New York, 1947), chaps. 3, 4, and passim.

Progress and Progressivism

The man who insists upon consent, who moves with the people, is bound to consult the feasible right as well as the absolute right. . . . Progress has been slower perpendicularly, but incomparably greater because lateral.

He has not taught his contemporaries to climb mountains, but he has persuaded the villagers to move up a few feet higher. It is doubtful if personal ambition, whatever may have been its commercial results, has ever been of any value as a motive power in social reform. But whatever it may have accomplished in the past, it is certainly too archaic to accomplish anything now. Our thoughts, at least for this generation, cannot be too much directed from mutual relations and responsibilities. They will be warped, unless we look all men in the face, as if a community of interests lay in between, unless we hold the mind open, to take strength and cheer from a hundred connections.[1]

Progressivism did not necessarily mean progress, that is, a faith that human affairs advanced with some evolutionary logic over what they had been. There were, of course, those who did believe this. Numerous businesses proudly prefixed their dry-cleaning, toolmaking, or other enterprises with the word "progressive"; innumerable people pointed to electric and electronic devices of every kind, available to plain people, as evidence that there was indubitable progress in human affairs. Some of these advocates may even have "worshipped" their car, television set, or motorized boat as others had worshipped the sun.

Many people practiced a species of belly faith in progress, as others practiced belly patriotism, loving life or their country so long as it fed them. They could be distinguished from more earnest ones who labored to improve their country, to keep it abreast of their dream of what it had been. Some of them were idealists of the stamp of George Bancroft, the historian and fugleman of America, who also served as speech-writer and statesman to more hardheaded Democratic party politicians. In general, such people mixed generous social premises with an appreciation of the need of people, including themselves, for material returns. And although they denounced Whigs and later Republicans for spouting idealism from a highpoint of financial gains, they themselves stirred democratic rhetoric into pots that bubbled with emoluments and slush-fund ingredients.

A later President persuaded himself that his sincere belief in the American system and its system of payoffs would protect him from opponents eager to find legal entanglements for his rough and ready experience. He would have been better advised to have noticed that Martin Van Buren, exposed by the passionately romantic Mackenzie, thought it wiser to lie low and let his sympathizers ride the storm with him. As it was, Van Buren had not been able to reweave his political threads, at least enough to give him the presidency again.

Progressives of later vintage were impatient of all such considerations and preferred to consider how they could improve society, not perfectly, but enough to enable them to look forward to more advances. Theodore Roosevelt began as a goo goo seeking better social structure. He went on to progressivism, working with politicians for power while assessing the will of the people and his ability to influence it. The public needed leaders, as well as democratic processes. All of this made for half-measures but in a cloud of affirmations that promised more.

Thus, efficiency seemed important in creating better government and industrial machines. But the machines could be run only by people, and who they were to be could only result from an equation of inside groups and pressures outside the statehouse or factory.

David Graham Phillips's optimism persuaded him, in his posthumous *George Helm* (1912), that the people by some mysterious social process found honest men when they needed them. Some such process had, during his time, made conspicuous a Tom L. Johnson, a La Follette, a Joseph W. Folk, a Louis R. Glavis, and muckraking writers from one end of the country to the other, from Fremont Older in San Francisco to Norman Hapgood in New York. That process had given Americans Theodore Roosevelt and Woodrow Wilson.

But some of these became legends rather than realities with techniques and experiences to contribute. Some like Folk were totally forgotten. Some were of the quality of William Randolph Hearst, with demagogic characteristics so muddled as to create as much evil as good. Roosevelt, who should have become a model of opportunism and legitimate goals to the young, was reduced from an inspirational cliché in the grammar schools—the weak boy who overcame his puniness by sheer will—to a target for undergraduate darts proving his racism and prototypical fascism. Most Americans gave no thought to him at all.

To be sure, they could, and probably did, consider his brand of progressivism in contrast with that of Franklin D. Roosevelt, the earlier Al Smith, Henry A. Wallace, and possibly the nonmartial Lyndon B. Johnson. But whatever they did and concluded, citizens were required to come to terms with questions that had plagued Americans almost from their very beginnings about the nature of their alleged programs and their capacity for carrying them out. Ever since the establishment of the Republic, with its illimitable resources, the world had marvelled at the restlessness of Americans, their dissatisfaction with opportunities that would have made ecstatic most peoples of the world, their "poverty in the midst of plenty."

All this seemed to reflect on politicos and political-minded citizens who were supposed to be first of all practical, mediating, compromising—in short, progressive. If, however, it was accepted that Americans did not necessarily follow the most reasonable routes to their desires or could not foresee what would come of their particular commitments, the hectic course of progressivism became more understandable.

Americans had imagined that the processes of democracy would give the most practical results; pragmatism was an adjunct of progressivism and rose along with it. An era of Progressive jurists, of Progressive historians, of Progressive educators accompanied Progressives on their historic journey to World War I. Their democratic decisions were implemented by a substantial measure of undemocratic actions. Notorious was "100% Americanism," which, during World War I, reversed the established American tradition that the reformer was the best patriot.

The collapse of the democratic dialogue in the face of "100%ism" made reform seem absurd and gave arms to "radicals" who claimed to be changing the rules of the game. Over the years, they even, when seeking wider suffrage, claimed the mantle of the Populists or Progressives. All such developments embittered some genuine Progressives and made them conscious of the fact that their countrymen, whom they had once advised on civic morals and humanistic goals, had lost interest in their competence and ideals. The cynicism of the 1920s and the desperation that accompanied the economic crises of the 1930s suggested new solutions to life's problems, ranging from those inherent in Ernest Hemingway's despairing prose to the technocratic and Keynesian ideas that influenced the New Deal.

In addition the world grew smaller and smaller as revolutions influenced the politics of American life and such inventions as supersonic planes, television, and atomic weaponry made war and peace decisions more crucial. It was nevertheless difficult to create a more responsible atmosphere for social endeavor in view of the public's penchant for keeping its options open, those options including the right to be lax as well as alert.

No one could foresee in 1906 the day when the Pure Food and Drug Administration and such associated agencies as the Surgeon-General's Office would be more generally conscientious about the public's health than the public itself. The original offices had been created by public pressure, by public advocates who had demanded social protection in the face of opinion that it was the government's business to hold power at a minimum, leaving the individual as much right as possible to head for heaven or hell as he pleased. The muckrakers had raised such a storm of indignation against such a philosophy as to increase the government's responsibility in such areas. The use of the cigarette became symbolic of the public's uncertainty about its own expectations in government. Some grew cynical about the public's ability to formulate or sustain worthwhile goals.[2]

"Public interest" persons and organizations worked to rouse both government agencies and the public to their need for greater efforts in fields of health, resources, and the just claims of posterity. They found themselves in competition with existentialist attitudes that advised that one only went around once, and with millennarian shoutings that governmental half-measures were a form of treason to the people. More deadly to the public-interest outlook was the stolid conviction of many who had considered public-interest careers that the public would not support them sufficiently for them to make a career and that, therefore, it was the better part of wisdom for them to fit themselves into secure, money-making jobs.[3]

Neither existentialist nor 'tis-the-final-conflict attitudes appeared in 1975 to have much prospect for social credibility, with simple survival becoming a desirable goal in itself. Under such circumstances a recrudescence of some form of progressivism or neo-progressivism seemed possible. It if emerged, it would doubtless offend some social experimenters of both a cultural and political variety. Those who persisted in being deliberately obscure, narcissistic, perverse, insulting to readers might seem less a challenge than a bore. Attitudes tolerated—even exploited—in good times might find themselves in devastated conditions. As one commentator put it:

> This year . . . [New York] has been inherited by a cash-and-carry crowd. Anonymous insurance men, bond underwriters, mob loan sharks, investment bankers, and political manipulators now control much of the city, and they are all business. No more fun. No more public fun, anyway. No more charismatic politicians. . . . No more talk of alternate life-styles, affirmative action, or incentive zoning.
>
> "The party's over," builder Sam Lefrak said recently. "Everyone in the government and in the housing business is up to their ass in debt."[4]

This was hardly progressivism under any guise. Perhaps it was some species of realism. One conjectured that the people the writer referred to, and he himself, would be glad to begin the party again, if given the chance, and, if called upon to do so, would be glad to find new equivalents for such phrases as alternative life-styles and affirmative action. But a positive view of American prospects based on real conditions and defensible wants could, possibly, create a different approach. It might bring forth social and cultural partisans not chained to illusions, not self-serving at the expense of the public interest, able and willing to reconsider with their readers or co-workers aspects of their experience. They might assess with a certain objectivity Progressivism in theory and fact.

They might ask for "social significance" again, but of a more native quality than had often been sought during the 1930s. They might wish to take into account a spectrum of Americans rather than a number of formalized types such as had attracted patrons of avant-garde traditions who often shifted readily to formalized "radical" types, and sometimes back again.

It was possible to know better, rather than casually to categorize or flatter, working men and women, farmers, seamen, and civic-minded men and women in all categories such as had studded the Progressive tradition. Whether the idea of Progress could be recaptured for a tired generation was unclear. But the idea of progressivism was in arm's reach.

NOTES

1. Jane Addams, "A Modern Lear," in Graham Romeyn Taylor, *Satellite Cities: A Study of Industrial Suburbs* (New York, 1915), 89-90.

2. Ferdinand Lundberg, *The Treason of the People* (New York, 1954), is by a New Dealer who found himself unable to sustain the democratic faith.

3. Mark J. Green, "The Young Lawyer, 1972: Goodbye to Pro Bono," *New York* 5 (February 21, 1972): 29-34. This publication often has an oddly "muckraking" tone, as it "exposes" venal politicians and deals, chicanery among ethic leaders, and hopeless conditions facing New York's citizens. This muckraking quality, however, is limited by a meagerness of program. The magazine no more than consoled its harassed subscribers with the information that other New Yorkers are suffering, too, and with the soft dream that the reader, too, like selected instances of fortunate New Yorkers, might hit a jackpot of success.

4. Nicholas Pileggi, "The Power Game, 1975," *New York* 8 (January 13, 1975): 30.

Bibliographical Note

The dimensions of progressivism are still to be fully delineated because definitions of its character and career are yet to be determined and agreed upon. Agreed upon more than accepted, for though a democracy requires a certain amount of "consensus," it requires even more a sense of its own variety of interests, all of which demand their place in the social scheme.

Academically, we have been through an era of monographs that dug deeply into aspects of the subject, but not infrequently contained assumptions that did not take into account interpretations of others in the field. In time, it may be hoped, there will be meetings of minds on such topics as Progressive beginnings, differences between social and political reform, the limits of radicalism, and related concepts. In the meantime, there must be forays into progressivism that attempt to transcend hypotheses which exclude the experiences of others.

I have prepared a narrative and descriptive bibliography of the overall subject of this book that seeks to put into one structure the numerous movements and causes which reached their apogee in the 1912 elections. *Muckraking and Progressivism: An Interpretive Bibliography* (1976) first inquires into the problem of discovering "A Meaning for Modern Times" in the subject. It recognizes that progressivism has fallen on evil decades, and that its uses to us must be considered in breadth as well as length. In this section I discuss such matters as morality, women, gentility, and ethnics. The main body of the book deals with muckraking and progressivism in their classic phase. The book's third section treats post-World War I progressivism. It makes efforts to distinguish between the sensationalist reputation of muckraking—the "muckraking" of *True* and Walter Winchell—and that highlighted by such activist-journalists as George Seldes and Drew Pearson. A final section sees both muckraking and progressivism as involved in our most recent "Search for Values." It features such social phenomena as Ralph Nader, the Pentagon Papers, and Watergate, but involves as well such valuable members of the community as I. F. Stone and Frank Serpico, the tenaciously honest New York policeman whose story is told in Peter Maas, *Serpico* (1973). Incidentally, this fine officer, who defied traditionally corrupt practices among his peers, has not yet been given any place in any other ongoing tradition of reform.

Several briefer treatments of muckraking and progressivism are presently available which list or describe leaders in the field and their experiences. See George E. Mowery, *The Progressive Movement* (1958) and Arthur S. Link and William M. Leary, Jr., *The Progressive Era and the Great War* (1969). The latter pamphlet gives no assessments, but lists more items than the first. The Great War was the King Charles head of the entire Progressive era (if one may make a literary reference to Dickens's *David Copperfield* without bewildering a sadly troubled generation). In time, I suppose, we will be able to see World War I as a tragedy rather than a conspiracy, and be no more angered by it than by the Battle of Agincourt, or by death itself.

In the meantime it behooves us by all means to try to see not only the war's irreparable agony, but also its many manifestations of graciousness, courage, and humanity, as in Brand Whitlock's unforgettable *Belgium: A Personal Record* (1919), Franz Werfel's *The Pure in Heart* (1932, translation), and Romain Rolland's *Above the Battle* (1916, translation), among other works of high nobility; I will never apologize for keeping in tender memory Rolland's *Jean-Christophe*, and other writings which dignify humanity.

Mark Sullivan's *Our Times, 1900-1925* (1927-1935) I deem vital to putting muckraking and progressivism into perspective, even though Sullivan, himself once a muckraker, repudiated that aspect of his era and was later only halfway sold on progressivism. Harold U. Faulkner, a fine historian, in his *The Quest for Social Justice* (1931) saw Sullivan's series as filled with "peculiar" emphases. But those emphases—involving fads, fancies, and forgotten heroes—affected events, and help explain them, as certainly as did elections, industrial innovations, and the condition of labor. We have yet to assess for our own time the presidency in its relation to Congress, Billy Mitchell (most of my students have forgotten who he was, or why he is memorable), and Samuel Gompers. Sullivan helps us in our re-assessments.

A remarkable fact of our era is that "populism" is being reaffirmed as of value to us, but that progressivism is not. Jack Newfield and Jeff Greenfield (no historians, but more immediately in touch with vibrant political "activists" than many historians who no more than contrive to keep their students's suffrage and attention), offer *A Populist Manifesto: The Making of a New Majority* (1972). It has received the approval of Jimmy Breslin, if of no one else. There is no comparable volume in the popular field for progressivism at the present time.

The historical profession has made efforts to create centers for discussion and controversy. These include an apotheosis for Richard Hofstadter, as expressed in the section devoted to him in Richard L. Rapson, ed., *Major Interpretations of the American Past* (1971). A number of other works have suggested centers for concern. These have included Forrest McDonald's *The Presidency of George Washington* (1974), a basically conservative view of revolutionary politics and society; Bertram Wyatt-Brown's *Lewis Tappan and the Evangelical War against Slavery* (1969), which treats Tappan as a repressed and neurotic Puritan; and Gabriel Kolko's *The Triumph of Conservatism: A Reinterpretation of American History, 1900-1916* (1963), which sees American capitalism as in a conspiracy to dominate the American government. Although this was probably true in a sense, since all social tendencies including Kolko's naturally hope for power and authority over others, it fails to explain why the "socialistic tendency" that seemed strong in 1912 so drastically declined in succeeding decades.

So long as we honor negative views of American experience that make no effort to put it into perspective or to make realistic comparisons between the workings of American social processes and those of other nations, we are unlikely to be able to utilize Progressive experience adequately or to adapt it to modern conditions. Such a book as Marvin E. Gettleman and David Mermelstein, eds.,

The Failure of American Liberalism: After the Great Society (1970) leaves us nowhere, and nowhere to go, except perhaps as followers of other nations. And it leaves us without anything to contribute to their national or international programs.

The most serious loss in present times has been the lack of exploitation of available materials that could modify or enrich academics' conjectures about the nature of American society, or the real experiences of its "activists." For example, Charles Edward Russell was "active" with respect to American betterment from the 1880s until his death in 1940. He left a vast assortment of papers to the Library of Congress, where I have myself consulted them on various missions. By this time, I estimate, they should have inspired perhaps half a dozen completed Ph.D. theses. So far, none has materialized to my knowledge. Some ten years ago, a person professed to be serious about completing one of them and negotiated with me on the subject, but disappeared into a void. I can't understand why theses, mediocre or otherwise, have not blossomed on Russell, unless progressivism at present should be too thick and murky to recent aspirants or their mentors. The papers should be "exploited."

But in addition, there are numerous projects in the area that could be readily and profitably pursued. In my narrative and descriptive bibliography I include a section "Work that Needs to Be Done." My point is that it could be readily done, even though muckrakers and Progressives were often much too "existentialist" to give thought to yearning Ph.D. candidates of an up-coming generation. *American Literary Manuscripts. A Checklist of Holdings in Academic, Historical and Public Libraries in the United States* (1960) is a mine of rich—sometimes extremely rich—materials dealing with muckrakers and Progressives. It ought to give birth to a hundred strong and useful theses not shackled by sweeping *a priori* judgments of the validity of this or that litterateur—judgments that restrain people from so much as *enjoying* the reading of essays, articles, stories, even poems. Must they wait to be passed upon as legitimate topics of research by cardinals of culture who are themselves fearful of that crime of crimes: their inability to make profits for hardheaded publishers?

Progressivism and muckraking were dependent on understanding and ministering to the informational and psychological wants of their reading public. An unbiased view of the reading public of 1920 and 1975 suggests that there was not too wide a difference between publics. Both sought respect, understanding, and a rather specific grasp of such needs as security and leeway. Both publics also sought a prideful sense of American opportunities not available to peoples elsewhere in the world whose heads were chopped off when they transgressed civil or religious laws. My preceding chapters invoke a variety of references from readings past and present. Their main value is that of providing *continuity*, not in behalf of ancestor worship, but of inevitable choices and preferences. It is hoped that an objective view of the references utilized in the text will suggest to creative readers the broad possibilities in research open to creative academics. For readers can be as evocative to researchers as researchers to readers. This is democracy's privilege as it is its problem.

The challenge to research in both muckraking and progressivism, as I discern it, involves two areas. One poses the simple task of seeing the earlier time with clear lenses, in both larger and specific terms. The second requires a firm mastering of its implicit cultural component. In several later editions of my *Muckraking/Crusaders of American Liberalism*, including the latest, I added an essay entitled "Toward a Bibliography of Muckraking." In it I suggested some of the varied topics to which contributions had been made, and indicated that more topics as well as volumes could be advantageously subjoined.

Tendentious movements help, when they do not somehow muddle the field. For example, Anne Royall has been recently "rediscovered," mainly because of the contemporary efforts to place women, their roles and achievements, into modern perspective. My own treatment of Royall in this volume is the one present effort to put her in the mainstream of American history and progressivism. Josephine Shaw Lowell has not yet been rediscovered for general purposes at all, probably because she was "genteel," and gentility has been viewed for decades through distorted glasses. And so it is with many others. William Lyon Mackenzie obviously needs more work, even though he is a national hero in Canada; my chapter in this volume no more than introduces him in his American phase, and demands further attention to his life and works.

There is no biography of W. S. U'Ren. There is no follow-up on Ben Hampton's short but brilliant career in muckraking. Yet his last decades and those of others among his contemporaries would help enlighten us on what happens to Americans when "the name died before the man." There are, for example, rich "Golden Rule" Samuel M. Jones papers in the Toledo, Ohio, Public Library. But there is no biography of him, or collection of his letters. John Kenneth Turner was a highly competent socialist critic of American ways and Woodrow Wilson's war, but Turner ran out his years in universal silence, and I have no idea at this time what may have happened to his papers, if he left any.

We can use more books like David M. Chalmers's *The Social and Political Ideas of the Muckrakers* (1964), which dealt with some thirteen major muckraking figures. All of them merit still further research and explication of purposes and achievements, as do their direct Progressive counterparts.

It would help to incorporate into our materials such a work as Ross E. Paulson, *Radicalism & Reform: The Vrooman Family and American Social Thought, 1837-1937* (1968), a far from sensational volume but one throwing important light on the fact that radicalism and reform are much closer to conservatism in America than is generally realized. Indeed, spelling out the nuances of American social thought should be a major concern of responsible cultural and political historians. This would cut out numerous foolish books which imagine they have proved something by revealing that their "radical" was, in fact, conservative in one way or another.

The Ballinger affair demonstrates how a legend may be securely established, deemed satisfactory by teachers and their students, and so not advanced through new research, or research that transgresses established cliches. Samuel Untermyer, whom I treat briefly in these pages, is utterly unknown to public or historians. Yet his career, adequately examined, could add important riders to the presumptions of "specialists" in progressivism and muckraking, and aid the work of placing in full view the positive as well as the negative aspects of American corporations and their lawyers.

Colonel E. M. House believed that Woodrow Wilson was nominated by Democrats for the presidency because of the labors of his Texas delegation. House may or may not have been correct, but the point is worth following up; it will be buried in the great Link *et al.* edited *The Papers of Woodrow Wilson*, when the series gets to the House-Wilson relationship. Labor, too, needs new, fresh approaches; at present it lies fallow between old, sentimentalized descriptions of the agencies of the poor and oppressed, and labor's uninvestigated status as the Big Labor of recent years.

Part of the problem of advancing muckraking-Progressive understanding is to distinguish the relevant from the irrelevant in its history. I once had occasion to reprimand Kenneth Stampp for his bland use of the word "sub-marginal": it being anything he had not heard of or worked with. There are indeed priorities in history as elsewhere. But these have to be established in open and fruitful discussion, if we are not to be mentally handcuffed by presumptive concepts.

All such considerations overlap into the problem of cultural assessments and investigations. Thus, John D. Hicks's *The Populist Revolt* (1931) is, indeed, in many ways a "classic," or at least a definitive work in the field. The limitation of the book is that it totally lacks a sense of awareness of what the cultural artifacts of the era could tell us. Farmers were human beings as well as economic integers. So were their wives and children. Although students in the field have some idea of how to use the "populist" fiction of Hamlin Garland (as though his nonreform writings do not also tell us something about the contours of his mind and feelings, and those of his forebears), they forget that man, even when a Populist, does not live by bread alone. He needs to be understood as E. W. Howe understood him in *The Story of a Country Town* (1883), as Harold Frederic understood him in *The Damnation of Theron Ware* (1896), and as such others as William Dean Howells, Willa Cather, and Frank Norris understood him.

In my *The Unknown Edwin Markham* (1966), I remarked (p. 101) that "[a]ny treatment of the 'Reform Era' which does not also cope with ['The Man with the Hoe'], as poetry as well as reform attitude, is automatically foolish and infirm." Although this opinion did not provoke violent repercussions in the field, or cause texts in reform to reconsider some of their casual phrases, my suggestion still seems to me one indicator of progress, if there is to be any progress in progressivism.

An interesting example of the confusion caused by an unwillingness to deal with the fact that progressivism was culture as well as politics is shown in Judith Mara Gutman's picture-and-text book, *Lewis W. Hine and the American Social Conscience* (1967). Hine was a sociologist and conscious Progressive reformer who utilized photographs to establish his points about child labor. He worked for the National Child Labor Committee and published his photographs in *Charities and the Commons.* He was also aware that he wielded his camera with artistic effect. Gutman sought our attention with Hine's art. But it also seemed to her necessary to separate him from what she imagined to be Hine's less arty Progressive contemporaries to identify him (rather far-fetchedly) with Picasso rather than Progressives. It was an ill-considered endeavor that deprived Hine of the strength a firm association with a great movement should have given him.

In addition, Gutman could have noted that patent artists had been associated with progressivism, including such artist-journalists of the "Ash Can School" as John Sloan. She could have noted, among others involved in muckraking and Progressive events, Finley Peter Dunne, universally admired for his enduring humor, the Jack London of a dozen social fictions and essays, the Edith Wharton of *The House of Mirth,* and others. But even more, the era is laced with controversial or poorly-recalled figures who need to be, at this late date, given patterns to explain their qualities and uses to us. Charles M. Flandrau is one of the finest modern American essayists, and almost a cult figure to the earlier Sinclair Lewis, the later Alexander Woolcott, and others. Flandrau's *Viva Mexico!* (1908) is a recognized classic. Yet his highly esteemed essays, as in *Prejudices* (1911), must be rediscovered, as must be his *Harvard Episodes* (1897). The fact that contemporary authors like Gutman have probably not heard of Flandrau should be racked up to their discredit rather than his.

Hutchins Hapgood developed an art-form during the Progressive period of depth studies in journalism, as in his *Autobiography of a Thief* (1903), *The Spirit of Labor* (1907), and *Types from City Streets* (1910). Yet all that is presently recalled of his work is *The Spirit of the*

Ghetto (1902), probably because it contained the youthful sketches of Jacob Epstein, and thus livened up the text at no extra cost to reprint publishers. Hapgood is still to be judged in the broader terms of his distinctly artistic accomplishment.

Theodore Dreiser needs to be more firmly grasped as *not* having been of the muckrakers, and indeed as having been their philosophical and practical foe. And until David Graham Phillips is actually read by his "critics," their views will continue to have no purpose but to impede the thought and due discrimination of their seminar students. But such are only a few obvious tasks in cultural understanding. In the body of this book I retell the classic tale of Theodore Roosevelt's rescue of Edwin Arlington Robinson, a tale that should be known to every school child. It is only one of many that needs to be regained for modern appreciation.

The story of Albert J. Beveridge's *Abraham Lincoln* (1928), written after his Progressive career was done, is worth knowing. It tells how Beveridge was shocked to find his hero engaged in less than noble ventures, but grimly set them down in the interests of truth. The longing of muckrakers to write novels aids insight into their psychological equipment. Lincoln Steffens's *Moses in Red: The Revolt of Israel as a Typical Revolution* (1926) was a poor book that E. A. Filene had to subsidize for publication. Such compulsions as Steffens's do not excuse bad art, but they do help explain the fine art that went into Steffens's *Autobiography* (1931), which those who derogate Progressive art should read carefully. They should also read Clarence Darrow's courtroom oratory, and Brand Whitlock's moving autobiographical *Forty Years of It* (1914).

Without understanding such muckrakers and Progressives, we not only cut ourselves off from much wisdom and American experience, we lose the means for judging later Progressive developments, and the capacity for creating our own. We cannot weigh with competence such Progressives as Frank P. Walsh and the Thomas J. Walsh of the Teapot Dome exposures, the stormy Burton K. Wheeler, the differences between a Drew Pearson and a Walter Winchell, the failures and successes of the New Deal and Franklin D. Roosevelt, and Henry A. Wallace's "Progressive" campaign of 1948.

Free speech has always been a precious American possession, and was vital to muckraking. But how do we distinguish between free speech and anarchy? Between patriotism and chauvinism? Between imperialism and a necessary posture in the world? It may be years before we can hope to feel that our national balance has been recovered, following our traumas of the sixties and early seventies. But we can never begin too early to find the roots of our expectations and confusions. Such probings into Progressive and muckraking experiences as are indicated above need to be undertaken, and undertaken now.

Index